The Power of Precedent

The Power of Precedent

Michael J. Gerhardt

OXFORD
UNIVERSITY PRESS

2008

OXFORD

UNIVERSITY PRESS

Oxford University Press, Inc., publishes works that further
Oxford University's objective of excellence
in research, scholarship, and education.

Oxford   New York

Auckland   Cape Town   Dar es Salaam   Hong Kong   Karachi
Kuala Lumpur   Madrid   Melbourne   Mexico City   Nairobi
New Delhi   Shanghai   Taipei   Toronto

With offices in

Argentina   Austria   Brazil   Chile   Czech Republic   France   Greece
Guatemala   Hungary   Italy   Japan   Poland   Portugal   Singapore
South Korea   Switzerland   Thailand   Turkey   Ukraine   Vietnam

Copyright © 2008 by Oxford University Press, Inc.

Published by Oxford University Press, Inc.
198 Madison Avenue, New York, New York 10016

www.oup.com

Oxford is a registered trademark of Oxford University Press

Library of Congress Cataloging-in-Publication Data
Gerhardt, Michael J., 1956–
The power of precedent / Michael J. Gerhardt.
p. cm.
Includes index.
ISBN 978-0-19-515050-6
1. Stare decisis—United States. 2. Law—United States—
Interpretation and construction. I. Title.
KF429.G47 2008
347.73'262—dc22   2007023693

2 4 6 8 9 7 5 3 1

Printed in the United States of America
on acid-free paper

For my mother, Shivia Lee Gerhardt

Acknowledgments

There are many people whom I cannot thank enough for giving me wonderful support and feedback on this project over the years. I am grateful to participants in faculty workshops on different chapters of the book at Princeton University's Politics Department and the Cleveland State, Creighton, University of Minnesota, University of Nevada–Las Vegas, University of North Carolina at Chapel Hill, University of Richmond, and William & Mary law schools. I have learned a lot from Robbie George and my fellow fellows in the James Madison Program for American Ideals and Institutions at Princeton University, and I have benefited enormously from extended conversations with Akhil Amar, Randy Barnett, Scott Baker, Chuck Cameron, Neal Devins, Lee Epstein, Ron Kahn, Ken Kersch, Sandy Levinson, Stefanie Lindquist, Bill Marshall, Kevin McGuire, Paul Schwartz, Neil Siegal, Keith Whittington, Jim Wilson, and John Yoo. I am particularly grateful to Ward Farnsworth and Mitu Gulati, who each read and gave me very useful feedback on an earlier draft of the entire manuscript. David Klein deserves special mention and thanks for reading and offering constructive comments on the entire manuscript twice! I am especially grateful for the support and advice I have received from Dedi Felman and David McBride, my editors at Oxford University Press. Further thanks are owed to my former students Laura Dalton, Paul Dame, Jimmy Finn, Alex May, and Paul Zimmerman. No one deserves more thanks for their patience and support than my wife Deborah and our wonderful children, Benjamin, Daniel, and Noah.

In addition, I would like to acknowledge *The George Washington Law Review* for kindly allowing me to present revised portions of my articel, "The Role of Precedent in Constitutional Decision-Making and Theory," in Chapters 1 and 5. My thanks are also owed to *The University of Pennsylvania Journal of Constitutional Law* for granting permission for me to reprint material from my 2005 article "The Limited Path Dependency of Precedent," which provides the basis for Chapter 3. Thanks as well to the *Minnesota Law Review* for granting permission to reprint, in a slightly different version, my 2006 article "Super Precedent" in Chapter 6. And finally, I am grateful to *The Vanderbilt Law Review* for allowing me to reprint in revised form my article "Non-Judicial Precedent" in Chapter 4.

In our progress toward political happiness my station is new, and if I may use the expression, I walk on untrodden ground. There is scarcely an action, the motive of which may not be subject to a double interpretation. There is scarcely any part of my conduct which may not hereafter be drawn into precedent. Under such a view of the duties inherent in my arduous office, I could not but feel a diffidence in myself on the one hand, and an anxiety for the community.

President George Washington (1789)

P]ractic[e] has fixed construction, which is too late to disturb. If open for discussion, it would merit serious consideration; but the practical exposition is too old and strong & obstinate to be shaken or controlled. The question is at rest.

Justice William Paterson (1802)

Mere precedent is a dangerous source of authority, and should not be regarded as deciding questions of constitutional power except where the acquiescence of the people and the States can be considered as well settled ... The opinion of the judges has no more authority over Congress than the opinion of Congress has over the judges, and on that point the President is independent of both. The authority of the Supreme Court must not, therefore, be permitted to control the Congress or the Executive when acting in their legislative capacities, but to have only such influence as the force of their reasoning may deserve.

President Andrew Jackson (1832)

Make no mistake about it—the precedents we set in this matter will remain part and parcel of our legal system for years to come, damaging or benefiting each of us, regardless of the political party to which we belong.

Representative Bob Barr (1998)

Contents

The Power of Precedent

When the 81st—or 181st—justice of the United States Supreme Court writes an opinion on an issue about which his predecessors have written, does he care what they wrote? Does he feel absolute freedom to write whatever he pleases, as if he were writing on a blank slate? Does he merely manipulate the Court's precedents to support his preferred result, or does he defer to what his predecessors wrote on the subject before him? Does, or should, he care about what his colleagues or successors think about what he writes?

This book tries to answer these and other questions about the constitutional significance of precedent, a subject which has divided constitutional scholars even more than Supreme Court justices and other public leaders. Some people believe that precedents do not constrain justices from doing what they please; they believe the justices merely vote their policy preferences or manipulate precedents to maximize their preferences. Many legal scholars apparently agree, as reflected in their signing of letters—or appearing before the Senate—supporting or opposing Supreme Court nominees based on their likely attitudes about precedent. In contrast, some people claim precedents have the force of law and cannot be understood through the quantitative methods popular among social scientists. Nor, they assert, can precedent be understood without fully appreciating the uniqueness of the law and the special skills required for its explication.

In this book, I propose a positive account of precedent that bridges the chasm dividing the people who believe precedent is (or should be) meaningless from those who believe it has special legal force. I define precedent as *any* past constitutional opinions, decisions, or events which the Supreme Court or nonjudicial authorities invest with normative authority. On the Court, precedents take many forms, including not only the Court's past opinions, but also norms (such as avoiding ruling on constitutional issues whenever possible), historical practices (such as the opening of legislative sessions with prayer), and traditions (such as producing opinions for the Court and not seriatim) that the justices have deliberately chosen to follow. In these forms, precedents exert more force than commonly acknowledged. This force is encapsulated in the implementation and recognition of a golden rule of precedent—justices must be prepared to treat others' precedents as they would like their own to be treated or risk their preferred precedents being treated with the same kind of disdain they show others'. This golden rule may explain why, for example, *Roe v. Wade* still stands even though Republican presidents have made 8 of the past 11 Supreme Court appointments for the express purpose of overturning *Roe*.[1]

The end of the Rehnquist Court and the advent of the Roberts Court provide an ideal opportunity to take stock of what we know about precedent. I will compare the Rehnquist Court's handling of precedent with that of other Courts, assess the competing perspectives on precedent in social science and legal scholarship, examine the significance of precedents made outside the Court, and conclude with some tentative predictions about how the Roberts Court (and other public institutions) will handle precedent. I hope my account of precedent will improve appreciation for the interdependence of judicial and nonjudicial precedents and the importance of synthesizing social science research with conventional legal analysis in studying precedent.

The book consists of six chapters, which together provide a multi-layered perspective on precedent. The first chapter surveys what the justices have said about the level of deference they owe to Supreme Court precedents. Because the justices' most extensive discussions of precedent occur in cases in which they are either expressly or clearly reconsidering prior decisions, I focus on these discussions in the first chapter. They provide the framework for the Court's doctrine—its developed case law—on precedent.

The second chapter moves beyond the Court to survey the two dominant outlooks within the legal academy on precedent. On the one hand, the weak view of precedent holds that precedent either carries—or ought to have—little or no weight in constitutional law. The principal problem with this view as a description of what the Court does is that it fails to comport with the fact that in constitutional adjudication the justices rarely focus on precedent to the exclusion of all other conventional sources of legal meaning and argumentation. Precedent is usually one of many items which the justices must coordinate to make decisions. The major problem with the scholars who propose the weak view of precedent as a normative prescription on the weight constitutional precedents ought to carry is that they need precedent as much as everyone else to ensure that their preferred precedents endure *and* that scarce judicial resources are not squandered over endless relitigation of every conceivable question of constitutional meaning. On the other hand, scholars with a strong view of precedent consider precedent as the principal if not the only meaningful source of constitutional meaning. But extensive social science data show precedents do not constrain justices from doing what they wish to do in constitutional adjudication. While the data are problematic, they cannot be easily dismissed because constitutional interpretation allows decision-makers some discretion in the prioritization and handling of legal materials. Moreover, social scientists often do better than legal scholars in predicting judicial outcomes.

Chapter 3 proposes ways to connect substantial social science data on precedent with conventional legal analysis.[2] There are a number of factors, such as constitutional design, the ambiguities or gaps in the constitutional text, the dynamics of collegial decision-making bodies, and network effects, which explain why many of the Court's decisions seem to fit within social science models. Yet, no factor may clarify what the justices do more than an essential dynamic commonly overlooked in constitutional adjudication. This dynamic functions like a golden rule—justices will generally recognize the value and utility of giving to the precedents of others the respect they would like for their preferred precedents to receive. Consequently justices will generally be rather selective and cautious in picking out precedents to weaken or overrule. The principal uncertainties in constitutional law—which are often exaggerated by scholars (and others) focusing on what is occurring on the ground, so to speak—pertain to (1) which will be the particular precedents the justices will agree to weaken or overrule and (2) by what means will the justices weaken or overrule these relatively few precedents. Yet, once the Court formally overrules a precedent, it usually tends not to reconsider what it has done in an effort to maintain stability and avoid chaos in constitutional adjudication.

In chapter 4 I examine the distinctive features of nonjudicial precedent, a phenomenon largely ignored in the social science literature on precedent. First, I demonstrate the unifying characteristic of all nonjudicial precedents—their discoverability, or the fact that the efforts of public authorities to invest some prior, nonjudicial acts with special normative force make them recognizable as precedents. To illustrate discoverability, I distinguish three easy cases from three hard cases for spotting nonjudicial precedents. The easy cases are simple because they involve nonjudicial precedents which are easily discoverable, and they are easily discoverable because of relatively high-profile public efforts to invest them with normative authority. The hard cases are difficult because of the problems or impossibility of finding public efforts to invest them with special, normative force. Other features distinguishing nonjudicial precedents from each other or judicial precedents include their extensiveness and their finality.

Chapter 5 examines the multiple functions performed by judicial and nonjudicial precedents. These include, among others, providing constraint, persuasive authority, modes of constitutional argumentation, and media through which to understand the Court and its operations; validating constitutional arguments; clarifying constitutional law; signaling agendas; settling constitutional disputes; educating the public; implementing constitutional values; and illuminating and shaping constitutional history, structure, and national identity. These various functions show how the Court both shapes and is shaped by the constitutional culture in which the Court operates.

The sixth and final chapter explores the phenomenon of super precedent and its ramifications for constitutional theory and practice. Super precedents are the judicial and nonjudicial decisions that have become so frequently cited with approval by courts and other public authorities that their meaning and value have become embedded into our law and culture. In this chapter I principally focus on examples of super precedents made by the Court, including decisions establishing (1) foundational practices (such as judicial review or vetoing laws presidents deem unconstitutional), (2) foundational doctrine (such as incorporation), and (3) foundational rulings on particular subjects (such as upholding the constitutionality of legal tender). After reviewing these different kinds of super precedents, I suggest that they pose serious obstacles to implementing most constitutional theories, particularly "grand" theories, which seek to explain constitutional law in terms of a single unifying concept. Because grand theories conflict with so much super precedent, their implementation is practically impossible. No approach to deciding cases is possible without implementation, and implementation is not possible unless an approach has enough normative appeal to pass muster through the confirmation process. Both presidents and senators are likely to use their powers as gatekeepers for the federal judiciary to filter out constitutional attitudes that are inimical to super precedents.

I close with several observations and tentative predictions about the future of precedent in constitutional law. First, returning to the image with which I began the book, I suggest that the Court's two newest justices—Chief Justice John Roberts and Associate Justice Samuel Alito, Jr.—basically adhered to the golden rule, just as most of their predecessors have done. In their first 2 years on the Court, neither questioned nor voted to overturn any of the Court's prior constitutional decisions. Each exhibited an awareness of the importance of collegiality, and each employed precedent as their principal mode of constitutional argumentation. Each demonstrated respect for the precedent of others, including tradition. Yet, each also did not feel bound to rigidly follow some precedents, and the primary basis on which they refused to follow some precedents was precedent. Their early performance has underscored the important fact that overruling precedent is now, as it has always been, the tip of the iceberg; the real action in constitutional adjudication is the construction, not the destruction, of precedent.

Justices who are genuinely committed to judicial modesty or constitutional humility, as Chief Justice Roberts and Justice Alito claimed to be, are generally respectful of precedent and particularly receptive to the power and appeal of the golden rule of precedent. Judicial modesty is not a constitutional philosophy, but rather a temperament or disposition to respect precedents (as embodying the opinions of others), to learn from their and others' experiences, and to decide cases incrementally to minimize conflicts with either earlier opinions of the Court or other constitutional actors.

Moreover, the golden rule of precedent has substantial force outside the Court. While nonjudicial authorities may have more political warrants (and electoral support) than the justices for deviating from the precedents they dislike, they nevertheless see value (and achieve legitimacy) in grounding their preferred outcomes in precedent and work within—rather than against—well-established frameworks. The golden rule of precedent may be especially appealing to nonjudicial authorities (as it is to most justices), for whom preserving institutional norms and maintaining collegiality and tradition are important if not indispensable.

Third, I expect judicial and nonjudicial precedents will continue to perform multiple functions beyond constraining some public action. They will continue to do such things as stabilizing constitutional doctrine and shaping the Court and the culture in which it and all other constitutional actors function.

Fourth, no theory of precedent—including the positive one I have put forward in this book—would be complete without addressing the phenomenon of nonjudicial precedents, including their impact on the Court. The extensiveness and finality of nonjudicial precedents expose the fallacies of judicial supremacy (the notion the Court is the ultimate authority in deciding questions of constitutional meaning) and most constitutional theory (which focuses almost exclusively on judicial, rather than nonjudicial, constitutional interpretation).

In closing, I think a few caveats are in order. First, the meaning of "precedent" ought to be clear from the context. I try to further clarify the meaning I or others intend when I think further clarification is needed.

Second, I use the terms *stare decisis*, which is the Latin phrase for "to stand by things decided." This phrase is popular among lawyers. They use it as a shorthand for either the Court's basic respect for its prior decisions or the basic principle that legal reasoning should be consistent with judicial precedent.

Third, I understand "constitutional law" to be the byproduct of the efforts undertaken by public authorities to determine constitutional meaning *and* to implement the Constitution. The term "doctrine" refers to the collected, or accumulated, rulings or judgments of the Court on particular questions of constitutional law.

Fourth, I do not purport to discuss lower court precedents or their functioning in the judicial system. The book primarily focuses on the horizontal and vertical influence of Supreme Court and nonjudicial precedents.

Fifth, the book is *not* an endorsement of the strong view of precedent. The limited path dependency of precedent that I describe is flatly inconsistent with a strong view of precedent. I further suggest that distinguishing, narrowing, and occasionally overruling precedent are acts which the Constitution authorizes. Moreover, these acts almost always are based on precedents and produce other precedents.

Sixth, my primary focus is a synthesis of both institutional and legal analysis. Institutional analysis requires appreciating the extent to which institutions shape the behavior of the people who lead or must work with them, while legal analysis requires closely reading cases and other legal materials and figuring out which precedent(s) the dispute before the Court most closely resembles. Through my interdisciplinary analysis of precedent, I seek to heighten appreciation for the complex role of precedent in constitutional law, and in particular to show why there is no constitutional law without precedent.

The Patterns of Supreme Court Precedent |

The most common place to which people turn for guidance on precedent is the Supreme Court. The Court talks a lot about precedents, particularly when it is deciding whether to overrule prior decisions. These discussions are important for two basic reasons. First, they comprise the Court's doctrine—its settled law and practice—regarding precedents. This doctrine provides the focus and primary material that academics and justices critically analyze in constructing their theories of precedent. Among the clearest, most extensive, and most direct discussions of any public institution on precedent, the justices' discussions reveal a lot about their attitudes on precedent.

Second, the most promising means for overturning Supreme Court precedents is persuading the Court to undo them. Only four Supreme Court decisions have been overturned through constitutional amendments—*Chisholm v. Georgia*,[1] through the Eleventh Amendment; *Dred Scott v. Sandford*,[2] through the Fourteenth Amendment; *Pollock v. Farmers' Loan and Trust Co.*,[3] through the Sixteenth Amendment; and *Oregon v. Mitchell*,[4] through the Twenty-sixth Amendment.[5] A basic principle of constitutional law, which all justices and most scholars recognize, is that the Congress may not overturn the Court's constitutional decisions through ordinary legislation,[6] and congressional efforts have generally failed to weaken or undo precedents through regulations stripping them from falling within the Court's jurisdiction. Similarly, Congress generally resists impeaching and removing judges and justices for their decisions, and it has yet to remove any justice because of his decisions. This leaves as the only alternative for politically retaliating against specific precedents the appointment of new justices dedicated to overturning them. In fact, changes in the Court's membership have been instrumental in persuading the Court to overrule precedents, and more precedents have been overturned by the Court by far than by any other method.

1. The Number and Rate of Overrulings

The first noteworthy pattern in the Court's handling of precedents is in the number and rate of overrulings. From 1789 through the end of the 2004 term, the Court, in 133 cases, expressly overruled 208 precedents. These cases are the instances in which the Court declared in so many words that it was overruling constitutional precedents. (Table A-1 in the Appendix lists these cases, including their subject matters and the cases which they overruled.)

The significance of this number is debatable. On the one hand, it may seem odd for Supreme Court justices, who pride themselves on their craftsmanship and expertise, to concede so many errors. On the other hand, a total of 162 express reversals averages out to be less than one explicit overruling per term. This total may be insignificant, because it constitutes a tiny fraction of the Court's constitutional decisions. Nor are overrulings the only means by which the Court modifies its rulings; there are other, subtler methods which the Court employs (which I discuss in the latter half of this chapter).

Moreover, the express overrulings are not evenly spread out in terms of subject matter—some subjects are covered more than others. (Table A-2 shows these data.) The explicit overrulings break down as follows: Fourteenth Amendment due process (19), commerce clause (18), Fifth Amendment (15), Fourth Amendment search and seizure (11), Sixth Amendment (11), equal protection (8), Eleventh Amendment (7), Article I (6), Article III (5), First Amendment freedom of speech and press (6), supremacy clause (4), and Tenth Amendment (4). In the remaining areas, the Court explicitly overruled itself three or fewer times. These statistics arguably raise an inference that the justices respect precedent more—or at least appear reluctant to expressly overrule themselves less—in some areas than others.

The Court's explicit overrulings are not spread evenly over time. The scope of the Court's docket has expanded along with the size of the national government. As the Court's jurisdiction has expanded, the Court's caseload has increased. As the Court's caseload has expanded, so too has the number of constitutional precedents overruled. From 1900 to 2005, the Court overruled more than seven times as many precedents as it overruled in the preceding years. These statistics raise the possibility that the Court may have had more room for maneuvering around possibly conflicting precedent in the 19th century than it did in the 20th century. Put slightly differently, there have been far more constitutional cases requiring reconciliation over the past 50 years than there were in the preceding 168 years, and the harder reconciling cases becomes, the more pressure there may be for overrulings.

Yet another arguably relevant factor is the rarity of the Court's over-turning a precedent without a change in membership. The average life span of an overruled precedent is 29.2 years, which exceeds the average length of service of a justice on the Court. Indeed, 29.2 years exceeds the tenures of all chief justices, with the exception of the great Chief Justice, John Marshall.[7] Only four precedents have been reversed with no changes in composition. In the remaining 159 cases, the overruling Court has had at least one different justice than the overruled Court. (Table A-3 categorizes overruled precedents according to changes in the Court's composition.) Of all the cases explicitly overruled,[8] 8 involved a Court with one new justice, 8 involved a Court with two new justices, 10 involved a Court with three new justices, 17 involved a Court with four new justices, 7 involved a Court with five new justices, 12 involved a Court with six new justices, 23 involved a Court with seven new justices, 9 involved a Court with eight new justices, and 101 involved a Court with nine different justices.

The breakdown of overrulings by each chief justice's tenure further illuminates the Court's pace of overruling. (Table A-4 categorizes overruled precedents according to the chief justice.) The Marshall Court did not overturn a single constitutional precedent, though Justice Joseph Story tried unsuccessfully to overturn one.[9] Many people expected Marshall's successor as chief justice, Roger Taney, to lead an effort to narrow if not overrule Marshall Court decisions with which Taney and the president who appointed him—Andrew Jackson—disagreed. But, the Taney Court overruled only a single constitutional precedent. Taney's successor, Salmon Chase, presided over the Court from 1864 to 1873, during which time the Court overruled only two constitutional precedents. Morrison Waite succeeded Chase as chief justice and presided for 14 years over a Court that overruled four constitutional precedents. Melville Fuller followed Waite as chief justice. From 1888 to 1910, the Fuller Court overruled only a single precedent, in spite of charges (made to this day) that it inaugurated an era of judicial activism on behalf of economic liberties. The first chief justice to preside in the 20th century was Edward Douglass White, whose Court overturned only three constitutional precedents. Following White for only eight years as chief justice, William Howard Taft oversaw a Court that actively protected property and economic liberties but overturned only four constitutional precedents. Taft's successor as chief justice, Charles Evans Hughes, oversaw a Court that significantly reconsidered constitutional precedents; it overturned 25 constitutional precedents—over eight times as many as the White Court. The next chief justice, Harlan Fiske Stone, presided over a fractured Court for five years, during which time the Court overruled 10 constitutional precedents. Fred Vinson, Stone's successor as chief justice, presided over the Court for seven years, during which time the Court overturned 11 constitutional precedents. The next chief justice, Earl Warren, became widely charged with leading an activist Court bent on protecting minority rights. His Court was more "activist" compared to its predecessors, at least in terms of overruling prior decisions; the Warren Court overturned 32 constitutional precedents, the most of any Court up until that time. Yet, the Warren Court's historic number of overrulings was eclipsed by the Court overseen by Warren's successor as chief justice, Warren Burger. The Burger Court was widely expected to curtail the expansions of individual liberties recognized by the Warren Court. During Burger's 17 years as chief justice, the Court overruled 76 precedents in 35 cases—the largest number of overrulings to date by a Court through a chief justice's tenure. Burger's successor, William Rehnquist, presided over the Court for 17 years, during which time the Court overruled 39 precedents.

Shifting the perspective from explicit overruling to specific calls for overruling illuminates individual justices' attitudes about precedents. For instance, the number of cases in which the justices who served on the Rehnquist Court in its last 11 years urged overruling and joined in overruling are as follows (with the approximate number of years of each justice's tenure in parentheses): 59 cases for Chief Justice Rehnquist (in over 33 years); 42 cases for Justice John Paul Stevens (in nearly 30 years); 42 cases for Justice Sandra Day O'Connor (in nearly 25 years); 35 cases for Justice Antonin Scalia (in 19 years); 32 cases for Justice Anthony Kennedy (in 18 years); 21 cases for Justice David Souter (in nearly 15 years); 29 cases for Justice Clarence Thomas (in nearly 14 years); 12 cases for Justice Ruth Bader Ginsburg (in 12 years); and 14 cases for Justice Stephen Breyer (in 11 years). The statistics for the average number of times per year each justice on the Rehnquist Court urged and joined in overruling precedents is 2.07 for Justice Thomas, 1.84 for Justice Scalia, 1.74 for Chief Justice Rehnquist, 1.78 for Justice Kennedy, 1.75 for Justice O'Connor, 1.45 for Justice Stevens, 1.4 for Justice Souter, 1.27 for Justice Breyer, and 1.0 for Justice Ginsburg. To the extent these statistics reflect attitudes about precedent, they may surprise some readers: For instance, the three justices who rank the closest in terms of their calls for overruling are Chief Justice Rehnquist and Justices O'Connor and Kennedy, though they disagreed on which cases they wanted to overrule. While it may not have been surprising that Justices Scalia and Thomas urge overruling most often, some people may be surprised that Chief Justice Rehnquist and Justice Kennedy had nearly identical averages for urging the overruling of precedent, while Justice Ginsburg has the lowest average calls for overruling.

Another arguably revealing statistic is the number of lines of decisions that justices have each thought were wrongly decided but agreed nonetheless to follow.[10] For example, Justices William Brennan and Thurgood Marshall repeatedly dissented in cases involving the death penalty because they disagreed with the Court's initial upholding of its constitutionality and believed every subsequent case involved the same unconstitutional exercise of state power.[11] One might say these justices consistently did not respect precedent, in at least one context. The problem is that these statistics may not be very useful. For one thing, it turns out that the vast majority of justices identify one or two lines of decisions they are prepared to disregard entirely. Thus the statistics may be important for what they do not show—general disdain for precedent. The absence of this showing is interesting given the absence of a norm for justices to adhere to lines of decisions with whose creation, or perpetuation, they disagree.

However, one must be careful in the inferences one draws from the foregoing statistics. The most that can be safely said about the foregoing data is they tell us something about the justices' preferences to overrule particular precedents. But they do not indicate either why or on what basis the justices urged overruling. For instance, they do not reveal how many requests for overruling were made for the sake of restoring or fortifying other precedent(s). Nor do they reflect the extent to which other factors influenced the justices' decisions on precedent, including their prioritization of other sources or preferences to weaken precedents by other means. Moreover, the data on justices' refusals to follow a line of decisions with whose i nitial precedents they disagreed are of limited relevance. While these data might demonstrate justices' attitudes regarding particular lines of precedents, it should not obscure the other lines of cases that the justices accept in spite of their disapproval, as well as the justices' acceptances of initial or originating precedents of lines of decisions, but disagree on the applications of these precedents. The other patterns explored in the remaining sections of this chapter help further to make sense of these statistics.

2. The Court's Consistent Reasoning for Following or Rejecting Precedent

Some scholars suggest the Court explained its constitutional decisions less extensively in the 19th and early 20th centuries than it did later.[12] Yet, a survey of the Court's opinions in which it has reversed itself indicate the justices are not necessarily any more thorough now in discussing their attitudes toward precedent than they once were. While many precedents are undertheorized (i.e., the Court did not exhaustively explain the reasons behind its decisions), the Court did not undertheorize about the conditions for overruling itself.

To be sure, the first instance in which the Court overruled itself, *Hudson v. Guestier*,[13] appears undertheorized: By a 4–1 vote, with Justice Brockholst Livingston delivering the majority opinion and Chief Justice John Marshall the sole dissenter, the Court overruled Marshall's two-year-old decision in *Rose v. Himley*.[14] At issue was the right of French warships to seize American vessels trading with the revolutionary forces of French-owned Santo Domingo, a right which a majority upheld the second time around. The majority did not defend its authority to overrule a precedent; it said it lacked the competence to acknowledge whether an overruling had occurred and left it to Chief Justice Marshall to note in his dissent that an overruling had occurred.[15] While the case seems implicitly to establish the Court's power to reverse itself, it is an international, not a constitutional, case; and the Court's practice in constitutional cases has not followed suit.

The first two constitutional cases in which the Court overruled precedents contain substantial reasoning. The first was *Propeller Genesee Chief v. Fitzhugh*,[16] in which the Taney Court decided in 1851 to overrule the earlier decision in *Thomas Jefferson*[17] on the scope of Congress' power to expand maritime jurisdiction in federal district courts. The Court devotes four pages to a defense of its overruling of the prior decision. In this discussion, the Court recognized, among other things, the

great weight to which [precedent] is entitled. But at the same
time we are convinced that, if we follow it, we follow an erroneous decision into which the court fell, when the great importance of the question as it now presents itself could not be
foreseen; and the subject did not receive that deliberate consideration which at this time would have been given to it by the
eminent men who presided here when that case was decided.[18]

After explaining why the prior decision was erroneous, the Court acknowledged that had it involved a question of property rights, the Court would
have followed precedent because

[i]n such a case, stare decisis is the safe and established rule
of judicial policy, and should always be adhered to. For if the
law, as pronounced by the court, ought not to stand, it is in the
power of the legislature to amend it, without impairing rights
acquired under it. But [the earlier decision] has no relation to
rights of property. It was a question of jurisdiction only, and
the judgment we now give can disturb no rights of property
nor interfere with any contracts heretofore made. The rights of
property and of parties will be the same by whatever court the
law is administered. And as we are convinced that the former
decision was founded in error, and that the error, if not cor-
rected, must produce serious public as well as private inconve-
nience and loss, it becomes our duty not to perpetuate it.[19]

The lengths to which the Court went to explain its reasons for overruling
are hardly evidence of undertheorized decision making.

The same is true for the next occasion on which the Court overruled
itself, one of the Court's most dramatic reversals. In 1870 the Court ruled
5–3 in *Hepburn v. Griswold*[20] that Congress lacked the authority to issue
unbacked paper money. In the year following *Hepburn*, Justice Grier, who
had been listed in the *Hepburn* majority, was replaced by Justice Strong,
and Congress added a ninth seat to the Court, filled by Justice Joseph
Bradley. In 1871 Justices Strong and Bradley joined the *Hepburn* dissenters
(Justices Miller, Swayne, and Davis) in overruling *Hepburn*, prompting a
bitter dissent from Chief Justice Salmon Chase, who had written *Hepburn*.
Chase charged *Hepburn* was being overruled under the unprecedented
circumstances in which none of the justices who had participated in the

earlier decision had been persuaded to vote differently on the issue before the Court, and in which "the then majority find themselves in a minority on the court."[21]

Neither Justice Strong nor Justice Bradley let the charge go unaddressed. Writing for the majority, Justice Strong explained that the case being overruled

> was decided by a divided court, and by a court having a less number of judges than the law then in existence provided this court shall have. These cases have been heard by a full court, and they have received our most careful consideration. The questions involved are constitutional questions of the most vital importance to the government and to the public at large. We have been in the habit of treating cases involving a consideration of constitutional power differently from those which concern merely private right. We are not accustomed to hear them in the absence of a full court, if it can be avoided. Even in cases involving private rights, if convinced we had made a mistake, we would hear another argument and correct our error. And it is no unprecedented thing in courts of last resort, both in this country and in England, to overrule decisions previously made. We agree this should not be done inconsiderately, but in a case of such far-reaching consequences as the present, thoroughly convinced as we are that Congress has not transgressed its power, we regard it as our duty so as to decide [to overrule the Court's prior judgment.][22]

In his concurring opinion, Justice Bradley declared:

> On a question relating to the power of the government, where I am perfectly satisfied that it has the power, I can never consent to abide by a decision denying it, unless made with reasonable unanimity and acquiesced in by the country. Where the decision is recent, and is only made by a bare majority of the court, and during a time of public excitement on the subject, when the question has largely entered into the political discussions of the day, I consider it our right and duty to subject it to a further examination, if the majority of the court are dissatisfied with the former decision. And in this case, with all deference and respect for the former judgment of the court, I am so fully convinced that it was erroneous, and prejudicial to the rights, interest, and

safety of the general government, that I, for one, have no hesitation in reviewing and overruling it.[23]

In further support, he noted,

> It should be remembered that this court, at the very term in which, and within a few weeks after, the decision in *Hepburn v. Griswold* was delivered, when the vacancies on the bench were filled, determined to hear the question reargued. This fact must necessarily have had the effect of apprising the country that the decision was not fully acquiesced in, and of obviating any injurious consequences to the business of the country by its reversal.[24]

In overruling *Hepburn*, the justices were obviously explaining themselves in detail rather than leaving the major questions undertheorized.

While there are other cases in which the Court gave little or no explanation for overruling precedents, these cases are not confined to any historical period. Nor should too much be made of the fact that in some 20th century cases the justices engaged in more protracted debates over the deference owed to precedent than they did in some earlier cases. Indeed, the Court generally engages in more extended discussion than it once did. For instance, Volume 158 of the *United States Supreme Court Reports*, covering the 1894 term, disposes of 54 cases in 715 pages, averaging 13.2 pages per case. Volume 534 of the *United States Supreme Court Reports*, covering part of the 2001 term, disposes of 24 cases in 554 pages, averaging 23.08 pages per case. The increase in the length of opinions may reflect greater conflict among the justices or pressure (from within the Court) to address more potentially relevant or conflicting law—including more case law—than they did in 19th century cases. Yet, the fact that the modern Court sometimes uses the same criteria as the Court did in earlier cases to evaluate precedent makes it hard to claim there has been a shift from undertheorizing to extensive theorizing about precedent. Indeed, as the next section shows, the Court usually employs the same criteria in reviewing its precedents.

3. Patterns in the Justifications for Overruling

Overrulings are easy to spot because the justices use such telling terms as "overrule," and they feature either sharp conflict or consensus among the justices over the authority of particular precedents. In 1988 Geoffrey Stone culled from the opinions in which the justices considered overruling precedents a list of the

> justifications [most] commonly offered for the doctrine of precedent. First, we do not have unlimited judicial resources. If every issue in every case is a question of first impression, our judicial system would simply be overwhelmed with endless litigation. Second, we need a degree of predictability in our affairs. Interests of fairness, efficiency, and the enhancement of social interaction require that governments and citizens have a reasonably settled sense of what they may and may not do. Third, the doctrine of precedent raises the stakes. The Justice who knows that each decision governs not only the litigants to the particular case, but the rights of millions of individuals in the present and future, will approach the issue with less concern with the merits of the litigants as individuals and more concern with the merits of the underlying legal question to be decided. Fourth, the doctrine of precedent reflects a generally cautious approach to the resolution of legal issues. It reflects the view that change poses unknown risks, and that we generally should prefer the risks we know to those we cannot foresee … Fifth, the doctrine of precedent reduces the potential politicization of the Court. It moderates ideological swings and thus preserves both the appearance and the reality of the Court as a legal rather than a purely political institution. And finally, from the perspective of the Justices themselves, the doctrine of precedent enhances the potential of the Justices to make lasting contributions. If a justice disregards the judgments of those who preceded him, he invites the very same treatment from those who succeed him. A justice who wants to preserve the value of his own coin must not devalue the coin of his predecessors.[25]

While the justices do not mention all these reasons for respecting precedent every time they are reconsidering precedent, they comprise the most common arguments for respecting precedent.[26]

The justices' consensus extends to the justifications for explicitly overruling. Usually the justices give more than one reason for overruling precedents, though they employ some reasons more than others. The most common explanations for the Court's overruling of precedent are inconsistency with later precedents (cited in at least 69 cases) and the case being wrongly decided (cited in 39 cases).[27] Employed less often as justifications for overruling are unworkability (16 cases)[28] and changed circumstances (11 cases).

Not surprisingly, the sharper the conflicts among the justices over precedent, the more expanded their discussions of the needs to follow or abandon precedent. These disagreements reflect the commonality of the positions taken by the justices over the years on the appropriate level of deference owed to precedent. For example, Justice Louis Brandeis, in one dissent, gave the following frequently cited statement on why the Court owes relatively little deference to its constitutional decisions:

> Stare decisis is usually the wise policy, because in most matters
> it is more important that the applicable rule be settled than it be
> settled right. ... But in cases involving the Federal Constitution,
> where correctness through legislative action is practically impos-
> sible, this Court has often overruled its earlier decisions. The
> Court bows to the lessons of experience and the force of better
> reasoning, recognizing that the process of trial and error, so
> fruitful in the physical sciences, is appropriate also in the judicial
> function.[29]

In another classic statement, Justice Owen Roberts expressed a less toler-ant view of overturning constitutional precedents. He once criticized the overruling of a decision that overruled another reached only nine years before as tending "to bring adjudications of this tribunal into the same class as a restricted railroad ticket, good for this day and train only. I have no assurance ... that the opinion announced today may not be shortly repudiated and overruled by justices who deem they have new light on the subject."[30]

In the 1960s the Warren Court's unusually large number of overruling precedents sparked sharp exchanges over the deference owed to precedent in constitutional adjudication. A particularly heated exchange occurred in *Mapp v. Ohio*.[31] In *Mapp*, a 5–4 majority of the Court overruled *Wolf v. Colorado*,[32] which had held that "in a prosecution in a State court for a State crime the Fourteenth Amendment does not forbid the admission of evidence obtained by an unreasonable search and seizure."[33] *Mapp* was noteworthy because the appellant had not raised the issue of whether *Wolf* should be reconsidered, nor even cited *Wolf* in her brief.[34] Writing for the

Mapp majority, Justice Tom Clark defended overruling *Wolf* nevertheless because it conflicted with several other recent precedents and because

> we can no longer permit [the Fourth Amendment] to be revocable at the whim of any police officer who, in the name of law enforcement itself, chooses to suspend its enjoyment. Our decision [that the Fourteenth Amendment makes the Fourth Amendment's exclusionary rule applicable to the states], founded on reason and truth, gives to the individual no more than that which the Constitution guarantees him, to the police officer no less than that to which honest law enforcement is entitled and, to the courts, that judicial integrity so necessary in the true administration of justice.[35]

Justice Black concurred with the overruling of *Wolf* (a decision in which he had concurred) because "the continued existence of mutually inconsistent precedents together with the Court's [recent] inability to settle upon a [standard for determining when illegally seized evidence could not be admitted in state prosecutions] left the situation at least as uncertain as it had been before."[36] Justice Douglas also concurred on the ground that he "believ[ed] that this is an appropriate case in which to put an end to the asymmetry which *Wolf* imported into the law."[37]

In dissent, Justice John Marshall Harlan chastised the majority for lightly disregarding "the sense of judicial restraint which, with due regard for stare decisis, is one element that should enter into deciding whether a past decision of this Court should be overruled."[38] Given the presence in the case of a First Amendment privacy issue concerning mere possession of obscene material, which the parties had briefed and argued, he found it "fair to say that five members of this Court have simply 'reached out' to overrule *Wolf*."[39] He further pointed to the substantial reliance of state law enforcement authorities on *Wolf* as a reason against abandoning that precedent in a case that had barely touched on the question.[40] Justice Harlan argued that the Court should have scheduled reargument rather than, in effect, summarily overruling *Wolf* without argument.[41] He concluded that "what has been done is not likely to promote respect either for the Court's adjudicatory process or for the stability of its decisions."[42]

Throughout much of its duration, the Rehnquist Court's narrowing of abortion rights, overruling and weakening of several important criminal procedure decisions, curtailment of affirmative action, and significant limitation of congressional authority to expand federal jurisdiction at the expense of state sovereignty prompted sharp exchanges among the justices about the weight due to precedent. For example, in *Payne v. Tennessee*,[43] the Court overruled two decisions in which it had held only a few years before that the Eighth Amendment prohibited the admission of victim impact statements in the sentencing phase of criminal murder trials. But the six-member majority reflected some differing emphases on the appropriate criteria for overruling those precedents. Speaking for the majority (consisting of himself and Justices White, O'Connor, Scalia, Kennedy, and Souter), Chief Justice William Rehnquist argued that the two decisions, *South Carolina v. Gathers*[44] and *Booth v. Maryland*,[45] deserved less deference than constitutional decisions usually receive because they had been recently decided by 5–4 votes with vigorous dissents;[46] did not involve commercial or business interests and thus matters in which there would be more widespread, significant private expectations;[47] and both had been erroneously reasoned.[48]

Justice O'Connor concurred on the grounds that *Booth* and *Gathers* ought to be overruled because they "were wrongly decided."[49] In another separate concurrence, Justice Scalia argued that contrary to the arguments made in the dissent of Justice Thurgood Marshall, the Court need not show any "special justification" for overruling *Booth* and *Gathers* and that those decisions did far more damage to the notion of stare decisis than *Payne* because they violated the "general principle that the settled practices and expectations of a democratic society should generally not be disturbed by the courts."[50] (In subsequent opinions, Justice Scalia explained these "settled practices and expectations" constitute "tradition"[51] and reflect the genuine or more traditional rule of stare decisis.[52]) In yet another separate concurrence, Justice Souter argued that *Booth* and *Gathers* should be overruled because they were erroneously reasoned and demonstrably unworkable.[53]

In what would be his final dissent, Justice Marshall castigated the majority for making "[p]ower, not reason ... the new currency of th[e] Court's decisionmaking."[54] He argued that (1) these overrulings could be traced to recent changes in the Court's personnel;[55] (2) overrulings based on prior close votes and disagreements with precedents' reasoning already expressed in dissents would disrupt constitutional law significantly;[56] and (3) the majority had failed to "come forward with the type of extraordinary showing that the Court has historically demanded before overruling one of its precedents."[57] Marshall argued further that the Chief Justice's position that 5–4 decisions with vigorous dissents deserve less than the usual deference owed to precedents threatened to "destroy" the Court's authority as the final decision maker on questions involving individual liberties, because it "invites" state actors to treat certain decisions as nonbinding and instead "to renew the very policies deemed unconstitutional in the hope that the Court may now reverse course, even if it has only recently reaffirmed the constitutional liberty in question."[58] In a separate dissent, Justice Stevens accused the majority of abandoning sound reasoning and stare decisis due to the "'hydraulic pressure' of public opinion."[59]

A year later the justices fractured further over whether to overrule *Roe v. Wade*[60] in *Planned Parenthood v. Casey*.[61] Justices O'Connor, Kennedy, and Souter, joined by *Payne* dissenters Blackmun and Stevens, made a bare majority to reaffirm the constitutional right of women to abortion that had been first recognized in *Roe*. The three swing justices made a controlling plurality to adopt a new "undue burden" standard for the validity of state abortion regulations. Chief Justice Rehnquist and Justices White and Scalia, joined by Justice Clarence Thomas, who replaced Justice Marshall on the Court, would have overruled *Roe* and permitted state regulations and restrictions that are rationally related to a legitimate state interest.

> In an extensive discussion of the doctrine of stare decisis, the majority explained that, when the Court reexamines a prior holding, its judgment is customarily informed by a series of prudential and pragmatic considerations designed to test the consistency of overruling a prior decision with the ideal of the rule of law, and to gauge the respective costs of reaffirming and overruling a prior case. Thus, for example, we may ask whether the rule has proved to be intolerable simply in defying practical workability; whether the rule is subject to a kind of reliance that would lend a special hardship to the consequences of overruling and add inequity to the cost of repudiation; whether related principles of law have so far developed as to have left the old rule no more than a remnant of abandoned doctrine; or whether facts have so changed or come to be seen so differently, as to have robbed the old rule of significant application or justification.[62]

The opinion dealt briefly with the workability question, finding that the determinations required under *Roe* "fall within judicial competence,"[63] and devoted more attention to the difficult issue of reliance. "Since the classic case for weighing reliance heavily in favor of following the earlier rule occurs in the commercial context [citing *Payne*,] where advance planning of great precision is most obviously a necessity, it is no cause for surprise that some would find no reliance worthy of consideration in support of *Roe*."[64] "[C]ognizable reliance," however, goes beyond "specific instances of sexual activity":

> [F]or two decades of economic and social developments, people have organized intimate relationships and made choices that define their views of themselves and their places in society, in reliance on the availability of abortion in the event that contraception should fail. The ability of women to participate equally in the economic and social life of the Nation has been facilitated by their ability to control their reproductive lives.[65]

The majority considered *Roe* in the context of other decisions, finding its abortion rights doctrine neither anomalous nor obsolete. And it saw supervening developments in medical knowledge and technology as requiring no more than flexibility in the application of *Roe*'s central holding, rather than its overruling.[66] Recognizing that *Roe* is no ordinary precedent, the majority broadened its discussion to consider arguable parallels with two abandoned lines of cases, those identified with recognition of the liberty of contract (or economic due process) in *Lochner v. New York*,[67] and validation of the separate but equal doctrine in *Plessy v. Ferguson*.[68] It viewed the abandonment of the constitutional doctrines of liberty of contract and separate but equal as resting on major changes in facts or in their understanding, beyond mere changes in Court membership or disagreement with the original holdings, that made reconsideration "not only justified but required."[69] With *Roe*, the majority saw not just a threat to the Court's legitimacy from too-frequent vacillation but an analogy to *Brown v. Board of Education*[70] in that there and in *Roe* the Court, in interpreting the Constitution, had called on "the contending sides of a national controversy to end their national division by accepting a common mandate rooted in the Constitution."[71] "A decision to overrule *Roe*'s essential holding under the existing circumstances," the majority explained, "would address error, if error there was, at the cost of both profound and unnecessary damage to the Court's legitimacy, and to the Nation's commitment to the rule of law. It is therefore imperative to adhere to the essence of *Roe*'s original decision."[72]

In dissents joined by Justices Thomas and White, Chief Justice Rehnquist and Justice Scalia both reconciled the overruling of *Roe* with the respect due to precedent generally. Both opinions strongly emphasized the gravity of what they viewed as *Roe*'s error, and Justice Scalia likened *Roe* to the Court's tragic mistake in *Dred Scott v. Sandford*[73] rather than to its abandonment of *Lochner* and *Plessy*.[74] Chief Justice Rehnquist's opinion contended that the prevailing opinion in *Casey* abandoned rather than adhered to stare decisis because it had modified the approach in *Roe* for measuring the constitutionality of state abortion regulations,[75] and disagreed point by point with its arguments on precedent and the plurality's reformulated "undue burden" standard.[76] In his view, "Strong and often misguided criticism of a decision should not render the decision immune from reconsideration, lest a fetish for legitimacy penalize freedom of expression."[77] He concluded,

> The sum of the joint opinion's labors in the name of stare
> decisis and "legitimacy" is this: *Roe v. Wade* stands as a sort of
> judicial Potemkin Village, which may be pointed out to passers
> as a monument to the importance of adhering to precedent. But
> behind the facade, an entirely new method of analysis, without
> any roots in constitutional law, is imported to decide the consti-
> tutionality of state laws regulating abortion. Neither stare decisis
> nor "legitimacy" [is] truly served by such an effort.[78]

Three years later *Casey*'s five-member majority split 2–3 in *Adarand Constructors, Inc. v. Pena*[79] over whether to overrule the Court's 1990 decision in *Metro Broadcasting v. FCC*.[80] (In the interim, Justice Breyer had replaced Justice Blackmun.) In *Metro Broadcasting*, the Court had upheld 5–4 the constitutionality of Federal Communications Commission policies allowing minority ownership to be taken into account in the awarding and transferring of broadcast licenses. In her opinion for the majority in *Adarand* (consisting of herself, the chief justice, and Justices Kennedy, Scalia, and Thomas), Justice O'Connor quoted approvingly Justice Felix Frankfurter's admonition that "'stare decisis is a principle of policy and not a mechanical formula of adherence to the latest decision, however recent and questionable, when such adherence involves collision with a prior doctrine more embracing in its scope, intrinsically sounder, and verified by experience.'"[81] Applying this principle to *Adarand*, Justice O'Connor found that *Metro Broadcasting* "undermined important principles of this Court's equal protection jurisprudence, established in a line of cases stretching back over 50 years."[82] The principles established in those cases, according to Justice O'Connor, "stood for an 'embracing' and 'intrinsically soun[d]' understanding of equal protection 'verified by experience,' namely, that the Constitution imposes upon federal, state, and local governmental actors the same obligation to respect the personal right to equal protection of the laws."[83] She concluded that *Adarand* "therefore presents precisely the situation described by Justice Frankfurter[:] We cannot adhere to our most recent decision without colliding with an accepted and established doctrine."[84] Moreover, she explained, the widespread scholarly criticism of *Metro Broadcasting* and the Court's "past practice in similar circumstances support our action today."[85]

Mindful that the Court's overruling of *Metro Broadcasting* might conflict with the Court's reaffirmation of *Roe* in *Casey*, Justice O'Connor took pains to distinguish the Court's approaches to precedent in *Adarand* and *Casey*. She argued that "*Casey* explained how considerations of stare decisis inform the decision whether to overrule a long-established precedent that has become integrated into the fabric of the law. Overruling precedent of that kind naturally may have consequences for 'the ideal of the rule of law'. … In addition, such precedent is likely to have engendered substantial reliance."[86] She suggested that whereas *Casey* had been consistent with a series of decisions reaffirming *Roe v. Wade*'s core holding, "*Metro Broadcasting* … departed from our prior cases—and did so quite recently. By refusing to follow *Metro Broadcasting* then, we do not depart from the fabric of the law; we restore it."[87]

In dissent, Justice Stevens argued that *Metro Broadcasting* could hardly conflict with well-established constitutional law because it had only been the Court's third opinion "consider[ing] the constitutionality of a federal affirmative-action program."[88] The first such case had been *Fullilove v. Klutznick*,[89] in which six justices had agreed to uphold (but without a majority agreeing on the reasons for upholding) a congressional enactment providing that at least 10 percent of federal funds granted for local public works must be used to obtain services or supplies from minority-owned businesses. The second decision had been *City of Richmond v. J. A. Croson Co.*,[90] in which the Court's 5–4 decision had struck down a city plan modeled on the federal program upheld in *Fullilove*. In *Adarand*, Justice Stevens explained, "*Metro Broadcasting* involved a federal program, whereas *Croson* involved a city ordinance. *Metro Broadcasting* thus drew support from *Fullilove* which predated *Croson* and which *Croson* [had] distinguished on the grounds of the federal-state dichotomy that the majority today discredits. ... [T]he law at the time of [*Fullilove* had been] entirely open to the result that the Court reached. Today's decision is an unjustified departure from settled law."[91]

Departure from clearly settled law, including subsequent cases, served as the primary basis for the Court's overrulings of two precedents raising fundamental questions about the scope of federal power to restrict state sovereignty in spite of the Eleventh Amendment. The Eleventh Amendment provides, "The judicial power of the United States shall not be construed to extend to any suit in law or equity, commenced or prosecuted against one of the United States by Citizens of another State, or by Citizens or Subjects of any foreign State." Though the text of the Eleventh Amendment explicitly bars only suits brought against a state by citizens of another state (or country), the Court held more than a century ago in *Hans v. Louisiana*[92] that the Eleventh Amendment also bars suits in federal court brought against a state by its own citizens. In 1989 a plurality of the Court in *Pennsylvania v. Union Gas*[93] joined in the outcome, but not in the reasoning by Justice White, that the interstate commerce clause[94] granted Congress the power to abrogate state sovereign immunity under the Eleventh Amendment. The plurality reasoned that the power to regulate interstate commerce would be "incomplete without the authority to render States liable in damages." The other four justices—Chief Justice Rehnquist and Justices O'Connor, Scalia, and Kennedy—vigorously dissented on the grounds that the decision could not be squared with the original understanding of the Eleventh Amendment or the Court's other precedents in the area, including *Hans*.

Seven years later the Court, in *Seminole Tribe v. Florida*,[95] readdressed the issue in the course of adjudicating a challenge to a congressional enactment under the Indian commerce clause permitting an Indian tribe to sue a state for failing to perform its statutory duty to negotiate in good faith a compact with the tribes to provide gaming activities within the state. Split precisely along the same lines as it had been in *Adarand*, the Court in *Seminole Tribe* overruled *Union Gas*. In a lengthy opinion for the majority, Chief Justice Rehnquist "conclude[d] that none of the policies underlying stare decisis require our continuing adherence to [the] holding in *Union Gas*."[96] First, he noted that the 5–4 decision in *Union Gas* lacked "an express rationale agreed upon by the majority of the Court."[97] Consequently the decision, in his view, "ha[d] created confusion among the lower courts that have sought to understand and apply the deeply fractured decision."[98] Second, Chief Justice Rehnquist found that the "result in *Union Gas* and the plurality's rationale depart[ed] from our established understanding of the Eleventh Amendment and undermine[d] the accepted function of Article III."[99] Relying instead on a rationale put forward by Justice Scalia in his dissent in *Union Gas*,[100] he explained that *Hans* and subsequent case law made clear that Article III, as amended by the Eleventh Amendment, defined the outer limits of federal court jurisdiction. On his view, the case law clearly dictated that the Fourteenth Amendment was the only constitutional provision that conceivably empowered the Congress to expand federal court jurisdiction under Article III at the expense of state sovereignty. By upholding an attempt by Congress to use its commerce clause authority to expand federal jurisdiction at the expense of state sovereignty, *Union Gas* "proved to be a solitary departure from established law."[101]

In their respective dissents, Justices Stevens and Souter gave different reasons for opposing the overruling of *Union Gas*. Writing for himself, Justice Stevens denounced the majority's characterization of *Union Gas'* holding as a novel or incomprehensible "plurality decision."[102] He found "far more significant than the 'plurality' character of the … opinions supporting the holding in *Union Gas* [is] the fact that the issue confronted today has been squarely addressed by a total of 13 justices [in prior cases], of whom 8 cast their positions with [the position of] the so-called 'plurality.'"[103]

Justice Souter suggested in his dissent that the majority's extension of *Hans* did more damage to settled law than did the plurality's opinion in *Union Gas*. Justice Souter explained that federal jurisdiction could be based on the diversity of citizenship between the parties to a lawsuit or the presence of a question of federal law. The major error in *Hans*, he suggested, was the Court's mistaken "assum[ption] that a State could plead sovereign immunity against a noncitizen suing under federal-question jurisdiction, and for that reason h[olding] that a State must enjoy the same protection in a suit by one of its own citizens."[104] This assumption was mistaken because it transformed a preconstitutional common law rule, which had recognized state sovereign immunity in diversity cases, into a constitutional prohibition on Congress' power to expand federal-question jurisdiction in a case involving diverse parties. Thus Justice Souter argued, *Hans* only answered the narrow question whether the Constitution, without more, permits a State to plead sovereign immunity to bar the exercise of federal-question jurisdiction. … Although the Court invoked a principle of sovereign immunity to cure what it took to be the Eleventh Amendment's anomaly of barring only those state suits brought by noncitizen plaintiffs, the *Hans* Court had no occasion to consider whether Congress could abrogate that background immunity by statute. Indeed (except in the special circumstance of Congress' power to enforce the Civil War Amendments), this question never came before the Court until *Union Gas* and any intimations of an immunity recognized in *Hans* had no constitutional status and was subject to congressional abrogation. Today the Court overrules *Union Gas* and holds just the opposite. In deciding how to choose between these two positions, the place to begin is with *Hans*' holding that a principle of sovereign immunity derived from the common law insulates a State from federal-question jurisdiction at the suit of its own citizens. A critical examination of that case will show that it was wrongly decided, as virtually every recent commentator has concluded.[105]

Justice Souter maintained that the transformation of a common law rule into a constitutional principle was reminiscent of the Court's widely criticized opinion in *Lochner* in which it had recognized a constitutionally enforceable right to contract. He warned that in taking such a discredited and dangerous approach, the *Seminole Tribe* Court was "follow[ing] a course that has brought it to grief before in our history, and promises to do so again."[106] He explained,

It was the defining characteristic of the *Lochner* era, and its characteristic vice, that the Court treated the common-law background (in those days, common-law property rights and contractual autonomy) as paramount, while regarding congressional legislation to abrogate the common law in these economic matters as constitutionally suspect. … And yet the superseding lesson that seemed clear in *West Coast Hotel v. Parrish* … that action within the legislative power is not subject to greater scrutiny merely because it trenches upon the case law's ordering of economic and social relationships, seems to have been lost on the Court.[107]

If there were any difference between *Lochner* and *Seminole Tribe*, Justice Souter suggested, it was that *Lochner* made

> an ostensible effort to give content to some other written provision of the Constitution, like the Due Process Clause, the very object of which is to limit the exercise of governmental power. … Some textual argument, at least, could be made that the Court was doing no more than defining one provision that happened to be at odds with another. Today, however, the Court is not struggling to fulfill a responsibility to reconcile two arguably conflicting and Delphic constitutional provisions, nor is it struggling with any Delphic text at all. For even the Court concedes that the Constitution's grant of plenary power over relations with Indian tribes at the expense of any state claim to the contrary is unmistakably clear, and this case does not arguably implicate a textual trump to the grant of federal-question jurisdiction.[108]

Justice Souter's protracted criticisms of *Hans* did not, however, lead him to support overruling *Hans*. Instead, he concluded that "for reasons of stare decisis I would not disturb the century-old precedent" of *Hans*.[109] He acknowledged that *Hans*

> was erroneous, but it has not previously proven to be unworkable or to conflict with later doctrine or to suffer from the effects of facts developed since its decision (apart from those indicating its original errors). I would therefore treat *Hans* as it has always been treated in fact until today, as a doctrine of federal common law. For, as so understood, it has formed one of the strands of the federal-state relationship for over a century now, and the stability of that relationship is itself a value that stare decisis ought to respect.[110]

Three years after *Seminole Tribe*, the Court in *College Savings Bank v. Florida*[111] split exactly along the same lines as it had in *Adarand* and *Seminole Tribe* to overturn another precedent dealing with the scope of federal power to limit state sovereign immunity. The precedent at issue was *Parden v. Terminal Railway Co. of Alabama*.[112] In *Parden*, the Court unanimously held that a state may constructively or implicitly waive its Eleventh Amendment sovereign immunity by engaging in a commercial activity in a federally regulated marketplace. *College Savings Bank* revisited this question in the context of a federal lawsuit brought against a state by a private business claiming that the state had engaged in commercial activities that constituted false and misleading advertising in violation of federal trademark law.

In his opinion for the Court in *College Savings Bank*, Justice Scalia described in detail the Court's long retreat from and persistent questioning of *Parden*. He noted, for instance, that in 1987 the Court in part of an opinion—the part that Justice Scalia had joined—had overruled *Parden* "to the extent [it] is inconsistent with the requirement that an abrogation of Eleventh Amendment immunity by Congress must be expressed in unmistakably clear language."[113] Justice Scalia then summarized the Court's reasons for overruling whatever remained of *Parden*:

> We think that the constructive-waiver experiment of *Parden*
> was ill-conceived, and see no merit in attempting to salvage any
> remnant of it ... *Parden* broke sharply with other cases, and
> is fundamentally incompatible with later ones. We have never
> applied the holding of *Parden* to another statute, and in fact
> have narrowed the case in every subsequent opinion in which
> it has been under consideration. In short, *Parden* stands as
> an anomaly in the jurisprudence of sovereign immunity, and
> indeed in the jurisprudence of constitutional law. Today, we
> drop the other shoe: Whatever may remain of our decision is
> expressly overruled.[114]

In dissent, Justice Breyer initially disputed that *Parden* had "br[oken] 'sharply with prior cases.'"[115] *Parden* itself cited authority that found related "waivers in at least roughly comparable circumstances."[116] Moreover, *Parden* had support from both earlier and subsequent cases. Second, Justice Breyer argued that the case law claimed by the majority as supporting its rejection of *Parden*, including *Seminole Tribe*, did no such thing. He claimed that *Seminole Tribe*, rather than *Parden*, was the genuine anomaly in Eleventh Amendment jurisprudence. After arguing that *Seminole Tribe* lacked support from constitutional text, history, and precedent, Justice Breyer suggested that the most serious problem with *Seminole Tribe* was that it marked a return to discredited Lochnerism. He explained, "The similarity to *Lochner* lies in the risk that *Seminole Tribe* and the Court's subsequent cases will deprive Congress of necessary legislative flexibility … to achieve one of federalism's basic objectives … the protection of liberty."[117] He concluded with a plea to overrule *Seminole Tribe*:

> Unfortunately, *Seminole Tribe* and today's related decisions, separate one formal strand from the federalist skein—a strand that has been understood as anti-Republican since the time of Cicero—and they elevate that strand to the level of an immutable constitutional principle more akin to the thought of James I than of James Madison. They do so when the role sovereign immunity once played in helping to assure the States that their political independence would remain after joining the Union no longer holds center stage. … They do so when a federal court's ability to enforce its judgment against a State is no longer a major concern. … And they do so without adequate legal support grounded in either history or practical need. To the contrary, by making that doctrine immune from congressional Article I modification, the Court makes it more difficult for Congress to decentralize governmental decisionmaking and to provide individual citizens, or local communities, with a variety of enforcement powers. By diminishing congressional flexibility to do so, the Court makes it somewhat more difficult to satisfy modern federalism's more important liberty-protecting needs. In this sense, it is counterproductive.[118]

Since the *College Savings Bank* case in 1999, the Supreme Court has explicitly overruled seven other constitutional precedents. Each time, the Court's primary justification for overruling a precedent was its irreconcilability with subsequent case law. *Mitchell v. Helms*,[119] for example, involved the question of the constitutionality of the expenditure of state funds by private schools, including some parochial schools, on instructional materials, including textbooks. In two earlier cases, *Meek v. Pittenger*[120] and *Wolman v. Walter*,[121] the Court held programs that provided many of the same kinds of materials as the practice at issue in *Mitchell* violated the establishment clause. As Justice O'Connor summarized the reasoning of those cases in her concurrence in *Mitchell*, "We reasoned that, because the religious schools receiving the materials and equipment were pervasively sectarian, any assistance in support of the schools' educational missions would inevitably have the impermissible effect of advancing religion."[122] Thus a major question for the Court in *Mitchell* involved the continued viability of the rule in the earlier cases that barred aid to religious schools that was potentially divertible to religious use. In *Mitchell v. Helms*, the Court upheld the challenged program and rejected the divertibility rule set forth in *Meek* and *Wolman*. On behalf of himself and four other justices, Justice Clarence Thomas "acknowledged [that in so holding] *Meek* and *Wolman* are anomalies [and] therefore conclude[d] that they are no longer good law."[123] He explained that the overrulings of these cases "should [have] come as no surprise" because of several subsequent cases that were decided to be incompatible with their reasoning.[124]

In her concurrence, Justice O'Connor expanded on the reasons for overruling *Meek* and *Wolman*. She suggested that "[a]t the time they were decided, *Meek* and *Wolman* created an inexplicable rift within the establishment clause concerning government aid to schools," with those two cases effectively adopting an irrebutable presumption of unconstitutionality that secular instructional materials would be diverted to use in religious instruction and thus advance religion impermissibly and many others upholding assistance to parochial schools without any evidence of actual diversion.[125] She concluded,

> Because divertability fails to explain the distinction our cases have drawn between textbooks and instructional materials and equipment, there remains the question of which of the two irreconcilable strands of our establishment clause jurisprudence we should now follow. Between the two, I would adhere to the rule we have applied in the context of textbook lending programs: To establish a First Amendment violation, plaintiffs must prove that the aid in question actually is, or has been, used for religious purposes. [Subsequent case law has] undermined the assumptions underlying *Meek* and *Wolman*.[126]

In dissent, Justice Souter challenged the Court's presumption that its decisions on aid to religious schools created any "single test of constitutional sufficiency"[127] and thus maintained the presumption underlying *Meek* and *Wolman* was both consistent with the First Amendment and not in conflict with any coherent or settled line of decisions.

Perhaps the Rehnquist Court's most dramatic, unexpected overruling occurred in *Lawrence v. Texas*.[128] *Lawrence* involved the constitutionality of a Texas law making it a crime for two persons of the same sex to engage in certain intimate sexual conduct. The Court explained that in order to resolve this question it had to reconsider its 1986 decision in *Bowers v. Hardwick*.[129] In *Bowers*, the Court upheld 5–4 the constitutionality of a law restricting sodomy between any two persons. In upholding the law, the Court rejected that the Fourteenth Amendment guarantees an implicitly fundamental right to engage in homosexual sodomy. In *Lawrence*, the Court wasted no time in rejecting the basis for the Court's holding in *Bowers*. Five of the six justices overturning the criminal convictions in *Lawrence* agreed that "[t]he foundations of *Bowers* have sustained serious erosion from our recent decisions in *Casey* and [*Romer v. Evans*]."[130] The Court found the liberty interest at stake in *Lawrence* was indistinguishable from the implied fundamental right (under the due process clause) it had recognized in *Casey* for women to choose to have abortions (at least until the point of viability) and the guarantee of the equal protection clause that the Court had recognized in *Romer* as protecting gay and lesbian citizens from being singled out solely on the basis of animus.[131] The Court found further that the usual justifications for fidelity to erroneous decisions, such as social reliance, were inapplicable to *Bowers*.

In dissent, Justice Scalia stridently denounced the majority for not faithfully applying the doctrine of stare decisis. He argued the doctrine called for reaffirming *Bowers*, rather than reversing it, because it was not erroneous and was consistent with the Court's substantive due process opinions generally.[132] He found no evidence that the rights being protected by the Court in *Lawrence* were, as the Court's precedents required, "'deeply-rooted in this Nation's history and tradition.'"[133] He concluded that the decision was nothing more than the "product of a Court, which is the product of a law profession culture, that has largely signed on to the so-called homosexual agenda, by which I mean the agenda promoted by some homosexual activists directed at eliminating the moral opprobrium that has traditionally attached to homosexual conduct."[134] Justice Scalia suggested his problem was not with gays, lesbians, or their agenda, but rather with the Court's failure to appreciate that "[w]hat Texas has chosen to do is well within the range of traditional democratic action, and its hand should not be stayed through the invention of a brand-new constitutional 'right' by a Court that is impatient of democratic change … [It] is the premise of our system that judgments [such as those made by the Texas legislature] are to be made by the people, and not imposed by a governing caste that knows best."[135]

At the end of the 2004 term, the Rehnquist Court again surprisingly overruled a precedent with which many conservative politicians and scholars strongly agreed. In *Roper v. Simmons*,[136] the Court considered the issue, resolved 16 years earlier in *Stanford v. Kentucky*,[137] of whether states could lawfully execute juveniles. Justice Kennedy, writing for the majority, concluded that executing juveniles was now disfavored by a majority of jurisdictions: "These considerations mean *Stanford v. Kentucky* should be deemed no longer controlling on this issue. To the extent *Stanford* was based on review of the objective indicia of consensus that obtained in 1989 … it suffices to note that those indicia have changed."[138] Thus the Court overruled *Stanford*. The majority also indicated, however, that *Stanford* was wrongly decided when it was issued:

> It should be observed, furthermore, that the *Stanford* Court
> should have considered those States that had abandoned the
> death penalty altogether as part of the consensus against the
> juvenile death penalty; a State's decision to bar the death penalty
> altogether of necessity demonstrates a judgment that the death
> penalty is inappropriate for all offenders, including juveniles.
> Last, to the extent *Stanford* was based on a rejection of the idea
> that this Court is required to bring its independent judgment to
> bear on the proportionality of the death penalty for a particu-
> lar class of crimes or offenders [citations omitted], it suffices
> to note that this rejection was inconsistent with prior Eighth
> Amendment decisions.[139]

In their dissents, Justices O'Connor and Scalia defended retaining *Stanford* as correctly decided. Justice O'Connor preferred "not [to] substitute our judgment about the moral propriety of capital punishment for 17-year-old murderers for the judgments of the Nation's legislatures,"[140] while Justice Scalia chided the majority for treating "less than 50% of death penalty States [as] constitute[ing] a national consensus."[141]

4. The Art of Overruling

Expressly overruling constitutional precedents constitutes a tiny fraction of what the Court does.[142] In most cases, the Court simply applies its precedents, usually in conjunction with other sources, such as the constitutional text, original meaning, and structure. Applying precedents requires interpreting them, interpreting them frequently entails modifying them, and modifying them often entails extending or contracting them. Consequently many cases may be weakened, but without being formally overruled.

In fact, cases may be weakened through implicit overrulings or narrowing construction. Overrulings *sub silentio*—overrulings that are not characterized in so many words—have different practical effects from decisions weakening other decisions through distinctions. An implicitly overruled precedent no longer is law, even as applied to the fact situation it initially purported to resolve, while a seriously narrowed precedent retains sufficient vitality to resolve fact situations identical to that which it originally settled. Not surprisingly, the Court can cause confusion when it does not clarify whether it is distinguishing or implicitly overruling precedents. For example, the Court generated considerable confusion in a series of inconsistent precedents on whether private shopping centers could regulate political speech, and it ultimately had to clarify it was overruling and not merely distinguishing an earlier decision.[143]

Finding overrulings *sub silentio* requires closely reading cases to assess the exact consequences of their decisions. With this in mind, I identified at least 17 occasions in which the Court has implicitly overruled earlier decisions. (Table A-7 shows that in 17 cases the Court has overruled 24 precedents *sub silentio*.) The first is one of the most important—the implicit overruling of *Lochner v. New York*[144] by the Court in *Bunting v. Oregon*.[145] *Lochner* symbolized the Court's aggressive protection of the right to contract; it struck down maximum-hour legislation for bakery employees because it interfered with a constitutionally recognized and protected right to contract. But in *Bunting* the Court upheld a statute establishing a maximum 10-hour day for factory workers. Although judicial activism on behalf of economic liberties persisted after *Bunting*, *Lochner*'s specific ruling did not.

Later, the Warren Court implicitly overruled the 8–1 decision in *Plessy v. Ferguson*[146] upholding state-mandated segregation in public railways. This did not occur, however, in *Brown v. Board of Education*,[147] as many people suppose. Rather than overrule *Plessy* entirely, the Court in *Brown* declared, "Whatever may have been the extent of psychological knowledge at the time of [*Plessy*,] this finding is amply supported by modern authority. Any language in [*Plessy*] contrary to this finding is rejected."[148] The Court acknowledged further "that in the field of public education the doctrine of 'separate but equal' has no place." This language could be read as overruling some of the reasoning underlying *Plessy*, but it left unaddressed state-mandated segregation in other public facilities, including railways. Not long thereafter, the Court removed any doubt about *Plessy*'s status by overruling it, with no fanfare, in *Gayle v. Browder*.[149] In that case, a special three-judge panel of the district court held that the Warren Court's decision in *Brown* effectively overruled *Plessy* and thus held state-mandated segregation of the races in public buses violated the equal protection clause.[150] The Supreme Court affirmed the district court without commenting on what it said about *Brown*'s overruling *Plessy*. Thus the Court implicitly overruled *Plessy*.

The reluctance to overrule *Plessy* outright is understandable. In *Brown*, the justices wanted to avoid the social disruption and harsh political backlash they expected an explicit overruling to produce. The Court delayed oral argument in *Brown* until after the 1952 presidential election to avoid *Brown* becoming an issue in the election. Moreover, the Court in *Brown* implicitly abandoned its prior practice of allowing separate but equal facilities in public education, with the effects of (1) partially deflecting controversy about precisely how much the Court would undo segregation outside the public school context; (2) adhering to the Court's practice of issuing separate lines of decision for each of the different contexts in which the state mandated segregation of the races;[151] and (3) suggesting that the stigma from segregation in public education had may have had more severe, harmful, immediate, and lasting consequences on its victims than those on the victims of segregation in other areas.[152]

In 1991, in *Arizona v. Fulminante*,[153] all five of Presidents Reagan's and Bush's appointees joined in implicitly overruling a prior decision that had automatically invalidated the criminal conviction of a defendant whose coerced confession had been admitted into evidence. By calling attention to the consequences of the majority's decision, the dissent made the implicit overruling easier to identify. As the next section shows, not all eviscerations of precedent are so easily spotted.

5. Weakening Precedents Through Narrowing

Constitutional adjudication frequently entails adjusting principles recognized in earlier cases. For example, in *BedRoc Ltd., LLC v. United States*,[154] the Rehnquist Court considered overruling *Watt v. Western Nuclear, Inc.*[155] The plurality—Rehnquist, O'Connor, Scalia, and Kennedy—expressed its discomfort with *Western Nuclear*, but it declined to expressly overrule the case: "While we share the concerns expressed in the *Western Nuclear* dissent, [we] decline to overrule our recent precedent. By the same token, we will not extend *Western Nuclear*'s holding."[156] The concurrence, by Justice Thomas, joined by Justice Breyer, noted "the Government identifies significant reliance interests that would be upset by overruling *Western Nuclear*" and thus he voted not to overrule it.[157] Justice Stevens' dissent, joined by Justices Souter and Ginsburg, preferred to uphold *Western Nuclear*, noting "Congress' acceptance of [its] holding ... for the past two decades should control our decision, and any residual doubt should be eliminated by the deference owed to the executive agency."[158]

Sometimes a series of distinctions clearly weaken precedents or set the stage for overruling. For example, the Court explicitly overruled *National League of Cities v. Usery*[159] in *Garcia v. San Antonio Metropolitan Transit Authority*,[160] but only after deciding several cases in the interim that had undermined *National League of Cities*. In the nine years between *National League of Cities* and *Garcia*, the Court, in four cases, tried to apply *National League of Cities*' rule prohibiting congressional regulations of traditional state functions, but in each case the Court found that federal regulations did not interfere with states' traditional functions.[161] These rulings led Justice Blackmun, who had concurred in *National League of Cities*, to conclude in *Garcia* that *National League of Cities* should be overruled because its test for determining the traditional state functions protected from commerce clause regulation was unworkable; the Court could not figure out what constituted states' traditional functions. *Garcia*, though, is not the end of the story, as threatened by then-Justice Rehnquist, who vowed in his *Garcia* dissent that *Garcia* would eventually be overruled and *National League of Cities* would be restored.[162] Seven years after *Garcia*, the Court in *New York v. United States*[163] partially overruled *Garcia* in the course of striking down a federal law for coercing states to participate in a federal plan to dispose of hazardous waste. *Garcia* has been further weakened through several decisions in which the Court has found that congressional commandeering of state activities violates the Tenth Amendment.[164] *Garcia* has been increasingly confined to its facts, and it seems only a matter of time before the Court declares *Garcia* as so inconsistent with its commerce clause and Tenth Amendment decisions as to require overruling.

More than a few commentators predict *Roe* will follow a similar path. Indeed, while working for the Justice Department, Justice Samuel Alito, Jr., had suggested a strategy for overruling *Roe* that entailed persuading the Court to uphold laws weakening *Roe* and thus allowing the Court to dismantle it bit by bit, so that eventually the Court would recognize there was nothing left of *Roe*. For his part, John Roberts wrote and signed a brief urging the Court in *Casey* to overrule *Roe*. While in their respective confirmation hearings Justice Alito promised to keep an "open mind" on *Roe* and Chief Justice Roberts characterized *Roe* as "settled," many believe President Bush would not have appointed them unless he had some reason to be confident they would severely weaken if not join others in formally overruling *Roe*.

Distinctions have also played a significant role in the Court's proportionality of punishment decisions. In 1980 *Rummel v. Estelle*[165] held by a 5–4 vote that Texas' statutory requirement of a mandatory life sentence for a defendant convicted of three felonies, consisting in that case of fraudulent practices cumulatively depriving people of property totaling less than two hundred dollars, did not violate the Eighth Amendment's prohibition against cruel and unusual punishment. This holding cast doubt on the Court's prior practice dating back to earlier in the century of applying, beyond the death penalty context, the standard that the Eighth Amendment prohibited imposition of a sentence that is grossly disproportionate to the severity of the crime.[166]

Subsequently the Court, by a 5–4 vote in *Solem v. Helms*,[167] struck down a punishment scheme almost identical to *Rummel*, except that *Solem* involved a mandatory life sentence without the possibility of parole. Justice Blackmun was the swing vote in *Solem* (as he was in both *Garcia* and *National League of Cities*), but he did not write an opinion. Instead, Justice Powell's opinion for the Court in *Solem* was virtually identical to his dissent in *Rummel*, prompting the dissenters in *Solem* to claim *Rummel* was being overruled *sub silentio*.[168]

In *Harmelin v. Michigan*,[169] the Court tried to resolve the confusion generated by the Court's deciding both *Rummel* and *Solem*. The five-member majority upheld Michigan's imposition of a mandatory life sentence without parole for drug possession, but split over how to deal with *Solem*. Chief Justice Rehnquist and Justice Scalia argued that *Solem* should be overruled because it set forth an unworkable standard and was inconsistent with prior decisions and original understanding.[170] In a separate concurrence, Justice Kennedy, joined by Justices Souter and O'Connor, refused the entreaty to overrule *Solem* and instead tried to reconcile *Solem* and *Harmelin* on the ground that the Eighth Amendment "forbids only extreme sentences that are 'grossly disproportionate to the crime.'"[171]

Harmelin has hardly been the Court's last word on proportionality of punishment. In 2002 the Court, in *Lockyer v. Andrade*, agreed to revisit the constitutionality of that state's law imposing a mandatory life sentence on someone convicted of at least three felonies or serious misdemeanors.[172] The Ninth Circuit judges split over the constitutionality of the law, though all recognized the need to reconcile *Solem* and *Harmelin*. Though the Court upheld the California law,[173] it did so without explicitly or implicitly overruling *Solem*. At the outset of her opinion for a five-member majority, Justice O'Connor acknowledged that "in determining whether a particular sentence for a term of years can violate the Eighth Amendment, we have not established a clear or consistent path for courts to follow." She acknowledged further that "[o]ur cases exhibit a lack of certainty regarding what factors may indicate gross proportionality."[174] Yet, the uncertainty did not lead the Court to overrule *Solem*. Andrade's sentence was disproportionate only if it were "'contrary to or [an] unreasonable application of' … the gross proportionality principle, the precise contours of which are unclear." The Court recognized that such a principle would be violated "only in the 'exceedingly rare' and 'extreme' case."[175] *Andrade* was not such a case. The Court concluded that in upholding Andrade's sentence the state courts had not violated the "'uncertainty' of the scope of the proportionality principle."

Oftentimes, factual differences among cases provide the bases for distinctions. For example, in *Stanley v. Georgia*,[176] the Court held the Fourth Amendment prohibited searching a person's home for obscene materials, but in *Osborne v. Ohio*[177] the Court held *Stanley* did not apply to the possession of pornography. In *R.A.V. v. St. Paul*,[178] the Court upheld a First Amendment challenge to a St. Paul ordinance criminalizing cross burning and certain other activities "which one knows or has reasonable grounds to know causes anger, alarm or resentment in others on the basis of race." A year later the Court unanimously rejected a First Amendment challenge to a hate-crimes statute.[179] Subsequently, in *Virginia v. Black*,[180] the Court upheld a Virginia law banning cross burning with "an intent to intimidate a person or group of persons" without narrowing or undermining either of these prior rulings as well as its prior extension of First Amendment protection to flag burning.[181]

In some cases, the Court claims that it is relying on a precedent in a decision, but mischaracterizes it with the effect, if not for the purpose, of undermining it. For example, in *Brandenburg v. Ohio*,[182] the Court did not overrule, but grossly mischaracterized its earlier decision in *Dennis v. United States*,[183] as having "fashioned the principle that the constitutional guarantee of free speech ... do[es] not permit a State to forbid ... advocacy of the use of force or of law violation except where such advocacy is directed to incit[e] or produc[e] imminent lawless action and is likely to incite or produce such action."[184] In fact, *Dennis* had upheld the federal antisubversive law, the Smith Act, under a very different test that required the Court to "ask whether the gravity of the 'evil,' discounted by its improbability, justifies such invasion of free speech as is necessary to avoid the danger."[185] Nevertheless, after *Brandenburg*, the Court relied on *Dennis* on at least one occasion.[186] Even more surprising may be the fact that after *Brandenburg* explicitly overruled another First Amendment case, *Whitney v. California*,[187] the Court subsequently relied on Justice Brandeis' concurrence in *Whitney* in its decision striking down state laws forbidding flag burning as violating the First Amendment.[188]

A common complaint about the Warren Court is that it failed to adopt a common law approach to constitutional adjudication, under which the justices could have built upon their predecessors' experience and reasoning while maintaining a healthy degree of stability and continuity in constitutional law.[189] When overrulings, express or otherwise, have been made possible primarily as a result of the votes of new justices, the new justices are open to charges that they have abandoned the doctrinal approach to constitutional adjudication for no good reason and instead have exercised raw power to reject prior experiences.[190] This charge has been leveled repeatedly against Chief Justice Rehnquist and Justices O'Connor, Scalia, Kennedy, and Thomas for trying to overrule or weaken precedents in many of the areas in which the presidents who appointed them had called for new directions, including criminal procedure,[191] interstate commerce,[192] church and state,[193] and equal protection.[194] The charges have less bite when the justices are ostensibly, if not actually, engaged in incremental decision making. Indeed, there is no meaningful difference between incremental decision making that weakens a precedent and incremental decision making that largely leaves a precedent intact.

6. Reaffirming Precedents

Occasionally justices will surprise—or disappoint—the presidents appointing them by affirming rather than overruling precedents with which the appointing presidents disagreed. One such case may have been

Minnick v. Mississippi.[195] Many commentators had expected the Rehnquist Court to curtail two earlier precedents, *Edwards v. Arizona*[196] and *Miranda v. Arizona*,[197] which had restricted police interrogation of suspects held in custody. In fact, the Court expanded both *Edwards* and *Miranda* in *Minnick* by establishing a bright-line rule that once a detained suspect declines to talk to police without a lawyer, the police can never thereafter initiate questioning without the suspect's attorney being present.[198]

These earlier cases set the stage for the Rehnquist Court's reconsideration of *Miranda* in *Dickerson v. United States*.[199] *Dickerson* involved the question of whether the warnings recommended in *Miranda* to be given a person prior to any custodial interrogation were constitutionally required. If the warnings were nonbinding policy recommendations, then there would be no constitutional problem with a law enacted by Congress post-*Miranda* setting forth a rule that the admissibility of statements made by someone in custodial interrogation before *Miranda* warnings were administered should turn only on whether the statements were made voluntarily. If, however, the warnings were constitutionally required, the law was unconstitutional unless the Court determined it was mistaken in deciding in *Miranda* that they were constitutionally required.

In a 7–2 decision, the Court reaffirmed *Miranda*. It decided the warnings recommended in *Miranda* were constitutionally required and thus struck down the congressional enactment and reaffirmed *Miranda*. Four of the six justices appointed by Presidents Reagan and Bush joined Justices Stevens, Breyer, and Ginsburg in the majority opinion, which was delivered by the Chief Justice. According to Chief Justice Rehnquist, "the principles of stare decisis weigh[ed] heavily against overruling [*Miranda*]."[200] He approvingly cited the Court's declaration in *Agostini v. Felton*[201] that "'in constitutional cases, the doctrine [of stare decisis] carries such persuasive force that we have always required a departure from precedent to be supported by some 'special justification.'"[202] The Court found no such justification in *Dickerson*. Instead, he declared,

> *Miranda* has become embedded in routine police practice to
> the point where the warnings have become part of our national
> culture. See *Mitchell v. United States*, 526 U.S. 314, 331–332 (1999)
> (Scalia, J., dissenting) (stating that the fact that a rule has found
> "wide acceptance in the legal culture" is "adequate reason not to
> overrule" it.) While we have overruled our precedents when subsequent cases have undermined their doctrinal underpinnings,

> ... we do not believe this has happened to ... *Miranda* ... If anything, our subsequent cases have reduced the impact of the *Miranda* rule on legitimate law enforcement while reaffirming the decision's core ruling that unwarned statements may not be used as evidence in the prosecution's case in chief.[203]

While Rehnquist recognized that the "disadvantage of the *Miranda* rule is that statements which may be by no means made involuntarily, made by a defendant who is aware of his 'rights,' may nonetheless be excluded and a guilty defendant go free as a result[,]"[204] he explained that it did not necessitate overruling *Miranda*, because "experience suggests that the totality-of-the-circumstances test which [the federal law at issue in the case] seeks to revive is more difficult than *Miranda* for law enforcement officers to conform to, and for our courts to apply in a consistent manner."[205] In short, he concluded, "Following the rule of stare decisis, we decline to overrule *Miranda* ourselves."[206]

In dissent, Justice Scalia suggested the majority had distorted *Miranda* in order to uphold it. He recalled that the original decision held inadmissible a statement made by someone in custody without being informed (or aware) of his Fifth Amendment privilege against self-incrimination. "So understood, *Miranda* was objectionable for innumerable reasons, not least the fact that cases spanning more than 70 years had rejected its core premise that, absent the warnings and an effective waiver of the right to remain silent and of the (hitherto unknown) right to have an attorney present, a statement obtained pursuant to custodial interrogation was necessarily the product of compulsion."[207] The statute enacted by Congress shortly after *Miranda* did nothing more, in his judgment, than facilitate the achievement of the same objective as *Miranda* to preclude involuntary statements made by defendants in custody from being admitted into evidence. As for the particular rule set forth in *Miranda*, he demonstrated that in many cases decided post-*Miranda* the "Court has squarely concluded that it is possible—indeed not uncommon—for the police to violate *Miranda* without also violating the Constitution. [Hence,] it is ... no longer possible for the Court to conclude, even if it wanted to, that a violation of *Miranda*'s rules [violates] the Constitution."[208] Moreover, he found that subsequent case law has "'undermined [*Miranda*'s doctrinal underpinnings,' ... denying constitutional violation and thus stripping the holding of its only constitutionally legitimate support. *Miranda*'s critics and supporters alike have long made this point."[209] In addition, Justice Scalia was

> not convinced by petitioner's argument that *Miranda* should be preserved because the decision occupies a special place in the "public's consciousness." … As far as I am aware, the public is not under the illusion that we are infallible. I see little harm in admitting that we made a mistake in taking away from the people the ability to decide for themselves what protections (beyond those required by the Constitution) are reasonably affordable in the criminal investigatory process. And I see much to be gained by reaffirming for the people the wonderful reality that they govern themselves—which means that the "power not delegated to the United States by the Constitution" that the people adopted, "nor prohibited to the States" by that Constitution, "are reserved to the States respectively, or to the people."[210]

He concluded, "Far from believing that stare decisis compels this result, I believe we cannot allow to remain on the books even a celebrated decision—especially a celebrated decision—that has come to stand for the proposition that the Supreme Court has the power to impose extraconstitutional constraints upon Congress and the States. This is not the system that was established by the Framers."[211]

One of Justice Scalia's arguments underscores an important dynamic in the Court's handling of precedent. Subsequent to *Miranda*, the Court has rendered a series of decisions creating loopholes and exceptions to *Miranda*. Reaffirming *Miranda* hardly reduced the significance of these rulings, which have unquestionably narrowed *Miranda*. They suggest *Miranda*'s reaffirmation is largely symbolic. Indeed, it calls to mind Chief Justice Rehnquist's description of *Roe v. Wade* in the aftermath of its reaffirmation in *Casey* as remaining only as "a sort of judicial Potemkin Village, which may be pointed out to passers by as a monument to the importance of adhering to precedent," but is nevertheless a "facade." *Miranda* may be in the same class—largely eviscerated but still standing.

The same cannot be said for *Buckley v. Valeo*.[212] There the Court upheld federal limitations on campaign contributions, but not on campaign expenditures. The *Buckley* dissent, as well as many (mostly conservative) scholars and Republican leaders, maintained the First Amendment fully protects both campaign contributions and expenditures as political speech and lambasted *Buckley*'s distinction between the two as incoherent. Yet, the Court reaffirmed *Buckley* in its 5–4 decision upholding the Bipartisan Campaign Reform Act of 2002 in *McConnell v. FEC*[213] and in its 6–3 decision in *Randall v. Sorrell*[214] in 2006 striking down a Vermont law establishing extremely low limits on campaign contributions. Chief Justice Roberts and Justice Alito joined Justice Breyer's opinion for the Court in *Randall*, expressly reaffirming *Buckley*. Three justices urged the Court to overrule *Buckley*—Justices Scalia and Thomas, in order to eliminate all regulations of contributions and expenditures, and Justice Stevens, in order to allow government more regulatory discretion.

7. The Subtle Significance of Precedent

Focusing on the cases in which justices discuss the weight they would attach to particular precedents risks overlooking what Richard Fallon describes as the "quiet fronts" in which precedent continues to influence the path of the Court's decision making.[215] Fallon identifies several areas in which the Court has shifted the direction of the case law, but without overruling any precedents, including the Court's widely reported and criticized shift since 1995 to limit congressional power to regulate private activity under the commerce clause.[216] By the time the Court decided *United States v. Lopez*,[217] the Court had not struck down a commerce clause regulation of private activity for almost six decades; however, the Court in *Lopez* struck down just such an enactment. In *Lopez* and subsequent commerce clause cases, notably *United States v. Morrison*,[218] in which the Court struck down the Violence Against Women Act, the Court clarified its framework for analyzing the constitutionality of congressional regulations of private economic activity.[219] While a popular critique of *Lopez* characterizes it as a revolutionary shift in commerce clause jurisprudence, *Lopez* is more credibly understood as a clarification of the law rather than a radical overhauling of commerce clause doctrine. Indeed, in both *Lopez* and *Morrison*, the Court did not overrule any precedents, and Chief Justice Rehnquist went to great lengths to reconcile the decisions with commerce clause doctrine dating back to the advent of the New Deal.

Lopez and its progeny fit into a larger pattern of decision making in which the Court has foregone refashioning or overruling precedents in many areas of constitutional law. This pattern is evident if one examines the lines of cases in which it no longer entertains constitutional arguments. These lines of cases involve many settled areas of constitutional law.

To appreciate the extent and number of the settled areas of constitutional law, one needs to look behind the published opinions (and actions) of the Court. Once one does, it becomes clear that an important function of precedent is framing the Court's agenda on whether to grant certiorari. After the virtual abolition of mandatory jurisdiction,[220] the Court has nearly complete discretion over its docket through the certiorari process. When petitioners apply for grants of certiorari, the Court must decide whether the questions they raise require consideration. It is practically impossible for the Court to decide any constitutional issue without initially determining the scope, legitimacy, and coherence of prior case law. The justices' respect for the Court's precedents is evident in their choices of which matters not to hear. Thus, in the certiorari process, the justices often demonstrate their desire to adhere to or accept precedents they might not have decided the same way in the first place.

There are many areas in which the Court no longer decides cases. Some areas of settled doctrine are evident from the Court's denials of certiorari to reconsider precedents.[221] Reconsideration of many cases is simply off the table. For example, the Court no longer considers incorporation questions—whether the liberty component of the Fourteenth Amendment due process clause applies the Bill of Rights, in whole or in part, to the states.[222] Nor does the Court revisit the Court's modern decisions on reapportionment (with the exception of its ruling political gerrymandering justiciable) or the precedents recognizing equal protection fundamental rights.[223] Moreover, the Court shows no disposition to reconsider its highly protective test for political expression in *Brandenburg v. Ohio*.[224] Nor has the Court revisited its standard restricting libel actions against the press for reporting on public figures. Moreover, the Court retains its fundamental standards for evaluating the scope of Congress' spending, war, and taxing powers.[225] The Court still accepts rulings that private corporations are "persons" for purposes of the Fourteenth Amendment and that paper money is constitutional. Moreover, the Rehnquist Court "never called into question the constitutionality of New Deal-type regulatory legislation and, of comparable salience, the 1964 Civil Rights Act,"[226] and reaffirmed decisions upholding civil rights legislation restricting practices, such as literacy tests, likely to be used "to deny and abridge voting rights on racial grounds."[227]

Although these preceding discussions from Supreme Court case law on precedents are typical, many legal scholars are harshly critical of them. These critics take issue with the Court's approach to precedent and construct theories for guiding the Court's handling of precedent. Understanding these theories and their problems, as I discuss in the next chapter, is crucial for developing a coherent perspective on the role of precedent in constitutional law.

Legal scholars and social scientists propose what they proclaim as superior positive accounts of the legal and constitutional significance of precedent. In this chapter I discuss the most prominent theories of precedent proposed by legal scholars and social scientists, their relative merits, and the tensions among them.

1. The Relative Merits of the Weak View of Precedent

Legal scholars generally advance a weak or strong view of precedent. In the weak view of precedent, the Court owes little or no deference to precedents. The strong view of precedent perceives precedents as the principal, or most meaningful, touchstone in constitutional law. As I explain below, neither view withstands close scrutiny.

1.1 The Origins of the Weak View of Precedent

In an excellent article,[1] Thomas Lee places in historical context what I understand as the weak view of precedent. He explains the Framers and Ratifiers were heavily influenced in their thinking about precedent by leading 17th- and 18th-century British scholars and judges, particularly William Blackstone.[2] According to Lee, Blackstone conceived of precedent in terms of the "declaratory theory" of law. This theory "h[eld] that the Law had a 'Platonic or ideal existence' before it was ever reduced to a judicial opinion. On this view, any decision deemed inconsistent with this 'ideal' need not be overruled but could be simply superseded by a new decision as a 'reconsidered declaration as a law from the beginning.'"[3] Lee explains that those who shared this view believed that "a judicial decision was not law, but mere evidence of it, and accordingly could be disregarded by a subsequent court. Subsequently, common-law courts and commentators 'began to speak of a qualified obligation to abide by past decisions,' under which precedents could still be set aside, but only if manifestly absurd or contrary to reason or custom."[4] Lee suggests the transformation toward the modern approach of requiring special justifications for overruling did not stabilize until the late 19th century.[5]

While Lee's account is consistent with other scholarship,[6] modern readers may find it odd to treat common law as the model for constitutional adjudication, given that statutes may displace common-law decisions but not constitutional rulings. Yet, the common law, like a good deal of the Court's decisions, was predicated on incremental decision making. In common-law adjudication, a single decision was less important and binding on other judges than a series of precedents that set forth the law more fully and clearly over time.[7] Nineteenth-century judges who followed this approach—and most did—clarified constitutional law through distinctions and analogies rather than overruling.[8]

As Lee shows, the general conception of constitutional precedent during this era was not static but rather in flux.[9] Although, as we saw in the first chapter, justices sometimes discussed at length their justifications for overruling prior decisions, they discussed less rarely and comprehensively the particular differences among constitutional, statutory, and common-law precedents.[10] Indeed, nineteenth century commentators generally neglected to discuss either the relationships among the different kinds of precedents or where precedents fit within the hierarchy of sources of constitutional meaning. For instance, Thomas Cooley, an eminent constitutional commentator in the 19th century, barely addresses these subjects in his major constitutional treatise. He offers no extended analysis of the nature of precedent beyond merely asserting (with apparent approval) that the Court approached its precedents in common law like fashion.[11] Near the end of the 19th century, D. H. Chamberlain observed, "We know of no authorities which have discussed or answered [whether the doctrine of stare decisis ought to apply in the same way to both constitutional and common-law adjudication]; we do not even know that it is regarded in the forum of the profession or of jurists and judicious law-writers as an open question."[12]

It is plausible that the reticence about the propriety of analogizing constitutional adjudication to the common law in the late 18th and early 19th century might be attributable to the fact that constitutional adjudication was novel to the Framers. Prior to the drafting and ratification of the Constitution, Americans had little, if any, meaningful experience with constitutional adjudication. The Framers and Ratifiers had firsthand experience with common law precedents, but not with constitutional ones; they had no precedent for handling constitutional precedents. Consequently, American lawyers and jurists may have needed time—almost a century—

to develop a coherent doctrine to clarify the relationships among the different kinds of precedents in the legal system.

The Framers' apparent reticence to talk at length about the relationships among the different kinds of precedents (and where, in particular, precedents fit within the hierarchy of sources of constitutional meaning) requires some explanation. The most obvious is that the Framers were fallible; they failed to anticipate every problem that could arise under the Constitution. As Larry Kramer suggests,[13] the Framers and Ratifiers primarily focused on the big picture. While constitutional stare decisis was not a part of their big picture, it is a part of ours. The Framers and Ratifiers may not have expected much litigation over constitutional issues. The filing of lawsuits raising constitutional issues is a modern phenomenon. The fact that constitutional litigation was rare meant justices easily could distinguish precedents and avoid direct conflicts among the precedents.

Yet, as early as the late 18th century, Supreme Court justices recognized the importance of avoiding questions of constitutional law to minimize their constitutional decision making and to leave as much play within the joints of the public sector as possible.[14] The Court continues to follow the avoidance canon, which is predicated on recognizing the near impossibility of overturning constitutional precedents.

Moreover, other developments suggest the likelihood that justices appreciated the constitutional significance of precedents as early as the 1790s. The fact that the Court's first major mistake in constitutional interpretation—allowing a state to be sued by a citizen from another state, *Chisholm v. Georgia*[15]—was overturned by a constitutional amendment, not a statute, is strong evidence that national leaders at the time recognized an essential difference between constitutional and common-law precedents. After all, federal authorities at the time moved quickly to overturn the precedent not through a statute (to which they would have resorted had they been dealing with a common law precedent) but a constitutional amendment. In the early years of the republic, national leaders employed various mechanisms to retaliate against constitutional precedents with which they disagreed, including abolishing the Court's term, regulating the Court's size and jurisdiction, and trying to remove federal judges with obnoxious views.[16] They quickly recognized that the most promising means for modifying precedents was appointing justices committed to deciding issues differently. Supreme Court selection up until the Civil War was intense, and its intensity suggests the awareness that appointments could transform the Court and its precedents.

The fact that the Court barely overruled a handful of cases within its first 100 years not only confirms its incremental approach to constitutional decision making, but also raises a strong inference—confirmed further by discussions in several opinions—that the Court did not lightly overturn its constitutional precedents.[17] For instance, some 19th-century justices had relatively settled views on the legal status of constitutional precedents well before the end of the century. Consider, again, Justice Strong's opinion from *Knox v. Lee*: "We have been in the habit of treating cases involving a consideration of constitutional power differently from those which concern merely private right."

Justice Strong's reference to the Court's "habit" might have alluded "to the rule of practice requiring ordinarily the concurrence of a majority of a full court in the decision of constitutional cases" as the Court held years before in *Briscoe v. Bank*.[19] Alternatively, Strong's statement might refer to the well-settled differences in the Court's approach to reconsidering constitutional and common-law precedents. The rule requiring "the concurrence of a majority of a full court in the decision of constitutional cases" appears to derive from the Court's recognition that constitutional cases are different and special care needs to be taken when they are being reconsidered. It is telling that the Court deferred to a precedent—*Briscoe*—in the course of explaining its approach to reviewing constitutional precedents.

Recall, in his concurrence, Justice Bradley states, "On a question relating to the power of government, where I am perfectly satisfied that it has the power, I can never consent to abide by a decision denying it, unless made with reasonable unanimity and acquiesced in by the country."[20] Justice Bradley may be suggesting the conditions under which constitutional precedents may be transformed from weak to strong. In dissent, Justice Stephen Field disputed that there had been any defects in the process by which the Court decided the first legal tender decision and expressed his "hope that a judgment thus reached would not be lightly disturbed."[21] These comments similarly suggest that at least some, if not most, justices of the era recognized that constitutional precedents should be given some deference by the Court and overruled only for special reason(s).

1.2 The Weak View of Precedent in the Modern Era

The Court's jurisdiction and docket expanded in the New Deal era, during which pleas to overrule precedent intensified. These pleas coincided with (and may have been encouraged by) some justices' expressions of a weak view of precedent.[22]

William O. Douglas was one such justice. In an article published midcentury, he vigorously defended his weak view of precedent. He explained,

> A judge looking at a constitutional decision may have compulsions to revere past history and accept what was once written. But he remembers above all else that it is the Constitution which he swore to support and defend, not the gloss which his predecessors may have put on it. So he comes to formulate his own views, rejecting some earlier ones as false and embracing others. He cannot do otherwise, unless he lets men long dead and unaware of the problems of the age in which he lives do his thinking for him.[23]

Even though the mind-set Justice Douglas describes risks destabilizing constitutional law, he defended any

> flux [as] healthy ... The alternative is to let the Constitution freeze in the pattern which one generation gave it. But the Constitution w as designed for the vicissitudes of time. It must never become a code which carries the overtones of one period that may be hostile to another.[24]

Justice Douglas' weak view of precedent derived from his perspective as an intellectual leader of the legal realist movement. Douglas, like other legal realists, believed legal doctrine was written primarily to protect or extend the ruling elite's power. Legal realists dismissed the formalities of legal reasoning as obfuscating what was really happening; so they insisted, like Douglas, on clarity and candor in judicial decision making as well as receptivity to insights (and methods) from the social sciences. Douglas praised the Hughes Court's overruling of precedents as "removing from constitutional doctrine excrescences produced early in the century. The tendency has been to return to older views of constitutional interpretation, and to sanction governmental power over social and economic affairs which the Court beginning in the [18]80's and particularly in the preceding ten to thirty years had denied. Only if this is understood can the work of the period be put into clear perspective."[25] Douglas stressed the importance of candor in deciding cases: "[T]he more blunt, open, and direct course is truer to democratic traditions … The principle of full disclosure has as much place in government as it does in the market place. A judiciary that discloses what it is doing and why it does it will breed understanding. And confidence based on that understanding is more enduring than confidence based on awe."[26]

Justice Douglas' weak view of precedent is apparent in his judicial opinions. In one dissent, he declared, for instance, the Court's "decisions … do not bind us, for they [have] dealt with matters of constitutional interpretation which are always open."[27] He reiterated the "irrelevan[ce of stare decisis] if we dealt with a constitutional matter, as issues of that magnitude are always open for reexamination."[28] He never hesitated to express his disagreement with the Court's failure to overrule decisions with which he disagreed.[29]

Douglas' fellow New Dealer and colleague, Justice Black, shared his disdain for precedent as authority for decision making. Justice Black thought of himself as a textualist who rigidly adhered to the plain meaning of the Constitution's language.[30] In an early dissent, he declared, "A constitutional interpretation that is wrong should not stand."[31] His weak view of precedent is evident from the fact that during his 34 years on the Court no one with whom Black served urged more overruling of precedents than he did.[32]

The Warren Court's defense of the rights of minorities was often challenged as deviating from the common-law method of adjudication. While the late Philip Kurland never described the Warren Court as having been motivated by a "weak view of precedent," it appears to be consistent with his complaint that the

> list of opinions destroyed by the Warren Court reads like a table of contents from an old constitutional law casebook. The willingness to disregard stare decisis … has a worthy pedigree. But the volume and speed of the Warren Court as it engaged in this enterprise have never been witnessed before. One can only think that the Warren Court was taking its guidance from a quotation

from a position used by Mr. Justice Sam Ervin, Jr., of the North Carolina Supreme Court: "There is no virtue in sinning against light or persisting in palpable error, for nothing is settled until it is settled right." On the other hand, it was early in the Supreme Court's history that Mr. Justice Baldwin said: "There is no more certainty that a late opinion is more correct than the first."[33]

Kurland urged the Court "to adhere to the step-by-step process that has long characterized the common-law and constitutional forms of adjudication."[34]

On the Rehnquist Court, the justices who most often expressed a weak view of precedent were Justices Scalia and Thomas. Immediately after his appointment to the Court in 1986, Justice Scalia directly challenged decisions he deemed mistaken. His challenges extended to numerous areas of constitutional law, including the establishment clause, abortion rights, separation of powers, freedom of speech, criminal procedure, abortion, the takings clause, and affirmative action.[35] His apparent attachment to a weak view of precedent was further reflected by his citing Justice Douglas as a precursor to his own position on precedent.[36] Over the years, Justice Scalia has urged overruling precedent with less frequency, but when he has done so he has increasingly cited both error and special justifications in support of overruling. This is partly because he is defending decisions in which he joined. For instance, he sharply questioned the special justifications the majority claimed in support of its overruling of *Bowers v. Hardwick*, and suggested that various factors argued against overruling the 1890 decision in *Hans v. Louisiana*, even though it might have been erroneous. In 2005, Justice Scalia declared that he, unlike Thomas, really respected precedent.

Justice Thomas expressed a weak view of precedent more often than Justice Scalia. Their different attitudes about precedent are evident in *Van Orden v. Perry*,[37] in which the Court, 5–4, held the establishment clause does not forbid a public display of the Ten Commandments along with other historical and religious markers . Although Chief Justice Rehnquist's plurality opinion did not question the validity of any precedents, Justice Scalia suggested in concurrence that he would prefer to reach the same result "by adopting an Establishment Clause jurisprudence that is in accord with our Nation's past and present practices, and that can be consistently applied—the central relevant feature of which is that there is nothing unconstitutional in a State's favoring religion, generally."[38] In his concurrence, Justice Thomas suggested that the case would have been easy if the Court were willing to abandon the inconsistent guideposts it has adopted for addressing Establishment Clause challenges, and return to the original meaning of the Clause ... I have previously suggested that the Clause's text and history resist 'incorporation' against the States. If the Establishment Clause does not restrain the States, then it has no application here, where only state action is at issue. Even if the Clause is incorporated, or if the Free Exercise Clause limits the powers of the States to establish religions, our task would be far simpler if we returned to the original meaning of the word "establishment" than it is under the various approaches this Court ... uses.[39]

While Justices Scalia and Thomas appear willing to overrule many precedents, Justice Thomas seems prepared to overrule more of them than Justice Scalia.

1.3 The Academic Defense of the Weak View of Precedent

Over the last two decades, the weak view of precedent has been popular among conservative commentators. While some liberal scholars have expressed a similar view,[40] conservatives have asserted a weak view of precedent more openly and boldly than their liberal counterparts. Because of the possible appeal of their assertions, they merit close attention.

One of the most prominent proponents of a weak view of precedent is Robert Bork. Indeed, this view was one basis for the Senate's rejection of his nomination to the Court.[41] In a book written shortly after his rejection, Bork responded to the charge made against his nomination that his unyielding commitment to original meaning could not be implemented without producing havoc in constitutional law.[42] Bork reconciled this tension by proposing three guidelines for reconsidering constitutional precedents: (1) lower courts should respect precedent more rigorously than the Court itself; (2) the Court should never overrule any decision unless it finds that the case was wrongly decided; and (3) the Court should not overrule prior erroneous decisions when that would seriously disrupt well-established government structures or practices, such as the printing of paper money.[43]

The late Raoul Berger asserted a more aggressive weak view of precedent. Berger argued that, with few practical limitations, it was more important for the Court to answer constitutional questions correctly than to perpetuate errors. He expected the Court's willingness to uphold mistaken precedents to produce instability (and incoherence), whereas the Court's renewed commitment to original meaning would promote stability over the long run. He explained that in considering the appropriate criteria for overruling constitutional precedents "we should separate legal from pragmatic considerations. On the legal issue, ... 'that which is wrong in the beginning cannot become right in the course of time.' Usurpation is not legitimated by repetition."[44] While Berger conceded "[w]hatever consequences might follow [from a particular overruling] should be weighed against the integrity of the Constitution and the unconstitutional revision of the instrument by the judiciary,"[45] he rarely found "consequences" to be sufficiently weighty to warrant foregoing the overruling of erroneous interpretations.[46]

Several conservative constitutional scholars who came of age in the 1980s reject Bork's and Berger's willingness to balance competing considerations. They propose mistaken precedents are unlawful, any wrongly decided cases should be overruled, the doctrine of constitutional stare decisis is policymaking (which the Court or Congress may displace), and mistaken decisions should have no binding effect other than on the parties to the original lawsuits.[47] But their weak view of precedents turns out to be more problematic than Bork's or Berger's.

1.4 The Limits of the Weak View of Precedent

There are several problems with the weak view of precedent advanced in recent scholarship. First, the Court has never actually embraced a weak view of precedent. At most, this perspective has been expressed in some concurrences and dissents, but not in majority opinions. Even justices who apparently favored a weak view of precedent did not consistently follow it. While one of Justice Black's sympathetic commentators observed that he "accorded to long established precedent a minimum of respect and showed scant compunction in overruling it,"[48] Black's disdain for precedent was not absolutist. In dissenting to the Court's holding in *Green v. United States*[49] that criminal contempt is not subject to the same constitutional guarantees as other criminal proceedings, Justice Black explained,

> Ordinarily it is sound policy to adhere to prior decisions but this practice has quite properly never been a blind, inflexible rule.

Courts are not omniscient. Like every other human agency, they too can profit from trial and error, from experience and reflection. As others have demonstrated, the principle commonly referred to as stare decisis has never been thought to extend so far as to prevent the courts from correcting their own errors. Accordingly, this Court has time and time again from the very beginning reconsidered the merits of its earlier decisions even though they claimed great longevity and repeated reaffirmation … Indeed, the Court has a special responsibility where questions of constitutional law are involved to review its decisions from time to time and where compelling reasons present themselves to refuse to follow erroneous precedents; otherwise its mistakes in interpreting the Constitution are extremely difficult to alleviate and needlessly so.[50]

Black's statement sounds as if he is rejecting a strong view of precedent rather than unequivocally embracing a weak view of precedent.[51]

Felix Frankfurter, Black's intellectual nemesis on the Court, began his career with a weak view of precedent but gradually moved away from it as a justice. More than 20 years before joining the Court, Frankfurter suggested that "the doctrine of stare decisis has no legitimate application to constitutional decisions where the court is presented with a new body of knowledge, largely non-existing at the time of its prior decision."[52] A decade later, Frankfurter added that "historic continuity in constitutional construction does not necessarily mean historic stereotype in application. To what extent respect for continuity demands adherence merely to what was, involves the art of adjudication—raises those questions of more or less that ultimately decide cases."[53] The degree to which precedent constrained decision making depended, in other words, on determining its relevance to a current dispute; and Frankfurter did not seem reluctant to draw distinctions to advance his preferred constitutional visions.

On the Court, Frankfurter gravitated toward a strong view of precedent. In 1946 he explained in a letter to then-Chief Justice Harlan Fiske Stone,

Law as a living force in society must make adaptation and from time to time and slough off the past, but … law implies certain continuities, or, at the very least, a permeating feeling that stability as well as change is an element in law. Past decisions ought not to be needlessly overruled. If this is done with sufficient frequency, the whole notion of law is discredited.[54]

Frankfurter considered consistency and stability in constitutional law as essential and thus held onto a relatively consistent (but nonabsolutist) respect for precedent over time. In 1950 he declared, "Especially ought the Court not to reinforce needlessly the instability of our day by giving fair ground for the belief that Law is the expression of chance—for instance, of unexpected changes in the Court's composition and contingencies in the choice of successors."[55] He explained that "shifts of opinion" on the Court "should not derive from mere private judgment. They must be duly mindful of the necessary demands of continuity in civilized society. A reversal of a long current of decisions can be justified only if rooted in the Constitution itself as an historic document designed for a developing nation."[56] In one concurrence, Frankfurter emphasized that the past behavior of the Court as reflected in more than 40 cases on the legitimacy of the justices' contempt power carried a good deal of weight. He even listed all of the past justices who had sustained the exercise of power that the Court reaffirmed in the case.[57] While agreeing with Black that the Court was free to correct obvious mistakes or to modify a rule of law that had been only occasionally applied, Justice Frankfurter did not agree with Black that "everybody on the Court has been wrong for 150 years and that which has been deemed part of the bone and sinew of the law should now be extirpated."[58]

Both Chief Justice Rehnquist and Justice Scalia appeared to increasingly distance themselves from a weak view of precedent. After becoming Chief Justice, Rehnquist apparently modified his attitude toward precedent. As Chief Justice, he rarely urged overruling precedents simply because they were wrongly decided. Since 1987, the closest he came to that position was his partial dissent in *Casey*, in which he suggests that *Roe* was erroneous from the day it was decided and that its error, combined with other factors, necessitates its overruling.[59] After boldly urging his colleagues to overrule a wide range of wrongly decided precedents in his first few years on the Court,[60] Justice Scalia acknowledged in 1996 that the Court's traditional approach had been to overrule constitutional precedents if it had "special justifications" to do so.[61] In First Amendment cases, he defended relying on precedent despite its potential conflict with the original meaning:

> Originalism, like any theory of interpretation put into practice in an ongoing system of law, must accommodate the doctrine of stare decisis; it cannot remake the world anew. It is of no more consequence at this point whether the Alien and Sedition Acts of 1798 were in accord with the original understanding of the First Amendment than it is whether *Marbury v. Madison* was decided correctly.[62]

Thus, he explained, "originalism will make a difference … not in the rolling back of accepted old principles of constitutional law but in the rejection of usurpatious new ones."[63] Subsequently Justice Scalia did not back down from challenging precedents with whose reasoning he disagrees, but he has modified his opposition by consistently including many reasons for overruling them, not just their having been initially wrongly decided.[64]

Even Justice William Brennan, who some commentators say had a weak view of precedent,[65] acknowledged that a justice can routinely dissent in no more than a handful of areas before he has impaired his ability to build coalitions.[66] Justice Brennan routinely dissented in only a few areas of constitutional law, including capital punishment, obscenity, the Eleventh Amendment, and double jeopardy.[67] While some critics suggest Justice Brennan manipulated precedent and lacked the candor to challenge precedent directly, they fail to explain why the manipulation or distortion of precedent is a common practice on the Court or why Justice Douglas' or Scalia's candor has not been embraced more often by the former's liberal or the latter's conservative colleagues.

Apart from its lacking support from the Court, a weak view of precedent conflicts with the primary sources of constitutional meaning—text, structure, and original meaning. These sources fully support the lawfulness of precedent. For example, the Constitution explicitly authorizes the lawfulness of precedent. Article III provides that the judicial power of the United States extends to "cases or controversies."[68] The plain implication of this grant of authority is that the cases or controversies decided by the Court are legitimate exercises of its authority. The creation of precedents is a lawful exercise of judicial authority. Moreover, Article III's grant of authority to the federal judiciary is not restricted to a single case or controversy.

The Court may exercise judicial review over more than one case arising in a given area of constitutional law. The more cases the Court decides in particular doctrinal areas, the more precedents it makes in those areas.

The exercise of Article III judicial power entails deliberating over how it ought to be exercised. Deciding cases entails determining how much weight to accord to precedent and other sources of constitutional meaning. As Richard Fallon argues, "The power to say what the Constitution means or requires—recognized since *Marbury v. Madison*—implies a power to determine the sources of authority on which constitutional rulings properly rest."[69] Deciding a case or controversy necessarily requires making choices about which sources to use and how. Given the implications of the Court's explicit power to decide cases or controversies, it is hard to see how any statute that restricts this power—e.g., dictating the scope of things the Court may consider in deciding cases or controversies—could avoid violating the core judicial power "to say what the law is."[70]

Three hypothetical statutes illustrate the limits of congressional power to direct the Court to increase or decrease its deference to precedent. Imagine, first, a statute that mandates in deciding questions of constitutional meaning that the Court may only consider the original meaning. Imagine the second directs that in exercising judicial review the Court should adopt James Bradley Thayer's classic test for determining the constitutionality of legislation, that is, that the Court may overrule only those legislative interpretations of the Constitution embodied in statutes that are "clearly erroneous."[71] Suppose a third statute requires that once the Court correctly decides a constitutional question it must never address the merits of that question again.

Each of these statutes is unconstitutional, and each is unconstitutional for the same reason: Each violates the boundaries separating judicial from legislative power. The first statute restricts the Court from deciding a case or controversy on the basis of sources of constitutional meaning on whose legitimacy virtually everyone would agree, including the text and structure of the Constitution. The second statute effectively imposes a standard of review for the Court to follow in every case involving the constitutionality of a congressional enactment that is likely to conflict with some if not many of the constitutional principles or standards governing the exercises of congressional power at issue. Even if the third statute were understood as defining how correct interpretations of the Constitution may be made, it is hard to square with our Constitution, which sets forth no such instructions explicitly. The Constitution is silent on how the Court should go about deciding constitutional questions. Moreover, the third statute requires the Court to accept another branch's interpretations of the Constitution as correct and therefore final (and thus immune to further judicial review). It would, therefore, force at least some justices to follow constitutional interpretations with which they disagree. It is one thing for the Court to defer to an interpretation of the Constitution which both the Court and Congress agree is within the Congress' power to make, but it is another for Congress to dictate to the Court which interpretations it must follow in deciding cases. Justices' constitutional duties and oaths argue in favor of their having the freedom to decide for themselves the basic matter of what the Constitution means or requires in a case that falls within their jurisdiction.[72] If some subsequent justices have reason to view some prior interpretation of the Constitution as incorrect, they may argue that foreclosing them from expressing this view allows a mistake in constitutional law to persist. The mistake might foreclose a right from protection, preclude a lawful power from being exercised, or allow a power to be employed illegitimately. But, in determining what the law requiring their interpretation in the cases that come before them, justices may not be compelled by political authorities to perpetuate what the justices regard as errors in constitutional law.

Other constitutional provisions further restrict congressional regulation of the Court's reasoning about precedents. For example, the Constitution provides limited means for directly regulating the Court, including adjusting the Court's size and jurisdiction, impeaching and removing justices for "treason, bribery or other high crimes and misdemeanors,"[73] appointing new justices, and amending the Constitution. Of these methods, amending the Constitution seems ideally suited to directly overturn mistaken constitutional interpretations.[74] The amendment procedure authorized by Article V is predicated on the addition of amendments to the Constitution in the order in which they have been ratified. The amendment procedure entails sequencing or incremental changes in the Constitution. The sequencing implies a gradual development in constitutional law during which there will be times when some understandings of the Constitution are in effect unless or until they are overturned by an amendment. In other words, the amendment procedure contemplates that constitutional law will not be static. It will develop over time, and as it develops, presumably choices in implementing the Constitution will be made by the Court and other actors in the course of exercising their respective powers that presumably will remain in effect unless they are displaced by constitutional amendment.

The Court's inherent authority obviously extends to doing what courts conventionally do—produce opinions. But when the Court shifted from its practice of issuing seriatim opinions to Chief Justice Marshall's preferred practice of having opinions given in the name of the Court, the shift was compelled not by the Constitution, but by Marshall's management of court personnel and resources. The discretion to package Court opinions as it sees fit falls squarely within the scope of the Court's inherent authority. The Court retains the discretion to return, if it chooses, to its prior practice of issuing a series of opinions from the justices rather than a single opinion of the Court. The Court thus could choose not to issue an opinion of the Court (or a majority) on anything, including stare decisis. There would be nothing to which one could point as the Court's "reasons" for a constitutional judgment. At most, there would only be some justices' explanations for their votes in a constitutional case or controversy, and these explanations would only be made to the length or in the depth to which each justice saw fit.

The Court could go further. The Court might choose simply to forego issuing any opinions whatsoever, including opinions seriatim. Nothing precludes the Court from deciding to forego opinion writing of any kind and to issue instead a terse statement on the bottom line of its judgment on affirming or reversing the case on appeal.

If the Court were to make any of these choices on the packaging of its opinions, it is hard to see how the Constitution allows the Congress to order them to do otherwise. Article III's grant of power to Congress to make exceptions to the Court's jurisdiction as it deems appropriate hardly constitutes a grant of authority to Congress to dictate to the Court the forms, much less the content, of its opinions. Congress could not compel the Court to disclose or elaborate on why it decided a particular case or controversy the way it did. Even the stated reasons of a decision are not necessarily an exhaustive account of what the Court considered in resolving the merits of a constitutional question. One need only briefly peruse the papers of particular justices to get some idea of the volume of communications or exchanges between the justices that never enter into the official reports of the Court.

Moreover, there are no rules governing the contents of written opinions. They contain as little or as much as the justices choose to write. Nothing in the Constitution directs them to issue opinions, much less what to say in them. The reasoning in opinions need not be exhaustive. The building of coalitions necessarily involves strategic choices not just with respect to outcomes but also content.[75] Consequently the content is a function of the majority's preferences. The choices of whether and what to publish are inherently judicial, not legislative. The Constitution, in short, does not compel the Court to announce anything more than the bottom line of its judgment—that is, who wins or loses.

Prior to Chief Justice Marshall's tenure, the actual precedential affect of a decision could be determined only by stitching together the reasoning of the justices in the majority. Given that there was no opinion for the Court, but rather seriatim opinions, one would have had to develop a matrix to determine how many justices agreed to what. What became precedent under these circumstances depended on what subsequent justices calculated had been done in earlier series of opinions. There was, in effect, no precedent until a later majority declared what it was. The legitimacy of prior judgments depended on the Court's judgment, which would presumably have been immune to interference except by the narrow means of the Court's overturning itself or a constitutional amendment.

An additional inference from the structure of the Constitution (and from historical practices) is that the doctrine of constitutional stare decisis is best understood as the justices' assessments of the likely consequences of affirming or overruling precedents. Consequentialist reasoning is a lawful exercise of judicial power; the justices are merely assessing how their decisions will fit within the constitutional structure (of which the legal system is a part). The assessment of decisions' consequences has long been recognized by the Court as a traditional source of constitutional decision making.[76]

This practice is so long-standing and common that it would be hard, if not impossible, to list all of the occasions on which some or all justices considered institutional ramifications in resolving constitutional disputes. Two early, now classic instances in which the Court decided cases on such grounds are *Martin v. Hunter's Lessee*[77] and *McCulloch v. Maryland*.[78]

Many scholars have not only acknowledged the propriety of the Supreme Court's reliance on such assessments in its constitutional decision making,[79] but some, such as Judge Richard Posner,[80] have gone further to argue that balancing the costs and benefits of possible rulings is the only coherent and intellectually honest way to formulate constitutional doctrine. In short, it is more accurate to think of the doctrine of stare decisis as constituting consequentialist reasoning rather than judicial policymaking and as such a traditional mode of constitutional argumentation. If the Congress had no power to preclude the Court from employing consequentialist reasoning, the same holds true for the doctrine of constitutional stare decisis, which is a species of it. Indeed, the doctrine reflects the Court's taking into account the institutional and social ramifications of overruling constitutional decisions. Few would dispute that, regardless of whether one disagrees with the legitimacy of the Court's grounding of its decisions on institutional analysis, the Congress lacks any authority to restrict the Court from taking such considerations into account in disposing of cases or controversies. Assessing these considerations is a core judicial function and as such is immune to direct attack by Congress.

An additional difficulty with the argument that only the "correct" judicial decisions are constitutional law is that a reasonable inference from the structure of the Constitution is that the Court will sometimes not decide constitutional questions correctly, however one measures correctness. Otherwise the Framers would never have provided for checking mechanisms against the Court's decisions, including congressional control over the size and funding of the Court and, in particular, a process for overturning decisions through constitutional amendment. The Framers did not expect any branch of government, including the judiciary, to have a monopoly on perfection. There is nothing to suggest they did. Nor did they ever suggest that mistaken constitutional judgments by any branch of government, particularly the Court, were something other than law.

Lastly, the justices' standards for reviewing their precedents have the same legal stature as their criteria for protecting substantive constitutional interests. Congress has no power to dictate to the Court the principles it ought to use in deciding constitutional cases, because requiring the Court to follow some principles rather than others is an unlawful exercise of judicial power by Congress, and the choice of what principles to apply in constitutional cases is left to the Court's judgment. If it chooses to apply a standard or principle from an earlier case (or line of cases), that choice, too, is for the Court to make. And if the Court reconsiders standards or principles it has previously employed in the course of trying to figure out which standards or principles ought to apply in particular cases, those are just other choices which fall within the Court's inherent judicial power.

2. The Relative Merits of the Strong View of Precedent

The preceding arguments against the weak view of precedent are hardly definitive. At best, they undermine the weak view in its most aggressive manifestation. They leave open the possibility that a weak view of precedent, albeit problematic, may be less problematic than competing perspectives. To assess the relative appeal of the weak view of precedent, we must turn to its opposite. Yet, the strong view of precedent is, as the next section shows, at least as problematic as its counterpart, particularly in light of the implications of the empirical data gathered by social scientists.

2.1 The Case for the Strong View of Precedent

Support for a strong view of precedent derives from all the traditional sources of constitutional meaning. For instance, Article III explicitly empowers the Supreme Court to decide cases or controversies,[81] and decided cases or controversies are precedents. Moreover, the structure of the amendment process is predicated on precedents as expressions of constitutional law. Until such time as an amendment is formally ratified, the governing, or pertinent, law is dictated and shaped at least in part by what the Constitution and the Court say. The status quo constitutionally is left intact until the Constitution has been amended, and judicial precedent fills the void in the meantime.

Further support for the strong view of precedent derives from two long-standing practices. The first is the Court's steadfast adherence to some constitutional decisions generally regarded as wrongly decided. Examples may be the decisions upholding the constitutionality of legal tender[82] and counting corporations as "persons" who are entitled to the protections of the Fourteenth Amendment due process clause.[83] While some scholarship casts these holdings into doubt,[84] the Court adheres to them.

A second, long-standing practice is the Court's commitment to doctrine grounded primarily on judicial precedent. One example is the Court's Eleventh Amendment jurisprudence. After the Supreme Court ruled in *Chisholm v. Georgia*[85] that the Constitution did not preclude a lawsuit from being filed against the state of Georgia by a citizen from another state, the

Eleventh Amendment was quickly ratified to overrule it. The plain meaning of the language in the amendment[86] suggests it establishes a flat rule forbidding any federal lawsuit filed by or against a state by a citizen from another state.

The Court has not, however, construed the Eleventh Amendment so narrowly. Instead, it has held that the Eleventh Amendment reflects a broad conception of state sovereignty that bars any federal or state lawsuits filed by or against a state by citizens of the same or different states. The principal source for these holdings is not constitutional text or original meaning,[87] but rather precedent. Indeed, Justice Stevens characterized the state sovereign immunity protected by the Eleventh Amendment as deriving principally from "judge-made law."[88] The foundation for the modern Eleventh Amendment doctrine is the Court's 1890 decision in *Hans v. Louisiana*.[89] Though Justice Scalia acknowledges *Hans* might have been erroneous,[90] he supports *Hans* as firmly settled, and joined opinions expanding *Hans* to support broad, robust state sovereignty protected by the Eleventh Amendment.[91]

The Seventh Amendment[92] is another area in which judicial precedent constitutes the primary source for the doctrine constructed by the Supreme Court. Seventh Amendment doctrine deals with the right to jury trials and judicial authority to review jury verdicts, but it is frequently criticized for inconsistency and incoherence.[93] The primary source for the doctrine is precedent, not original meaning or the text of the Constitution.[94]

These examples hardly definitively establish the strong view of precedent. Nor has the Court endorsed such a view. Indeed, everyone is bound to consider certain decisions as so awful as to require overruling. Moreover, the Court's position on constitutional stare decisis—granting precedents some but not much deference[95]—hardly reflects a strong view of precedent.

Nevertheless, the strong view of precedent merits close attention. First, it is evident in some areas of constitutional law and in particular opinions of some justices. Even limited applications, or endorsements, of a strong view of precedent may help to illuminate precedent's role in constitutional law. Second, it appeals to anyone who puts a premium on stability and consistency in constitutional law, or has a Burkean affinity for tradition.[96] Third, precedent is the most cited source in constitutional adjudication. The extreme frequency with which the justices cite, or ground their opinions in, precedent establishes precedent as a, if not the, principal mode of constitutional argumentation.[97] Fourth, some prominent legal scholars treat "elaborated precedent" as effectively displacing the constitutional text.[98] In the next section, I examine some theories grounded in a strong view of precedent and their limitations.

2.2 The Strong View of Precedent in Legal Scholarship

Several prominent legal scholars propose theories that make uprooting certain precedents more difficult. For instance, Bruce Ackerman advances a provocative theory of constitutional moments.[99] On his view, constitutional moments as rare instances in which the American people bypass the formal amendment process to work with national political leaders to produce enduring constitutional changes. Ackerman identifies three such moments—the Founding, Reconstruction, and the New Deal—which did not conform to Article V's formal rules for constitutional amendments. To Ackerman, these moments are important precedents that judges and justices must not only respect, but are obliged to explicate "long after the reformers [who framed them] have left the scene of political struggle."[100] He understands "[t]hese precedents are unconventional, but they provide a key to the American success in sustaining self-government for two centuries."[101]

Ronald Dworkin has a judge-centered theory of precedent. For him, the critical question is what judges regard as the law in hard cases. In hard cases (those in which legal materials do not present clear or determinate answers), judges forge concrete, if contestable, understandings of what the law requires.[102] In doing this, they strive to find the moral principle that provides the best possible explanation of earlier cases.

Dworkin analogizes judging to writing a "chain novel" in which someone is asked to write the final chapter of an unfinished work of fiction.[103] Far from being an unconstrained choice about how to complete the narrative, writers are constrained by many factors, including character development and the writer's depiction of the social world. Dworkin maintains it is implausible for the writer of a chain novel or a judge to credibly claim that she has discretion to write whatever she pleases.[104]

Unlike Ackerman or Dworkin, David Strauss explains the Court's doctrine determined by what he calls "common law constitutional interpretation." He believes constitutional meaning derives not "from some authoritative source," but rather from "understandings that evolve over time," especially as reflected in precedents.[105]

Like Strauss, Kathleen Sullivan eschews any grand theory of constitutional law. Sullivan closely reads cases to clarify constitutional doctrine. She demonstrates in one article how it was possible to understand the Court's most recent decisions as reflecting sharp differences among the justices over formulating decisions as rules (bright-line, inflexible principles) or as standards (multifactored criteria).[106] She later rejects characterizing the Republican appointees on the Rehnquist Court in simplistic ideological terms.[107] She shows that, instead, so-called conservatives on the Rehnquist Court divide over the weight and propriety of considering nine different factors, or preferences, including originalism, textualism, judicial restrain and deference to legislatures, libertarianism and deregulation, states' rights, tradition, judicial precedent, free market capitalism, and law and order.

None of these scholars proposes adopting formal rules as a way to entrench precedents more deeply into constitutional law. For example, the justices could adopt a rule forbidding them to overrule constitutional precedents unless a majority of justices in the overruling case is larger than the majority in the case(s) being overruled. This structural change would surely lead to fewer express overrulings. But it might encourage more subtle, less candid eviscerations of precedent. More importantly, the justices would never adopt such a rule[108] because they are strongly committed to allowing each other the freedom to decide the level of deference each will give to precedent.[109]

Without formal rules for construing precedent,[110] proponents of a strong view of precedent must depend on the force of their reasoning to persuade others. Yet, the absence of formal rules for constructing precedents leaves justices, particularly in hard cases, free to interpret prior decisions in accordance with other factors.[111]

The biggest problem for the strong view of precedent is, however, posed by the empirical data amassed by social scientists (and some legal scholars) suggesting that judicial precedents do not strongly constrain courts. The data merit close inspection because of their widespread acceptance among social scientists and devastating implications.

2.3 The Empirical Challenge to the Strong View of Precedent

Social scientists who study Supreme Court precedent split roughly into five camps: (1) strong attitudinalists; (2) strong rational choice theorists; (3) empiricists synthesizing rational choice and attitudinal models; (4) postpositivists, including historical institutionalists; and (5) skeptics who are not convinced by the dominant models. In this section, I examine the research done by scholars in the first three camps because they pose the most serious problems for the strong view of precedent. In the next chapter I examine the empirical work done by those in the other groups because they question or reject the claims of scholars in the first three groups and support a more nuanced perspective than the weak or strong view of precedent.

3. Rational Choice, Attitudinal, and Mixed Models of Precedent

The dominant social science models of precedent are the attitudinal model and rational choice theory. Those who favor, or combine, these models have long been conducting extensive empirical tests of precedent's influence on judicial behavior. These scholars suggest that their testing reveals that precedent does not constrain the Court. They claim that the most meaningful predictors—and constraints—on what justices decide are factors external to the law, such as the justices' personal or policy preferences, and not factors internal to the law, including the Constitution or precedent. Rational choice theorists and attitudinalists diverge over how and which external factors drive judicial behavior. While there are variants of the rational choice and attitudinal models (and their combinations), they are subject to the same problems which I suggest undermine the two basic models.

Harold Spaeth is the leading and strongest attitudinalist. Building on social psychology research and theory, Spaeth initially constructed the attitudinal model, which he later refined with the help of Jeffrey Segal. In 1993[112] Spaeth and Segal demonstrated the empirical support for the attitudinal model, and in 1999 they published extensive empirical findings demonstrating that precedent did not constrain the justices from voting their personal policy preferences.[113] In 2002 they revised their thesis to incorporate strategic behavior among the justices and to take into account a more sophisticated understanding of law.

In their revised thesis, Spaeth and Segal identify the legal model as their primary target. They define the legal model as "the belief that, in one form or another, the decisions of the Court are substantially influenced by the facts of the case in light of the plain meaning of statutes and the Constitution, the intent of the framers, and/or precedent."[114] They identify Dworkin as a principal proponent of the legal model because he believes that "stare decisis plays a vital role in judicial decision-making"[115] and that the quest to fit past cases and "hard" ones leads judges to "eliminate interpretations that some judges would otherwise prefer, so that the brute facts of legal history will in this way limit the role any judge's personal concoctions can play in his decisions."[116] Spaeth and Segal were not persuaded. They claimed Dworkin and the legal model failed to meet the exacting standards of scientific research, under which the "[legal] model must be able to state a priori the potential conditions that, if observed, would refute the model."[117] Because the legal model posits no such conditions, it is irrefutable.

Spaeth and Segal consider

> the best evidence for the influence of precedent must come from [justices who dissented] to … the majority opinion under question, for we *know* that these justices disagree with the precedent. If the precedent established in the case influences them, that influence should be felt in that case's progeny, through their votes and opinion writing. Thus, determining the influence of precedent requires examining the extent to which justices who disagree with a precedent move toward that position in subsequent cases.[118]

Segal and Spaeth searched 2418 votes and cases for evidence of the "gravitational force" of precedent claimed by Dworkin,[119] the "'respect for precedent'" Ronald Kahn suggests justices exhibit,[120] or the validity of C. Herman Pritchett's statement that "'[j]udges make choices, but they are not the 'free choices of congressmen.'"[121] In categorizing attitudes towards precedent, Spaeth and Segal treated justices who supported challenged precedents as "precedentialists" (ranging from strong to weak) and justices who did not as "preferentialists" (ranging from strong to weak).[122] They further broke down cases into "ordinary" and "landmark" cases as rated by *Congressional Quarterly's Guide to the U.S. Supreme Court*. Their data showed that "[t]he justices are rarely influenced by stare decisis."[123] It demonstrated "beyond doubt that the modern Courts, heavily criticized for their activism, did not invent or even perfect preferential behavior; it has been with us since Washington packed the Court with Federalists."[124] Segal and Spaeth suggested the few precedentialist acts are irrelevant because they are "more likely to be found in cases of the lowest salience: ordinary cases compared with landmark cases and, among ordinary cases, statutory cases over constitutional cases and modern economic cases over modern civil liberties cases. The influence of precedent appears to be quite minor, but it does not appear to be completely idiosyncratic."[125] They found "not one justice of the Rehnquist Court exercised deference to precedent by voting to uphold both conservative and liberal precedents."[126]

In contrast to the strong attitudinal model, rational choice theorists—sometimes called positive political theorists[127]—argue that precedent is principally instrumental as a means to an end. They suggest justices employ various strategies to manipulate precedents to implement their preferences. These preferences include (but are not limited to) preserving the Court's reputation and dominance in interpreting the Constitution. Attitudinalists dispute the extent (and significance) of the manipulation,[128] whereas rational choice theorists suggest justices are not completely free to vote their policy preferences, but rather operate in a specific institutional environment that sometimes forces them to take various factors into consideration, such as the norm of stare decisis, when formulating strategies to implement their objectives.

Spaeth and Segal suggest that a major problem with rational choice theory is its failure to develop models that satisfy equilibrium theory, which posits that in competitive circumstances parties tend to move toward stable outcomes. This theory provides the means by which to measure the parties' achievements of their respective strategies and goals:

> Equilibria … are crucial to most rational choice theorists. They represent "a prediction, for a specified circumstance, about the choices of people and the corresponding outcomes. This prediction generally takes the form of 'if the institutional context of a choice is … and if people's preferences are … then the only choices and outcomes that can endure are …,'"[129]

Thus, equilibrium theory "provid[es] necessary and sufficient conditions for choices to occur."[130] Spaeth and Segal acknowledge other theorists—particularly two leading rational choice theorists, Lee Epstein and Jack Knight—who "dispute the centrality of equilibrium analysis for rational choice models, labeling the positions taken by each side of the debate a play 'to its competitive advantage.'"[131] Nevertheless, Segal and Spaeth consider equilibrium theory as the "most powerful and important advantage that rational choice theory has over other theories" because it provides the means by which to construct falsifiable models of strategic behavior by "demonstrat[ing] that interactions among the justices constitute a best response to a best response, or alternative equilibrium solutions."[132] Rational choice theorists mistakenly infer strategies from the outcomes achieved in particular cases, even though this is circular; and they "allow [justices to pursue] any goals whatsoever," making every objective achieved rational.[133]

The clash between the attitudinal model and Epstein and Knight's work is most evident in Segal and Spaeth's discussion of the extent to which precedent genuinely constrains the justices from voting their policy preferences. In 1996 Epstein and Knight argued that "precedent can serve as a constraint on justices acting on their personal policy preferences."[134] Although judges and justices might prefer to ignore precedent in favor of their preferred policies, they are constrained by the utility of precedent in fostering social stability and judicial legitimacy. Others might react negatively if the Court violated precedent. In support of the significance of precedent in judicial decision making, they point to the ubiquity of citations of precedent in judges' published opinions, litigants' arguments, and justices' private discussions. Spaeth and Segal responded that ubiquity was not influence and the evidence actually demonstrated that the justices felt little social pressure to adhere to precedents.[135] Spaeth and Segal's quarrel is less with Epstein and Knight's empirical methods than with the implications of their data.

Beyond the strongest attitudinalists and rational choice theorists are scholars who combine the dominant models, including rational choice theorists who agree with attitudinalists about the centrality of attitudes to judicial decision making. For instance, one variant posits that justices' votes in some areas of constitutional law are predictable according to a single "ideal point" symbolizing, or summarizing, their respective preferences.[136]

4. The Limits of Strong Attitudinal and Rational Choice Theories

Many if not most legal scholars ignore the dominant social science models of the Court or argue judging cannot be quantified and consider empirical analysis untrustworthy because it can be easily manipulated. The impasse between legal scholars and many social scientists does not bode well for understanding precedent. It allows perpetuation of misconceptions about precedent, law, and the relevance of the empirical analysis of judging. In this section I examine several problems with the empirical analyses of attitudinalists and rational choice theorists. These problems underscore the need for more refined data analysis and theories of precedent.

First, attitudinalists and rational choice theorists attack a nonexistent foe. Legal scholars do not propose a scientific model of judging and insist law is not a science. This

> refusal is ... common among social scientists. In fact, legal
> scholarship frequently pursues doctrinal, interpretive, and nor-
> mative purposes rather than empirical ones. Legal scholars often
> are just playing a different game than the empiricists play, which
> means that no amount of insistence on the empiricists' rules can
> indict legal scholarship—any more than strict adherence to the
> rules of baseball supports an indictment of cricket.[137]

Other fields, such as presidential studies, paleontology, and anthropology, employ similar methods. Attitudinalists' and rational choice theorists' "empirical methodology blinds them to legal scholarship's internal perspective" or legal scholars' efforts to explain the process by which judges and justices "interpret" the law, including precedent.[138] The internal perspective includes analytical methods for assessing the coherence of legal reasoning and different constructions of the Constitution. Many attitudinalists and rational choice theorists too quickly dismiss the significance lawyers attach to interpretive methodologies. Justices' interpretive methodologies are endemic, not exogenous, to the adjudicative process, because they derive from traditional sources of constitutional law. Moreover, attitudinalists and rational choice theorists do not appreciate how judges critique alternative interpretive approaches based on their internal coherence and achievement of their stated objectives. Thus Dworkin's theory of law should be evaluated on how well it makes sense on its own terms and as compared to other positive accounts of what justices do.[139]

Some scholars may respond that judicial ideologies are not law, but rather personal preferences. This response reflects, however, a basic misunderstanding of law. Law is not just what legislatures make, and not all laws have the same constraining force. Judicial interpretations of legal materials are law, and they exert legal force. The particular perspectives which many social scientists claim are constraining the justices are their legal interpretations. The fact that the justices assert different legal interpretations does not make them any less law. The Constitution—the supreme law in the land—authorizes these interpretations by empowering the Court to decide cases, by requiring justices to take oaths prior to performing their constitutional duties, and by authorizing their decisions to stand as constitutional law unless or until they are displaced through formal constitutional amendments. The Constitution establishes multiple processes for filtering these interpretations out, for implementing them, and for altering them. One such process is the judicial system. It consists of a hierarchical decision-making process for courts, including internal rules for legal argumentation. The Constitution also authorizes a process that is external to the courts (but with possible ramifications within them) for testing and correcting their interpretations of the Constitution.

Second, many attitudinalists and rational choice theorists do not recognize the possibility of good faith differences of opinion over interpretation of the law. For example, variations in judicial votes might not be evidence of hypocrisy, as claimed by Spaeth and Segal. Instead, "what the two call 'subjective preferences' may be nothing more than honest attempts to apply consistent interpretive philosophy to the facts."[140] Any correlation between justices' decisions and (possible) political preferences is designated as a policy choice rather than a good faith attempt to construe the law. Many attitudinalists (and some rational choice theorists) go further to dismiss the significance of the fact that the Court decides hard cases. "Virtually none of the disputes that reach the Court are easy cases. Most of them concern issues for which sources of legal authority—constitutional text, original understanding, evolving tradition, precedent—do not yield determinate answers."[141] The Court's docket consists of cases in which no single source points to a simple or obvious answer. More importantly, precedent is not an isolated issue or subject in the cases decided by the Court. To the contrary, it arises in relation to the possible relevance of other possible sources of constitutional meaning. Consequently the justices are usually required to coordinate sources in deciding cases[142]—something that most attitudinalist and rational choice theorists ignore.[143]

In making judgments about coordinating sources, justices' ideological preferences or commitments may come into play. Yet, these preferences or commitments are not the same as partisan policy preferences. They purport to be principled approaches to deciding cases.[144] They can be dismissed as unprincipled only if they fail to be grounded in coherent constructions of legal materials and to comport with normatively superior principles, which attitudinalists and rational choice theorists generally fail to propose.

Third, many attitudinalists and rational choice theorists minimize the extent to which legal variables may explain constitutional cases. For instance, Spaeth and Segal exclude unanimous opinions from their data set on the justices' fidelity to precedent because they lack the friction that presumably provides the impetus for justices to express their respective policy preferences.[145] Unanimity is difficult to square, however, with a critique of the legal model that suggests Supreme Court justices never, or almost never, make decisions based on legal variables. Even worse for the critique of the legal model, there are numerous cases involving salient issues on which the justices transcend their ideological differences to reach agreement about the law. Many of these cases are unanimous,[146] while others are nearly unanimous. For instance, a six-member majority of the Supreme Court upheld Virginia's statutory ban on cross burning.[147] The six justices in the majority were Chief Justice Rehnquist and Justices Sandra Day O'Connor, Antonin Scalia, Clarence Thomas, and Stephen Breyer. Justices Souter, Ginsburg, and Kennedy dissented. These are not easily predictable or explicable coalitions. None of the justices sympathized with cross burning. Instead, they divided into coalitions based on their interpretations of the Court's doctrine on symbolic conduct. Their positions are explainable on the bases of legal variables.

Fourth, attitudinalists' supposition that justices should follow all the precedents to which they dissented is dubious. There is no basis for believing justices should rigidly follow every precedent to which they dissented. The same obligation that lower court judges have to obey Supreme Court precedent does not extend to the Court's dissenters; they are not considered subordinate in any way to their colleagues and thus have no obligation to accept their colleagues' positions. There is, in other words, no norm that obligates justices to defer to precedents to which they dissented. The legal model allows dissent.

Fifth, the dominant social science models assume, but do not prove, that the primary interest which justices are interested in maximizing is influence over policymaking. Supreme Court justices have many possible interests they might wish to maximize. It is true that the conventional assumption of economics that individuals seek to maximize wealth is largely inapplicable to federal judges, whose salaries are fixed and tenure is secure.[148] While justices cannot get better salaries by improving their performances, they may try to maximize other interests, including pre-serving leisure time, desire for prestige, promoting the public interest, avoiding reversal, or enhancing reputation.

"[P]ersonal dislike of a lawyer or litigant, gratitude to the appoint-ing authorities, desire for advancement, irritation with or even a desire to undermine a judicial colleague or subordinate, willingness to trade votes, desire to be on good terms with colleagues, not wanting to disagree with people one likes or respects, fear for personal safety, fear of ridicule, reluc-tance to offend one's spouse or close friends, and racial or class solidarity" may also represent interests justices maximize.[149] Further, justices might seek to maximize their sense of duty, for example, they might seek to make the best decision in light of the relevant legal materials. These different interests suggest that the search for a single, universal, invariable maxi-mand, such as influencing policy, is futile.

Sixth, the dominant social science models cannot explain constitutional change in the short or long term.[150] The attitudinal model is based in part on the presumption that individual justices have fixed ideological preferences at the start of their respective tenures. Fixed preferences are appealing to social scientists because they can be easily measured. If, however, they shift, there would be no tangible measure of a justice's ideology against which to assess her subsequent decisions. Unfortunately, there are no data confirming that justices generally have firmly fixed preferences at the outset of, much less throughout, their respective appointments. The search for these firmly fixed preferences leads many social scientists around in circles.

This problem is evident in Spaeth and Segal's treatment of John Marshall. They accept the misconception of Marshall as dominating his Court intellectually to further the Federalist party's policy preferences.[151] They fail to acknowledge, much less appreciate the fact that nearly all of Marshall's constitutional opinions were delivered for a Court with a hand-picked Jeffersonian majority. Most of the justices with whom Marshall served were chosen because of their antipathy towards Federalist policies and sympathy towards the Jeffersonian constitutional vision.[152] Thus the Court, with Marshall as Chief Justice, actually repudiated Federalist pref-erences that the Constitution be construed rigorously, with any ambigui-ties in its language resolved according to the "rule of choosing the meaning that best comported with the objects, or purposes, of the Constitution as stated in the Preamble";[153] that our Constitution is not one of enumer-ated powers but rather invests the Congress with "a general lawmaking authority for all the objects of the government that the Preamble of the Constitution states,"[154] that the "United States formed a single nation as to 'all commercial regulations'";[155] and that the common law was part of the law of the United States and thus allowed for Supreme Court supremacy over the state courts with respect to all questions of state law and common law.[156] The attitudinal model cannot explain why Marshall abdicated these strongly held Federalist views as chief justice.

Nor can the dominant models explain why the ideological categories to which their proponents assign justices shift over time. Spaeth and Segal, for instance, gloss over shifts in the meanings of these categories, merely defining them on the extent to which they favor or support policies which are popularly viewed as liberal or conservative.[157] If, however, the meanings of these categories shift, the model cannot explain why. The model cannot account for, and is in fact undermined by, ideological drift, which is the phenomenon by which a view generally associated with one political faction is over time appropriated by or becomes associated with a different one.[158] Thus aggressive judicial review might in one period appear to be liberal, while in another it might appear to be conservative. The fact that such alterations occur is beyond doubt, even assuming particular justices' attitudes are fixed.

For instance, Frankfurter was among the strongest advocates for judicial restraint during his 22 years on the Court. Praised by liberals for his staunch defense of judicial restraint in evaluating progressive economic regulations through his first decade on the Court, Frankfurter was upset to find that in the late 1940s and early 1950s liberals were denouncing him.

> Now, when he advocated judicial restraint, he was attacked by those very same liberals [who had once praised him]. In his earlier years, pillars of the legal community like Henry Stimson, Emory Buckner, and Charles Burlingham praised him. Now, they were either dead or silent. [In] the Truman years, there was little White House contact. Frankfurter had never believed he was "the single most influential man" in Washington, but sometimes he had enjoyed the notoriety. Now there was no more notoriety; he was only one of nine, and one under increasing criticism from those once his friends.[159]

In the years that followed, Frankfurter's status as a liberal increasingly declined. Coincidentally, he shifted from a weak view of precedent before his appointment to the Court to acknowledging once he was on the Court the tendency to "encrust" the Constitution with precedents and "thereafter to consider merely what has been judicially said."[160]

Moreover, the dominant models fail to fully explain stability in constitutional doctrine. The strongest attitudinalists insist that justices will not vote against the interests of governing political coalitions, but sometimes these coalitions do not get the change they want. The strongest attitudinalists cannot account for rather frequent periods in which new justices have failed to alter constitutional doctrine to the extent preferred by the political forces responsible for their appointments.[161] Indeed, there are many areas in which judicial closure is achieved, even though many justices might personally disagree with the position(s) reached.[162] A striking example is the Court's 7–2 decision, in an opinion by Chief Justice Rehnquist, reaffirming *Miranda v. Arizona*[163] in *Dickerson v. United States*,[164] in spite of conservatives' long-standing efforts to dismantle *Miranda*.

Lastly, many attitudinalists (and some rational choice theorists) ignore the phenomenon of institutional path dependence. A decision has path dependency if it compels or forces judges to forego or accept other choices.[165] While attitudinalists claim precedents do not generate much if any path dependency in constitutional law,

> [i]nstitutions are relatively persistent, and thus carry forward in time past political decisions and mediate the effects of new political ones. The creation of institutions closes off options by making it more costly to reverse course, by differentially distributing resources, and by tying interests and identities to the status quo. [Moreover,] the persistence of institutions across time can foster political crises and change as they enter radically changed social environments or abrade discordant institutions.[166]

Many attitudinalists and rational choice theorists discount the link among constitutional design, doctrinal stability, and legal change.

The difficulties which I have found in the dominant social science models of precedent are not merely knit-picking. They reveal the need for a theory of precedent that better explains the Court's handling of precedent. In the next chapter I propose a theory that synthesizes conventional legal analysis and social science research to explain the construction and evolution of precedent.

In this chapter I propose a moderate view of precedent as an alternative to the weak and strong perspectives on precedent. On my view, an essential dynamic in constitutional law is what I call the golden rule of precedent: Justices (and, as we will see in the next chapter, other public officials) generally know from experience, training, and temperament they cannot be too disdainful of precedents or else they risk having other justices show the same, or even more, disdain for their preferred precedents. This realization leads most justices to carefully pick and choose which particular precedents to challenge. With respect to the image with which I began this book, this means that the 81st justice to consider an issue previously decided by the Court will not write about that issue as if he were writing on a blank slate and ignore what the previous 80 justices have said—or the next 80 may say—about the issue before him.

I combine conventional legal analysis with social science research (particularly historical institutionalism[1]) to show that while justices express respect for precedent in the abstract, the actual process of deciding cases has enough play in the joints to make it difficult, if not impossible, to predict which particular precedents the justices will agree to weaken, if not overrule. But in studying precedent, many social scientists appear not to understand this dynamic, and so they often miss the forest for the trees. They infer a good deal from studies showing that in many doctrinal areas specific precedents do not generate strong path dependency—they do not, in other words, foreclose or mandate particular choices or outcomes.[2] The absence of strong path dependency within specific doctrinal areas is not proof, however, that precedent generally lacks the force of law. Nor do these studies disprove the golden rule of precedent or most justices' genuine respect for precedent. Rather, it is merely a consequence of the interaction of a number of unique, endogenous factors shaping constitutional adjudication in specific cases. In the remainder of this chapter I examine these factors in detail.

1. The Significance of the Forecasting Study and Other Data

The discussion in the last chapter of the dominant social science models for analyzing precedent is hardly all that could be said about them.

As I suggested in chapter 2, there are at least two other groups of social scientists whose empirical work challenges legal scholars' conventional attitudes about precedent. In this section, I examine this other research and the forecasting study which supports important claims of attitudinalists and rational choice theorists.[3] First, some social scientists and legal scholars, sometimes called postpositivists or institutionalists, differ in significant ways from attitudinalists and rational choice theorists. The former are not troubled by the indeterminacy of the law. They believe, as Howard Gillman explains, "judging 'in good faith' is all we can expect of judges." Postpositivists have amassed considerable empirical data to support their beliefs that justices try to "make the best decision possible in light of [their] training and sense of professional obligation."[4]

While critics suggest these claims are impossible to falsify and are merely results of motivated reasoning—the process by which people rationalize behavior to which they are already committed—they fail to grapple with the implications of historical institutionalists' research. Institutionalists recognize that understanding the Court requires more than merely aggregating the justices' individual votes. Institutionalists appreciate the significance of the specific institutional and cultural contexts in which justices operate. Fundamental to their approach is recognizing that these contexts have substantive effects (for instance, by supporting or imposing certain norms), while attitudinalists and rational choice theorists generally claim the Court primarily functions as a cipher for justices' expressions of their individual preferences. While rational choice theory suggests that the justices' different orderings and intensities of preference might produce inconsistent outcomes, institutionalists illuminate the patterns in decision making that can be attributable to the Court as an institution. The institutionalist objective is to determine the operative norms of constitutional adjudication, including the Court's distinctive practices.

Historical institutionalists have gathered an impressive amount of empirical support for their claim that structure, including norms relating to precedent, shapes judicial decisions. Though not strictly falsifiable, the evidence may be assessed on the bases of logic, coherence, experience, and history.

Howard Gillman has summarized some of the most important recent empirical work of postpositivists.[5] Some of their research shows how legal variables explain and shape how constitutional doctrine has evolved, including the Court's due process and commerce clause decisions from the late 19th century to the New Deal era,[6] the Warren Court's failure to constitutionalize welfare rights,[7] and the evolution of modern free speech[8] and death penalty jurisprudence.[9] Other research demonstrates how the judicial process shapes practices and choices within constitutional adjudication, including "the use of precedent by lawyers in case briefs and by Justices in conference discussions, where discussion of legal materials cannot be merely a matter of public relations";[10] "precedential effects on [lower] courts";[11] "judicial practices, such as writing concurring and dissenting opinions (forms of expressive behavior that are not about policymaking), inviting legislative overrides, and patterns of case selection during the cert-granting process";[12] and how "distinctive jurisprudential categories or doctrines have influenced voting and opinion writing on the Supreme Court."[13] At the very least, postpositivist research has "[a]ll [been] written by scholars who were mindful of the debates in the literature about legal versus personal influences on decision making, and all attempted to show how the judges' expressed beliefs and patterns of behavior could only be explained with reference to distinctive legal norms."[14] Moreover, this research arguably counters the attempts by attitudinalists, rational choice theorists, and others to rule out the relevance of legal variables to judicial decision making.

A second group of social scientists share postpositivists' suspicions that the strong attitudinal model oversimplifies judicial decision making and that law matters, but they are not persuaded by the evidence offered by postpositivists. For example, Herbert Kritzer and Mark Richards found that certain precedents established new "jurisprudential regimes"—particular constitutional doctrines firmly grounded in precedent—that dictated how justices analyzed later cases.[15] They found these decisions had influence by "establishing which case factors are relevant for decision making and/or by setting the level of scrutiny or balancing the justices are to employ in assessing case factors."[16]

Another prominent scholar, Lawrence Baum, agrees precedent matters, but for more complex reasons than proponents of the dominant models recognize. He suggests these models rest on the mistaken assumption that the justices are principally concerned with making good policy. Baum suggests that this assumption is mistaken because it "does not comport well with what we know about human motivations."[17] He urges scholars not merely to accept judges as interested in improving public policy. He suggests another influential factor in judicial decision making is "judges' interest in the esteem of audiences that are important to them."[18] Baum's research

> offers a means to consider what we know and still need to learn about judicial behavior. It helps in interpreting patterns of behavior that scholars have identified, such as ideologically structured voting on the Supreme Court. It assists in thinking about issues that lie on the fringes of the current models, such as the sources of temporal change in judges' policy positions. [Lastly,] it provides a way to reopen issues that particular models close by assumption, such as the balance between legal and policy considerations in judges' choices.[19]

In two other, recent studies of federal appellate court decisions, researchers confirmed that precedents have limited path dependency. In one, Cass Sunstein and three coauthors found that ideological and group influence effects grew over time.[20] In the other, Stefanie Lindquist and Frank Cross reached a similar conclusion. They empirically tested Dworkin's claim that the judicial use of precedent can be likened to a group of authors writing a novel seriatim, in which the accumulation of chapters increasingly constrains writers' choices.[21] Based on their analysis of 700 federal appellate decisions, Lindquist and Cross found that judges had the most latitude in "cases of first impression," but "[f]ollowing the development of some clear precedents, [the] influence of attitudes may be moderated as judges feel bound by those clear and controlling decisions. As more time passes and more precedents are decided, [the] proliferation of available prior decisions in turn expands judges' discretion to decide cases in accordance with their attitudes simply because they have more precedents from which to choose."[22]

Besides the fact that studies of the federal courts of appeals have little relevance for understanding the Court (on which there is more constancy in composition and no norm requiring justices to strictly follow decisions to which they dissented), one has to wonder whether analogizing judging to a chain-written novel is more apt than analogizing it to umpiring (as Chief Justice Roberts suggests) or jazz (as Charles Fried suggests). None of these metaphors fully captures the uniqueness of judging. Judging allows for more discretion and creativity than umpiring, but is far less creative than jazz or chain-writing a novel. Whereas each of these other enterprises puts a premium on creativity, legal scholars, public officials, and the general public hardly agree that creativity and imagination are appropriate attributes of judging.

Another interesting empirical analysis of precedent is the "forecasting study" done by some legal scholars and social scientists. The study compared whether legal scholars or their statistical model did a better job of predicting the outcomes in one Supreme Court term. The model forecasted outcomes based on six general case characteristics: the circuit from which the cases originated, the issues in the cases, the types of petitioners, the types of respondents, the ideological directions of the lower court rulings, and whether petitioners argued the law or practice being challenged was unconstitutional. The competing set of predictions was taken from 83 legal experts.[23] The statistical model predicted 75% of the Court's affirm/reverse results correctly, while the experts (in panels of three) predicted only 59.1% of the affirm/reverse results correctly.[24] The legal experts correctly predicted 67.9% of individual votes correctly, while the statistical model predicted 66.7% of individual votes correctly.[25]

There are two significant problems with the forecasting study. First, like the attitudinal and rational choice models, it needs justices to be path dependent, or how else could it measure the consistency and predictability of justices' voting. Ironically, the study and these models assume justices will follow their prior votes and hence need path dependency at the individual rather than the institutional level.

Second, the group that best predicted outcomes was neither the model nor the legal experts, but rather experienced Supreme Court advocates. They predicted 92% of the affirm/reverse results correctly, while legal scholars correctly predicted only 53% of those results.[26] The study dismissed the relative success of the attorneys as a statistically insignificant sample because they constituted only 12 of 83 legal experts consulted.[27] The attorneys' relative success suggests, however, their potential as the most meaningful group to consult on the likely outcomes and individual votes in pending cases. This likelihood stands to reason since practitioners make their living knowing the Court better than anyone else.

In another study, Thomas Hansford and James Spriggs II fused the attitudinal model with legal analysis.[28] Based on the empirical analysis of precedents decided between 1946 and 1999, they found

> that while precedent can operate as a constraint on the justices' decisions, it also represents an opportunity. It represents a

constraint in that justices may respond to the need to legitimize their policy choices and thus gravitate toward some precedents rather than others. It represents an opportunity in the sense the justices utilize precedent to constrain other actors, thereby promoting the outcomes they prefer. By specifying the benefits the justices receive from interpreting precedent positively [by expanding it] or negatively [by narrowing it] based on both the desire to make existing precedent compatible with their policy preferences and their need to justify and legitimize their holdings, we gain a better handle on how these variables influence the Court.[29]

Hansford and Spriggs recognized that the "meaning and clout of precedent hangs centrally on how the Court treats it in subsequent cases"[30] and not just on what happens in cases involving the overruling of precedent.

I find little to dispute here, except Hansford and Spriggs treat all precedents the same. They do not distinguish between constitutional and other precedents, even though the Court does, by deferring more to statutory than to constitutional precedents. They do not measure how faithfully the Court maintains this distinction or whether the greater deference given to statutory precedents skews the results. Moreover, they minimize the importance of how people with different levels of experience and skills may read cases differently. After all, a tentative finding of the forecasting study is that people specializing in Supreme Court advocacy may have excellent—if not superior—insights into the Court's manipulation of precedent. In the next section, I examine more closely the factors that complicate predicting precedents.

2. The Prerequisites of Path Dependency

For precedents to impose path dependency, they need to have five properties. This section examines each of these.

2.1 Path Dependency Requires Permanence

The first essential element of path dependency is permanence. Permanence refers to a particular judicial decision's enduring resolution of some disputed constitutional issue(s). Judicial decisions cannot be said to impose path dependency if they do not alter justices' choices in some enduring way. Permanence requires the closure of questions of constitutional meaning for all time.

There are, however, many decisions that did not permanently settle constitutional conflicts. While the Court has achieved closure in many discrete constitutional areas (discussed in chapter 1), the closure was often unpredictable. For instance, I previously noted the Court shows no inclination to revisit a number of landmark decisions, including those upholding the incorporation of most of the Bill of Rights through the Fourteenth Amendment due process clause. Nor does it show any inclination to reconsider its decisions upholding the constitutionality of the Voting Rights Act, the 1964 Civil Rights Act, and landmark environmental regulations. These are some examples of precedents that have become "entrenched," or so widely accepted by the Court, the government, and society generally that they are practically immune to modification by the Court. Yet, some of these lines of decisions, such as those pertaining to incorporation, were hardly linear; they did not follow a straight or inexorable path to their present state of entrenchment.

Even some seemingly settled areas of constitutional law might not be. An example is commerce clause jurisprudence.[31] Richard Fallon suggests that the Rehnquist Court, in the course of reviving constitutional federalism, never overruled any commerce clause precedents.[32] Yet, as Fallon admits, these precedents have been stable for only about six decades. In the mid to late 1930s, the Court apparently began to tinker with its prior commerce clause precedents, thus denying them much path dependency. The current precedents governing congressional power to regulate commercial activities, dating back to the 1930s, can claim some path dependency, but then the preceding string of commerce clause decisions could have made similar claims until 1937. Just how long the current doctrine will generate some path dependency is unknown.

In the constitutional cases in which the Court has explicitly overruled itself,[33] the plurality is commerce clause cases. Yet, Fallon identifies the constitutionality of congressional regulation of commercial activity as one of the few issues arising under the commerce clause that has been settled for a significant period of time. Even though Fallon claims that path dependency explains the doctrine on congressional regulation of private economic activity, the Court has arguably signaled in recent commerce clause opinions its intention to refine its articulation of what constitutes a commercial activity.[34] This fine-tuning requires the justices to tinker with precedents on such far-ranging topics as environmental and criminal law. The full extent of path dependency in commerce clause cases thus remains to be seen.

2.2 Path Dependency Requires Sequentialism

The second prerequisite for path dependency is sequentialism. Sequentialism requires the order in which the Court decides cases to influence outcomes. Sequentialism presupposes that what came before has some definitive or measurable effect(s) on what follows. It is, however, impossible to prove sequentialism determines specific outcomes. It is pure speculation whether the Court would have ruled differently if it were to have decided some cases in a different sequence.

The Court's privacy decisions illustrate the difficulty of proving sequentialism in constitutional adjudication. A common assumption is that the sequence of the Court's decisions on privacy led to *Roe v. Wade*.[35] Many people suspect that had the Court decided *Roe* prior to, say, *Griswold v. Connecticut*,[36] the Court might have had more trouble deciding *Roe* as it did. This assumption is mistaken. First, there is no consensus on the precedents that might qualify as the Court's so-called privacy decisions. Legal scholars, if not the justices, hardly agree on the particular decisions that are indispensable to *Roe*'s formulation or that support *Roe* or any other privacy decisions. Path dependency presumes that prior decisions not only set the stage for *Roe* but led inexorably to it. This was not the case. The path of the Court's privacy decisions, to the extent there has been a discernible one, is far from clear and highly contentious. While some scholars might claim the path begins with the Court's 1920s decisions in *Meyer v. Nebraska*[37] and *Pierce v. Society of Sisters*,[38] the connections between those cases and *Roe* are dubious because they did not directly involve a person's autonomy over his or her body, much less procreative or sexual activity. While others might argue the path of the privacy opinions begins with *Skinner v. Oklahoma ex rel. Williamson*,[39] *Skinner* was an equal protection case, not a due process case. If, however, one were to think that the path of privacy decisions begins with *Griswold*, *Griswold* hardly leads inexorably to *Roe*. Several justices in *Griswold* explicitly distinguished abortion from a married couple's use of conception in *Griswold*,[40] and the Court in *Roe* distinguished *Roe*'s facts from those in prior cases dealing with privacy interests.[41] *Griswold* is only one of the many cases cited in *Roe*,[42] none of which *Roe* cites as compelling its result. Nor did the decision in *Roe* lead the Court—except notably in *Lawrence v. Texas*[43]—to uphold other substantive due process claims. Indeed, *Roe* did not bar the Court from rejecting the substantive due process claims in *Bowers v. Hardwick*.[44] Nor did the majority in *Lawrence* follow *Bowers'* lead; in fact, it did the opposite, by overruling *Bowers*. And it is not immediately apparent that the liberty interest at stake in *Lawrence*—homosexual sodomy—is the same or similar to the liberty interest in *Roe*—terminating pregnancies. Some say the cases both involve personal autonomy or bodily integrity, while others say that the Court has never recognized an absolute right to bodily integrity or personal autonomy and that the cases involve quite different contexts and the government's interest is different in each.

Nor is it possible to show how reversing the path of privacy decisions would alter outcomes. The Court rarely takes cases in which the outcomes are clearly dictated by a single precedent or set of precedents. Even in cases in which the fate of a particular precedent is at issue, the Court rarely bases its decision on a single, earlier decision. Further, one might suppose that had the Court decided *Roe* before *Griswold*, the fallout from *Roe* might have discouraged the Court from recognizing substantive due process claims in cases such as *Griswold*. Alternatively, some people could plausibly argue that *Roe* differs from *Griswold* in that *Roe* involves much more extensive and intrusive coercion on a class of citizens than did *Griswold*. As long as cases are distinguishable from each other, they are not inexorably connected. If they can be disconnected, then the sequence in which the Court decides them does not dictate their respective outcomes. Distinguishing one decision from another means the decisions are not dependent on each other.

Nor, as I have suggested, does *Lawrence* follow inexorably from *Roe*, or other precedents. In *Lawrence*, the justices could have declared that overturning the Texas antisodomy statute had been foreclosed by *Bowers*, the position maintained in Justice Scalia's dissent.[45] That would constitute some evidence of path dependency. Prior to *Lawrence*, the Court had refused to extend the notion of privacy recognized in *Roe* to contexts other than abortion, including the right to die and homosexual sodomy.[46]

While the Court upheld the equal protection challenge in *Romer v. Evans*,[47] *Evans* did not inexorably follow from prior decisions. *Evans* deviated from several precedents upholding state constitutional referenda and overturned for the first time on constitutional grounds a law disadvantaging gays and lesbians. *Evans* argues in favor of the Court's deciding *Lawrence* not on due process grounds, but rather on equal protection grounds, as suggested by Justice O'Connor's concurrence in *Lawrence*.[48] Indeed, Justice O'Connor's concurrence in *Lawrence* dramatically underscores the limited path dependency of *Bowers*, in which she joined the majority's opinion.[49]

2.3 Path Dependency Requires Consistency

The third property required for path dependency is consistency. Consistency requires precedents fit logically or coherently into particular lines of decisions. It requires that the precedents forged in particular areas of constitutional law are analogous to each other and are based on, or employ, similar reasoning.

Consistency is an elusive condition. On the one hand, justices can satisfy the demands of consistency relatively easily in areas in which there are few prior cases, such as the Second Amendment. In such areas, there may not be a clear or settled framework through which the justices could analyze the constitutionality of gun regulations. Even if there were a framework in place, its elements might be sufficiently capacious to allow justices substantial maneuverability to fit particular judicial decisions coherently together. For instance, in *Lopez v. United States*,[50] Chief Justice Rehnquist inferred from the Court's commerce clause decisions from 1937 through 1995 a three-part test for measuring the constitutionality of a congressional regulation of private activity enacted pursuant to the commerce clause. He then demonstrated how the Gun-Free School Zones Act at issue in *Lopez* did not satisfy any of the elements of that framework. The Chief Justice went so far as to reconcile all preceding commerce clause decisions with the framework.[51] He could not reconcile the Gun-Free School Zone Act with the other laws upheld by the Court because it covered an activity—carrying a gun into a school—that differed in kind rather than degree from the "economic" or "commercial" activities which the Court had previously held as congressionally regulable under the commerce clause.

On the other hand, consistency may sometimes be hard to achieve or maintain. Even if a precedent were consistent with past decisions, it may not be consistent with all precedents on the same subject. Free exercise and establishment clause precedents illustrate the problem. In *Locke v. Davey*,[52] the Supreme Court acknowledged that these two clauses are in "tension," and it is not surprising to find as a result that many of its precedents in these two areas are also in "tension." In *Locke*, the Court upheld, against a free exercise challenge, a Washington state law that had awarded merit scholarships to college students but had excluded students pursuing degrees in "devotional theology." On behalf of the majority, Chief Justice Rehnquist read the Court's prior decisions as having enough "play in the joints" to allow the state of Washington to enact the law at issue in the case.[53] The Court found *Locke* to be analogous to its decision in *Zelman v. Simmons-Harris*,[54] which upheld a school voucher program available to certain public and private schools (including parochial schools) in the Cleveland area. But the Court says little in response to Justice Scalia's argument in dissent[55] that *Locke* is more analogous to *Church of Lukumi Babalou Aye, Inc. v. City of Hialeah*, in which the Court had declared that "[a] law burdening religious practice that is not neutral … must undergo the most rigorous of scrutiny"[56] and that "the minimum requirement of neutrality is that a law not discriminate on its face."[57] Moreover, it is hard to reconcile *Employment Division v. Smith*,[58] in which the Court used the rational basis test to analyze the constitutionality of generally applicable, neutral laws burdening religion with other precedents in which the Court used heightened scrutiny to examine the constitutionality of generally applicable, neutral laws significantly burdening religious practices.[59]

These freedom of religion cases illustrate a related problem with expecting perfect consistency in constitutional adjudication. The difficulty is that a particular decision's significance depends on how subsequent justices define it, and it is common for justices to take liberties in characterizing prior decisions. For instance, in *Brandenburg v. Ohio*,[60] the Supreme Court developed a highly protective test for political speech, which it claimed to have derived from prior freedom of speech cases. This, however, was not true. The test in *Brandenburg* required courts examining laws regulating advocacy to commit lawless action to determine whether "such advocacy is directed to inciting or producing imminent lawless action and is likely to produce such action."[61] The cases from which the Court supposedly took this test never, however, articulated such a test. These cases suggested a "clear and present danger" test, which the *Brandenburg* Court did not discuss in any meaningful detail.[62] The latter phrase does not even appear in *Brandenburg*.

Similarly, a majority in *Adarand Constructors, Inc. v. Pena*[63] overruled *Metro Broadcasting, Inc. v. FCC*[64] on the ground that it could not be reconciled with the Court's earlier decisions on affirmative action—the use of race-based classifications supposedly to benefit minorities.[65] The problem with *Adarand* is that there had only been one earlier decision, reached only six years before, in which the Court had struck down a similar program.[66] The other intervening precedents, including *Metro Broadcasting*,[67] had all gone the other way. Prior precedents thus could be plausibly read, as Justice Stevens did in dissent, as upholding exactly the opposite outcome as the one reached in *Adarand*.[68]

2.4 Path Dependency Requires Compulsion

The fourth property required for path dependency is compulsion. Compulsion entails forcing justices to make some decisions they prefer not to make. Yet, there are many precedents that do not appear to have been compelled.

Consider, for instance, the path of voting rights decisions, beginning with *Baker v. Carr*, in which the Court held challenges to racial gerrymandering to be justiciable,[69] and its divisive opinion in *Bush v. Gore*, in which it found Florida's manual recount procedures to be unconstitutional.[70] A conventional critique of *Bush v. Gore* is that it deviated from the path of the Court's voting rights decisions, in which the Court had generally subjected to heightened scrutiny only those governmental actions or decisions that impeded the voting rights of racial minorities, particularly African Americans.[71] Moreover, some scholars maintain the Court should have treated then-Governor Bush's equal protection claims either as nonjusticiable or as not meriting heightened judicial review.[72]

There are several problems with these criticisms. First, no precedents clearly compelled the Court to recognize Bush's claim as nonjusticiable. *Baker* arguably did the opposite by recognizing the constitutionality of judicial review over governmental decision making affecting voting rights. *Baker*, however, is a classic case demonstrating the non-path dependency of precedent, because it rejected the Court's earlier decision in *Colegrove v. Green*,[73] holding that the Court lacked the power to intervene on election district apportionment issues.

Second, *Baker v. Carr* initiated a path of decisions which has hardly been linear, predictable, or coherent. *Baker v. Carr* upheld judicial review of racial gerrymandering, but this ruling did not clarify the constitutionality of political gerrymandering, which has raised different questions and produced a less than coherent body of law. In *Vieth v. Jubelirer*,[74] the Court fell a single vote short of overturning *Davis v. Bandemer*,[75] in which the Court allowed judicial review of political gerrymandering. Nevertheless, Justice Scalia, speaking for a plurality of justices in *Vieth*, declared *Davis* "wrongly decided"[76] and urged its overruling to make way for a clear ruling from the Court that the Constitution did not provide "a judicially enforceable limit on the political considerations that the states and Congress may take into account when districting."[77]

Third, the Court's voting rights decisions hardly lead inexorably to a single conclusion. It is possible to read them as having been largely, if not wholly, about protecting minority voting rights from unfair and discriminatory treatment. One could, however, read them differently, as did seven justices, to overturn a scheme for allowing recounts in a contested election without some clear test for determining which votes to count.[78] The chances for mischief within such a scheme were enormous. The prior case law could be read as disallowing any electoral scheme with a high potential for mischief against a candidate or minority voters. Thus precedents made Bush's claim possible, but not compelling.

Due process of lawmaking is another area in which precedents fail to compel particular outcomes. In *Hampton v. Mow Sung Wong*,[79] the Court struck down a Civil Service Commission rule barring noncitizens, including lawfully admitted aliens, from employment in the federal civil service, on the ground that the rule violated the equal protection component of the Fifth Amendment due process clause. But, as the editors of a leading casebook on the legislative process note, "*Mow Sung Wong* has never directly controlled the result in any subsequent Supreme Court decision, although it has been cited [many] times."[80]

2.5 Path Dependency Requires Predictability

The final property required for path dependency is predictability. Path dependency is predicated on the likelihood that past choices make forecasting future ones easier. Predictability requires that the choices the justices make create expectations about the path of constitutional adjudication and that these expectations are largely justified and realized.

The path of constitutional adjudication is, however, not always predictable. For instance, since the Court reaffirmed *Roe* in *Planned Parenthood of Southeastern Pennsylvania v. Casey*,[81] it has not entertained challenges to *Roe* since, not something many Court observers would have predicted. But once the Court decided *Nixon v. United States*,[82] one could have reasonably expected that it would probably not entertain other challenges to Senate impeachment trial procedures. Once *Nixon* held judicial challenges to Senate impeachment trial procedures to be nonjusticiable, the decision strongly discourages similar challenges and relieves the Court from adjudicating similar questions in the future.[83]

Sometimes predictability is possible. A notable example is the Court's Eleventh Amendment jurisprudence.[84] One can trace one path of Eleventh Amendment decisions back to at least the 1890 decision in *Hans v. Louisiana*.[85] There the Court held the Eleventh Amendment barred federal lawsuits against a state by its own citizens or by citizens of other states. In spite of acknowledging serious questions about the merits of this ruling, particularly its inconsistency with the amendment's plain language,[86] several justices as we have seen, have not only insisted that it is too late to reconsider *Hans*, but have joined together to extend it.[87]

Notwithstanding, the predictability of constitutional adjudication should not be overstated. A significant implication of the forecasting study becomes apparent in the area of predictability. Path dependency requires that outcomes, as well as individual votes, are predictable because they supposedly follow both logically and inexorably as a consequence from a prior sequence of decisions. Yet, none of the groups surveyed in the forecasting study perfectly predicted the outcomes, or individual votes, in the cases from the 2002 term.[88] Most groups fell short of Spaeth and Segal's rate of success—77%—in predicting outcomes.[89] The outcomes of the Court's cases might have been consistent with prior precedents, but consistency is not the same as predictability. The question is the extent to which the outcomes, or individual votes, were foreseeable. The failure to predict outcomes and individual votes flawlessly suggests that they were not all compelled by prior decisions.

One might counter that the forecasting study did not rule out predictability as a requirement for path dependency. Nor did the forecasting study assess the degree of certitude of the experts' predictions of the range of possible outcomes in given cases. Nevertheless, some of the Court's most famous—or infamous—decisions have defied prediction. For instance, immediately after *Griswold*, few if any experts were predicting it would lead to a case like *Roe*. In *Griswold*, the majority set forth five theories for recognizing the privacy claim in the case;[90] and no one could have known or predicted which, if any, of these a majority might follow in a subsequent case involving a claim of either a right to terminate unwanted pregnancies or to engage in homosexual sodomy. Nor after the Court reaffirmed *Roe* could anyone have predicted with certainty which abortion regulations would be found to be unconstitutional under the new "undue burden" standard set forth in *Casey*.[91] Prior to the Court's historic decision in *Brown v. Board of Education*,[92] mandating the end of segregation in public schools, constitutional doctrine as it existed at the time hardly made such a decision predictable or likely. As David Strauss explains, *Brown* did not set forth a clear principle of equal protection. Instead, he argues, *Brown* set forth one of at least five different principles of equal protection.[93] No one after *Brown* could be sure which of these principles, if any, the Court might subsequently follow. Nor was it clear after *Brown* whether or to what extent the Court intended to strike down segregation of public facilities other than schools.

Predictability was also difficult in some commerce clause cases. In *Lopez*,[94] the Court's striking down of the Gun-Free School Zones Act was its first decision in almost six decades to overturn a federal regulation of private conduct for violating the commerce clause. But the Court explicitly declared its refusal to abide by its earlier deference to commerce clause regulations.[95] Moreover, after the Supreme Court held in *Garcia v. San Antonio Metropolitan Transit Authority*[96] that the political safeguards states had in the federal political process obviated the need for judicial review of federal regulation of the states under the commerce clause, no one could be sure how long *Garcia* would be good law. *Garcia* had overruled[97] another decision issued only nine years before, *National League of Cities v. Usery*, which had overruled[98] another precedent.[99] Given that then-Justice Rehnquist threatened in dissent in *Garcia* to secure *Garcia's* overruling,[100] its status was in doubt from the start. Indeed, *Garcia* was overruled partially in one of the next major cases on the scope of congressional authority to regulate state activity under the commerce clause.[101] *Garcia* gave no hint, and few if any at the time it was decided expected, that the bases on which the Court would recognize congressional authority under the commerce clause would be further limited by the Eleventh Amendment in *Florida v. Seminole Tribe*.[102]

Nor, for that matter, had any voting rights experts prior to Election Day 2000 predicted the outcome of *Bush v. Gore*.[103] Nor did any experts envision a decision like *Bush v. Gore* was possible. Nor, for that matter, is anyone sure whether, or to what extent, *Bush v. Gore* will apply outside the context of presidential elections.[104] If one were to believe the Court, the case has no precedential effect.[105] It declared, in effect, that the decision would not impose any path dependency.

As *Bush v. Gore* and other cases demonstrate, it is relatively easy to demonstrate the absence of path dependency in constitutional adjudication. All one must do is show a precedent lacks at least one essential property required for path dependency. It is harder to predict why, when, and how cases generate path dependency. The next part lays the groundwork for explaining why some, but not other, precedents can do this.

3. The Limited Path Dependency of Precedent in Constitutional Adjudication

I propose here that Supreme Court precedent cannot play the role that many social scientists (and some legal scholars) insist that it must play. These social scientists maintain that factors external to the law—personal attitudes, for instances—drive the Court's decision making. Yet, there are at least eight related factors endogenous to constitutional adjudication that demonstrate how and why some, but not other, precedents generate path dependency. These factors include (1) constitutional design; (2) the peculiar nature of constitutional adjudication; (3) how the Court frames its judgments; (4) the phenomenon of entrenchment in constitutional law; (5) changes in the Court's composition; (6) the dynamics of the Court as a multimembered institution that makes decisions by majority vote; (7) the absence of formal rules for construing precedents; and (8) the X factor—the term I use to refer to the hard-to-nail-down reasons that produce change in constitutional law. The operation of and interaction among these factors undercut the boldest claims of social scientists that path dependency is absent in constitutional adjudication. They provide some support for the limited path dependency in constitutional adjudication, and thus provide a bridge between conventional legal analysis and the work of political scientists not wedded to the purest forms of the dominant models.

3.1 Constitutional Design and Legal Indeterminacy

Many social scientists are bothered by the indeterminacy of the law, but legal scholars generally are not. Moreover, legal scholars agree on the reasons for the indeterminacy of the law. The first is the nature of the

Constitution. A written constitution, like other laws reduced to writing, must be abstract; it must speak in "broad outlines" and generalities, as Chief Justice Marshall famously suggested.[106] The abstractness of a written constitution limits its ability to guide concrete decisions taken in its name, and increases the likelihood of unpredictability in its construction.[107]

The abstractness of the Constitution is evident in its broad, non-self-defining terms. No one has yet comprehensively identified the full extent to which its terms are not-self-defining. Nor do legal scholars agree precisely on how widespread the ambiguity is in our Constitution. There are, however, more than enough vague, open-ended terms—as well as troublesome questions raised by the silence and design of the Constitution—to make the legal indeterminacy of the Constitution a real problem. The range of vague, ambiguous, non-self-defining terms within the Constitution is daunting. These terms are not, by nature of design, subject to several plausible interpretations. The Constitution provides no guidance on how its terms ought to be interpreted or on which interpretation is superior.

Second, several practical problems exacerbate the indeterminacy of constitutional law. The Framers and Ratifiers failed to anticipate every contingency, they often failed to reach consensus on more specific language, and they agreed on general terms for different, often complex reasons. As Michael Dorf explains, the difficulty of achieving consensus on more specific language in the Constitution "is particularly problematic for constitutional interpretation. Given profound disagreement, any foundational set of procedures or principles sufficiently abstract to secure consensus and thereby work its way into a popularly chosen constitution will be too abstract to resolve the most acute subsequently arising constitutional controversies."[108]

The text of the Constitution is, however, not the only source of constitutional meaning that is open-ended, lacks consensus on rules for its construction, and is subject to multiple interpretations. Similarly the structure of the Constitution raises inferences, but the Constitution does not dictate which inferences ought to be controlling. In a classic dispute, some people support construing the Constitution as setting forth the full range of areas in which the branches may share power, while others argue that the Constitution limits only how much power may be shared by the heads of each branch, but not how much may be shared by officials operating below the apexes. In another long-standing (and bloodier) dispute, authorities disagreed over the areas in which the federal government is supreme to the states, as well as the scope of state sovereignty protected by the Constitution. The open-ended terms of the Constitution, as well as the inferences raised by the Constitution's design, lend themselves to several plausible interpretations; however, the Constitution provides no guidance on how it ought to be interpreted, much less on which one of several plausible interpretations is superior.

My purpose in raising the indeterminacy of constitutional design or meaning is not to express agreement with some attitudinalists that the indeterminacy of law impedes principled interpretation altogether. Scholars who make this claim misunderstand what legal reasoning entails and have not bothered to empirically support their claim that all law is indeterminate. Sometimes constitutional text is relatively clear (suggesting, for instance, Congress has two chambers), but the ambiguities in the Constitution do not preclude all principled interpretation.

3.2 The Significance of the Distinctions Among Constitutional Adjudication, Legislating, and Common-Law Judging

Many social scientists have the wrong paradigm in mind when they analyze courts. They presume mistakenly that the Court functions like a legislature. Yet, deciding cases is different than legislating: Legislating entails creating a code to govern future conduct, while judging entails interpreting the law, in its various forms, to resolve particular disputes. Justices, by definition, training, and practice, do not create statutes. Legislators make statutes which primarily apply prospectively, while justices primarily apply the law retrospectively. Legislators are directly subject to political pressure and accountability, but justices are not.

Moreover, many social scientists—and some legal scholars—believe constitutional adjudication functions like common-law judging. For instance, Oona Hathaway defines path dependency in common-law adjudication as "a causal relationship between stages in a temporal sequence, with each stage strongly influencing the direction of the following stage."[109] This is almost precisely the same causal relationship that many legal scholars presume exists in constitutional adjudication. Even prominent legal scholars such as Frank Easterbrook and Richard Posner have acknowledged that precedent imposes a degree of path dependency in constitutional adjudication similar if not identical to path dependency in the common law.[110] Other scholars go further not only to treat constitutional adjudication as akin to common-law judging, but also to treat the path dependency in constitutional adjudication as akin to that in the common law.[111]

Yet, justices do not treat constitutional precedents as they treat common-law ones. To begin with, the structure of the legal system reflects these differences. The structural differences between constitutional adjudication and judicial resolution of common-law and statutory issues dictate a different status for precedent in each context. In a common-law system, precedents are the exclusive source of legal authority. By definition, common-law cases are those in which a legislature or higher authority has not yet spoken (at least explicitly) to the issues. While it is true that in common-law cases the judges may be trying to resolve particular disputes in light of some abstract principles of the law, they are common-law cases precisely because these abstract notions have not been codified. In the common-law system, cases thus are the primary constituents. What follows is that path dependency then becomes a basic expectation in the common-law system. While cases are not the primary or sole constituent of litigation over the meaning or application of a statute, statutory and common-law cases have one essential feature in common: a legislature may overrule or displace a court's decision on the meaning of either the common law or a statute. Because of this common feature, judges have tended to defer to earlier common-law or statutory decisions so as to give legislatures a fixed target they may regulate.

But the Court shows less deference to precedent in constitutional adjudication. There, the primary constituent is the Constitution. There is nothing analogous to the Constitution in the American common-law system. In common-law adjudication, cases—precedents, if you will—are the principal framework. Precedent is the only medium of exchange in the common law, while it is not in constitutional adjudication. In common-law cases, arguments are based solely on precedent. In constitutional adjudication, arguments may be based not only on precedent, but also on other conventional modes of constitutional discourse—text, original meaning, structure, moral reasoning, and consequences. The choice of which arguments to make in a common-law case is almost always defined by prior cases; the primary issue is which prior case is most like the one before the court. But the choices of which arguments to make in constitutional adjudication and which are persuasive are not just based on which precedent(s) ought to control. We know from social science research and other data that many factors—such as the relative quality of the briefs and lawyers appearing before the Court, the audiences which the justices are addressing, and the nature and clarity of the supposedly relevant case law, the political and legal salience of the issues, and the clarity of the text, doctrine, or other pertinent legal materials—influence the justices' interpretive choices. The important thing to keep in mind is that the justices' decisions in any given case may turn on any combination of these or other factors. Moreover, in every case the Court must choose how to frame its decision, which I discuss in the next subsection.

3.3 The Significance of Rules and Standards

The justices' training, duties, and norms narrow their options for packaging their decisions. Generally they frame their judgments as rules or standards. Rules and standards constrain the Court's decision making differently, and these differences illuminate how precedent has limited constraint on judicial decision making.

By design, rules constrain choices more than do standards.[112] Rules constitute broad, inflexible principles that provide clear notice to those to whom they apply and that allow minimal discretion from those charged with implementing or enforcing them. Speed limits are prime examples of rules. Any driver who exceeds the speed limit is violating the law. The law makes no exceptions. The only discretion permitted by the law is measuring the speed of the driver and matching that speed against the maximum allowed to determine compliance.

The more absolutist the rule set forth by the Supreme Court in a given area, the more strongly it imposes path dependency on constitutional law. Interestingly, the Court frames relatively few judgments as rules. Good examples are the Court's holdings that Section Five of the Fourteenth Amendment does not authorize Congress to regulate private activity and that the Tenth Amendment forbids Congress to commandeer states' policymaking. In racial discrimination cases, Justice Scalia also has proposed a virtually absolute rule prohibiting race-based classifications. If the Court were to adopt his preferred rule, it would significantly constrain the path of the Court's rulings in racial discrimination cases. Such constraint is Justice Scalia's objective.

In contrast, standards set forth criteria against which governmental action is measured.[113] Compliance with a standard entails discretion because a standard's implementation requires a decision maker to interpret the criteria in order to determine whether they have been satisfied. A classic example of a standard is a parent's will leaving all his money to his children as long as they eat healthily. Eating healthy is not self-evident. Someone must adjudicate what constitutes healthy eating for purposes of implementing the will.

Standards abound in constitutional law. A few examples include the balancing tests the Court employs for determining the reasonableness of searches or seizures,[114] the propriety of some congressional encroachments on the powers of other branches, and the Court's varying levels of scrutiny for discrimination in cases not involving racial discrimination. Even the kind of heightened scrutiny adopted by the majority in affirmative action cases such as *City of Richmond v. Croson*,[115] *Adarand Constructors, Inc. v. Pena*,[116] and *Grutter v. Bollinger*[117] is a standard. It does not operate mechanically like a rule, but it allows judges to use their discretion to determine if the government has demonstrated the requisite compelling justification.

Though the Supreme Court rarely addresses the significance of the difference between rules and standards, it did in *Crawford v. Washington*.[118] *Crawford* involved the constitutionality of a conviction based in part on the admission into evidence of the statement of a woman who later refused to testify against her husband based on the marital privilege. Prior precedent had allowed such admissions as long as the evidence was "reliable." The Court overturned the conviction. In a unanimous opinion by Justice Scalia, the Court discussed the importance of framing its judgment as a rule rather than as a standard. Justice Scalia condemned the practice of employing standards, which allowed unpredictable, manipulative balancing by the justices.[119] He defended the Court's deciding the case on the basis of an absolute rule,[120] because the Court could apply it more easily, other courts and authors could follow (and be bound by) it more easily, and it comported with the confrontation clause's apparently flat requirement that in every criminal case defendants are entitled to confront adverse witnesses.[121] Accordingly, the Court overturned its precedent.

The Court's judgments can be subdivided beyond rules and standards. Some scholars have suggested categorizing cases on the basis of whether they define the meaning or scope of particular constitutional provisions or measure particular actions against those definitions.[122] Categorizing precedents along these lines ought to remind us that not all constitutional precedents are the same, even though the justices themselves do not recognize the distinctions on which these categories depend as relevant to their determinations of how to construe, follow, and otherwise interpret their precedents.

3.4 The Constitutional Significance of Entrenchment

Many Supreme Court decisions are entrenched or deeply engrained within our legal system. While I discuss this phenomenon in detail in chapter 6, I stress its relevance as a factor contributing to the limited path dependency of precedent. Any effort to explain how the justices decide cases must account for the entrenchment of constitutional law. One possible explanation is that the entrenchment of some precedents reflects the network effects of different judicial practices and decisions. Once other institutions invested in, or relied upon, particular judicial practices and decisions, they became more ingrained into our legal system. The more ingrained a particular judicial practice or decision, the more difficult it is to undo.[123] As layers become deeply embedded and encrusted, the more immune they become to judicial tinkering or excavation. Of course, why some judicial decisions and practices become entrenched (at least to the extent of becoming effectively immune to overturning) remains a difficult question. Because these may be network effects, it might be useful to examine more closely the network within which the justices operate. In particular, certain features of constitutional adjudication may be pertinent to the phenomenon of entrenchment. I turn next to perhaps the most obvious of these.

3.5 The Significance of Changes in the Court's Composition

A change in composition is unquestionably an important factor in triggering either a shift in, or reconsideration of, a Supreme Court precedent.[124] It has been extremely rare for justices to join in overruling a prior decision that they wrote or joined. As I mentioned in the first chapter, in only four cases has a Court with no change in membership overruled itself, and more than half of the overrulings occurred with at least six new justices. Interestingly, the figures suggest that, at least with respect to overruling, a Supreme Court decision probably has its strongest claim to generating path dependency within a relatively short period after it has been created.

Its path dependency is more unpredictable over time, depending on the various factors discussed in this section.

The fact that the most significant, explicit lack of deference to Supreme Court precedent coincides with the arrival of new justices on the Supreme Court is not surprising. The easiest way to overrule a decision is by persuading the Court to change its mind rather than amending the Constitution. To be sure, it is difficult to convince the justices who rendered an opinion that their opinion was wrong. As the statistics in the first chapter (and above) indicate, that method rarely succeeds. Justices might resist overturning cases they joined in deciding for many reasons. One is to protect scarce judicial resources. Standing by their decisions simply allows the Court to build doctrine and to spend time on other cases and areas of the law. Another reason is the justices' reluctance to admit they have made mistakes. Such admissions might make the justices appear to be indecisive or incompetent.

It is easier to persuade justices that the Court erred in opinions in which they did not participate. Indeed, it is possible new justices might be more inclined to reconsider precedent. Many presidents appoint justices with the hope and expectation that they will vote to overrule particular decisions or doctrines. Life tenure allows justices to serve for a substantial amount of time on the Court, but they cannot serve forever. Vacancies on the Court provide presidents and senators with their best and only chances to directly shape the composition and direction of the Court.

Presidents generally recognize the significance of filling vacancies on the Court. In many presidential campaigns the candidates have even made assurances, if not pledges, with respect to the kinds of justices they would nominate. For instance, Richard Nixon campaigned against the Warren Court's activism, particularly its decisions favoring criminal defendants and curbing states' rights.[125] He vowed that if elected he would appoint "strict constructionists" who would be tough on criminals.[126] Nixon's appointees helped to close some of the loopholes created or recognized by the Warren Court to help criminal defendants. Subsequently Presidents Ronald Reagan and George H. W. Bush both campaigned against liberal judicial activism to stifle school prayer and other majoritarian preferences, singled out *Roe* for especially virulent criticism, and vowed to appoint justices who would, inter alia, overrule *Roe* and be tougher on criminals.[127] Their appointees helped to make overturning convictions and abortion regulations more difficult.[128] More recently, President George W. Bush won reelection based in part on his vows to appoint "strict constructionists" to the Court, and the platform on which he ran denounced the "activist" judges deciding *Roe v. Wade*, removing school prayer and the Ten Commandments from public life and schools, striking down laws criminalizing homosexual sodomy, and requiring a state to accept gay marriages.[129]

Newly appointed justices are likely to arrive on the Court with several possible attitudes regarding precedent. Some may not feel any personal stake in decisions in which they did not participate. Alternatively, some newly appointed justices might defer to earlier decisions because they want to show the respect for other decisions they would like for their opinions to receive. Yet another possibility is that newly appointed justices might recognize the need to respect precedent as a means to protect the Supreme Court institutionally from attacks for inadequately respecting the rule of law. Newly appointed justices might also believe that the Court's status will be enhanced if they undo its mistakes and therefore improve the quality of the Court's output. And, of course, an entirely new set of possibilities might arise if the vacancy being filled is that of the Chief Justice. The person who acts as Chief Justice may feel different institutional pressures than Associate Justices. They may feel greater pressures, for instance, to forge majorities, to maintain cordial relations on the Court, to facilitate greater stability on the Court (and its decisions), to promote respect for the Court that bears their name, or to pay more attention to how the public perceives the Court.

In spite of the attitudes of new justices about precedents, they may not be fixed. Interaction on the Court might shape justices' attitudes about precedent and even produce some surprising outcomes. Yet, as the next section shows, justices' abilities to control the path of constitutional adjudication are limited.

3.6 Rational Choice Theory

The path dependency of a particular judicial decision depends in part on the size and jurisdiction of the court creating it. A single judge on an inferior court will not decide cases in the same manner (or be subject to the same pressures or norms) as a three-judge panel or the nine-member Supreme Court of the United States. A federal district judge, for instance, has relatively little discretion in handling precedent.[130] She is bound by a directly superior court's precedents; they impose an order—indeed, they often contain directions—on what she must do.[131] If a district judge is deciding a question on which the federal appeals court for her circuit has not yet ruled, she has the discretion to follow whichever reasoning she finds to be the most persuasive.[132] As for her own rulings, a judge is bound to the practical extent to which she strives for consistency and coherence.[133]

The Court's dynamics are unique. It is common to refer to the Court as an "it," though Adrian Vermeule emphasizes it is usually more useful to treat the Court as a "they" and not an "it."[134] Nor do the Court's precedents relate to its decision making as they do to other courts. Whereas the Supreme Court's precedents are binding on inferior courts, its judgments are, by definition and design, not subject to review by any other tribunal. The Court's precedents apply horizontally to each of the justices, or as persuasive authority from an equal rather than a superior authority. Rational choice theory posits that under such circumstances in which decisions are made by majority vote and not subject to review by a higher authority, the Court will not act as a single person would. Instead, it will produce inconsistent, unpredictable, and even irrational decisions because its members have different orderings and intensities of preferences and because of the ensuing phenomenon of cycling.[135] Rational choice theory suggests that the justices will differ in how they prioritize precedent, and they will differ in how strongly they each feel about the institutional benefits and costs of fidelity to precedent. These differences ensure that the Court will often produce outcomes that are not the primary preferences of each of the justices in the majority. Its reasoning and holdings will thus tend to be inconsistent and lack an essential element of path dependency. Periodic changes in the Court's composition exacerbate the potential inconsistencies in outcomes because new members will introduce into the decision-making process new or different orderings, or intensities, of preferences from those held by their colleagues.

It is hardly impossible for members of a multimembered institution, such as the Court, to share some similar or nearly identical orderings of preference. For instance, one can expect justices to agree, if ever asked, not to overrule either *Brown* or the *Legal Tender Cases*.[136] We also know that the Court will not be asked (at least for the foreseeable future) to reconsider either of those cases. At the very least, we can expect the Court to be asked to consider more difficult, more divisive questions and not whether it ought to stand by a precedent as well settled as *Brown*.

Presidents (and their advisers) have yearned to control the justices' individual or collective orderings of preferences. This desire has led them to try to control those orderings, if only at the margins, by choosing Supreme Court nominees based on their likely ideologies.[137] Ideologies supposedly constrict or preclude preferences. They presumably restrict how judges approach certain questions, regardless of the facts in particular cases. Hence presidents will often choose nominees with the ideologies— or commitments to approaching constitutional issues in particular ways— they would prefer to drive the Court's jurisprudence. The more vacancies a president can fill, the greater control he can hope to have over the Court's decision making, particularly if his appointees share certain precommitments on the issues likely to come before the Court. Consequently it can hardly be a surprise that the presidents who have filled the most vacancies have had the most influence over the course of the Court's decision making: George Washington with 11, Andrew Jackson with 5, Abraham Lincoln with 5, William Howard Taft with 6, and Franklin Roosevelt with 8. These presidents each preferred to choose nominees based on their likely judicial ideologies.

A major problem with efforts to pack the Court, assuming the opportunities for them arise, is that sometimes presidents guess wrong. Sometimes presidents, or their advisers, simply fail to accurately predict the path of the Court's docket.[138] It is not unusual for justices who have all been appointed by the same president to eventually fracture over unexpected issues that come before the Court.[139] Over time, justices, even when they have been selected pursuant to the same criteria, find themselves at odds, fracturing over the rulings or outcomes in particular cases and over how to interpret, or apply, the precedents they have created.

3.7 The Absence of Rules Governing Precedents

The absence of formal rules for the Court to follow in construing its decisions further undermines the path dependency of precedent in constitutional adjudication.[140] The Court has no rules for determining the breadth or narrowness of a particular ruling, how much or how little deference a justice ought to give a prior decision, the requisite conditions for determining error in constitutional law or for overruling constitutional precedents, how to prioritize sources of decision, or how to read prior cases, including the appropriate level of generality at which to state the principles set forth within precedents.

If we genuinely want precedents to have path dependency, we should be prepared to change the conditions under which they are made and interpreted. Rational choice theory suggests that one way to preclude or inhibit the Court from producing inconsistent (and thus not path dependent) precedents is through structural alterations to the Court's decision-making process. These changes could include requiring a supermajority vote of the justices or the passage of a minimal amount of time before formally reconsidering one of its rulings.

It is no accident that the Court has never had such rules (or will, in all likelihood). The first reason is structural. The supermajority requirement for an overruling would undoubtedly transform the dynamics on the Court in particularly undesirable ways. It would, for instance, allow a minority to prevent a simple majority from resolving a particular constitutional claim as long as there were a potential for its decision to weaken a precedent. The requirement would make changing constitutional doctrine more difficult than it already is. Moreover, raising the requirements for the Court to overrule itself conflicts with the independence of the justices. Most, if not all, justices are likely to want for themselves, and therefore for each other, the complete, unfettered discretion to rule as they see fit in a given case. The current system allows each an equal opportunity to influence outcomes, but the supermajority requirement would give simple majorities a distinct advantage in enabling their decisions to become entrenched.

Second, the Court might not be able to perform its constitutional duty to decide cases or controversies if it were unable to review its precedents. During a period in which the Court lacks a supermajority disposed to overrule some contested decision(s), a majority might be precluded from reaching any decisions that might be construed as narrowing and therefore effectively overruling any precedents. Litigants who perceive that they might benefit from such hesitancy would rush to have their claims adjudicated in the interim. Furthermore, the supermajority requirement might pressure a majority to avoid being candid about its attitudes towards a precedent for fear that their candor might preclude them from reviewing a case in which the fate of precedent is at risk.

Third, requiring a supermajority vote for the Court to overrule itself might allow errors in constitutional interpretation to be preserved indefinitely or needlessly. No matter how compelling the reasons may be for overruling a precedent, no overruling could be achieved without the requisite minimum number of votes. If those votes were not forthcoming, whatever harm that the erroneously decided precedent has caused would remain in effect.

Even if the justices were to craft rules to guide their decision making on precedent, they may not constrain their preferences. Adrian Vermeule's notion of a "veil rule" nicely captures this dimension of constitutional adjudication.[141] He is interested in demonstrating the difficulty of the Court's developing rules of decision making that will genuinely constrain how it decides cases. To illustrate his point, he suggests that if the justices were to adopt a rule beforehand to govern their decision making in constitutional cases—the one realm in which they are completely free from legislative correction—the knowledge that they would have to live or comply with this rule would lead them to avoid rules that would unduly restrict their discretion and instead develop rules that allow themselves a lot of wiggle room.[142] In other words, they would develop a rule that does not preclude them from achieving their preferences. He thus suggests that while the justices might have developed the basic rule of limited deference to precedent as a veil rule designed presumably to tie their hands in constitutional adjudication, it does no such thing. It does not constrain outcomes, in part because the parties are free to construe past cases as broadly or as narrowly as they wish, depending on whether they want to follow or distinguish them. Even if there were rules for constructing or construing precedents, there is no way to ensure uniform application of them. It is unlikely the justices would unanimously or consistently agree on such basic things as how to apply the rules and how to implement or revise them.

The likely impossibility of implementing rules for constructing or construing precedents is maddening to many people. Even more maddening is the fact that predicting long-term change in constitutional law is harder to explain and to control than short-term changes.

3.8 The X-Factor

More than 200 years after the original Constitution's ratification, we still have more questions than answers about how enduring shifts in constitutional understanding and law occur. The enduring constitutional changes to which I refer include more than the formal constitutional amendments.

Article V sets forth relatively difficult procedures for formal amendments to the Constitution.[143] Hence, in spite of support from President George W. Bush, a constitutional amendment prohibiting gay marriage is quite unlikely to succeed.[144] This is not a comment on the merits of the proposal. Instead, this is merely an acknowledgment of the unlikelihood that at least two-thirds of each chamber of Congress and three-fourths of the states would support an amendment prohibiting, or impeding, gay marriage. The odds are always against supermajorities in the Congress and among the states for formally amending the Constitution. Less formal changes in constitutional law, such as shifts in the Court's doctrine or popular understandings of the Constitution, are easier to achieve than formal amendments. For instance, no one predicted the boldness of the Massachusetts Supreme Judicial Court in declaring that the state's constitution prohibited denying marriage to two people of the same gender, much less that three members of the majority would have been justices appointed by Republican governors.[145]

I refer to the unpredictable elements of enduring shifts in constitutional understandings and doctrine as the X-factor. Social scientists are more comfortable and adept than legal scholars at examining the possible connections between doctrine and social, political, and economic developments. For instance, social scientists have demonstrated how interest groups (and other organizations) have helped to frame the Court's agenda.[146] Another interesting study indicates a pattern in which the Court apparently favors the side with the largest number of amicus briefs filed on its behalf.[147] This pattern surfaced in *Grutter v. Bollinger*,[148] in which most amicus briefs supported the University of Michigan Law School's admissions program. The same pattern held in *Dickerson v. United States*,[149] in which the vast majority of police departments and other law enforcement organizations asked the Court to reaffirm *Miranda*.[150] But neither *Dickerson* nor *Grutter* involved an enduring shift in doctrine; *Dickerson* reaffirmed *Miranda*, while *Grutter* reaffirmed Justice Powell's test for determining the constitutionality of affirmative action in graduate or professional school admissions.

Legal scholars increasingly suggest that the Court is much more of a follower than a leader with respect to constitutional change. They suggest, for instance, that the Court largely tracks majoritarian preferences.[151] Recently, legal scholars have begun to show how the justices do this, although I will argue in the remainder of this book that much of what the justices do in constitutional adjudication is choose which majoritarian preferences to follow—prior decisions (made by a prior majority of justices); the Constitution and its amendments (ratified by prior supermajorities in Congress and the states, legislation (made by majorities, if not supermajorities, in Congress, oftentimes with presidential approval, or by majorities or supermajorities in the States); or custom, tradition, or historical practices (fashioned by either majorities or supermajorities in either the states or the Congress over time). If there were precedents at odds with majoritarian preferences, then we would expect to see either some backlash or the embattled precedents to be preserved through reinforcement by, or sustained support from, national political leaders.

Almost seven decades after the Court began to defer more to progressive economic regulations in 1937, scholars still argue over whether it was the result of pressure exerted on the Court by President Roosevelt's Court-packing plan, a genuine change of mind for some justices, a radical shift in commerce clause doctrine, or other factors. The difficulties scholars have had in reaching consensus on the constitutional significance of the events of 1937 derives in part from several factors that complicate analysis of the Court.

The first is the impossibility of proving a negative. Proving that a particular factor, or set of factors, had no effect on or relevance to an outcome is impossible, though we can use our common sense to calculate the odds. For instance, I am unable to prove the sun will rise tomorrow morning, but the odds, based on past experience (and our knowledge of astrophysics) favor it. Moreover, some events might be so removed in time and space from the event we are studying that we can exclude, or at least substantially discount, their relevance on the bases of logic and human experience. Within the boundaries of our experience and logic, we search for relatively plausible influences on certain outcomes.

The second complication in searching for the elusive X-factor is figuring out the significance of the justices' choices about what to reveal and not to reveal in their opinions. This complication calls attention to the question of the relative importance of the Court's legal reasoning. Poking holes in the Court's reasoning hardly proves it was irrelevant to the outcome, or to the votes, in particular cases. Nor does supposing a different explanation for the outcomes or votes establish its relevance. For instance, one explanation for *Bush v. Gore*,[152]—the need for the Court to have averted a constitutional crisis[153]—does not appear in any of the opinions. No doubt, this explanation is consistent with the outcome, as is the possible disdain some justices might have had for Congress or other political authorities to settle the dispute between Bush and Gore. This explanation provides the motivation for finding an equal protection violation in the case, but it does not constitute proof of one. Moreover, the justices had to make a showing as a group that there was such a violation of the Constitution; the group dynamics within the Court are not irrelevant to the choices that justices must make in both reaching decisions and formulating how to express them. Explaining how coalitions are reached and maintained, as well as the choices made in opinion writing, are perennially fruitful sources of inquiry in constitutional theory.

Third, the Court is the branch least understood by and most mysterious to the public. Almost everything we know about the Court is based on public statements and actions. One reason for the great fanfare surrounding the publication of a justice's private papers is because it partially relieves our ignorance of the influences on the justice's deliberations.

3.9 Network Effects

The meaning and value of precedent depends on how subsequent justices conceive it. For instance, the justices who decided *Korematsu v. United States*[154] and *Brown* did not frame either decision with affirmative action in mind. Yet, in *Adarand* and *Croson*, a majority of justices relied on *Brown* and *Korematsu* for the proposition that all race-based classifications must be subjected to strict scrutiny.[155] It did not matter that *Brown* had not clarified the level of scrutiny it had employed or that *Korematsu* plainly involved a race-based classification directed against a relatively powerless ethnic minority. What mattered was how subsequent justices would construe *Brown* and *Korematsu*. Path dependency depends, in short, on how justices construe the work of their predecessors.

Social scientists and legal scholars study the implications of subsequent uses of precedents by analyzing their network effects. When we study network effects, we find that the values of precedents increase the more often they are cited. Conversely, the values of precedents decrease the less often they are cited—or the more often they are criticized. So, for example, *Brown*'s value as a precedent has increased with the frequency with which it has been cited by not only the Court but also other constitutional authorities. Moreover, we can expect the value of *Korematsu* to drop dramatically based on how rarely it is cited, and even then without approval.

In their network analysis of precedent, James Fowler and Sangick Jeon reached several conclusions with implications for the attitudinal model and the golden rule.[156] They found that by the early 20th century "the norm [of stare decisis] had taken hold, even though there is strong evidence that the activist Warren Court later deviated from it. Later Courts also tended to skip over the decisions of the Warren Court, reaching back in time to rulings that were more firmly rooted in precedent."[157] Of greater significance is their finding "that reversed cases tended to be much more important [or salient] than other decisions, and the cases overrul[ing] them quickly become and remain … more important as the reversed decisions decline. We also show the Court is careful to ground overruling decisions in past precedent, and the care it exercises is increasing in the importance of the decision that is overruled."[158] These findings are more significant because they indicate the Court avoids repetitive overrulings or tends to limit the number of times it revisits previously litigated questions of constitutional law. The Court does not repeatedly reopen issues, regardless of the justices' ideological preferences and salience of issues.[159]

There are, however, phenomena which the study of network effects neglects. First, the network effects of precedent extend beyond courts. If the meanings or values of precedents depend on their frequency of their citation, we should pay more attention to citations by nonjudicial authorities. Moreover, nonjudicial authorities produce precedents whose meanings or values depend, in turn, on the frequency of their citation by courts or other institutions. Second, citations are not fungible. In fact, public authorities use precedents for different reasons. In the next two chapters I examine these two phenomena.

U p to this point, I have generally tracked the conventional understanding of precedent as synonymous with judicial decisions, particularly those of the Supreme Court.[1] This conception derives from the common practice of viewing constitutional law from the Court's vantage point,[2] but it is incomplete. In fact, nonjudicial authorities produce precedents, which merit closer inspection for many reasons. First, introducing nonjudicial precedent into the lexicon of constitutional discourse will improve the precision and clarity of the terms we employ in constitutional analysis. I understand the term "nonjudicial precedent" to refer to any past constitutional judgments made outside the courts which public authorities try to invest with normative authority.

Second, shifting perspective on constitutional law to the vantage point of nonjudicial precedent exposes the fallacy of common complaints about judicial arrogance or supremacy.[3] Every constitutional question addressed by the Court has already been decided by at least one nonjudicial authority, and the Court leaves intact most of the nonjudicial activities it reviews. When we further recognize the range of nonjudicial activities not subject to judicial review—extending from the manner in which the first presidential inaugural address was delivered and the first use of senatorial courtesy to block presidential nominations to President George W. Bush's abundant signing statements and the threat of the "nuclear option" to stop judicial filibusters—it is apparent the domain of nonjudicial precedents dwarfs that of judicial precedents. Given that most nonjudicial precedents endure or elude judicial review, it is evident that the Court is not supreme in the realm of constitutional law generally, but rather only within its relatively narrow jurisdiction.

Third, nonjudicial precedents exert substantial influence over the content and direction of constitutional law. The Court is shaped by nonjudicial precedents—prior constitutional decisions—on the Court's size, composition, jurisdiction, and funding.[4] Moreover, the Court's doctrine is shaped by nonjudicial precedents in such diverse forms as administrative and historical practices, traditions, and customs.

In this chapter I lay out the distinctive features of nonjudicial precedents. First, I examine the basic characteristic which all nonjudicial precedents share—their discoverability, which makes both the recognition and network effects of nonjudicial precedents possible. Second, I examine other distinctive features of various kinds of nonjudicial precedents. Finally, I consider the consequences of a positive account of precedent in which nonjudicial precedents, as I describe them, are a fundamental dimension of constitutional law.

1. Discoverability

Not all nonjudicial activity qualifies as a precedent. When, for instance, George Washington acknowledged that as the nation's first president "[t]here is scarcely any part of my conduct which may not hereafter be drawn into precedent," few if any of us would expect that *everything* he did, no matter how trivial, should count as a precedent. Surely, what he ate for breakfast and how long he slept are not precedents, but why not? Similarly, when then-Representative Bob Barr declared that "the precedents we set in" the Clinton impeachment proceedings "will remain part and parcel of our legal system for years to come," it is doubtful everything done in those proceedings should count as precedents. It is likely some events, but not others, comprise precedents, but which ones? It is reasonable to resist a notion of nonjudicial precedent that is so capacious that it counts every nonjudicial activity as a precedent and thus ceases to be meaningful or manageable.

The point is not, however, that every nonjudicial activity is a precedent. Rather, the point is that all nonjudicial activities have the potential to become precedents, but only those nonjudicial activities which are *discoverable* should count as precedents. Discoverability is what transforms nonjudicial activities into precedents. Discoverability is the culmination of public efforts to invest certain past nonjudicial activities with normative force. These efforts may be undertaken at any time—when nonjudicial activities first take place or later. The important thing is that it is the public efforts to invest nonjudicial acts with normative authority that makes these acts discoverable, and their discoverability is what makes them recognizable as precedents. Discoverability is a necessary, but not a sufficient, condition for path dependency. It is impossible for something that is not discoverable to be a precedent, because no one knows about it, much less has tried to invest it with normative power. In order for nonjudicial precedents to be precedents they must be at least knowable. Discoverability is thus important as an essential, indispensable prerequisite for a nonjudicial activity to count as a precedent in the first place. So, what President Washington ate for breakfast is not a precedent, because neither he nor anyone else tried to invest it with special authority. Similarly, not everything done in the Clinton impeachment proceedings constituted precedents—only those things which public authorities have tried, or will later try, to invest with special legal force. Thus discoverability is a useful means to separate the nonjudicial activities that count as precedents from those that do not count.

The discoverability of nonjudicial precedents makes their network effects possible. The normative authority of nonjudicial activities, just like that of judicial precedents, is linked to the frequency with which they are cited. The more often public authorities, including courts, cite or seek to invest past nonjudicial activities with normative power, the more discoverable they become and the more their meaning and value increase. Because not all nonjudicial authorities have the same citation practices or feel the same compulsion or necessity as courts do to explain their decisions through reasoned elaboration, it is not surprising that some nonjudicial precedents will be harder to find than others. In the next two sections, I illustrate how frequency of citation and other public efforts to invest certain past nonjudicial activities with normative authority differentiate the cases in which nonjudicial precedents are easily identified from those in which they are not.

1.1 Three Easy Cases

In this section, I discuss three easily discoverable nonjudicial precedents. These precedents are easy to spot because of repetition, formal codification, and consistent, long-standing public recognition and construction.

1.1.1 Vice Presidential Succession to the Presidency

When President William Henry Harrison died barely a month after his inauguration, Vice President John Tyler's legal status was unclear. For years, many people had anticipated the problem of a vice president's status upon a president's death, but there was no consensus on the proper construction of the pertinent portion of the Constitution, Article II, section 1, paragraph 6, which provided,

> In case of the removal of the President from office, or of his death, resignation, or inability to discharge the powers and duties of the said office, the same shall devolve on the Vice President, declaring what officer shall then act as President, and such officer shall act accordingly, and until the disability be removed, or a President shall be elected.

The question was whether "the same" refers to the office or the powers and duties of the presidency. Prior to Harrison's death, leading constitutional scholars split over whether a vice president formally succeeded to the presidency upon a president's death. Justice Story, in his *Commentaries on the Constitution of the United States*, agreed with William Rawle's 1825 treatise, *View of the Constitution of the United States*, that a vice president should succeed to the presidential office and continue therein until the expiration of the term. Chancellor James Kent disagreed, arguing in his *Commentaries on American Law*, that a vice president could only act as president upon the incumbent president's death or disability.

Since Tyler was in Williamsburg, Virginia, when Harrison died, congressional leaders and the cabinet had at least a day to ponder his status before he returned to Washington, D.C. Henry Clay, the Whig leader in the Senate, argued that the powers and duties of the office of the president, but not the office itself, devolved upon Tyler. Harrison's cabinet agreed with Clay, and thus addressed Tyler as vice president in its first contact with him after Harrison's death. Just before Tyler arrived in Washington, Secretary of State Daniel Webster took the initiative to ask the clerk of the Supreme Court to send a message to Chief Justice Roger Taney requesting his counsel on the proper constitutional procedure, but Taney demurred.[5]

Tyler arrived in Washington on April 6, 1841, with a well-conceived strategy in mind. His first order of business was to meet with the six members of Harrison's cabinet. He told them in no uncertain terms that he believed the office, which included the powers and duties of the presidency, fully devolved upon him, automatically and immediately, at the moment of Harrison's death.[6] After Webster mentioned Harrison's practice of making decisions on the basis of a majority vote of his cabinet, Tyler rejected the practice because he did not believe cabinet members were co-equal with the president. Tyler vowed that he "would never consent to being dictated to" by his cabinet.[7] By the end of the meeting, the cabinet agreed to recognize Tyler as the duly authorized President of the United States.

Tyler's next step was to publicly take another oath to certify his claim to the presidency. Although Tyler believed his succession was automatic, he agreed to take the oath of office with the entire cabinet present, after the persistent urging of the presiding judge, William Cranch, of the Circuit Court of the District of Columbia. Cranch believed the new oath was necessary to forestall any doubts about the legality of Tyler's status.[8] Cranch appended a statement with his beliefs to the copy of the oath he administered to Tyler, along with Tyler's objection. Three days later, Tyler delivered an inaugural address, in which he explained why he believed he had succeeded to the presidency and referred to himself several times as "chief magistrate" and "president."[9] Almost immediately thereafter, Tyler moved into the White House, called for a public day of prayer and fasting to honor Harrison's memory, and met with several foreign ministers to allay international concerns about the legality of the transfer of power.[10]

Nevertheless, some doubts persisted in Congress, where Whigs distrusted him because he had been a Democrat and Democrats disliked him for leaving their party to protest the party's support of the National Bank. A little less than two months after Tyler took the presidential oath, Congress held a special session, in which it formally addressed Tyler's status. On May 31, 1841, Representative Henry Wise of Virginia proposed a resolution referring to Tyler as the President of the United States. After a heated exchange, the resolution passed without any change in wording.[11] On the following day, the same matter came before the Senate, in which Ohio's two senators led a protest against Tyler's succession. After some debate, the Senate voted 38–8 to recognize Tyler as the president.[12] This generally settled the matter, though some people, including John Quincy Adams, persisted in referring to Tyler as "Acting President," while others disparagingly called him "His Accidency." Even near the end of Tyler's presidency, some detractors continued to address letters to Tyler as "Vice President-Acting President," but Tyler routinely returned them unopened.[13]

Tyler's succession to the presidency became a precedent because of the persistent efforts of Tyler and other national leaders to make it one. Tyler's succession became a precedent because of public efforts to invest his succession to the presidency with special force. After Tyler left office, seven vice presidents followed Tyler's example.[14] The repetition reinforced Tyler's succession as a precedent. In 1967, Tyler's precedent was officially codified with the adoption of the Twenty-Fifth Amendment, which provides that, "In case of the removal of the President from office or of his death or resignation, the Vice President shall become President." In the only application of this amendment to date, Gerald Ford became president when Richard Nixon resigned from office in 1974.

1.1.2 Presidential Signing Statements

While President George W. Bush's signing statements have been controversial,[15] their status as nonjudicial precedents is quite easy to establish. In the course of both exercising their constitutional authority to "sign" bills into law[16] and fulfilling their constitutional oath, presidents, beginning with James Monroe, have exercised the prerogative of issuing public statements along with their signatures on bills.[17] The commonality of signing statements intensified with President Reagan, who issued 276 of them, 71 of which contained provisions questioning the constitutionality of one or more of the statutory provisions signed into law.[18] President George H. W. Bush issued 214 signing statements, 146 of which raised constitutional objections.[19] President Clinton issued 391 signing statements, of which 105 raised constitutional concerns or objections.[20] While President George W. Bush has rendered 128 signing statements as of the fall of 2006, 110 of these—the largest percentage of any president—contain constitutional challenges or objections to more than 700 statutory provisions.[21] Many of these signing statements have provoked widespread criticism in the media and Congress, and an American Bar Association commission issued a report protesting that they were unconstitutional presidential attempts to create legislative history, which the report regarded as the sole province of Congress, to define the inherent scope of the president's power beyond its limits, or to refuse to enforce laws which the president should have been obliged to enforce because he had signed them.[22]

Controversy over signing statements does not necessarily diminish them as precedents. Controversies merely call more public attention to them and thus make them more discoverable. The discoverability of presidential signing statements as precedents turns on presidents' public efforts to make them special, asserting them as a presidential prerogative, using them to send signals or to bind executive officials, and seeking to get others to accept their legitimacy.

As long as the opinions expressed in signing statements are just opinions, their principal legal significance is as persuasive authority to Congress, executive officials, states, and subsequent presidents. Efforts to implement the opinions—for instance, through vetoes or executive orders—are different acts than signing statements, and have different legal force and consequences than the opinions expressed in signing statements.

1.1.3 The Nonimpeachability of Members of Congress

Another, easily discoverable nonjudicial precedent is the first federal impeachment. On July 7, 1797, the House of Representatives impeached U.S. Senator William Blount, a Tennessee Federalist.[23] The House impeached Blount based on evidence provided by President John Adams that Blount had attempted to help the British capture Spanish-controlled Florida and Louisiana by inciting the Creek and Cherokee Indians to attack the Spanish settlers there. The House principally charged Blount with engaging in a conspiracy to compromise the neutrality of the United States, in disregard of the constitutional provisions for conducting foreign affairs.[24] The next day the Senate expelled Blount by a vote of 25–1. When the Senate began its impeachment trial against Blount several months later, Blount's lawyers challenged the Senate's jurisdiction on three grounds.[25] First, they argued that since he was no longer a senator, the Senate no longer had jurisdiction to convict, remove, or disqualify him. Second, they argued that senators were not impeachable, since only "civil officers of the United States" were impeachable and senators were not "civil officers of the United States."[26] Third, they argued his misconduct was strictly personal and involved no abuse of official powers and thus did not provide the proper basis for his impeachment, much less removal and disqualification. On January 10, 1798, the Senate voted 14–11 to defeat a resolution declaring that Blount was a "civil officer" and therefore subject to impeachment.[27] On January 11, 1798, the Senate voted, by the same margin, to dismiss the impeachment articles against Blount since he no longer held office, and again voted 14–11 on January 14, 1798, to dismiss the impeachment resolution against Blount for lack of jurisdiction.[28]

Public authorities (and commentators) have subsequently construed the first basis on which the Senate voted to dismiss Blount's impeachment as the most significant—that members of Congress are not impeachable.[29] While the Senate's votes dismissing jurisdiction over Blount's impeachment bound the Senate and other public authorities at the time, members of Congress and most scholars then and since have maintained its significance as authority for the proposition that members of Congress are not impeachable. Until senators rule differently on whether members of

Congress are impeachable,[30] Blount's acquittal continues to clearly stand as the first, authoritative precedent on the impeachability of members of Congress.

1.2 The Hard Cases

In this section, I discuss three cases whose discoverability as nonjudicial precedents is difficult if not impossible. These cases demonstrate the difficulties of discovering precedents when there are incomplete historical records, conflicting precedents, or few if any citations.

1.2.1 Presidential Censure: The Problem of Incomplete or Conflicting Records

Censure—a resolution condemning presidential conduct by the House or Senate—is typical of nonjudicial activities that are hard to characterize as precedents because of three problems with the historical record. First, the Senate expunged the only resolution which it has ever formally characterized as a censure of a president. In 1834, President Jackson instructed his then-Acting Treasury Secretary Roger Taney to remove deposits from the National Bank and place them in state banks.[31] Jackson believed the National Bank was corrupt and antidemocratic, while his critics, led by Henry Clay in the Senate, believed that the order was illegal. In response to Jackson's refusal to share with the Senate a copy of a message he had read to his cabinet on the subject, Clay proposed a formal resolution censuring Jackson for assuming power not conferred by the Constitution. After a 10-week debate, the Senate approved the resolution, 26–20.[32] Jackson responded publicly in two formal protests, which questioned the constitutionality of the censure resolution, but which the Senate refused to allow into the *Congressional Record*.[33] Two years later, after Jackson had succeeded in helping to elect a slim Democratic majority in the Senate, the Senate expunged the resolution pursuant to a motion by Senator Thomas Hart Benton.[34] Hence it is difficult to claim a precedent clearly in favor of the constitutionality of presidential censure resolutions. While other arguments may be made, the only possible precedent that could constitute a precedent, at least directly on point, for censuring a president was formally repudiated. Indeed, the expunging of the censure may be viewed as nonbinding or persuasive authority to Congress or the president on the wrongfulness of the president's conduct and on the Senate's authority to condemn the conduct through a resolution rather than impeachment and removal. Similarly, failure to get either the House or the Senate to censure, rather than to impeach or remove, President Clinton[35] may be construed as a nonbinding nonjudicial precedent against censure.

The second problem with establishing a precedent for censuring presidents is the fact that the resolutions that are critical of presidents and other public figures are not called censures. The House and the Senate have each passed resolutions that were critical of presidents and other public figures,[36] but none of these was formally titled, then or since, as a censure resolution. On the one hand, the discovery of these resolutions may mean that they are nonjudicial precedents even though we lack, at least as of yet, consensus for denominating them (if not on their constitutionality). On the other hand, the failure of these other resolutions to characterize themselves as censures may be construed as other precedents against censure. Whatever we may call these resolutions, they are not censure resolutions.

Third, establishing a precedent on censure is hard because of the significant gaps in the historical record. Even if people were to treat resolutions critical of presidents and other public figures as censure resolutions, finding such resolutions is hard. The *Annals of Congress* (1789–1824) and its successor volume, the *Register of Debates* (1824–1837), provide abstracts of congressional debates, but the editors only included the abstracts of debates that they considered to be "important."[37] The *Congressional Globe* (1833–1873) initially contained a condensed report rather than a verbatim report of the debates and transcription, but Congress voted in 1873 to replace the *Globe* with the *Congressional Record*, an in-house publication that continues to provide the most comprehensive record of congressional activities.[38] A 1989 report to the National Archives describes the pre-1873 difficulties with congressional records:

> The Constitution stipulates in Article I, section 5, that Congress simply maintain a journal of its proceedings. Production of an accurate record of the actual speeches and debates developed slowly. In part this was due to congressional traditions. All Senate proceedings held during the period 1789 to December 1795, for example, were closed to the public. Senate proceedings on its executive business (treaties and nominations) were also closed to the public until the 1920s. House deliberations on the other

hand, have, except on rare occasions, always been open to the public. Because of the poor quality of early efforts at transcription, legislators insisted on their right to edit their remarks. . . Members of Congress have also been permitted to submit materials for incorporation into the record that they did not actually read on the floor.[39]

While external events, such as the British invasion of Washington, D.C., in 1814, destroyed early House records, Senate records from the same period have also not survived.[40] Before 1946, it was unclear whether Senate rules required records of special and select committees, as well as the records of subcommittees, to be returned to the Congress at the end of the session.[41] Due to ambiguities in the rules, some committee records were probably not preserved. Moreover, a combination of unsuitable storage conditions, loss of records, and other administrative issues finally led Congress to pass the Legislative Reorganization Act of 1946,[42] which required House and Senate committees to maintain, for the first time, a continuous record of all committee proceedings. This act also required that a legislator's committee staff and personal staff remain separate to reduce the possibility of mixing committee records with personal papers. Before the act, a legislative file might have included published items such as bills and resolutions. While the deficiencies of congressional records prior to 1946 are not unique to censure,[43] they ought to sensitize us to the possibilities that actual citations or efforts to transform certain past activities into precedents may either never have been recorded or may have been left out of the official records.

1.2.2 Majority Rule in the Senate

From 2002 through 2005, many Republican senators maintained majority rule in the Senate as a fixed constitutional principle. They asserted that Senate Rule XXII,[44] which requires a two-thirds vote to invoke cloture against filibusters—endless debate—of motions to amend Senate rules, is unconstitutional because the rule bars a simple majority from voting to change the rules of the Senate.[45] They argued that this kind of blockage constitutes an unconstitutional entrenchment of the filibuster—it allows past Senate majorities to prevent or impede current or future ones to change Rule XXII as they prefer.[46] The Senate majority leader and other leading Republicans endorsed a plan, called the "constitutional" or "nuclear" option,[47] through which a simple majority in the Senate could engage in a series of procedural maneuvers bypassing Senate rules and culminating in a vote to forbid judicial filibusters. Although the plan was put on hold as a result of an agreement reached between seven Republican and seven Democratic senators,[48] it may be threatened again, if not employed, the next time a minority filibusters judicial nominations.

There are, however, several problems with claiming a precedent establishing majority rule in the Senate as a fixed constitutional principle. First, there is no precedent establishing such a principle. Even the two Senate staffers who coined the term "nuclear option" acknowledged it would constitute "a new precedent" if it were triggered.[49] Similarly, in the Senate Rules Committee's hearing on the nuclear option, every witness, including all three Republican experts, conceded that the "nuclear option" was unprecedented.[50] Moreover, as the Congressional Research Service found, there is no existing precedent supporting the "nuclear option."[51]

Second, there are several easily discoverable precedents flatly rejecting antientrenchment or majority rule as a fixed constitutional principle in the Senate. First, in 1925, Vice President Dawes, on his first day in office, invited a majority of the Senate to bypass Senate rules to amend the rules as they saw fit, but more than 80% of the senators polled rejected his invitation.[52]

Next, in 1957, Vice President Richard Nixon declared that "he believed the Senate could adopt new rules 'under whatever procedures the majority of the Senate approves.'"[53] After Nixon urged the Senate to determine for itself Rule XXII's constitutionality, it proceeded to ignore Nixon's statement and adhere to the requirements in Rule XXII for changing the rules. In 1961, Nixon reiterated his belief in majority rule in the Senate, but it again took no action to vindicate his point.

In 1967, then-Senator McGovern proposed a resolution to require only a three-fifths vote of the Senate to invoke cloture, or to end filibusters.[54] McGovern proposed ending debate on a motion to consider his proposed resolution, and suggested—contrary to the rules—that only a majority was needed to end the debate. Some senators construed his request as asking that proposals to amend Rule XXII be subject to a majority vote to invoke cloture. Vice President Hubert Humphrey refused to comment on McGovern's request. Instead, he relied on precedent allowing the Senate, rather than the Vice President, to decide constitutional questions.[55] The Senate then voted to reject McGovern's proposal for ending debate, 61–37, and voted 59–37 to sustain a point of order raised by Senator Dirksen, who had challenged the constitutionality of McGovern's motion that only a majority was needed to end Senate debate.[56] These votes are construed as determinations that McGovern's proposal was unconstitutional.

The Senate again debated the constitutionality of Rule XXII in 1969. In the course of the debate, Senator Church asked the chair—Vice President Humphrey—whether a majority had the power to invoke cloture, contrary to the rules of the Senate. Humphrey answered "yes," and then explained that "if a majority of the Senators present and voting but fewer than two-thirds vote [as required by the rule] in favor of the pending motion for cloture, the Chair will announce that a majority having agreed to limit the debate [on the resolution under consideration,] to amend XXII, at the opening of a new Congress, debate will proceed under the cloture provisions of that rule."[57] Humphrey acknowledged this ruling was subject to appeal to the full body without debate. The Senate initially voted 51–47 to invoke cloture, after which Humphrey invoked cloture. But the Senate immediately voted to reverse Humphrey's ruling by a 53–45 roll call vote, thereby requiring the Senate to revert to its two-thirds rule to invoke cloture.

In 1975, the incident arose on which proponents of the "nuclear" option rely. Senator Mondale proposed to amend Rule XXII to require only three-fifths vote to invoke cloture.[58] In the course of the debate over the motion, he asked whether a majority of the Senate may "change the rules of the Senate, uninhibited by the past rules of the Senate?"[59] Vice President Nelson Rockefeller refused to answer the answer, submitting it instead to the full Senate's consideration. Subsequently Senator Pierson made a point of order, which may not be filibustered under the Senate rules, to consider Mondale's proposal and suggested a majority vote was sufficient to invoke cloture.[60] Senator Mansfield responded with another point of order that Pierson's motion was out of order, but the Senate rejected Mansfield's point of order, 51–42, arguably signaling to some senators approval of Mondale's claim that a majority vote was sufficient to invoke cloture.[61] This latter vote is treated by proponents of the "nuclear option" as a supportive precedent, even though two weeks later the Senate voted 53–48 to reconsider what it had done, and voted 53–43 to sustain Mansfield's point of order that a majority lacked the authority to bypass the rules to amend Rule XXII.[62] Through the latter two votes, the Senate "erased the [only] precedent of majority cloture established two weeks before, and reaffirmed the [Senate] rules."[63] Subsequently the Senate agreed to a compromise proposed by Senator Byrd, and voted 73–21 on

March 7, 1975, to end debate on Mondale's proposal to amend Rule XXII and formally amended Rule XXII by a vote of 56–27 (pursuant to Rule XXII, which allows a simple majority to amend the rules after a vote to invoke cloture) to require three-fifths to invoke cloture.[64]

Historical practices further undermine the claim of majority rule as a fixed constitutional law. The Senate's long-standing traditions and rules include countermajoritarian measures such as unanimous consent requirements, holds, and of course filibusters.[65] Nevertheless, then-Senate Majority Leader Bill Frist suggested that there had been a 214-year-old tradition of the Senate having up-or-down votes on judicial nominations.[66] The assertion is counterfactual: As Thomas Mann and Norman Ornstein observe, "For more than two hundred years, hundreds of judicial nominees at all levels had their nominations buried, killed, or asphyxiated by the Senate, either by one individual, a committee, or a small group of senators, before the nominations got anywhere near the floor."[67] Senator Frist and other leading Republicans could only argue that judicial filibusters were unprecedented by trying to rewrite the easily discoverable filibuster that forced the withdrawal of President Lyndon Johnson's nomination of Abe Fortas as chief justice.[68]

The third problem with establishing a precedent for majority rule as a fixed constitutional principle is that it is easy to distinguish the four precedents that are sometimes cited in support. These precedents involve Senator Robert Byrd's successful efforts to secure majority votes to (1) end postcloture filibustering, (2) limit amendments to appropriation bills, (3) require nominations rather than treaties as the first piece of business in executive sessions, and (4) alter voting sequences on some measures.[69] While some proponents of the "nuclear option" cite these as precedents of majorities amending rules,[70] they are the only ones. Neither the Parliamentarian nor the Congressional Research Service, nor anyone other than the losing minority in Senate debates over the constitutionality of Rule XXII, construe them as such. The failure of a Senate majority ever to cite (or to rely on them) in support of a fixed constitutional principle of majority rule in the Senate undermines their authority. Instead, these precedents merely involved enforcing, rather than formally amending, Senate rules.

1.2.3 Presidential Reliance on Treaty Authorization to Authorize Military Force

Whereas establishing majority rule in the Senate as a precedent depends on characterizing events that are discoverable,[71] there is no discoverable precedent supporting treaty authorizations for presidents to go to war. The problem is determining the significance of something that never happened—the Senate's failure to ratify treaties with such authorizations.

The fact that the Senate has never ratified treaties with such authorizations could be construed as precedent against the constitutionality of any such treaty authorizations. Indeed, one easily discoverable precedent apparently makes this point—the Senate's rejection of the League of Nations based in part on senators' fears that it would have allowed this country to go to war without congressional authorization and subjected American forces to the control of foreign leaders.[72] Treaties usually contain no such authorizations, as, for instance, the North American Treaty Organization's provision that an armed attack on any member "shall be considered an attack against them all" and "each party will assist the Party or Parties so attacked by taking forthwith ... such action as it deems necessary."[73] Moreover, there appear to be structural limitations on treaty power, as, for instance, the origination clause's requirement that the House alone has the power to initiate appropriations.[74]

The persistent refusal of the Senate to endorse certain outcomes does not necessarily constitute a discoverable precedent. Whereas consistent, long-standing construction of Blount's impeachment clearly rules out impeaching members of Congress, national political leaders and some scholars have not ruled out the constitutionality of treaty authorizations of the president's use of military force.[75] First, some people may argue that while there may not be any precedents authorizing such treaties, there are no precedents disallowing them. Second, because there are no subject matter limitations on the treaty power, it may be used to expand the powers that the Congress or the president otherwise have.[76] Third, since the supremacy clause[77] makes both treaties and laws made in accordance with the Constitution the supreme law of the land, and laws authorizing presidential use of force are constitutional, then treaties that do the same thing should be, too.[78] But the question of the constitutionality of such treaties is not answered by the supremacy clause. To be sure, it is unlikely something that courts would review.[79] Once the Senate ratifies a treaty, the matter of its constitutionality is effectively left to the president and Senate, who, because they are acting concurrently, provide (according to Justice Robert Jackson's popular framework for separation of powers analysis[80]) the strongest constitutional foundation for presidents to authorize military force. And while there may be easier ways for presidents to secure authorization to go to war than treaties (which require at least two-thirds of the Senate for ratification),[81] presidents have no incentive to rule treaties out as options they may need some day along with the myriad of alternatives they already have.

Yet, what few cites there are to treaty authorizations of presidential use of force are to their rejection. Without any apparent precedent supporting the constitutionality of such authorizations, much less any subsequent reliance on or citation to such a precedent, there is literally no network of supportive citation, much less any effects from it. In other words, precedent provides no authority for allowing treaties to sanction presidential use of force. The absence of a precedent on point is not, however, incontrovertible proof of the unconstitutionality of such treaties. It is still possible to derive support for them from other sources of constitutional argumentation, such as text or original meaning. The absence of a precedent on point is thus not determinative of the ultimate question.

2. Other Distinctive Features of Nonjudicial Precedents

While discoverability is the essential precondition for nonjudicial precedents, they have other features. Below, I examine other features that differentiate nonjudicial precedents from each other and judicial precedents.

2.1 Categorizing Nonjudicial Precedents

Nonjudicial precedents may be discovered in all sorts of places and forms. In this section, I depict their remarkable extensiveness and how they may possibly be categorized.

2.1.1 The Extensive Variety of Nonjudicial Actors

One way to measure the range of nonjudicial precedents is by the range of actors making them. As Philip Bobbitt observes, "there are as many kinds of precedent as there are constitutional institutions creating them."[82] Some of these institutions are familiar, including Congress and presidents, while others, including cabinet officials or the heads of federal agencies, may be less so. Moreover, in each of the 50 states there are state and local officials, including governors, state legislatures, and mayors, who have the power to make precedents.

The public are also actors who have the potential to make precedents through their interactions with public leaders. Constitution-making is one example. While the Framers drafted the Constitution behind closed doors,[83] the ratification process was a public event with many formal and informal participants.[84] The process by which our Constitution, its 27 amendments, and state constitutions are made or amended may serve as precedents in the course of people's efforts to fashion new constitutional protections at the federal and state levels or abroad. Popular elections are important means through which political leaders interact with the public to ratify constitutional agendas, as Franklin Roosevelt, Ronald Reagan, and Richard Nixon each did in seeking public approval of their pledges to transform the Court. How these presidents achieved their agendas—Roosevelt to make the Court more hospitable to the New Deal, Nixon to appoint "strict constructionists," and Reagan to end liberal judicial activism—provide potential precedents for future presidents to emulate. Moreover, legal scholars, civil rights and other organized interest groups, and the American Bar Association may create precedents of their own—for instance, the American Bar Association in evaluating judicial nominees and proposed legislation,[85] and the Lawyers' Committee for Civil Rights Under Law in commenting on nominations, sponsoring or coordinating litigation, and lobbying for civil rights legislation.[86]

2.1.2 The Different Kinds of Constitutional Judgments

Nonjudicial precedents may be categorized on the basis of their substantive content. First, there are nonjudicial precedents with purely constitutional content. These precedents are decisions in which nonjudicial authorities directly address constitutional questions. For example, nonjudicial precedent apparently guided the national archivist in resolving the legality of the Twenty-Seventh Amendment.[87] The amendment was first proposed in 1791, but an insufficient number of states had voted to ratify the amendment by the end of the First Congress. Without any time limit or deadline for ratification imposed by Congress, it was unclear whether states joining the Union after the amendment was proposed were precluded from voting on its ratification. By 1992, 38 states had ratified the amendment. Following precedent, the national archivist deferred to states' decisions and certified the amendment's adoption,[88] and Congress by joint resolution declared the amendment valid.

Second, nonjudicial precedents may consist of mixtures of constitutional and policy judgments. An example is the Senate's rejection of President

Franklin D. Roosevelt's Court-packing plan. In opposing the plan, senators relied on constitutional and policy justifications.[89]

Third, nonjudicial precedents may consist of primarily policy. Indeed, most nonjudicial activities have this kind of content. For instance, voting on tax increases obviously entails making policy choices, though it may involve implicit judgments about their constitutionality.

2.1.3 Categorizing on the Basis of Form or Context

Nonjudicial precedents may be categorized according to the forms or contexts in which they are made. For instance, nonjudicial precedents may consist of floor votes and rule making in the House or Senate.[90] While not all of these activities may be expressly based on constitutional judgments, the formulations, retentions, and attempted amendments of House or Senate rules depends on the members' understandings of their constitutional power to undertake these activities.

But members of Congress do not just create precedent through formal lawmaking or rule making. Their inaction may produce precedents. Members of Congress may not authorize things—as with President Roosevelt's Court-packing plan. They may create precedents when they vote against legislation they deem unconstitutional or when they vote not to impeach or convict someone because they do not believe his misconduct qualifies as impeachable. Their refusals to declare war may also create potential precedents about the prerequisites for such declarations. Similarly, they may be creating precedents when they vote against judicial nominations based on their disapproval of the nominees' constitutional opinions.

In fact, most congressional activity occurs off the House and Senate floors. Legislative committees may create precedent through what they approve or disapprove. Nothing reaches the floor of the House or Senate without first being considered in committee. Committees are Congress' gatekeepers.[91] Usually a committee's disapproval is fatal, though exceptions are made through discharge petitions (requiring majority approval in the House and unanimous consent in the Senate).[92]

Congressional constitutional judgments may further take the forms of informal practices, norms, and traditions.[93] For instance, seniority has been a long-standing, but not binding criterion for committee assignments in the House and Senate.[94] The practice constitutes a continuing exercise of each chamber's authority to "determine Rules for its proceedings."[95]

The rules on seniority, like all the other formal rules of either chamber, derive from the same explicit constitutional authority.

Presidents and other executive officials may produce precedent in at least as many forms as Congress does. They may create precedents through executive orders, federal regulations, and the official opinions and memoranda of legal counsel in every executive department and agency. Presidents and executive officials also render constitutional judgments in the forms of informal practices, norms, and traditions. For instance, presidents from Thomas Jefferson to Woodrow Wilson delivered their States of the Union by letter, but Wilson inaugurated what has become the customary presidential practice of delivering the address before a joint session of the Congress.[96] The practice has enhanced the prestige of the president. The choice of delivering the State of the Union is the consequence of presidents' judgments about how they would like to deliver their address and Congress' acquiescence.

State officials render constitutional judgments in at least as many forms as federal officials do. State constitutions are the states' most prominent constitutional judgments; they provide additional governmental obligations and powers beyond those the federal Constitution requires. State law, for instance, generally sets forth the legal definitions of life, marriage, and death.[97] In 2004, 18 states amended their state constitutions to expressly prohibit gay marriage.[98] In addition, state law defines the authority of state attorneys general to issue legal opinions.[99] Because governors usually do not appoint state attorneys general, these officials may disagree over constitutional issues, and some states have developed special processes for resolving such disagreements.[100] Moreover, state legislatures create precedents similar to those made by Congress. All state legislators make judgments about legislation, and state constitutions set forth procedures for removing or recalling certain officials under certain conditions.[101] For instance, in 2003, the voters of California agreed to recall (and thus remove) then-Governor Gray Davis and replace him with Arnold Schwarzenegger.[102] In 2004, Connecticut Governor John Rowland resigned when confronted with the enormous likelihood of impeachment and removal for misappropriating funds,[103] while New Jersey Governor James McGreevey resigned in anticipation of an effort to remove him based on charges that he had sexually harassed a male employee and used his office to bestow favors upon the employee.[104]

Moreover, state law serves as the primary basis for some constitutionally protected interests. Contracts clause, takings, Eighth Amendment, and due process cases illustrate this aspect of state law. In cases requiring interpretation and application of the contracts clause,[105] courts need to determine whether a contract exists before deciding whether a particular contractual obligation has been impaired. Whether a contract exists depends on the relevant state law on the formation of contracts.[106] In cases involving construction of the due process clause[107] or the takings clause,[108] the Court consults state law to determine whether an interest qualifies as "property."[109] Moreover, the Court must determine whether a particular criminal sentence is "unusual" and therefore violates the Eighth Amendment[110] by determining its consistency with state punishment schemes.[111] In substantive due process cases, the Court defers to state practices as establishing a benchmark in the form of tradition against which to measure the legality of a particular measure or action. In *Lawrence v. Texas*,[112] the majority found "an emerging awareness that liberty gives substantial protection to adult persons in deciding how to conduct their private lives in matters pertaining to sex."[113] The Court found no tradition or "long-standing history in this country of laws directed at homosexual conduct as a distinct matter"[114] and thus overruled *Bowers v. Hardwick*[115] because it had mistakenly identified a tradition supporting the criminalization of homosexual activity.

The ways in which the public expresses constitutional judgments may also have the potential to become precedents. Direct democracy implements popular sovereignty, and popular sovereignty is a major theme and influence in our constitutional development.[116]

In addition, the efforts of nonjudicial authorities to fortify judicial precedents constitute another set of nonjudicial precedents. While judicial decisions helped the civil rights movement to flourish, they did so with the aid of significant presidential and congressional activities,[117] including the 1958 and 1964 Civil Rights Acts.[118] The civil rights movement, particularly the cohesive litigation strategy to end state-mandated segregation, is the model for contemporary interest groups to advance their agendas through litigation over such diverse issues as gay marriage, abortion rights, and church-state relations.[119]

2.1.4 Congressional and Presidential Authorities

Nonjudicial precedents may be categorized on the basis of the powers producing them. For instance, the Constitution explicitly vests Congress with 75 powers, presidents with 14, and vice presidents with five. Each and every one of the exercises of these official powers has the potential to be a precedent. For instance, pursuant to express authority set forth in Article I, the House of Representatives has excluded 10 people from being seated because of their failures to satisfy the requirements for membership in the House,[120] expelled 4 people and almost expelled a fifth,[121] censured 22 members for misconduct,[122] and reprimanded 8 members for misconduct;[123] and the Senate has excluded 6 people from being seated,[124] expelled 15 people,[125] and reprimanded or censured 9 people.[126] Although these legislative decisions are routinely ignored in the study of precedent, they obviously serve as precedents on the ticklish problem of how to handle the misconduct of members of the House or Senate.

Presidents may create precedents, as well, through the exercise of their official powers. For instance, President Jackson's veto of the second National Bank is one of the most famous statements and precedents bolstering the proposition that the "opinion of the judges has no more authority over Congress than the opinion of the Congress has over the judges, and on that point the President is independent of both."[127] Moreover, presidents have vetoed more than 2000 federal laws—far more than the 160 struck down by the Court. These vetoes may comprise an important set of precedents on executive power.[128]

Many other powers are discounted, but still significant. For instance, presidents choose how to structure their office.[129] For instance, President Nixon had only one White House counsel—John Dean—while President George W. Bush has fewer than 20 people in the White House counsel's office.[130] Other executive officials create precedents through their exercises of their respective authorities. For instance, the president may ask the attorney general for formal advice on particular constitutional questions.[131] This advice is given in the form of official opinions of the Office of Legal Counsel of the Justice Department.[132]

Similarly, we may discount the vice president's authority, which Al Gore, Jr., undertook on his last day in office to settle the 2000 presidential election, as "president of the Senate" to oversee the final counting of electoral votes for the presidency, including opening "all the certificates" of electoral votes cast.[133] Thomas Jefferson effectively exercised this nonreviewable power to his advantage after the closely contested presidential election of 1800.[134]

Another overlooked, but not insignificant power is the explicit authority within the House to "choose their Speaker and other Officers"[135] and the Senate to "choose their Officers."[136] Pursuant to these authorizations, these chambers have chosen their leadership for more than 200 years. Many other implicit powers are rarely reviewed, but when the Court has done so it has not questioned their exercise. For instance, the principal dispute among the justices in *Goldwater v. Carter*[137] was not whether, but why they should avoid adjudicating whether presidents have the authority to rescind treaties unilaterally.[138]

The range of presidential and congressional powers says nothing about their finality. The next part examines the durability and finality of the overwhelming number of nonjudicial authorities' constitutional judgments, even when subject to judicial review.

2.2 The Finality of Nonjudicial Precedents

Judicial review of nonjudicial constitutional activities is much more limited than commonly thought. In this section, I examine the different ways in which nonjudicial precedents are the last word on constitutional matters.

2.2.1 The Limited Scope of Judicial Review

Anyone familiar with constitutional law knows the Court does not have the power to decide every constitutional issue it wants to decide.[139] By design, the Court must wait for constitutional questions to come to it. Indeed, the Court has never had jurisdiction to hear all possible constitutional claims.[140] Nor are all constitutional questions litigated. Of the constitutional questions that are litigated, not all are appealed to the Supreme Court.[141] Of those that are appealed, the Court chooses not to hear them all. It has never agreed to decide the merits of every constitutional question brought before it. Of the questions that the Court chooses to decide, not all are constitutional cases, and most constitutional cases involve the constitutional judgments of nonjudicial authorities.[142] Hence virtually every question of constitutional law that the Court hears has already been considered by one or more nonjudicial actors. Thus it is an exaggeration to assume judicial review makes the Court supreme in fashioning constitutional law.

In fact, most constitutional judgments of nonjudicial actors survive judicial review.[143] First, the Supreme Court may not take cases in which lower courts have upheld nonjudicial constitutional activity. For much of its history, the Court had the jurisdiction to review lower court decisions overturning, but not upholding, federal laws or rights.[144]

Second, in most constitutional cases, the Court uses extremely deferential review. Judicial review primarily involves the application of the rational basis test, which is the most deferential standard available for assessing the constitutionality of governmental action.[145] It is rare for the Court to strike down governmental action for violating the rational basis test.[146]

Third, the standing and political question doctrines have precluded judicial review of several areas of constitutional law. Standing doctrine restricts who may litigate certain constitutional claims in Article III courts.[147] For instance, the Court decided on standing grounds not to address the constitutionality of public schools' daily recitation of the Pledge of Allegiance.[148] By overturning on standing grounds a Ninth Circuit holding that the pledge violated the First Amendment's prohibition against establishment of religion,[149] the Court left intact the words "under God" inserted into the pledge by Congress at the outset of the Cold War.[150] When a district court subsequently ruled that Ninth Circuit precedent required overturning the pledge on establishment clause grounds, members of Congress wasted no time in denouncing the decision and ratifying their earlier decision to include the words "under God" in the pledge.[151]

Through the political question doctrine, the Supreme Court avoids reviewing the merits of several matters involving the powers of nonjudicial actors.[152] The Court has held nonjusticiable judicial challenges to the process for ratifying constitutional amendments,[153] using Senate trial committees to gather evidence and take testimony for judicial impeachment trials,[154] and enforcing the Republican guarantee clause.[155]

Fourth, the Court defers to nonjudicial precedents in the forms of traditions,[156] customs,[157] and historical[158] and administrative practices.[159] These terms usually refer to separate actions. Tradition refers to a state's long-standing understanding about the scope of personal autonomy in certain realms of behavior or their powers to restrict, or proscribe, personal autonomy.[160] Historical practices refer to the federal government's long-standing exercising of powers over certain domains.[161] Indeed, the Court's deference to long-standing historical practice is long-standing. In *Stuart v. Laird*,[162] the Court upheld Congress' requiring Supreme Court justices to ride circuit in a stunning endorsement of nonjudicial precedent. Justice William Paterson explained for the unanimous Court "that practice and acquiescence . . . for a period of several years, commencing with the organization of the judicial system, affords an irrestistible [sic] answer, and has indeed fixed the construction. It is a contemporary interpretation of the most forcible nature. This practical exposition is too strong and obstinate to be shaken or controlled, and ought not now to be disturbed."[163] Custom, institutional or cultural habits, and conventions are bases for decisions in such diverse contexts as separation of powers, establishment of religion, international law,[164] and municipal liability under section 1983. Administrative practices, which are the most common federal nonjudicial activities, entail agencies' constructions of ambiguous federal statutes.[165] While the Court defers to these constructions most of the time,[166] it is even more deferential to historical practices, customs, and traditions, which it only rarely overturns.[167]

Moreover, the Court allows the states to render final judgments on the scope of their sovereign immunity.[168] Eleventh Amendment[169] jurisprudence recognizes that states may waive their immunity from being forced to pay damages in federal court.[170] The Court also allows states to determine the actions for which they may be held accountable under the Fourteenth Amendment's state action doctrine.[171]

Fifth, preoccupation with judicial review sometimes blinds commentators to the Court's deference to nonjudicial precedent. For instance, the stridency of the dissents about the majority's activism in two recent cases deflected attention from the fact that the common link between the cases was the Court's deference to nonjudicial authority. In *Gonzales v. Raich*,[172] the Court concluded that federal law criminalizing possession and distribution of marijuana preempted states from allowing doctors to authorize their patients to use marijuana for medical purposes. While the dissent complained that the majority had failed to give adequate deference to the states operating as laboratories,[173] the majority deferred to Congress' formulation of a comprehensive national policy to regulate drugs. Similarly, in *Kelo v. City of New London*,[174] the majority upheld a locality's decision to take private property in a relatively poor neighborhood in order to develop the land to benefit wealthier residents. The dissent complained that the majority's deference eviscerated the takings clause. Yet, the majority in *Kelo* effectively allowed the locality—a nonjudicial authority—the final say on the scope of its power. *Kelo* allows localities to reach different conclusions about the "public uses[s]" for which they may exercise control over private property.[175] Localities could make more restrictive determinations of what constitutes "public use" for purposes of eminent domain, and such determinations would be just as constitutional as New London's judgment (and for the same reasons). Similarly, *Raich* does not preclude Congress from exempting medical marijuana from the coverage of its drug policies.

Similarly, in *Eldred v. Ashcroft*,[176] the Supreme Court upheld the constitutionality of the Copyright Extension Act on the basis of "an unbroken congressional practice of granting to authors of works and existing copyrights the benefit of term extensions."[177] *Eldred* recognized Congress had the last word on the scope of its power to regulate copyrights for "limited times."[178] The Constitution does not compel Congress to repeatedly extend, or to stop extending, copyright terms. A different Congress could interpret its power differently.

Sixth, there are numerous subjects the Court is unlikely to subject to judicial review. For instance, the federal impeachment process is rife with final congressional judgments on constitutional questions, such as which kinds of misconduct qualify as lawful grounds for removal from office and whether censure is constitutional.[179] Similarly, presidents and senators make the final, constitutional judgments on the criteria for assessing judicial, cabinet, and subcabinet nominations.[180] Other areas of effectively final, nonreviewable decision making are presidential transitions,[181] the powers of congressional committees and their respective jurisdictions,[182] rule making within the House and Senate,[183] and reorganizing the federal government (such as the recent creation of the Department of Homeland Security[184]). Presidential decisions on vetoes and pardons are invariably final.[185]

Even when the Court uses heightened scrutiny, it is not invariably fatal.[186] The Court reviewed the constitutionality of the University of Michigan law school admissions program under strict scrutiny, but upheld it nevertheless.[187] It adopted Justice Lewis Powell's approach in his pivotal concurrence in *California Regents v. Bakke*[188] to uphold for the first time a racial preference for professional schools. While the Court subjected the Bi-Partisan Campaign Finance Reform Bill[189] and Family Leave Act[190] to heightened scrutiny, it upheld both.

Indeed, the number of laws struck down by the Court is relatively small. It has overturned less than 200 federal laws.[191] This rate of overturning averages less than one federal law per year. Even though the Rehnquist Court overturned more federal laws than did any previous Court,[192] this number is minuscule compared to the number of federal laws enacted during the same period.[193]

Over nearly 19 years, the Rehnquist Court struck down a tiny fraction of the constitutional activities of political authorities besides Congress. For instance, it struck down only a small number of state constitutional judgments in its last few years.[194] The Court overturns presidential judgments more rarely than it does congressional actions. Over the past half century, the Court has overturned less than a dozen presidential acts, most of which involved presidential efforts to thwart judicial inquiries into their conduct.[195] The Court overturned the constitutional judgments of executive officials, including President George W. Bush, in three cases—each involving the constitutional foundations for President Bush's restrictions on access to courts by people detained in the military conflicts in Afghanistan and Iraq.[196] Yet, compliance with the Court's rulings remains unclear.[197] The few other cases in which the Court has overturned presidents' actions involved presidential usurpations of legislative authority.[198]

2.2.2 The Timing of Judicial Review

The timing of judicial review has significant ramifications for some nonjudicial decisions. The longer it takes for the Court to review such decisions, the longer they endure. An excellent example of this dynamic is the Tenure in Office Act, which Congress passed to curb President Andrew Johnson's power to remove Republicans from his cabinet.[199] Johnson vetoed the act, and Congress overrode his veto. Subsequently Johnson refused to comply with the act, and the House impeached, but the Senate barely acquitted him.[200] More than five decades later, the Court struck down the act,[201] but in the meantime 12 presidents and members of Congress had to accommodate their differing opinions about its constitutionality.

The significance of the ramifications of belated judicial review is evident with respect to the ways in which the moral and ethical dilemmas raised by advancements in medical technology—the field of bioethics—are handled prior to their relatively rare disposition by the Supreme Court. For instance, Oregon's assisted suicide law had been in effect for a number of years before a challenge to its constitutionality came before the Supreme Court.[202] The Court did not render a judgment on the constitutionality of this law until 2005, more than a decade after the state had enacted the legislation.[203] Since no court had barred implementing the statute in the meantime, almost 200 people had chosen to die pursuant to its procedures. The law was final for these people, their health care providers, and their families.

2.3 The Power of Nonjudicial Precedent

Nonjudicial precedents do not all have the same power. Their constraining power, for instance, differs depending on whether they exert influence vertically—from the top down—as binding authority imposed by superior authorities upon inferior ones, or horizontally, as persuasive authority within or across equally situated, or powerful, institutions. Consequently the power of nonjudicial precedent may be categorized in the following four ways:

2.3.1 Vertical-Vertical Nonjudicial Precedents

Vertical-vertical nonjudicial precedents operate as binding authority within the branch creating them and on other branches. Presidential pardons are examples of such precedents. Presidents have the unique power to pardon people for federal crimes.[204] Once pardons are issued, they are binding on other authorities. No other constitutional authority may undo, or undermine, a presidential pardon. Not even a subsequent president may withdraw a predecessor's pardon. Pardons bind every branch at the top as well as every inferior federal and state official.

President Ford's pardon of Richard Nixon illustrates the binding effect of presidential pardons.[205] Congress lacks the authority to erase the pardon through legislation.[206] The most that Congress may do is to hold oversight hearings, as it did to inquire into Ford's reasons for pardoning Nixon.[207] No subsequent president had the power to undo Nixon's pardon. Moreover, state and federal courts had to accept the pardon; it barred any prosecutor from prosecuting Nixon for the misconduct for which he had been pardoned.[208] Federal and state prosecutors may not prosecute people for the criminal misconduct for which they have been formally pardoned.

2.3.2 Vertical-Horizontal Nonjudicial Precedents

Vertical-horizontal nonjudicial precedents impose binding authority from the top down within the institutions producing them, but are persuasive authority in other institutions. Official opinions from the attorney general are examples of vertical-horizontal precedents. The Office of Legal Counsel produces official opinions for the attorney general in response to requests made by him or her, other executive branch officials, and the president.[209] These opinions have strict binding authority throughout the executive branch, but they are merely persuasive authority in Congress, the courts, and the states.

Similarly, presidential decisions on what material to keep confidential bind the executive branch, but they do not bind Congress. At most, they are persuasive authority in Congress and the courts. Hence presidential and congressional disputes over executive privilege are usually resolved through mutual accommodations reached between presidents and Congress.[210]

2.3.3 Horizontal-Horizontal Nonjudicial Precedent

Horizontal-horizontal nonjudicial precedents operate as persuasive authority within the institutions creating them and in other institutions. These precedents encompass what we commonly refer to as traditions, customs, and historical practices. Horizontal-horizontal nonjudicial precedents came into play after Chief Justice William Rehnquist's death. President Bush had to decide initially whether he would follow the norm of not naming a sitting justice as chief justice of the United States. Presidents usually have appointed someone from outside the Court as chief justice, in part to avoid friction among sitting justices who might have lusted for the job or oppose one of their colleagues becoming chief justice. President Bush chose to follow the norm.

Timing was another issue: President Bush had to decide whether to fill two vacancies on the Court at the same time or, instead, nominate a successor to the chief justice and forego naming someone to replace Justice O'Connor until after the Senate had confirmed Rehnquist's successor.[211] The circumstance was unprecedented—never before had a chief justice died pending hearings on a nomination to replace another justice, and never before had a president had the opportunity to withdraw a nomination so that he could renominate the person to be chief justice. President Bush made precedent with his nomination of John Roberts to two different seats on the Court within a short time.

2.3.4 Horizontal-Vertical Nonjudicial Precedents

Some nonjudicial precedents have horizontal effects within the institutions creating them, but vertical effects on other institutions. For example, when the Senate Judiciary Committee approves judicial nominations, the decisions are not binding on senators in casting their votes on the floor. These decisions are regarded as recommendations for the senators to follow. When senators do follow the recommendations (as they did with the committee's recommendations of both the Roberts and Alito nominations), they do so because they are persuaded, not bound, to approve them. But officials in other branches are formally bound to accept the committee's recommendations; they have no formal power to interfere with, or change, the recommendations.

2.4 The Limited Path Dependency of Nonjudicial Precedents

Even when nonjudicial precedents are designed or intended to constrain, they have limited constraining force. Below, I consider the most significant reasons for this.

2.4.1 Beyond Standards and Rules

While judicial precedents are generally framed as rules or standards,[212] the same is not true for nonjudicial precedents. Nonjudicial precedents arise in numerous circumstances and take multiple forms. They may be expressed in various ways and through various means, and nonjudicial authorities rarely explain in detail the reasons for their actions or inaction.[213] In many instances, nonjudicial precedents are the outcomes of an institutional decision-making process or conflict. Much of the underlying reasoning that has gone into the making of a nonjudicial precedent is never reduced to writing. Consequently it is difficult, if not impossible, to know why certain things happened or did not happen in the legislative process at both the federal and state levels.

Rational choice theory, as noted before, suggests that collegial institutions such as the Congress will reach inconsistent, incoherent results, in part because of the different orderings and intensities of preference among its members.[214] Without knowing the orderings or intensities of preferences, it may be hard to know why the House or Senate did what it did. Nevertheless, the outcome may take on a life of its own; an acquittal in an impeachment trial, for instance, may depend more on how subsequent generations come to understand it than on what senators said at the time they rendered judgment. Yet, the reasons given for particular actions may also matter. Just as the significance of a judicial precedent may oftentimes depend on the quality, or persuasiveness, of its reasoning, the same could be said of nonjudicial precedent. To understand why particular senators voted in the ways they did (in impeachment trials or on other matters), it would help if they explained their votes; however, not all senators provide such explanations. Moreover, members of Congress might have had different reasons for their votes, might have prioritized the reasons for their votes differently, and might not have disclosed fully (or perhaps at all) the reasons for their votes.

President Clinton's acquittal in his impeachment trial is another precedent whose meaning is uncertain. At the end of Clinton's trial, only 72 senators formally explained their votes.[215] These 72 included 34 of the 45 Democrats who voted not guilty on both articles of impeachment, 4 of the 5 Republicans who voted not guilty on both impeachment articles, and 3 of the 5 Republicans who voted not guilty on the first article but guilty on the second article. With most of the senators voting guilty on both articles not bothering to explain their votes publicly, we are left to speculate about the precise reasons for their votes. While more than half of those voting to acquit Clinton explained their votes, we still do not know for sure why the Senate voted to acquit Clinton, and we still face the challenge of finding the common ground among the statements that we do have. Most importantly, the fact that there have been no subsequent impeachment trials, much less any presidential impeachment trials, means that as a precedent, Clinton's trial has virtually no network effects—its value and meaning are substantially reduced because public actors have not yet defined its significance.

Similarly, the precise meaning or significance of the nation's second impeachment is a subject of ongoing debate. It involved District Judge John Pickering, whom the House impeached on March 2, 1803, by a vote of 45–8.[216] The impeachment articles charged drunkenness and profanity on the bench and the rendering of judicial opinions based neither on law nor fact. Although Pickering did not appear on his own behalf before the Senate, his son filed a petition claiming that Pickering was so ill and deranged that he was incapable of exercising any sound judgment whatsoever and that he should therefore not be removed from office for misconduct attributable to insanity. Nevertheless, the Senate voted 18–2 to accept evidence of his insanity, 19–7 to convict, and 20–6 to remove him from office. Consequently he became the first federal official to be impeached and removed from office.

Yet, disagreement among scholars and members of Congress persists about whether Pickering's removal established a precedent for removal based on nonindictable misconduct, that is, misbehavior that is violative of some criminal law. On the one hand, Simon Rifkind, counsel for Justice Douglas in the House's impeachment inquiry against him in 1970, suggested Pickering was charged "with three counts of willfully violating a federal statute relating to the posting of bond in certain attachment situations, and the misdemeanors of public drunkenness and blasphemy."[217] On the other hand, some experts claim that "no federal statute made violation of the bond-posting act a crime, nor obviously were drunkenness or blasphemy federal crimes. The Pickering impeachment [confirms] that the concept of high crimes and misdemeanors is not limited to criminal offenses."[218]

Both of these views have merit, "because the question of guilt was put in the form of asking senators whether the judge stood guilty as charged," rather than whether the acts he allegedly committed constituted impeachment offenses.[219] The Senate's votes to convict may not reflect an acknowledgment by the Senate that violations of impeachable offenses were actually involved. Indeed, five senators withdrew from the court of impeachment when the Senate agreed to put the question in the form of "guilty as charged." Two senators—both Federalists—objected to procedural irregularities and claimed that the question put to them failed to ask whether the charges actually described high crimes and misdemeanors.[220] John Quincy Adams claimed that the other senators who withdrew—all Republicans—objected to procedural irregularities but did not want to separate from their party by voting to acquit the judge.

A related problem with using the Pickering impeachment and removal as a precedent is that party fidelity seems to have played a major role in the Senate's votes to admit the evidence of insanity and to remove Pickering. All 19 of the Senate's votes to acquit the Federalist judge were cast by Republicans, while Federalists cast the 7 acquittal votes.[221] Even the seemingly bipartisan vote to admit evidence on Pickering's insanity can be explained on partisan grounds: The Federalist senators may have wanted to introduce this evidence because they hoped that proof of his insanity would have led to an acquittal, given their position that insanity was not an impeachable offense, while the Republicans might have expected the admission of the evidence to lead to the judge's conviction because they thought it demonstrated the need to remove him before he damaged the political system any further. In any event, the party-line voting was consistent with an apparent Republican strategy to employ the impeachment process to create vacancies in the federal judiciary by ousting Federalist judges, of which one of the easiest to remove was Pickering.[222]

2.4.2 The Absence of Rules for Constructing Nonjudicial Precedents

The absence of rules for constructing nonjudicial precedents creates at least as many difficulties in recognizing or construing them as it does for judicial precedents. First, the significance of inaction may be hard to define. The fact that legislatures may have failed to do certain things—such as foregoing criminal prosecution of homosexual activity on a wide-scale basis—may be significant to the extent that the Court recognizes this failure as constituting a tradition.[223] Moreover, the Senate Judiciary Committee might have failed, for various reasons, to hold hearings or votes on pending judicial nominations.[224] But the absence of a hearing does not rob the event of precedential significance. It might have been the result of a chair's decision simply not to schedule a hearing or a vote, and the chair might have done this with, or without, consultation with other members of the committee.[225] A committee's prior failures to hold hearings are at least precedent on the authority of its chair to schedule matters as he sees fit.

Yet, this is hardly the extent of the legal significance that committee inaction may have. In the absence of a formal hearing, there is no occasion—and no need—for either the chair or the committee's members to explain themselves. The Senate rules provide, however, that a nomination lapses and becomes void if it is not approved or acted upon by the end of the legislative session in which it was made.[226] Senate rules invest inactivity with some significance. Failures to hold hearings or votes make the significance of inactivity malleable. Such failures can mean almost anything—or nothing—depending on the interpreter's needs. Thus the Senate Judiciary Committee's failure to hold a hearing on President Clinton's nomination of Elena Kagan to the U.S. Court of Appeals for the District of Columbia means different things to different senators. For some, it means nothing that the committee failed to hold a formal hearing or vote on her nomination.[227] For others, the failure to hold a hearing or vote resulted from the need to accommodate other pressing business. For still others, the failure was the consequence of a long-standing impasse between Democrats and Republicans over whether the court's caseload justified filling a vacant seat.[228] For others, the failure was a consequence of the desire to keep the seat open for the next president to fill.[229] And for others the failure to hold a hearing for Kagan was driven by a desire by some senators to prevent the confirmation of a potentially activist judge. Each of these interpretations is credible, and all can be measured in terms of how well each fits the facts.

A similar interpretive challenge arises when the Judiciary Committee formally recommends not sending nominations to the full Senate. Only occasionally do committee members explain their votes before casting them. Senators tend to be most expansive in high-profile hearings, as demonstrated in the confirmation proceedings on John Roberts' nomination as chief justice.[230] With the proceedings covered by the national media, including television, senators had a strong incentive to be there as much as possible. The committee members each had lengthy statements, and each had relatively long questions—or comments—to pose to the witness. In lower profile proceedings, the record tends to be more incomplete. Even when senators explain their votes, they may not make full statements, and it is possible their statements do not include all the reasons for their votes. Many statements might draw from prior proceedings, but not because the latter are binding, but rather because they are persuasive authority. Thus the Senate Judiciary Committee's rejection of President Bush's nomination of Priscilla Owen to the Fifth Circuit in 2001 meant different things to Democrats and Republicans. Many Democrats construed the event as an instance in which they blocked confirmation of a nominee with a judicial ideology with which they disapproved,[231] while most Republicans construed Owen's rejection as driven by a petty desire for payback for Republicans' failure to confirm some of President Clinton's judicial nominees or hostility to any jurisprudential outlooks other than liberal activist ones.[232] A similar interpretive problem arose with respect to the Democrats' successful filibuster against President Bush's nomination of William Pryor to the Eleventh Circuit in 2003. Many Democrats defended the filibuster as precluding the confirmation of a conservative ideologue or activist,[233] while some Republicans charged that Pryor's opposition was based on anti-Catholic bias.[234] The arguments opposing his nomination were identical to those held by devout Catholics, including opposition to abortion.

Second, the meanings or values of nonjudicial precedents depend, like those of judicial decisions, on their network effects. But subsequent citation (or reliance) may be impeded by the fact that there may have been so many opinions expressed in support, or opposition, to some past nonjudicial activity that subsequent authorities have great latitude in choosing which, if any, of these opinions to rely on for similar or analogous events. This may be true even for events that are cited or referenced frequently. Such is the case, for instance, with full Senate votes on particular nominations. The significance of a particular vote depends not just on how senators construe it at the time they vote, but also how subsequent senators understand it. Thus events such as the Senate's rejection of President Washington's nomination of John Rutledge as chief justice and President Reagan's nomination of Robert Bork do not have firmly fixed, clear constitutional significance. They have been cited more than enough times to have their authority firmly established, but the question for what particular proposition remains in some dispute. Rutledge's rejection is often cited as the first instance in which the Senate rejected a nominee based on his ideology,[235] while others argue that the rejection had at least as much to do with doubts about his sanity.[236] Bork's rejection stands as a watershed event in which the Senate targeted a nominee because of his ideology,[237] payback for Bork's firing of special prosecutor Archibald Cox and other misdeeds,[238] and Bork's confirmation conversion in which he appears to have abandoned prior positions he had taken for the sake of getting confirmed.[239] Others believe it resulted from the convergence of many factors, including President Reagan's belated defense of Bork against public attacks and Bork's alienating many senators in his public testimony.[240]

Third, the path dependency of nonjudicial precedent is limited by the congressional norm allowing every member the freedom to make their own independent judgments on constitutional matters.[241] In practice, this means that legislators are free to challenge procedures or prior judgments (made by committees or entire bodies) that they regard as unconstitutional. Their independence extends to making their own determinations in fact-finding and figuring out what standard governs their decision making in different contexts. For instance, in Supreme Court confirmation hearings, senators recognize that they each may decide for themselves the burden of proof that nominees must meet.[242] Similarly, in removal trials senators have long recognized that they may decide for themselves on the applicable burdens of proof (preponderance of the evidence, clear and convincing, or beyond a reasonable doubt) and evidentiary rules (pertaining to such things as relevance, reliability, and hearsay).[243] Senators may feel obliged to follow their earlier practices in addressing the same constitutional question, though this is not always the case,[244] but they may also change their minds for all sorts of reasons, including the dictates of party leaders, short-term political expediency, constitutional commitments, or their conceptions of what is in the best interest (then or later) of the country and the Constitution.

Ironically, this is the point at which a golden rule of precedent may be apparent outside the Court. To be sure, national political leaders may not follow as rigidly as justices do a golden rule which calls upon them to give as much respect to their predecessors' views on particular subjects as they would like for their successors to give theirs. Sometimes they will deviate from the constitutional opinions of their predecessors for what they regard as persuasive or compelling justifications. Nevertheless, they do not scrap altogether the prevailing traditions and norms within the institutions which they lead and the culture in which they live. Instead, they tend to pick their battles, and they generally adhere to basic institutional procedures set in place before them (unless they believe they have substantial political warrants to justify their deviation). For instance, senators may follow the golden rule when they generally recognize and protect each other's autonomy to exercise certain prerogatives, such as temporary holds, or to make judgments on nominations, treaties, removals, and impeachment trial procedures such as the governing burden of proof or rules of evidence.

Even when national leaders are seeking institutional or other reforms, they seek political warrants in the same traditional ways and are careful to legitimize their actions based on their willingness to preserve some traditions or structures in exchange for others. The golden rule is good politics, though there is more to politics (and constitutional adjudication, for that matter) than the golden rule. Eric Shickler captures this dynamic when he describes

> congressional development [a]s disjointed in that members
> incrementally add new institutional mechanisms, without
> dismantling preexisting institutions and without rationalizing
> the structure as a whole . . . The resulting tensions mean that
> significant numbers of members will ordinarily be dissatisfied
> with established ways of doing business. This enables
> entrepreneurs to devise innovations that serve as common
> carriers, momentarily uniting those dissatisfied with the status
> quo. As a result, institutional development is an ongoing,
> open-ended process. The interplay of coalitions promoting
> contradictory objectives produces institutions that are tense
> battlegrounds rather than stable, coherent solutions.[245]

Change, in other words, may be justified on the basis of past practice, and it may be possible in part because of the willingness of political leaders to accept some institutional features and traditions of which they disapprove in exchange for some innovations.

2.4.3 The Ramifications of Nonjudicial Precedents for Judicial Supremacy

Recognizing the constitutional significance of nonjudicial precedents poses serious consequences for both judicial supremacy and constitutional theory generally. The first is that their extensiveness, finality, and other features demonstrate why judicial supremacy is not a fact of constitutional life. It is not possible to credibly claim judicial supremacy as the distinctive pervasive feature of constitutional law, because it is not. Moreover, as we have seen in this chapter (and even more in the next chapter), nonjudicial functions significantly shape both the Court and its doctrine.

Second, judicial supremacy is problematic because it will discourage nonjudicial actors from taking constitutional interpretation seriously. The political checks on the Court—including congressional oversight of federal regulation, presidents' nominating powers, the Senate's "advice and consent" authority,[246] and the impeachment process—are meaningful only as long as they genuinely keep the Court in check. But in a regime of judicial supremacy, they would not. Indeed, presidents and members of Congress would have little if any incentive to be cautious, or responsible, when interpreting the Constitution; they would expect the Court to do all the heavy lifting in constitutional interpretation. Judicial supremacy demotes the leaders of the other branches to second-class, subordinate status in constitutional construction.

Third, judicial supremacy exacts a bigger price, for it comes at the expense of popular sovereignty. "We the People" are the ultimate sovereigns in our constitutional order,[247] but judicial supremacy leaves the American people with no meaningful opportunity to participate in constitutional interpretation except perhaps through their efforts to amend the Constitution. In a regime in which the people are at least as important to constitutional construction as the Court, the people will become more active (and interested) in participating in constitutional dialogues when they know their participation matters. This was evident with two recent exercises of direct democracy. In the first, eight states on November 7, 2006, enacted measures similar to those in 27 other states restricting their respective states' abilities to take private property for private redevelopment.[248] All these measures are repudiations of the Court's decision in *Kelo v. City of New London*[249] deferring to a city's determination that there was a "public use" for taking private property to benefit private developers because of the city's "broad latitude in determining what public needs justify the use of the takings power."[250] Similarly, within the past three years, only 1 state—Arizona—out of 28 rejected proposed constitutional amendments restricting same-sex marriage.[251] These efforts would probably not occur or would be meaningless in a regime of judicial supremacy.

A fourth problem with assertions of judicial supremacy is the Court's inability to settle the most pressing constitutional controversies. The most serious constitutional disputes are constitutional crises, which arise when public authorities disagree over whether the Constitution provides the means for settling a dispute. For instance, the Court did not resolve how the House should resolve the 1800 presidential election immediately in which Jefferson and Burr had tied in the Electoral College.[252] Instead, the House brokered a deal in favor of Jefferson, and then joined the Senate in successfully proposing the Twelfth Amendment.[253] Nor did the Court resolve the problem of secession. Nonjudicial actors settled that great dilemma through a series of actions, including the Civil War, President Lincoln's consolidation of presidential emergency powers, and the Reconstruction amendments.[254] After no candidate in the 1876 presidential election had a majority in the Electoral College, the controversy was resolved not by the Court, but by a special commission appointed by the House pursuant to its authority under the Twelfth Amendment.[255] After the commission split strictly along partisan lines to declare Rutherford Hayes the victor rather than Samuel Tilden, who had won the popular vote, it was not the Court, but rather Hayes and Democratic leaders who brokered a compromise that allowed Hayes to serve a single term in exchange for ending Reconstruction. In each of these events, nonjudicial authorities negotiated compromises that remain discoverable precedents to this day.

Finally, judicial supremacy is undercut by overlooking the fact that nonjudicial precedents, like judicial ones, perform many functions besides constraint. These multiple functions enable nonjudicial precedents to have an enormous influence on our law and culture. I explore these functions in the next chapter.

In this chapter I survey the many functions, including constraint, which judicial and nonjudicial precedents perform. Some scholars dismiss all of these functions except for constraint because they consider constraint as the only significant purpose of precedent. Yet, these other functions of precedent matter for several reasons. First, they illustrate how law matters in ways besides the force of constraint. Second, anyone interested in precedent should appreciate the significance of the rhetoric and reasoning employed in constitutional decision making. Outcomes are important, but so is the route by which the Court gets there. Third, the multiple functions of precedents show how public authorities understand their and other branches' respective powers. Fourth, they demonstrate the dynamic interaction among the Court, judicial doctrine, and culture. They show how public authorities are historically, legally, and culturally bound. In fact, one of the most significant constraints on the Court is that it "is historically conditioned and politically shaped."[1] Below, I give a few examples of each function (as performed by judicial and nonjudicial precedents) for illustrative purposes.

1. Precedent as a Modality of Argumentation

Perhaps the most common function of precedent is as a mode of constitutional argument. In a classic treatise, Philip Bobbitt describes precedent as one of the conventional modalities of constitutional argumentation.[2] Some scholars suggest that it is circular reasoning for any modality to try to establish its primacy based on its own terms, while others suggest that the "strongest" or "best" arguments depend on their moral foundation. Still others, including this author, maintain that the strongest arguments in constitutional law are based on the best or most coherent combinations of all the arguments made within each modality.

The popularity, or prevalence, of precedent as a modality of constitutional argumentation is evident from the fact that precedent-based arguments are among the most popular—if not the most popular—both in and apart from constitutional adjudication. For instance, it is practically impossible to find any modern Court decision that fails to cite at least some precedents in support. The same cannot be said for other sources, such as tradition or original meaning. Similarly, public authorities other than the Court express the need to coordinate any decision they make with both their own and judicial precedents. In some cases, the Court's primary basis for decision is precedent, as in *Bush v. Gore*.[3]

Serving as a modality of argumentation allows precedent to function as the medium through which public authorities, including the Court, recognize the lawfulness of precedent and other modes of constitutional argumentation.[4] Precedent serves as a forum, or testing ground, for arguments based on precedent and other sources. For example, some precedents rely principally on original meaning,[5] while others employ intratextual analysis—clarifying the meaning of a constitutional term by examining how it has been used throughout the Constitution.[6] In other cases, the Court essentially ratifies reliance on nonjudicial precedents in such forms as historical practices, cultural or professional norms, tradition, and custom.

Consistent with their functioning as a modality of argument, precedents may construct a conceptual framework for constitutional law or serve as a heuristic for judicial action.[7] In other words, precedents provide interpretive frameworks, or short-hand references, for understanding what courts do. For instance, some cases—*Dred Scott v. Sandford*[8] and *Lochner v. New York*[9]—have become synonymous with judicial activism. Chief Justice Marshall's opinion in *McCulloch v. Maryland*,[10] the Court's famous fourth footnote in *United States v. Carolene Products*,[11] and many other federalism and equal protection cases employ (and thus sanction recourse to) representation reinforcement as a standard methodology of constitutional interpretation.[12]

Justices and many other public officials are trained in the law and thus familiar with the special language of the law, which is expressed in and through precedents. Law schools train students to read cases and to argue from case law. Just as importantly, people who practice law, whether in the public or private sector, are deeply immersed in the art of reading cases. When people steeped in the law become public authorities, they enter office prepared to learn from and to justify actions in terms of precedent. They appreciate that precedent-based arguments are an important stock in trade and are aware that a natural part of their job is constructing precedents. Examples abound of nonjudicial authorities on both sides of issues making precedent-based arguments, as, for instance, senators did in their debate over deploying the "nuclear option" to ban judicial filibusters.[13]

Similarly, precedent was an important mode of argumentation during President Clinton's impeachment proceedings.[14] The critical question before the House and Senate was the extent to which President Clinton's misconduct was the same as the misconduct for which three judges had been impeached and removed from office in the 1980s. For proponents of Clinton's ouster from office, his misconduct was identical, or analogous, to that for which all of three of these judges had been impeached and removed from office—Harry Claiborne for income tax evasion, and thus for misconduct that had no formal connection to his duties as a judge; Alcee Hastings for perjury; and Walter Nixon for making false statements to a grand jury.[15] President Clinton's critics likened his misconduct further to the obstruction of justice charge in the second impeachment article approved by the House Judiciary Committee against Richard Nixon.[16] In contrast, President Clinton's defenders argued his misconduct was unlike any misconduct for which officials had been removed from office. They likened his behavior to either Richard Nixon's alleged income tax evasion, which the House Judiciary Committee had chosen not to make the basis of an impeachment article,[17] or Andrew Johnson's misconduct—failing to abide by the Tenure in Office Act[18]—for which the Senate had acquitted him.

2. Resolving Disputes

While both courts and nonjudicial authorities resolve disputes, the Constitution in Article III expressly authorizes the Court's jurisdiction to "extend to all Cases, in Law and Equity, arising under this Constitution." The plain meaning of these words is the Court has the power to decide every case "arising under the Constitution."

If judicial precedents do nothing else, they are the means through which the Court decides disputes. This is, for instance, the partial significance of the precedents involving the constitutionality of measures adopted by the Bush administration restricting federal jurisdiction over the conditions of detentions resulting from military conflicts in the aftermath of September 11, 2001. In *Rasul v. Bush*,[19] the Court had to adjudicate the conflict between the president and the courts, and the Court ultimately ruled that it was illegal for the president to unilaterally restrict habeas relief or federal jurisdiction altogether for Guantanamo detainees. Similarly, in *Hamdi v. Rumsfeld*,[20] the Court resolved the conflict posed by the legality of the Bush administration's policy to bar "enemy combatants" in detention from access to legal process. In both cases, the Court determined the restrictions on federal jurisdiction were unconstitutional.[21] In each case, resolving the conflict was a significant end in itself.

Two other well-known separation-of-powers decisions further illustrate how precedent resolves potentially explosive conflicts. The Court's unanimous decision in *United States v. Nixon*,[22] known as the Watergate Tapes case, is a landmark decision in part because it resolved the dispute over whether President Nixon was constitutionally obliged to comply with a judicial subpoena. The Court addressed—for the first time—whether presidents have an absolute privilege to maintain the confidentiality of internal White House communications. The Court rejected the claim of absolute privilege, but recognized a "qualified" executive privilege for presidents over communications in, or generated by, the White House. Similarly, in *Clinton v. Jones*,[23] the Court unanimously resolved the thorny question of whether presidents could be subjected to civil lawsuits based on prepresidential conduct. The Court emphatically said yes.

For some scholars, resolving cases or controversies cannot be separated from how the justices explain themselves. Cass Sunstein's theory of judicial minimalism[24] suggests, for example, the Court should generally undertheorize, which means leaving some things undecided. He proposes some decisions should be narrow (confined to their particular facts) and shallow (reasoned thinly), while others should be narrow and deep (more elaborately reasoned).[25] Minimalism has the principal virtue of reducing judicial interference as much as possible with democratic authorities' own, independent constitutional judgments.

While it does enable the justices to avoid candor or clarity in their opinions, minimalism is predicated on the Court's decisions serving one function—resolving disputes. The defense of judicial minimalism is its normative appeal—it reduces the risks of error and the costs and burdens of making decisions, and it "tends to promote social peace at the same time [it shows] a high degree of respect to those who disagree on big questions."[26] Proponents of minimalism discount—or minimize—the network effects of precedents, particularly those precedents whose meaning and value are shaped by substantial (approving) citations by nonjudicial authorities. The meaning and value of precedents increase the more often they are approvingly cited, and they may be cited approvingly for all sorts of reasons. I am not sure the Court has to combat—or go out of its way to influence—how nonjudicial authorities cite or shape its precedents. Nor should it rebel against the possibility that some precedents may come to mean something different or perform a different function than the Court initially intended. When this happens, the justices should consider whether to follow the meaning or value their precedents have acquired. Indeed, this is one way in which the Court is constrained by its historical, cultural, and social conditions.

Unlike Sunstein, I eschew taxonomies altogether as going beyond the incompletely theorized arguments he urges the Court to employ. Instead, I prefer for the Court to proceed, as Chief Justice Roberts suggested it ought, from the "bottom up," by which he means incrementally, one case at a time, and on the narrowest grounds possible. This is not to say that the Court ought to decide every question posed to it. Rather, it means that the Court ought to decide particular cases based on what it can learn from other actors and its experience. By deciding cases from the bottom up, the Court leaves more room for the other branches to operate and positions itself to learn from its and other constitutional actors' experiences.

Bottom-up judging is pragmatically superior to the alternative. The alternative is deciding cases from the "top down," which requires the Court to impose on lower courts or other authorities principles directly inferred from the Constitution. The risk of top-down judging is that it has no margin of error; the Court has to get it right from the start or risk having its error perpetuated and spread through the enforcement of its decisions. With bottom-up judging, the Court minimizes the risks of error, so it can avoid overreaching its competence, not unduly interfere with other branches' constitutional decision making, and learn from its own mistakes and the mistakes of other institutions. Among the things it will learn over time is how much, or little, it should explain the reasons for its decisions.

3. Precedent as Binding or Persuasive Authority

In the last chapter I explored the constraining (or persuasive) authority of nonjudicial precedents, while in this section I address the binding authority of judicial precedents. The binding power of the latter depends on at least three, interrelated factors. The first is the constituencies to which the judicial precedent applies. There are many possible constituencies for whom judicial precedents may have special meaning: (1) the parties to a case or controversy, (2) other actors confronting the identical legal issues, (3) other actors confronting similar but not identical legal questions, (4) lawyers, (5) other jurists, (6) the general public, (7) other public authorities, and (8) legal scholars and groups interested in the Court. Among these constituencies, the ones most tightly bound by nonjudicial precedents are the people or subjects which they purport directly to address or govern, while those most tightly bound by judicial decisions are the litigants or parties.[27] Other people who confront the same legal issue are not technically bound by judicial decisions, though they can reasonably expect that if they refuse to abide by the ruling in question, lower courts, if not the Supreme Court, will bind them to it. Otherwise a judicial precedent is likely to constitute persuasive authority, depending on the extent to which other actors find themselves in similar but not identical circumstances.[28] Disputants involved in controversies that are identical to those resolved in prior cases have strong incentives to settle, unless at least one of them has reason to believe something is to be gained from appealing. The more closely analogous a dispute is to one that the Court has previously decided, the more likely it will settle or not end up in the Court because lower courts will follow what they regard as binding or authoritative vertical precedent. Of course, lower courts retain ample discretion to challenge or revise doctrine (especially when they believe the Court is receptive to the challenges).

The second factor influencing judicial precedents' binding effects is context. The impact, or binding authority of precedents, depends on the purpose for which someone is using them. In the previous section I suggested precedent may constitute an important validation of other sources of constitutional meaning, constitutional arguments, or particular interpretive methodologies. Such validation need not be limited to actions within the judicial process, for judicial precedents give respectability, or a stamp of approval, to constitutional arguments or perspectives, lending a prestige these arguments may not otherwise have. Thus a judicial decision may be instrumental not just to a court, but also to other authorities, as validating the use of particular interpretive methods, such as original meaning.

Justices are not the only authorities who validate constitutional arguments. The validations of judicial precedents depend on the support they receive from political authorities. Political legitimacy entails approval of particular judicial decisions by national political authorities.[29] A judicial decision does not have political legitimacy—recognition as having legal force by political authorities—merely because it claims such support. The extent to which a judicial precedent achieves political legitimacy depends on several interrelated factors. First, a judicial decision's legitimacy depends on social acquiescence. Generally the American people may have come to accept a particular judicial decision as a rule of law—or at least an expression of the law. Second, a precedent has to receive the genuine, enduring commitment of political institutions to the principle(s) set forth within it. To the extent that the Court's decision in *Brown* can be fairly described as achieving its objective, it depended on critical backing from presidents and Congress (and subsequent Courts) over time. Third, persuasion is instrumental to the social and political acceptance of a particular judicial decision. I do not mean that judicial decisions can only achieve political legitimacy if their reasoning is so strong as to convince opponents that they have been correctly decided. Rather, I mean that judicial decisions need to be grounded in sufficiently persuasive reasoning, argumentation, rhetoric, or imagery as to cultivate, maintain, and win the longstanding support of at least the Court and the leadership of other public institutions.

A third factor affecting judicial precedents' binding force is how different constituencies consider its relevance. This construction is an aspect of network effects. As network effects studies show, a particular precedent cannot easily retain the meaning its creators assigned to it (assuming they had one). Instead, its value and meaning largely depend on how often it is cited or used by subsequent justices and other public authorities. It is only through the process of citation (and subsequent construction) that the meaning, value, and authority of a judicial decision becomes clearer (or more fixed) over time.

4. Setting Agendas

While both judicial and nonjudicial precedents perform agenda-setting functions, most people are more familiar with how the Court, rather than nonjudicial authorities, performs this function. In fact, judicial precedents frame the Court's agenda in at least two ways. First, the Court's precedents frame its choices of which constitutional matters *not* to hear.

The justices' respect for precedent is particularly evident in such choices. While the justices' decisions to deny certiorari are considered not to have any formal legal significance, refusals to hear cases may provide insights into the justices' priorities.[30] For instance, the Court's refusal, since 1939, to agree to hear a case involving a Second Amendment[31] issue discourages litigation to enforce the Second Amendment,[32] though as litigation over its scope percolates in the lower courts, pressure undoubtedly increases on the Court to hear Second Amendment claims.[33] Until the Court agrees to hear such claims, its silence is likely to provoke speculation; perhaps the justices prefer that the matter percolate longer in the lower courts, perhaps they would like to avoid the question for as long as possible, perhaps some justices find other issues more pressing, or perhaps some justices prefer to deal with other constitutional issues relating to gun control before confronting Second Amendment claims.

Second, the Court's precedents frame its choices of which matters to hear. Patterns in the Court's certiorari decisions reveal its agenda to reconsider or clarify certain precedents. For instance, from 1994 to 2005, federalism has been the area in which the Rehnquist Court had granted the most petitions for certiorari.[34] This trend contrasts sharply with the Rehnquist Court's first eight years, during which it granted certiorari most frequently in cases involving social issues, such as abortion and school prayer.[35]

The Court's patterns of decision making on certiorari send important signals to litigants, lower courts, and other public authorities. The Court may invite further litigation in some areas, particularly when its opinions are undertheorized, deliberately vague, or persistently contested, or leave issues unresolved. For instance, one such area is the scope of Congress' interstate commerce clause power to regulate noneconomic activities. While the Court has hinted at the extremely low probability that there are any noneconomic activities which Congress may regulate through this power, it has not ruled out the possibility altogether. Hence litigants, lower courts, and non-judicial actors may ponder the utility of pressing the Court to clarify which, if any, noneconomic activities the Congress may use its commerce clause power to regulate.

The Court's precedents also frame the agendas of nonjudicial authorities (and their agendas may influence what the Court does in cases to which they are parties). These authorities need to make decisions about the applicability of judicial decisions, whether to litigate certain matters, how to defend against constitutional challenges, and whether or how to comply with judicial decisions in which they have been parties. The Court's precedents are at least one factor the Court and nonjudicial actors will take into consideration in setting their agendas. Hence they will probably be sensitive to the signals being sent by the Court with respect to its agenda.

Nonjudicial precedents serve to shape agendas no less than judicial precedents. Sometimes nonjudicial authorities send signals to the Court, but not all these signals may be through precedents. Nonjudicial authorities may send signals in part to make the Court aware of pertinent nonjudicial precedents (as may have been the case with the efforts to restrict same-sex marriage or to toughen the punishments for three-time felony offenders), but nonjudicial authorities oftentimes construct precedents to influence their agendas and the agendas of other states (and Congress), as has been the case with the spate of state referenda and constitutional amendments restricting same-sex marriage. With these latter enactments, state authorities have tried to do many things at once—to make a point, to appease important constituencies, to encourage other states to follow suit, to fortify their marriage laws from judicial challenges, and to bolster (or impede) arguments that tradition supports prohibitions of same-sex marriage.

5. Facilitating Constitutional Dialogues

Judicial and nonjudicial precedents facilitate national dialogues about constitutional meaning.[36] The participants in this dialogue are varied; they are justices, the leaders of other public institutions, interest groups, the media, and the public. Precedents frame, inform, and facilitate a constitutional dialogue among these actors.

In performing this function, both judicial and nonjudicial precedents fulfill several possible objectives and strategies. For instance, they may define the range of possible outcomes in particular disputes. At the very least, justices must reconcile their preferred methodological approaches with those employed in prior cases. The reconciliation entails a dialogue among the justices, their predecessors, their successors, and those who will be affected by, or interested in, what the Court decides.

One of the best known theories of precedent as facilitating constitutional dialogues was made by the late Alexander Bickel. He maintained, "Virtually all important decisions of the Supreme Court are the beginnings of conversations between the Court and the people and their representatives."[37] For instance, *Brown v. Board of Education*[38] is often characterized as self-consciously framed to foster a national dialogue about the constitutionality of state-mandated segregation. As Bickel's colleague Robert Burt explains, "The justices acknowledged among themselves that, in pragmatic terms at least, nothing would follow from the *Brown* decision unless support voluntarily came from the President and Congress."[39] The Court in *Brown* thus asked for briefing on the question whether "future Congresses might, in the exercise of their power under section 5 of the Fourteenth Amendment, abolish" state-mandated segregation in public schools, even if "neither the Congress in submitting nor the States in ratifying the Fourteenth Amendment understood that compliance with it would require the immediate abolition of segregation in public schools."[40] The Court needed the support of the executive and legislative branches to ensure its decision became law.

Robert Post agrees that precedents perform this function and that dialogue is an essential means through which judicial decisions are tested and accepted socially. For instance, he construes the "best interpretation" of *Lawrence*, which struck down Texas' antisodomy law, "as the opening bid in a conversation that the Court expects to hold with the American public. The Court has advanced a powerful and passionate statement that is plainly designed to influence the ongoing national debate about the constitutional status of homosexuality."[41]

Post envisions a dialogue that shapes and is shaped by American culture, which he defines as "the beliefs and values of nonjudicial actors."[42] Although he recognizes culture "comes in a myriad different guises,"[43] he argues "constitutional law and culture are locked in a dialectical relationship, so that constitutional law both arises from and in turn regulates culture."[44] Post points to the Rehnquist Court's decisions construing the scope of Congress' power pursuant to section 5 of the Fourteenth Amendment as demonstrating "that the Court in fact commonly constructs constitutional law in the context of an ongoing dialogue with culture, so that culture is inevitably (and properly) incorporated into the warp and woof of constitutional law."[45] The Court is not "autonomous from culture."[46] Instead, the Court "defines the substance of constitutional law in the context of the beliefs and values of nonjudicial actors."[47]

The dynamic interactions between what the Court decides and non-judicial actors' beliefs and values are consistent with the limited path dependency of judicial precedents. A dialogue does not have to be linear, predictable, or cordial in order to be a dialogue. The discourse among the justices and interested parties may be about the correctness of particular decisions, the appropriate deference to give to constitutional decisions of nonjudicial actors, or the relative competency of each branch's authority to address particular problems.

Moreover, dialogue is antithetical to not only the notion that constraint is the only meaningful function of precedent, but also to judicial closure. Both judicial closure and constraint signify the end of debate, rather than its extension. Yet, the more flux in Supreme Court decisions, the richer the dialogue (both on and off the Court). Judicial precedents, in this view, matter not because they foreclose choices, but rather because they contribute to or extend public exchanges over constitutional values.

The Court is not, however, always part of, or a principal player in, these public exchanges. For instance, precedent was a central concern when President George W. Bush's then-National Security Adviser, Condoleezza Rice, was deciding whether to testify under oath before the September 11, 2001 Commission.[48] The exchanges between Rice and the White House on the one hand and the commission on the other (as an agent of Congress) constituted a classic constitutional dialogue. Initially Rice refused, based on precedent—no sitting National Security Adviser had ever previously testified under oath before Congress or a congressionally created commission. Public pressure mounted against her refusal, particularly after she had publicly appeared in the media and other places to counter statements made under oath by other witnesses. Eventually the president allowed her to testify under oath based on a special understanding, spelled out in a letter from the White House counsel to the commission that requested, inter alia, that her appearance not be construed as a "precedent" in similar proceedings in the future.[49]

6. Shaping Constitutional Structure

All precedents perform several structural functions, including shaping (and clarifying) constitutional structure in several significant ways. First, judicial precedents impose order on the legal system. As I previously indicated, judicial precedent, at its most basic, settles disputes between parties (including the other branches) and clarifies the rules of the game for what litigants need to do in order to prevail in constitutional adjudication. Besides framing legal analysis of a constitutional question, judicial precedents may clarify the operative principles for certain constitutional conditions, fashion doctrine,[50] influence the justices' different constitutional outlooks, shape how the legal system works, make settlement easier or harder, and "structure the future behavior of both governmental and nongovernmental decision makers."[51]

Second, the Court's precedents reflect its understanding of its powers and place within the legal order.[52] Precedents further reflect the Court's understanding of other public institutions' powers and responsibilities (and, of course, nonjudicial precedents reflect nonjudicial authorities' understanding of their and other institutions' powers). Moreover, precedents reflect the Court's awareness of political realities. For instance, the Court's famous declaration in *Brown II* that public school boards should end state-mandated segregation "with all deliberate speed" reflected the justices' awareness of the difficulties many jurisdictions would face in ending state-mandated segregation in public schools. The choice made not to press state authorities harder reflects the justices' awareness of the limits of their powers and the repercussions of stiff resistance in the South, though some scholars believe the justices' failure to press harder for immediate compliance with *Brown* sowed the seeds of its own destruction.

Third, judicial precedents clarify the proper steps for certain constitutional activities to follow. In many constitutional cases, the Court is laying out the steps that governmental actors must follow in order to do take certain actions. These are sometimes called the "existence conditions" required for certain activities, such as creating a lawful bill.[53]

Fourth, judicial precedents are outlets for airing differences of opinion about constitutional matters.[54] Precedents may reflect the justices' efforts to let off steam. At the same time, precedents without clear rulings or majority opinions may show that the justices' differences of opinion cannot be accommodated in a single opinion, as in cases dealing with such socially divisive issues as the rights of biological parents in *Michael H. v. Gerald D.*[55] and the right to die in *Washington v. Glucksburg*.[56] In addition, some precedents inflame political controversies, as was the case with *Dred Scott v. Sandford*,[57] which exacerbated the division over slavery,[58] while other opinions settled heated controversies without fisticuffs or blood-shed, as may have happened with *Bush v. Gore*.[59]

In other precedents, the Court may be trying to take the heat off the other branches by resolving issues which they would prefer not to decide. For instance, once the Court had struck down a state statute prohibiting flag burning for violating the First Amendment,[60] Congress quickly passed a federal anti-flag-burning statute that the Court wasted no time in overturning because it was not meaningfully different from the one it had previously struck down.[61] Many members of Congress, who may have felt it was politically expedient to publicly denounce flag burning, may have privately accepted the inevitability of the Court's striking down the federal anti-flag-burning statute.

Yet, other judicial precedents may perform the important function of giving legitimacy to the exercise of governmental power. Such is the case with the Roberts Court's 5-4 decision in *Gonzales v. Carhart*,[62] upholding a federal partial-birth abortion ban nearly identical to a state law which the Rehnquist Court had struck down in *Stenberg v. Carhart*.[63] Rather than overrule *Stenberg*, in which the Court had effectively taken the heat for striking down the state partial-birth abortion ban at issue there, it took on a different kind of heat in *Gonzales v. Carhart* by refusing to follow *Stenberg* and instead deferring to Congress' extensive fact-finding supporting the federal law (including its failure to include any exception for protecting the mother's health). Hence, the Court effectively lent its power and prestige in support of the controversial judgment embodied in the federal partial-birth abortion ban.

Moreover, the Court sometimes facilitates what James Scott describes as "projects of legibility."[64] Scott argues that the government cannot regulate something unless it is visible to, or known by, the government. Legibility is the process through which the government, often working with the Court (or other governmental institutions), makes something visible in order to facilitate its governmental regulation. Ken Kersch shows how precedents can facilitate the state's achievement of the law's regulatory imperatives.[65] This was particularly true, Kersch suggests, in the late 19th and early 20th centuries, during which the interaction among the national political and legal elites over the content of constitutional doctrine on privacy was indispensable to the project of constructing the scope of the Congress' commerce clause power.

Precedents might not only facilitate the process of government's seeing into the realms it is attempting to insert itself, but also clarify the point beyond which the government may not look. *United States v. Morrison*[66] demonstrates this phenomenon. In *Morrison*, the Court explained that the civil remedies provision of the Violence Against Women Act was defective in part because section 5 of the Fourteenth Amendment empowered the Congress to regulate only state activity.[67] The Court's ruling clarified that the Congress' authority under section 5 of the Fourteenth Amendment did not reach any private activity. This ruling is also telling, particularly with respect to the power of precedent, because it is entirely consistent with the Court's 1883 decision in the *Civil Rights Cases*,[68] in which the Court held precisely the same thing. *Morrison* thus closely follows the *Civil Rights Cases* in holding that congressional power does not extend to private activity. In addition, the Court in *Morrison* ruled that the commerce clause empowered the Congress to regulate private economic activity, but that the activity at issue in *Morrison* did not qualify as economic activity.[69] Consequently the Court held that the commerce clause did not authorize the Congress to manipulate private, non-economic activity. In short, *Morrison* clarified the realm into which the federal government may not extend its authority (under the commerce clause or the Fourteenth Amendment).

The final structural function performed by judicial precedents is stabilizing constitutional law. First, they do this by providing peaceful channeling of constitutional arguments. Here it is the function of precedents to allow not just justices, but the parties themselves, to blow off steam. Emotional outbursts do not persuade the Court. Nor do protestations about how strongly people feel about the rightness of their cause. The very fact that constitutional discourse is structured signals to the parties in constitutional disputes the channels through which they must go and the kinds of arguments they must use in order to prevail in constitutional adjudication. Precedents provide a peaceful, orderly means for settling disputes.

Second, some precedents purport to settle some controversies and thus stabilize constitutional law. For instance, there are firmly settled precedents defining governmental relations;[70] other precedents providing the foundations of modern administrative law[71] and environmental regulation;[72] and still other precedents defining fundamental rights with which government must not interfere.

For their part, nonjudicial precedents clarify and shape constitutional structure in at least two significant ways. First, they shape, or clarify, the organization and allocation of power outside the Court. The organizations of the executive and legislative branches, administrative agencies, and state governments depend largely on the discoverable constitutional judgments of presidents, members of Congress, administrative officials, and state leaders. Moreover, nonjudicial precedents shape the Court through choices made about its size, composition, funding, and jurisdiction. This is not to mention how, as I previously discussed, judicial doctrine is informed by nonjudicial precedents.

Second, nonjudicial precedents, like judicial ones, clarify the existence conditions for certain constitutional activities. They show the paths that nonjudicial authorities need to follow in order to achieve their desired objectives. International trade agreements are an excellent example of nonjudicial precedent shaping constitutional structure. Presidents and the Congress have worked out together several alternatives for reaching international trade agreements. The first and most obvious is a treaty. Ratification of treaties requires votes of approval by at least two-thirds of the Senate,[73] but questions regarding negotiation and termination of treaties have been largely left to the political branches to work out between themselves. Over time, presidents have claimed the prerogative to unilaterally terminate and negotiate treaties, though both are often done with substantial congressional consultation.[74]

A second alternative for international agreements is an executive agreement. Although the Constitution does not mention executive agreements, they were known even in President Washington's day, and have become the predominant form of international agreement for the United States.[75] Even Congress has recognized the constitutionality of negotiating executive agreements by enacting the Case Act, which requires the secretary of state to transmit the text of agreements other than treaties to each chamber for informational purposes.[76]

A third kind of international agreement is executive agreements, of which there are three types. First, treaty-based executive agreements are made pursuant to treaties.[77] They enjoy the same legal status as the treaties that authorize them so long as they are consistent with and within the scope of those treaties. Second, congressional-executive agreements are those authorized by statute. These agreements are complete alternatives to treaties.[78] They are approved not by a supermajority vote in the Senate, but rather by majority vote in each chamber of Congress. Like treaties, these agreements (including the North American Free Trade Agreement [NAFTA]) may become the supreme law of the land and thus supersede inconsistent state laws and any inconsistent provisions in earlier treaties, other international agreements, or statutes. Third, executive agreements are those international agreements that a president makes solely under his own authority.[79] Thus the president, as commander in chief, may make armistice agreements. Questions related to particular agreements are usually determined outside the courts, but even when litigated they have been approved by the courts. For instance, the Court has held that a president's authority to recognize foreign governments is sufficient to authorize unilateral executive agreements to settle issues that are necessary to establish diplomatic relations.[80]

Also, without any interference or input from the courts, presidents and members of Congress have worked out several routes by which the nation may lawfully go to war.[81] First, there are declarations of war, which usually follow the incidence of war and formally recognize a preexisting state.[82] Declarations might also initiate hostilities if they were, for instance, in the form of ultimata. Second, statutes may become the basis on which a president may validly commit the armed forces to combat without returning to Congress for further authorization.[83] Third, joint resolutions may provide a basis for using military force.[84] In recent years, joint resolutions have authorized military actions in Kuwait, Afghanistan, and, most recently, Iraq. Last but not least, the context of an emergency may provide the basis for warfare.[85] Thus military force may be used to rebuff an imminent threat to American forces, national security, Americans abroad, or civil order. Just as with international agreements, the constitutionality of taking the country to war by any of these routes depends not on courts, but on the judgments of national political leaders. Political accountability, rather than judicial review, provides a meaningful check on these judgments.

7. The Historical Functions of Precedent

Judicial and nonjudicial precedents perform three historical functions. I consider these functions in turn.

First, the Court's opinions and nonjudicial activities are frequently intertwined with historical events. Perhaps the most famous example of a judicial precedent performing this function is *Dred Scott v. Sandford*,[86] which divided the Court and the nation over the extent to which the Constitution protected slavery or empowered the Congress to restrict its spread. *Dred Scott* set the stage for the Civil War and was a major target of the Reconstruction amendments. *Dred Scott* is important to justices and others as the precedent overturned by the Reconstruction Amendments. Moreover, it is widely regarded as an important symbol for the consequences of the Court's reliance on questionable historical analysis and interference with socially divisive issues.

A more recent example of a judicial precedent intertwined with an historical event is *Bush v. Gore*.[87] The decision did not merely settle a dispute. By trying to resolve the dispute and preempting any political solution, the Court entered the fray and became the center of national attention. Rather than just end the dispute between Bush and Gore, the Court became part of the dispute.[88]

Judicial decisions also reflect the attitudes of a particular historical period. Justices—and nonjudicial authorities, for that matter—cannot stand apart from the culture, society, and historical period in which they live. The Court's decisions are not only shaped by the values of the society in which the Court operates, but also shape those values. For instance, the development of the civil rights movement in this country was intertwined with a long list of cases in which the justices' attitudes on race both mirrored and attempted to shape those of the era in which they lived. A modern example is that popular mobilization in support of the proposed Equal Rights Amendment strongly influenced the Court's doctrine. As Reva Siegel concludes, "The ERA was not ratified, but the amendment's proposal and defeat played a crucial role in enabling and shaping the modern law of sex discrimination."[89]

Similarly, nonjudicial precedents make constitutional history, as was the case with the series of congressional regulations in the territories before the Civil War.[90] These regulations were the product of extensive congressional debates over the extent of Congress' regulatory power over both slavery and the territories. Scholars agree that the compromises embodied in these laws were significant, but disagree over whether they stalled or provoked secession.

Moreover, historical practices are history in the making. So, President Thomas Jefferson's decision to forego congressional approval for the Louisiana Purchase not only significantly expanded the United States, but also set an important precedent on the necessity for getting congressional approval for similar acquisitions in the future.[91] Similarly, President Jefferson's decision to direct military force against the Barbary pirates without congressional approval not only helped to eliminate a threat to American commerce and lives, but also was one of the earliest in a series of unilateral presidential initiatives to employ military force without explicit congressional approval.[92] More recently, Southern resistance to civil rights legislation through filibusters explains the failure of such legislation to pass the Senate from the Reconstruction era until 1958.[93]

The second historical function performed by precedents is chronicling constitutional history. Because the Court is a critical interpreter of (and actor) in historical events, its precedents preserve, illuminate, and reflect contemporary perspectives on the nation's social, political, and legal traditions.[94] The Court attempts to define the relevant past for itself and the other branches. In doing so, the Court may not only legitimize recourse to original meaning or historical practices, but its precedents present to other institutions its understanding of original meaning or pertinent historical practices. The point is not that its historiography is binding or impervious to review, but rather that it has to be taken into account and may be accepted, built upon, or evaluated, in either constitutional adjudication or nonjudicial forums.

The Court's historiography is abundant.[95] There are many precedents in which the justices try to figure out the precise scope or original meaning (the basic understanding of the pertinent constitutional actors of the era). This enterprise entails writing the history of particular provisions or events, as the Court did in *Nixon v. United States* on the scope of Congress' impeachment authority,[96] *Jones v. Alfred H. Mayer Co.* on the history of the Thirteenth Amendment,[97] *New York Times v. Sullivan* on the original meaning of the scope of the First Amendment's protection of the press from libel actions,[98] *Harmelin v. Michigan* on the extent to which the Framers meant for the Eighth Amendment to guarantee proportionality of punishment,[99] and *Marsh v. Chambers* on the original meaning of the establishment clause and the practice of opening legislative sessions with prayers.[100]

The Court's mediations of past events are often thought to be at least as reliable—if not more reliable—than the historiography of nonjudicial actors. First, the Court is supposedly designed to perform retrospective analysis. The president and the Congress tend, for the most part, to be prospective, or forward-looking, when tackling constitutional problems. Second, political authorities have no tradition of reasoned elaboration, as courts do. Hence they rarely feel the need to explain fully the reasons for their constitutional judgments (and constructions of history). Third, political authorities are amenable, unlike Article III courts, to direct political pressure, and thus are frequently disposed to make decisions based on short-term advantage or political expediency. There may be some proceedings in which nonjudicial authorities take the long view, but there are many in which they do not. Fourth, a fundamental premise of the adversarial system is that strong advocacy on each side of a dispute will expose the flaws of the historical material submitted to the Court. The adversarial system provides a check on the Court's historiography. If there is a flaw in it, then the Court can make corrections in subsequent litigation.

No recent case better illustrates such self-correction than *Lawrence v. Texas*.[101] The Court rejected the earlier conclusion, reached in *Bowers v. Hardwick*,[102] that the states had traditionally criminalized homosexual sodomy.[103] Instead, the Court in *Lawrence* revised its historiography of governmental regulation of homosexuality to show that the states had not criminalized homosexual sodomy (as opposed to sodomy generally) and that the criminalization of homosexual sodomy is a relatively recent phenomenon in this country.[104]

Yet, *Lawrence* does not signify the end of the public debate over gay rights generally or the constitutionality of antisodomy laws. After *Lawrence*, the debate has evolved. It has moved into the public domain, where it has focused on the necessity for a constitutional amendment protecting traditional marriage and on the needs for states to amend their Constitutions to regulate same-sex marriages.[105] In short, the dialogue on same-sex marriage has become a dramatic instance of constitutional activity outside the Court.

The fact that courts may generally take greater care in writing about constitutional history does not mean nonjudicial authorities produce unreliable historiography. To the contrary, many nonjudicial authorities reach historical findings or produce their own histories of pertinent matters. For instance, many of the official memoranda of the Justice Department's Office of Legal Counsel include the office's own historiography on pertinent issues.[106] Opinions thus become important for both the counsel and the historical support or background they provide. Similarly, in preparation for its hearings on President Nixon's misconduct, the House Judiciary

Committee asked the eminent historian C. Vann Woodward to coordinate an historical inquiry into the origins and scope of the federal impeachment power.[107]

In producing their historiographies, nonjudicial authorities produce some valuable distillations of precedent. The *Congressional Record* is replete with Congress' prior constitutional activities, which can be assembled by anyone who wants to take the time and effort to plumb through it to assemble them. Consequently there are several noteworthy compilations of congressional precedents.[108] Moreover, members of Congress may direct constitutional questions to the Congressional Research Service, which routinely produces memoranda describing and analyzing pertinent precedents. In addition, past presidential decisions are reported in *The Messages and Papers of the President*, which includes executive orders, veto messages, State of the Union messages, and other official presidential directives and actions. Different units within the executive branch as well as the White House Counsel's Office also compile useful distillations of precedent. They may record their own past judgments or perhaps longer distillations of relevant precedents for some desired action(s). For example, in 1966 the State Department Legal Adviser's Office produced a memorandum collecting more than 125 incidents in which the president used the armed forces abroad without obtaining prior congressional authorization.[109]

A final historical function of precedents is they are a means by which judicial and nonjudicial authorities try to put themselves on the right side of history. For example, the justices try to foresee (maybe influence) where society or social trends are heading and to place the Court on the same path. *Brown*, *Roe v. Wade*, *Furman v. Georgia*,[110] and *Lawrence v. Texas* are all cases in which the justices may be seen as attempting to put the Court on the right side of history; and the critics of each of these cases object to "such a soothsaying role for the Court [as] normatively problematic."[111]

A similar dynamic is apparent outside the Court. Recently the House passed a nonbinding resolution that was critical of President Bush's proposed surge in Iraq. The resolution was supported by House members convinced that history would judge kindly their opposition to continuing to supply American armed forces in Iraq. Similarly, senators concerned about the constitutionality of the "nuclear option" or about the propriety of convicting or removing President Clinton from office openly expressed concerns about how history would likely judge their actions.

8. Education

A once popular notion of precedents was that they were the means through which the Court educates people about the Constitution.[112] Many scholars used to look to the Court as a leader in educating people about the Constitution. They believed that of all public institutions, the Court had more time, training, opportunity, resources, and independence from political pressure to produce relatively impartial, legally grounded insights on constitutional law. They further believed that the Court's institutional virtues, especially its detachment from everyday politics, imbued its constitutional pronouncements with a special authority no other governmental institution could match.

Within the past few years, the ideal of the Court as moral educator has diminished. For one thing, the notion of the Court as educator was hard to square with our democratic system of government. It treated popular discourse about the Constitution with disdain and granted an exalted status to Supreme Court justices that reinforced their elitist status in American society.

The most serious challenge to the Court as educator was directed against the claim that the justices have some special moral authority to speak about constitutional law. Some scholars reject as completely inappropriate the Court's employment of moral reasoning or interjection into matters of morality. Moreover, as the Court has increasingly injected itself into politically and socially divisive constitutional issues (such as abortion, school prayer, and capital punishment), it is no longer clear that the Court does a better job than other public authorities in constructing the Constitution. In addition, the notion of the Court as educator encouraged justices to expand on constitutional issues, while a number of scholars, including Bickel, favored reticence as a virtue.[113] Consequently admiration for the Court as an educator is widely disfavored, even though its precedents continue to provide perhaps a more visible and extensive discussion of constitutional meaning than any that the other branches provide.[114]

One need not agree with precedent's serving educative functions to see that some precedents in fact aim to serve this exact purpose. Some precedents that perform educative functions are well known, such as *Brown v. Board of Education*, in which the Court famously declared that "in the field of public education the doctrine of 'separate but equal' has no place."[115] In *Cooper v. Aaron*,[116] the Warren Court put its authority—political, moral, and otherwise—on the line to support its bold declaration that the Court was the final arbiter in disputes with states over constitutional meaning. The Court again—quite self-consciously—put its authority on the line when it defended *Roe* in *Planned Parenthood of Southeastern Pennsylvania v. Casey* as properly "calling the contending sides of a national controversy to end their national division by accepting a common mandate rooted in the Constitution."[117]

Another example of precedent's fulfilling educative purposes is the justices' debates about how to properly interpret the Constitution. These debates recently extended to disagreements over the propriety of the Court's relying on foreign law in constitutional adjudication. In *Roper v. Simmons*[118] and *Lawrence v. Texas*,[119] the majority relied on foreign law in striking down state laws. However, in both cases, Justice Scalia took the majorities to task for relying on foreign law in interpreting the Constitution in spite of protestations in each case that its reference to foreign law had no meaningful bearing on the outcome of the case.[120] There is little, if any, doubt that Justice Scalia, like Justices Oliver Wendell Holmes and Hugo Black before him, writes his dissents—including the two in these cases—with a larger audience (including the press) in mind. His dissents provided useful rhetoric for Republicans in the Congress to denounce *Roper* and *Lawrence*. Moreover, he and Justice Breyer, who joined the majority opinions in both cases, later appeared together in public to educate the public about their respective positions on the propriety of relying on foreign law in constitutional adjudication.

Again, nonjudicial precedents, no less than judicial ones, are designed in part to educate the public (and other actors) about constitutional law. For instance, judicial nominees may learn from prior judicial confirmation hearings what they should say (or not say) in order to get confirmed by the Senate. The Senate's confirmation hearings on Robert Bork's nomination as associate justice have been described sometimes as a seminar on constitutional law.[121] In its aftermath, Senator Joseph Biden pointed to those hearings as an example of the proper functioning of the Senate on Supreme Court nominations.[122] In the midst of the confirmation hearings on John Roberts' nomination as chief justice, Republican and Democratic senators disagreed over the extent to which the earlier confirmation hearings on Ruth Bader Ginsburg's nomination to the Court provided an example of either a candid or reticent nominee.[123] Senators treated her hearings as instructive on how forthcoming a Supreme Court nominee ought to be before the Senate Judiciary Committee.[124] Moreover, the 1987 confirmation hearings on Robert Bork's nomination as an associate justice are often construed as demonstrating the problems with a nominee's being too candid and expansive in responding to Judiciary Committee questions.[125] With this possible construction of the Bork precedent in mind, Chief Justice Roberts, immediately after being sworn into office, told his audience what lesson his confirmation taught—that his Senate confirmation ratified the principle that judging is distinct from politics.[126] The Roberts and earlier hearings influenced the next Supreme Court confirmation hearings, in which Justice Alito followed the examples of Chief Justice Roberts and Justice Ginsburg in answering questions and senators from both sides tried to educate the (listening) public about the nominee's virtues or flaws, the Court, and the proper scope of questioning.

9. Symbolism

While subsequent justices try to shape the symbolic importance of precedents, nonjudicial actors exert more influence in constructing not only the symbolic significance of nonjudicial precedents, but also how the Court perceives its precedents. *Brown* illustrates this dynamic interaction. When first decided, *Brown* symbolized to many Southerners the outrageous consequences of the federal government's efforts to interfere with their way of life. At the same time, as Michael Klarman suggests, *Brown* "dramatically raised the salience of the segregation issue, forcing many people to take a position for the first time. *Brown* was also enormously symbolic to African Americans, many of whom regarded it as the greatest victory for their race since the Emancipation Proclamation."[127] Subsequently, *Brown* has taken on additional symbolic significance as flatly rejecting the principle of "separate but equal" in public education. *Brown*'s symbolic importance has been reinforced through the Court's subsequent decisions and our political process, particularly in judicial confirmation proceedings in which, for all nominees but Justice Thomas, possibly, fealty to *Brown* is required. Robert Bork's Supreme Court nomination stumbled in part because of his harsh criticism of *Brown* earlier in his career. Today, the justices and political leaders wrestle over whether *Brown* signifies the rejection of all race-based laws or just those hurting racial minorities. For some people, *Brown* symbolizes the failure of will, particularly the Court's resolve to withstand political backlash, to stamp out segregation and its effects once and for all.

Dred Scott, too, assumed symbolic importance when it was first decided and since. When first decided, Southerners celebrated it as affirming their constitutional entitlements to own slaves and to maintain their preferred way of life. To others, *Dred Scott* symbolized the Court's misguided and corrupt efforts to preempt the efforts of abolitionists and Republicans to dismantle slavery through political means. Abraham Lincoln viewed *Dred Scott* with such derision as symbolizing the Court's failings that he rarely referred publicly to the Court afterwards. Today, *Dred Scott* still symbolizes different things to different people—to some it symbolizes the dangers of substantive due process, to others the consequences of manipulating original understanding, and to still others the tragic consequences of the Court's failure to recognize the limits of its power.

Korematsu is symbolic, like *Dred Scott*, of the Court's failings, dramatically underscored by President Reagan's signing into law an act authorizing reparations to be paid to Japanese Americans (or their families) for their detention in camps during World War II. *Korematsu* is almost universally condemned, though the fact that it has never been formally overruled allows the Court to cite it as authority for strictly scrutinizing all race-based classifications. Yet, just as affirming *Brown* is now required in judicial confirmation proceedings, rejecting *Korematsu* is pro forma for Supreme Court nominees.

More recently the Court's decision striking down the Virginia Military Institute's exclusion of women has been hailed as rejecting—in the Court's words—"separate but equal" facilities for women in higher education. Meanwhile, critics lambaste both *Lawrence* and *Goodridge v. Department of Public Health*,[128] in which the Massachusetts Supreme Judicial Court held the state constitution guaranteed same-sex couples the right to marry, as symbols of liberal judicial activism. Shortly after the Court decided *Lawrence*, some Republicans in the House of Representatives lambasted it as symbolizing an activist Court run amuck, while President Bush and other Republican candidates in 2004 used *Goodridge* to symbolize the activist judges they were dedicated to opposing and the need for a constitutional amendment protecting traditional marriage.

10. Shaping National Identity

One of the conventional modes of constitutional argumentation is *ethos*, or arguments about what makes the American people or nation distinctive. Many precedents, both judicial and nonjudicial, employ such arguments and draw on American culture to do so. For example, in *Marbury v. Madison*,[129] Chief Justice Marshall invoked in support of his decision "the whole American fabric," while in *McCulloch v. Maryland*[130] he famously described the necessary and proper clause as having been "made in a Constitution intended to endure for ages to come, and consequently to be adapted to the various crises of human affairs."[131] In another classic statement of the constitutional significance of the nation's collective identity, Justice Oliver Wendell Holmes, Jr., insisted that the "case before us must be considered in light of our whole experience and not merely in that of what was said a hundred years ago."[132] Similarly, Chief Justice Rehnquist supported his conclusion that the Constitution allows voluntary recitation of the Pledge of Allegiance in public schools by pointing to a series of "events" or nonjudicial precedents, including President Washington's inaugural address, President Lincoln's Gettysburg Address, President Franklin D. Roosevelt's first inaugural address, and the opening proclamation of the marshal of the Supreme Court, all of which "strongly suggest that our national culture allows public recognition of our Nation's religious history and character."[133]

But judicial precedents may do more than rely on perceptions of American identity; they may seek to shape it. Precedents are integral to the nation's understanding of itself and to how the public and public authorities conceive the nation. The rejections of *Dred Scott* and *Korematsu*, for instance, are essential elements of our distinctive national identity. Moreover, *Brown* has additional importance as a precedent that has become intertwined with national identity; many Americans view *Brown* as an expression of the nation's commitment to equality and to treating people based (as Martin Luther King, Jr., eloquently said) on the "content of their character" and not their race. Many people view *Marbury* as fashioning an important component of our national identity—our constitutional commitment to the principle of judicial review. The Court recognized there, and later in the Watergate tapes case and *Clinton v. Jones*, the basic principle that "no man is above the law," which many Americans consider a distinctive component of our national character. Similarly, the Court's decisions establishing and enforcing "one person, one vote" are popularly conceived as reflecting another essential facet of who we are as a nation.

Nonjudicial precedents are even more important than judicial precedents in shaping national identity. For one thing, they are instrumental in constructing national identity. For instance, "manifest destiny" was central to how Americans viewed their nation in the first half of the 19th century; it encapsulated the driving forces within the nation to acquire new territories and expand dominion over what has become the continental United States.[134] Similarly, both in the House and later in his Senate impeachment trial, the representatives who became the House managers insisted, time and again, that Clinton's removal was necessary to protect the "rule of law" and that allowing him to remain in office would be an affront to preserving the "rule of law" as an essential component of our national character. Moreover, it is common to measure the legality of the Bush administration's warrantless wiretapping and techniques in interrogating detainees on the basis of whether they fit or conflict with our national character or identity.[135] The repeated expressions of the commitment of President Bush and other Republican leaders to appointing judges "who will interpret the law and not legislate from the bench" is not only another ethos-based argument, but also an effort to ingrain this conception of judging into our national identity. Likewise, Chief Justice Roberts' analogizing judging to umpiring was another attempt to tap into what he and others understand as a common perception within our culture of how judges should act.

Moreover, nonjudicial precedents shape the background norms or default rules in constitutional adjudication. When justices employ these, they are revealing (perhaps unconsciously) the nonjudicial beliefs or values on which they are relying to decide constitutional questions. Among the default rules or norms that justices have derived from our culture (and which they may view as fundamental to our national character or identity) are Justice Scalia's certitude that legislative committee reports are primarily drafted to influence judicial construction;[136] Justice Thomas' default rule that constitutional ambiguities or gaps ought to be construed in favor of state sovereignty;[137] and Justice Stevens' default rule that constitutional ambiguities or gaps ought to be construed in favor of federal authority.[138]

11. Implementing Constitutional Values

One of precedent's most important functions is implementing the Constitution. The Constitution is not self-executing. The institutions, rights, and powers recognized in the Constitution did not come into being spontaneously upon the moment of ratification. Instead, the public, working in concert with national and state authorities, made the Constitution operational. The institutions which the Constitution authorizes materialize only when people (presumably duly authorized) put its directives and guarantees into effect. The interaction of judicial and nonjudicial precedents is instrumental to putting these directives and guarantees into effect. The Court, for instance, did not come into being (or receive its funding or even the building it occupies) without other responsible authorities making it happen. Moreover, the Court must rely on the other branches to enforce its opinions; the Court has had to turn more than once to the president for enforcement of its decrees. Meantime, the political branches are expected to keep each other in check while at the same time each is exploring the outer boundaries of its respective powers.

A growing number of scholars are grappling with the difficult questions of whether and how the Constitution may be fully implemented. Daryl Levinson, for example, argues that, as a practical matter, all constitutional rights are over- and underenforced, which makes it both "pointless and indeterminate" to figure out the precise scope or substance of the rights themselves.[139] As a descriptive matter, Levinson's assertion seems quite sound to me (though we lack empirical verification), given the impossibility of the Court's policing perfect compliance with all its decisions and with the other branches perfectly keeping each other in check and not trying to extend their authority (or to obstruct others' authority) as much as they can. Richard Fallon argues, instead, that there may be "a [permissible] gap ... between constitutional meaning and judicially enforced doctrine."[140] He suggests the "best rationalizing explanation" of the gap is that some "background rights" may be properly "aspirational, embodying ideals that do not command complete and immediate enforcement."[141] Fallon rejects Kermit Roosevelt's assertions that courts may not ignore "background rights" and may have different reasons than nonjudicial actors for underenforcing rights,[142] while Fallon and Levinson maintain that courts do not, as Roosevelt and Mitchell Berman claim,[143] decide cases first by identifying operative principles and then crafting decision rules.[144]

Missing from this discourse is the recognition that the perfect implementation of constitutional values depends on the interaction between judicial and nonjudicial precedents. The problem is not just with nonjudicial actors making comparative assessments about their relative competence to enforce certain norms or the costs associated with enforcing those norms. Sometimes nonjudicial actors directly oppose particular judicial precedents and take actions to undermine, rather than to facilitate, their implementation. For example, *Brown* did not fail to be fully implemented in the 1950s or later because nonjudicial actors decided manageability costs outweighed their compliance with *Brown*, but rather because there were, among other things, nonjudicial precedents in the forms of traditions, customs, and norms that were so deeply entrenched in the South that they impeded the implementation of *Brown*'s full promise. *Brown* and its progeny could not fully displace these precedents, much less achieve full implementation without enthusiastic, enduring, and extensive support from national political leaders.

Similarly Presidents Reagan, George H. W. Bush, and George W. Bush did not just underenforce *Roe*, but tried to circumvent it. They blocked as much as they could any federal support for *Roe*. They used all their prerogatives, including issuing executive orders, vetoing bills, and appointing judges and justices, to vindicate their judgment that *Roe* was a mistake.

Neal Devins and Lou Fisher argue that the interaction between nonjudicial actors and the Court is instrumental not just in implementing judicial precedents, but also in shaping constitutional doctrine. Through the ways in which nonjudicial actors influence how the Court's decisions may be implemented and are framed, nonjudicial actors help to democratize the implementation of the Constitution.[145] Nonjudicial precedents may be one essential means through which the public is allowed some say over the implementation of constitutional values.

An example of this dynamic is Congress' response to *INS v. Chadha*,[146] in which the Court struck down the legislative veto—an arrangement in which one or both chambers of Congress or a legislative committee may override an executive action. Constitutional and administrative law scholars for 20 years have emphasized this aspect of *Chadha*—that the Court on that day struck down parts of more statutes than it had previously in its entire history.[147] Yet, immediately after *Chadha*, an angry Congress began finding other ways to reassert its contrary views about the relationship between the executive and legislative branches, and in time turned the state of affairs back in the direction of the pre-*Chadha* world they wanted in the first place.[148] Through their active resistance to fully implementing *Chadha*, Congress reached a point of equilibrium with the Court over their different positions on the constitutionality of legislative vetoes,[149] and its resistance influenced how lower courts construed arrangements like the legislative veto after *Chadha*. For Devins and Fisher, this ensuing state of equilibrium reflects how nonjudicial actors, most of whom are politically accountable, bring to bear on the interpretive process their sensitivity to and awareness of public concerns and values.

The interaction between judicial and nonjudicial precedents is omnipresent in constitutional law. Perhaps the most dramatic way to illustrate how this interaction helps to democratize constitutional law is to rethink what judges may often be doing in constitutional adjudication—looking for which majoritarian decisions they should follow, support, or ground their decisions in. The sources that justices consult to decide cases are oftentimes majoritarian decisions in which someone is trying to persuade the Court to invest normative authority. For example, in *Lawrence*, the question before the justices was, in part, whether they were prepared to accept as controlling the statute before them (as enacted by a majority of the state legislature of Texas and presumably reflecting the approval of Texans), the Constitution (approved by a supermajority of the states pursuant to Article V), tradition (presumably reflecting either the nation's "collective conscience" or perhaps an overwhelming majority of state laws or state constitutions), and precedent (approved by at least one previous majority, if not more than one, on the Court). In *Hamdan v. Rumsfeld*, the justices considered deciding the case based on the Constitution, historical practices (reflecting how presidents and members of Congress have understood their powers over time), precedent, and congressional authorizations (which might reflect the approval or disapproval of majorities in the House and Senate). In *United States v. Lopez*, the Court had to decide on which of the following to ground its decision: precedent, the Constitution, historical practices, or federal law (as approved by Congress and signed by the president). The fact that one may disagree with particular decisions or that the justices made mistakes in construing some sources does not mean the justices failed to find a reflection of majoritarian—or even supermajoritarian—preferences on which to ground their decision.

Even in circumstances in which there is no prospect of judicial review, nonjudicial actors will follow a legal command which they find in some form of majoritarian or supermajoritarian expression of preference. In other words, they will follow a democratic command which they deem authoritative. For instance, Article IV largely leaves to the national government (but not the courts) enforcement of its directive that the "United States shall guarantee to every State in this Union a Republican form of

Government." In addition, the directive in Article VI that "no religious test shall ever be required as a Qualification to any Office or public Trust under the United States"[150] depends on nonjudicial authorities for its implementation. President Bush's nomination of Harriet Miers to the Supreme Court faltered partly because of White House efforts to defend her nomination on the basis of her religious beliefs. The defense provoked outcries from senators and commentators that the president had violated Article VI's directive against religious tests for federal office.[151] The president implicitly acknowledged his error by withdrawing the nomination and avoided defending the next nomination on the same basis. Accordingly, President Bush and most senators tailored their rhetoric (and focus) in the Alito hearings to fit the constitutional commitment, as it is understood within our culture, to treat nominees' religious convictions as irrelevant to their qualifications for federal offices.

One question not yet answered is how some precedents become more settled than others if complete or immediate implementation of all constitutional values is practically impossible. Does the Court's reliance on nonjudicial actors to implement its precedents inhibit their enduring legal significance? The answer is no, because when we say some issues are well settled—or that there is judicial closure—we mean that the Court and nonjudicial actors have reached an enduring equilibrium on these issues. The next chapter explores the rare precedents that reflect such enduring equilibria.

Throughout this book I have referred to some precedents as being so deeply embedded in our law and culture that they have become practically immune to overturning. I call these precedents super precedents, and in this chapter I examine their distinctive characteristics, why they matter, and their normative implications for constitutional theory and practice.

Courts have long recognized that some precedents are so well settled as to be beyond reconsideration. An early opinion from the King's Bench declared, "Those things that have so often been adjudged ought to rest in peace."[1] In *Stuart v. Laird*,[2] the Supreme Court expressed a similar sentiment when it upheld the constitutionality of Congress' requiring justices to ride circuit because "that practice and acquiescence under [the Constitution] for a period of several years, commencing with the organization of the judicial system, affords an irresistible answer, and has indeed fixed the construction. It is a contemporary interpretation of the most forceful nature. This practical experience is too strong and obstinate to be shaken or controlled, and ought not now to be disturbed."

In the course of denigrating *Dred Scott v. Sandford* in his 1858 Senate campaign against Stephen Douglas, Abraham Lincoln explained that if that decision had

> been made by the unanimous concurrence of the judges, and
> without any apparent partisan bias, and in accordance with
> legal and public expectation, and with the steady practice of the
> departments throughout our history, and had been, in no part
> based on assumed historical facts, which are really not true; or,
> if wanting in some of these, it had been before the [C]ourt more
> than once, and had been affirmed and re-affirmed through a
> course of years, it then might be, perhaps would be, factious,
> nay, even revolutionary to not acquiesce in it as a precedent.[3]

Lincoln was suggesting that some judicial decisions are akin to super precedents, but *Dred Scott* was not one of them.

In 2005, super precedent came to public attention when Senate Judiciary Committee Chairman Arlen Specter asked Chief Justice Roberts in his confirmation hearings whether he agreed there were "super-duper precedents" in constitutional law.[4] Roberts did not either endorse or reject the concept, but in asking about "super-duper precedents" Senator Specter was borrowing a notion of stare decisis initially recognized by Fourth Circuit Judge Michael Luttig, who once referred to *Roe v. Wade*[5] as having become "super-stare decisis" because of its repeated reaffirmation by the Court.[6]

Super precedents are not unique to the courts, but rather are constitutional decisions in which public institutions have heavily invested, repeatedly relied, and consistently approved over significant periods of time. These are decisions which have been so repeatedly and widely cited for so long that their meaning and value have increased to the point of being secured by enduring networks. They are deeply and irrevocably embedded into our culture and national consciousness, so much so that it seems un-American to attack, much less to formally reconsider them. These decisions are the clearest instances in which the institutional values promoted by fidelity to precedent—consistency, stability, predictability, and social reliance—are compelling.

I describe three kinds of super precedents in the first three parts of this chapter. The final section addresses several criticisms of super precedent, my responses, and the likely ramifications super precedents pose for constitutional theory and practice.

1. Foundational Institutional Practices

The first kind of super precedent consists of long-standing Supreme Court decisions establishing foundational institutional practices of the judiciary. (I hasten to add there are nonjudicial precedents that do the same for nonjudicial authorities—establishing, for instance, committees as gatekeepers on legislative business or nonreviewable presidential veto authority based on constitutional or other objections. Nevertheless, I will primarily focus on judicial decisions for illustrative purposes.) These decisions recognize and firmly support particular dimensions of the functioning of courts in our system of government.

The first example of a foundational institutional practice grounded in precedent is the widespread judicial and social recognition of precedent as a mode of argumentation and as indispensable to the implementation of constitutional law. The Court—and other public institutions—have jointly and repeatedly employed precedent-based arguments and recognized precedents are both law and instrumental to the implementation of many constitutional values.

A second example of a foundational institutional practice grounded in precedent is judicial review. For more than 200 years, judicial review has been a permanent fixture of our constitutional order. Its scope has generally grown over time. While a few academics and political leaders urge the abandonment of judicial review altogether,[7] there are no signs of any serious and sustainable political or social movements to severely restrict judicial review. Consider, for instance, the fact that Supreme Court nominees routinely accept the lawfulness of judicial review, and that a prospective judicial candidate who failed to do this would never be nominated, much less confirmed.

There are two good examples of super precedents that provide the foundation for the institutional practice of judicial review. *Marbury v. Madison*[8] was an early instance of the Court's exercising judicial review over the constitutionality of a federal statute. While some scholars question the Court's justifications for exercising judicial review (both generally and in the particular circumstances of a case), the practice which it sanctioned endures. The Court repeatedly cites *Marbury* as authority for the exercise of judicial review of the actions of federal authorities.[9] Countless other decisions by the Supreme Court (not to mention lesser judicial tribunals) rely on *Marbury*, for both what it says and what it has come to mean. The case is the standard citation in textbooks and treatises for the basic practice of judicial review. It has become legendary in the study of constitutional law, and it is widely accepted in our culture and an inextricable dimension of our national identity. Students (from grade school to law school), lawyers, justices and judges, members of Congress, and presidents accept *Marbury* as standing for the proposition that judicial review is a constitutionally authorized practice. The persistently positive citations of *Marbury* both by the Court and other institutions deeply entrenches it in the public consciousness and the fabric of American law.

A second example of a super precedent securing the institution of judicial review is *Martin v. Hunter's Lessee*.[10] There, the Supreme Court recognized the constitutional necessity for the exercise of Supreme Court review over a state court judgment resting on interpretation of federal law.[11] As Oliver Wendell Holmes famously remarked, "I do not think the

United States would come to an end if we lost our power to declare an Act of Congress void. I do think the Union would be imperiled if we could not make that declaration as to the laws of the several states."[12] While it is reasonable to assume the public (and perhaps many lawmakers) are not familiar with *Martin* by name, they are familiar with, and widely accept (if not assume), the fact that the Supreme Court may review the constitutionality of state action which might violate the Constitution or other federal laws. Every time the Court exercises judicial review over state actions it reinforces *Martin* and extends its legacy, and presidents and members of Congress stand by the constitutional necessity for federal judicial review of such state actions. While *Michigan v. Long*[13] clarifies the Court's review of state actions, raising a combination of state and federal issues,[14] neither it nor any other decisions have diminished its fundamental importance in constitutional law. And while state officials have sometimes resisted the logic and implications of *Martin*,[15] most state officials, particularly since the civil rights era, have accepted it and no longer question it as a permanent fixture of American constitutional law.

2. Foundational Doctrine

A second set of super precedents consists of Supreme Court decisions establishing foundational doctrine. Foundational doctrine refers to the Court's and other public institutions' persistent recognition of, and support for, enduring categories, frameworks, classes, and kinds of constitutional disputes.

I have previously alluded to one excellent example of this set of super precedents—the Court's decisions upholding the incorporation of most of the Bill of Rights against the states through the due process clause of the Fourteenth Amendment. To be sure, Justice Clarence Thomas has urged his colleagues to adopt his construction of the establishment clause, which would obviate its incorporation.[16] Yet, he stands alone with no support on the Court or any meaningful support off it. And while the Court has employed more than one standard for determining whether to incorporate a specific guarantee of the Bill of Rights,[17] the justices uniformly accept the incorporation doctrine as it stands today. They build on that doctrine every day. Whenever the Court reviews possible state violations of incorporated constitutional guarantees, it reinforces the incorporation doctrine. The bulk of First and Fourth Amendment jurisprudence has been forged in cases involving the constitutionality of state, rather than federal, actions. Incorporation of most of the Bill of Rights makes judicial review of many other constitutional disputes possible. The incorporation doctrine does not dictate how the Court should resolve particular claims of state violations of incorporated liberties, but it provides the basis for judicial review of these claims.

Consequently it is easy to see why a landmark opinion such as *Mapp v. Ohio*[18] is a super precedent. It recognized a principle that endures to this day—incorporating the Fourth Amendment's guarantee against unreasonable searches and seizures.[19] It is the foundation on which most judicial review of Fourth Amendment claims takes place. Indeed, one of the last cases in which the Court upheld the incorporation of a specific constitutional guarantee, *Duncan v. Louisiana*,[20] further anchors the enduring framework for incorporation doctrine.

Similarly the Court's repeated recognition of political questions as nonjusticiable is another example of super precedent establishing foundational doctrine. The doctrine traces its origins at least as far back as *Marbury*, in which Chief Justice Marshall recognized a distinction between a legal question, which a court may decide, and a political question, which is left to the discretion of nonjudicial authorities. In *Luther v. Borden*,[21] the Court found that claims brought under the Constitution's guaranty clause are nonjusticiable,[22] a judgment that endures to this day. Just as importantly, *Luther v. Borden* recognized the classical political question doctrine, which treats as nonjusticiable matters committed by the Constitution to other authorities' final decision making.[23] That understanding of the political question doctrine endured until the Court, in an opinion by Justice Brennan, expanded it in *Baker v. Carr*.[24] In that case, the Warren Court "clarified" the political question doctrine to include several prudential criteria for determining political questions.[25] *Baker*'s articulation of the political question doctrine has been followed by courts ever since. Thus *Baker v. Carr* is a super precedent because it both set forth an enduring test for determining nonjusticiable political questions and recognized the justiciability of constitutional challenges to gerrymandering. As the noted editors of a prominent constitutional law casebook observe:

> Powerfully supporting this reading of *Baker* are the dozens
> of post-1962 voting and school desegregation cases, where
> the Court has affirmed or required federal court civil rights

injunctions in the face of strong popular and official opposition. Even more dramatic have been the orders entered in other institutional reform litigation, especially in the many lawsuits seeking structural reform of state prison systems.[26]

If all that were not enough, *Baker* and its progeny provided the foundation for the Supreme Court's review of the dispute over the Florida recount in the 2000 presidential election. It was practically impossible to claim the dispute in *Bush v. Gore*[27] posed a nonjusticiable political question, given the many other decisions, beginning with *Baker*, allowing judicial review of electoral disputes.

3. Foundational Decisions

This brings us to the most potentially controversial super precedents. They are Supreme Court decisions on questions of constitutional law that have (1) endured over time; (2) been repeatedly cited with approval by public authorities; (3) shaped the development of doctrine in one or more areas of constitutional law; (4) enjoyed, in one form or another, widespread social acquiescence; and (5) been widely recognized by the courts as firmly settled and not requiring the expenditure of scarce judicial resources to revisit. Super precedents in this category satisfy all five conditions. After examining several precedents that probably qualify as super precedents, I explain why some well-known decisions, such as *Roe*, are not (yet) super precedents.

3.1 Illustrations of Foundational Doctrine

An early example of a super precedent establishing foundational doctrine is *Knox v. Lee* (or, the *Legal Tender Cases*).[28] Though not widely known outside constitutional law circles, it is familiar to the American people because they live with it, and rely on it, every day. The decision upholding the constitutionality of paper money[29] is a super precedent. There has been extraordinary social, political, and economic reliance on the decision in the public and private sectors. The pervasive and deep-seated social, political, and economic investment of our society and of the legal system in the constitutionality of paper money makes it a permanent fixture in American constitutional law. Overruling the decision would produce a level of instability beyond anything the Court or other institutions could possibly imagine.

Bill Eskridge and John Ferejohn's provocative work on super-statutes suggests some other examples of super precedent.[30] They suggest that the Civil Rights Act of 1964[31] and the Sherman Antitrust Act of 1890[32] are examples of "super-statutes."[33] Each statute has long been widely accepted into the public consciousness, and each provides the framework and foundation for other legislation.[34] One does not have to agree with Eskridge and Ferejohn, that these statutes have quasi-constitutional status,[35] in order to appreciate that the constitutional decisions supporting these grand pieces of legislation qualify as super precedents. These decisions (1) established fundamental institutional frameworks or principles in constitutional law; (2) have been consistently supported by national political leaders for decades; (3) provide support for additional case law and legislation; and (4) enjoy widespread public support or societal acquiescence. Consequently they are deeply embedded in our legal system.[36] The fact that the public may be generally unaware of these decisions does not matter. What is important is that the precedents supporting these laws, which are widely known and accepted, are as deeply embedded into law and culture as the legislation they upheld. Each time presidents renew these laws, expand them, sign others like them into law, praise them, and use them as models for other laws, they become more deeply embedded into our law and culture. Political institutions, social movements, economic forces, and the American people have heavily invested in the legislation upheld in these decisions. Nothing short of a constitutional revolution could undo these precedents.

Brown v. Board of Education[37] is a case in point. Initially the Warren Court's unanimous decision to strike down state-mandated segregation in public schools provoked considerable backlash, particularly in the South.[38] As Michael Klarman and others have shown, the dismantling of state-mandated segregation in public schools (and other public facilities) became more extensive (and settled) after national political leaders fell behind *Brown*, particularly through politically and socially significant legislation such as the 1964 Civil Rights Act and the 1965 Voting Rights Act.[39]

Brown may not have achieved "super" status, though, without the Court's systematically striking down state-mandated segregation in all public facilities, the Court's attribution of foundational status to it, and the widespread approbation it has received from all public authorities for decades. Its accepted status is evident, for example, from the fact that it has become pro forma for Supreme Court nominees to declare their allegiance to it. Robert Bork's nomination to the Court foundered in part because of his candid criticism of *Brown*.[40] While Clarence Thomas rebuked the Court to some extent for its decision in *Brown*, he never suggested in his confirmation hearings any agenda to undo it. Nor did Justice Thomas suggest he would question the landmark legislation that *Brown* and its progeny had spawned,[41] including the 1964 Civil Rights Act and the 1965 Voting Rights Act. Had he called these laws into question, the razor-thin majority he enjoyed might have come undone. Subsequent nominees, including Chief Justice John Roberts and Justice Samuel Alito, have declared unambiguously their fidelity to *Brown* and to the landmark legislation that embedded it deeply into American culture and constitutional law.[42]

Super precedents are not restricted to decisions popular with political liberals. For instance, the *Civil Rights Cases*,[43] decided in 1883, are a super precedent. There, the Court recognized a basic principle of constitutional law—that the Fourteenth Amendment prohibits only state action[44]—that endures to this day. The Court has reaffirmed this principle so often and in so many subsequent cases, including *United States v. Morrison*,[45] that it could be fairly described as a super precedent recognizing foundational doctrine in constitutional law. The Court has extended the principle set forth in the *Civil Rights Cases* for more than a century, and the principle applies to all Fourteenth Amendment doctrine. The Court has repeatedly fashioned other constitutional doctrine to be consistent with the state-action requirement.

Similarly, *Washington v. Davis*[46]—which requires rational basis review of laws disproportionately disadvantaging racial minorities in the absence of proof the disproportionate burden was intentional—is a super precedent. The Court has steadfastly stood by the principle associated with the decision,[47] so often in fact that it can be said to have imposed some path dependency on equal protection law.

Yet another super precedent is the Steel Seizure Case, *Youngstown Sheet and Tube Co. v. Sawyer*.[48] Chief Justice Roberts almost said as much in his confirmation hearings,[49] and Justice Alito spoke positively of it in his hearings.[50] Supreme Court Justices have paid tribute for decades to the concurring opinion of Justice Robert Jackson in *Youngstown*. Members of Congress similarly cite *Youngstown* with approval,[51] and they routinely declare fealty to Justice Jackson's framework for analyzing separation of powers conflicts. Similarly presidents have pledged fidelity to *Youngstown*, frequently citing Jackson's concurrence as authority. Jackson's concurrence is an enduring, popular heuristic for lawmakers and judges in analyzing separation of powers questions.

3.2 Distinguishing Super Precedents and Infamous Precedents

There is no simple test for identifying super precedents. Some cases are known because of the controversy they generated—*Lochner v. New York*[52] and *Dred Scott v. Sandford*[53] come to mind—but they are not super precedents, while other, less familiar decisions have become super precedents. Notoriety is not a necessary condition for something to be a super precedent.

A major factor in determining whether something is a super precedent—or what kind of super precedent it has become—is its network effects. While super precedents enjoy and are the product of extensive, supportive, reinforcing citations over time, the meaning and value which they come to have are often different than what the Court which created it may have intended. Consider, for instance, whether *Miranda v. Arizona*[54] is a super precedent. It has long had critics, but many factors—the Court's reaffirmation of the decision in *Dickerson v. United States*,[55] its persistent backing and long-standing support from law enforcement authorities (for decades) and from political leaders around the country, and the public's recognition and awareness of *Miranda*—have all given *Miranda* iconic status in our culture and law. Yet, the Court has recognized many exceptions severely weakening *Miranda*.[56] Persistent citations to *Miranda* over the years have clarified its meaning and value, but as having less force than it first had. *Miranda* is a super precedent, but with less force than it first had.[57]

Wickard v. Filburn[58] is another decision that is well established and frequently cited, albeit not always enthusiastically or without reservation. Though many conservative constitutional scholars harshly criticize the Court's upholding the constitutionality of a federal subsidy that prohibited wheat farmers from consuming wheat which they grew, *Wickard* endures. *Wickard* is one of several decisions establishing the New Deal's constitutional foundations.[59] Unanimously decided, it was reaffirmed by the Court in *United States v. Lopez*.[60] Indeed, Chief Justice Rehnquist went out of his way to reconcile *Lopez* with *Wickard* and to emphasize that the Court in *Lopez* was not reconsidering, much less over-turning, any prior commerce clause decisions.[61] The Court's more recent decision in *Gonzales v. Raich*[62] further reinforced *Wickard*. Nevertheless, Justice Thomas continues to express disagreement with *Wickard*,[63] and Chief Justice Roberts pointedly refused in his confirmation hearings to acknowledge *Wickard* as firmly settled. Instead, he suggested the question in *Wickard* could come back before the Court.[64] It thus appears that we have passed the point at which the Court would reconsider *Wickard* and that its meaning and value in commerce clause jurisprudence have increased to the point (through persistently positive and reinforcing cita-tions) that they are embedded in our culture and law even though some justices apparently feel the need to clarify its reach. That it has a reach is firmly settled, but how far that reach may extend remains unsettled for at least some justices.

Yet another decision that has clearly become a super precedent is *Griswold v. Connecticut*.[65] *Griswold* has become firmly embedded in our law and culture through repeated and widespread expressions of approval by the Court and other public authorities. On the Court, persistent, exten-sive, and supportive citations for decades have increased its meaning and value to the point of no return. Moreover, Supreme Court nominees over the past two decades have realized that accepting *Griswold* is a precondi-tion for confirmation. It was no accident that Justices David Souter and Samuel Alito picked Justice John Marshall Harlan II as one of the justices whom they admired most, because his eloquent concurrence in *Griswold* indicated that it had no bearing on other possible claims pertaining to abortion, euthanasia, and homosexual sodomy.[66] Among the reasons Robert Bork's nomination to the Supreme Court failed was his candid declaration that *Griswold* was wrongly decided, reinforcing the impres-sion he may have lacked a sufficient regard for precedent generally.[67] While Justice Scalia said nothing revealing his attitudes about particular prec-edents, including *Griswold*,[68] Chief Justice Roberts acknowledged in his confirmation hearings more than 80 years' worth of decisions supporting a marital right of privacy.[69] *Griswold* is firmly settled, even if, like *Wickard*, its precise reach may receive some adjustment in the future.

Loving v. Virginia is even more clearly a super precedent. Its network effects have firmly secured it as a fixture in American constitutional law, standing irrevocably for the Constitution's prohibition of any laws for-bidding, or restricting, interracial marriage (between men and women).

The Court has steadfastly adhered to the principle set forth in *Loving*, and there is no doubt that the fundamental right of women and men to marry is deeply and irrevocably embedded into our culture and law. The only remaining issue with respect to *Loving* is not whether the right of men and women to marry is fundamental (and thus could not be withdrawn by the states or the federal government), but rather whether the right recognized in *Loving* should be extended to same-sex marriage. The question, in other words, is whether *Loving* may be extended, not whether it may be retracted. However that question gets answered will not diminish *Loving*.

Justices and national leaders who support *Roe v. Wade*[70] are eager to give *Roe* "super precedent" status. Its reaffirmation nearly 30 times, coupled with an apparent majority of Americans' support for its construction in *Casey*, illustrates the extent of its entrenchment in our culture and law. Nevertheless, three presidents over the past decade openly condemned *Roe*, and a Senate majority in 2006 seemed opposed to *Roe*. The persistent political outcry against *Roe*, though not consistently from a majority of Americans or their leaders, precludes it from having the enduring, unambiguous support of all three branches and deep-seated entrenchment required for super precedents.

4. The Implications of Super Precedent for Supreme Court Practice and Design

In this section I consider the utility of introducing the notion of super precedent into constitutional analysis. First, I briefly address what I perceive as the major criticisms of super precedent as a theoretical construct. Second, I examine the significance of super precedent as crucial to constitutional practice.

4.1 Responses to Four Criticisms

Here I respond to four criticisms of super precedents (arguably applicable as well to the foregoing analysis of precedent in the preceding chapters). The first criticism is that the notion of super precedent may preclude reconsidering important questions of constitutional law.[71] The concern is that declaring something as super precedent makes it off limits for criticism or correction. For many scholars, the single most important factor for the Court is to get things right, for its authority depends on getting things right.[72]

An important premise of this criticism is that justices have not been sufficiently committed to strictly adhering to, and following, a preferred approach to constitutional interpretation, particularly original meaning. For many legal scholars, the problem with the modern Court is that it has not been sufficiently constrained in interpreting the Constitution. Their complaint is that the justices have abused their discretion by not rigidly adhering to a proper source of constitutional meaning—namely, the text or original meaning. For such scholars, an obvious solution is appointing justices with the right kind of ideological commitments. Their hope is that, if the Court were dominated by justices committed, say, to original meaning, then it would likely produce more decisions grounded in original meaning. The more the Court builds on and follows those decisions the more entrenched they become.

There are, however, two problems with this criticism. The first is that critics of super precedent need super precedent as much as everyone else, unless they are prepared to defend the relitigation of every single constitutional question. Justices appreciate their limited resources and do not wish to be inundated by the need to reconsider every constitutional question the Court has previously decided. Indeed, Justice Scalia, whom many people (wrongly) assume is eager for the Court to reopen a number of settled questions of constitutional law, declared that "if a constitutional line of authority is wrong, [Justice Thomas] would say, 'Let's get it right.' I wouldn't do that." I am not sure Justice Scalia is even right about Justice Thomas, who does not, at least statistically, urge more than three overrulings per term, thus indicating his willingness to leave a fairly broad spectrum of constitutional decisions intact. In fact, all the current justices, as well as the vast majority in American history, place a premium not just on correctly deciding questions, but on the institutional value of stability—avoiding needless chaos, uncertainty, and instability—in constitutional law. This is a pragmatic concern, to be sure, but no less legitimate for that reason, for there is a long-standing tradition and social and political expectations of (and support for) pragmatism as a conventional mode of constitutional argumentation. Nonjudicial and judicial precedents both support recourse to pragmatic considerations in at least some, if not a lot of, constitutional adjudication.

The second problem is the limited path dependency of precedent. As I argued in chapter 3, several factors—such as the structure of constitutional adjudication, the basic indeterminacy of the law, and the dynamic of collegial decision making—converge to produce unpredictable, inconsistent decisions. A uniform commitment to original meaning will not produce consistent decisions. Nor is it likely to produce decisions agreeable to politicians or scholars keen on the Court's strict adherence to original meaning because justices are likely to define it at different levels of generality and to make other mistakes, such as respecting precedent too much or caring too much about the social and political consequences of their decisions.

Moreover, judicial closure on some constitutional questions should not be equated with a precedent's constraining force. Merely designating some decisions as super precedents does not preclude scholars from questioning those decisions (as some scholars still do, for instance, with respect to the Court's incorporation doctrine) or developing a sustained attack on seemingly settled constitutional doctrine. A super precedent is the culmination of sustained support from political leaders and the Court over time. The enduring support of political institutions and the public is the answer to the concerns that the Court may not be free to reconsider some things.

A second criticism of super precedent is the apparent impossibility of determining the requisite length of time that judicial precedents must endure before they may become super precedents. For some people, the problem with super precedents is that time is not the only, or even a reliable, measure of their unique status.

I concede the impossibility of determining a requisite length of time for precedents to endure before they may be called super precedents. It is of course impossible to know what will happen many years or centuries from now. No one can prove the Court will refrain from reconsidering for all time some decisions which now appear firmly settled. The reluctance to foreclose some maneuvering room, even for the most settled precedents, may be the strongest argument against super precedents.

Nevertheless, strictly focusing on the longevity of a precedent misses the point. Long-standing precedents, especially in important cases, are rarely overturned in a single bound. Cases that can credibly be characterized as super precedents are distinctive in part because they are so deeply engrained in our culture and law that they cannot be reconsidered—much less overturned—without considerable excavation. In practice, this means that if and when the time comes to reconsider a super precedent, it would only occur after persistent warnings and attacks (on and off the Court). *Plessy v. Ferguson*,[73] for example, was not left untouched in a shrine until the Court began to dismantle it in *Brown*. To the contrary, it was attacked systematically in a series of lawsuits brought by the NAACP Inc. Fund, culminating in *Brown*.[74] Similarly the so-called right to contract recognized in *Lochner v. New York*[75] was not only overruled *sub silentio*[76] just a few years after it was decided, but the right to contract it recognized continued thereafter to be the target of persistent litigation (and political attacks) for decades.[77] Important cases do not disappear in the absence of concerted, sustained efforts to overrule them. Persistent challenges to precedents are merely one clear indication of the absence of its enduring support among the leaders of national political institutions.

The third criticism of super precedents is that the concept is hard to square with the fact that they may not have been fully implemented. The failure to implement a decision fully may reflect that it is not so deeply engrained as to merit special status in constitutional law or even among precedents.

It is important, however, to recall two things. The first is that the fact that a precedent may have become a super precedent in a different form than it had at some earlier point in time is not evidence it has failed to become a super precedent; it is evidence that what has become a super precedent; has a different form, meaning, or value than the earlier decision had. The repetitive citations to an earlier decision help to secure and clarify its meaning and value, but the meaning and value which it ultimately may have may differ from what it may have had at some earlier point in time. The transformation of a precedent is not evidence that it lacks the qualities of a super precedent; it merely clarifies what has become super precedent. Moreover, super precedents, like other precedents, may perform multiple purposes. A decision may become a super precedent for a particular purpose, not for every conceivable purpose.

The final criticism of super precedents is that it is unclear why judicial nominees' attitudes toward them should matter. If a precedent is really a super precedent, then what particular nominees think of it is irrelevant, because it is likely that political forces would mobilize to protect the values embodied in the decision, apart from what the Court does. The precedent is protected where it counts—society and national political forces will not turn their backs on the values it embodies.

This criticism ultimately misses the point. First, if a case is really a super precedent and society is willing to do whatever is necessary to protect the values it embodies, then it follows that the Senate would be one place in which social preferences could protect the values embodied in it. Otherwise the case might not really be a super precedent. If, for instance, a nominee expresses his belief that some precedent, say *Roe*, should be overruled, then the Senate's approval of that nominee is evidence that *Roe* is not a genuine super precedent. Second, the problem with a nominee who has declared a preference to overrule a case commonly regarded as a super precedent may be that his declaration shows his views may be outside the mainstream of constitutional law. His nomination might provoke justifiable opposition on the ground that his expressed preference to overrule a super precedent may reflect the extent to which he will wreak havoc in less well-settled areas of constitutional law. His unwillingness to accept a super precedent might reflect a fundamental disregard for the institutional values associated with fidelity to precedent. If a nominee does not respect super precedent, what precedents, if any, will he respect? If overruling a precedent is a shock to the legal system, a nominee disposed to overruling a super precedent may not be averse to shocking the legal system a good deal. A nominee's apparent indifference to the shocks to which he is willing to subject the legal system is a problem less because of the threat posed to a particular super precedent than because it demonstrates the nominee's lack of a minimally socially acceptable degree of respect for precedent generally. The nominee appears, in other words, to lack the requisite judicial temperament. Thus the confirmation process may be a useful place to look to illuminate super precedents further.

4.2 The Implications of Super Precedent for Constitutional Theory and Practice

Without super precedents, constitutional practice would be chaotic and filled with uncertainty. Yet, as Daniel Farber and Suzanna Sherry suggest, a fundamental tension exists between respecting precedent and rigid adherence to a judicial philosophy of original meaning.[78] In the 1980s and early 1990s, Supreme Court and other judicial nominees got into trouble because of their professed adherence to original meaning in spite of the fact that considerable constitutional doctrine is fundamentally irreconcilable with original meaning.[79] Principled originalists must acknowledge that any decision inconsistent with original meaning is wrongly decided. Yet, if they were to vote their principles, their preferred approach would produce instability, chaos, and havoc in constitutional law.

Any officials—even originalists—charged with constitutional authority cannot ignore the likelihood that the existence of super precedents reflects the intricate network effects of precedents in such various forms as non-judicial norms, values, and decisions. Each time other institutions invest in, and rely upon, judicial decisions, these decisions become more deeply ingrained in our legal system and culture. The more ingrained a particular decision, the more difficult it is to undo. As layers become deeply embedded and encrusted, the more difficult they are to excavate.[80] The more courts and other institutions approvingly cite precedents, the more their value increases and the clearer and more stable their meanings become. Of course, why some, rather than other, judicial decisions become deeply ingrained remains a difficult question. Because super precedents may be the product of network effects, it is useful to closely examine the network within which justices operate.

To begin with, the construction of the Supreme Court is the consequence of a series of choices by national political leaders. The Court is what others, including our national political leaders, make it. The Court has been shaped by various nonjudicial activities, some of which are recognizable as precedents. These activities—usually through presidential and congressional interaction—include choices made about the Court's size, jurisdiction, composition, and financial support. These nonjudicial decisions are an important link between what the justices decide and the culture in which they operate.

Thus it is interesting to note some patterns in recent Supreme Court nominations. For example, three successive Republican appointees as chief justice—Warren Burger, William Rehnquist, and John Roberts—were each appointed to steer the Court away from what it had become under Chief Justice Earl Warren. Each had served at one time as a political appointee in the Justice Department, and 6 of the last 8 Republican nominees to the Court had significant experience as executive officials. It is likely, as I have suggested, that the past three Republican presidents and their advisers may have believed that the nominees' executive experience might make them more sympathetic to executive branch claims (and increased the likelihood their ideological preferences were well known by people close to the judicial selection process.) Yet, much of the Warren Court's jurisprudence endures, in spite of the fact that in the 36 years since the Warren Court, Republican presidents have appointed 13 of 15 justices. It is possible that political circumstances have hindered the achievement of the stated goals of the last three Republican presidents to weaken *Roe* and other decisions they dislike. Political circumstances may have thus made some changes on the Court impossible.

Consider further that when some conservative commentators cite the three or four decisions they would most like to see overruled, they usually cite such cases as *Roe v. Wade, Lemon v. Kurtzman*,[81] and *Garcia v. San Antonio Metropolitan Transit Authority*.[82] These are Burger, not Warren, Court decisions; these are decisions produced by a Court dominated by Republican appointees, not liberals. Moreover, the decisions that often provoke exasperation with the Court these days are cases such as *Lawrence v. Texas*[83] and *Roper v. Simmons*.[84] As the Warren Court recedes into history, its precedents become harder, not easier, to excavate. They become more calcified. As they become more calcified, they become more entrenched, and as they become more entrenched, they come closer to becoming super precedents—a frightening prospect, to say the least, for politicians, scholars, or others convinced of the Court's liberal slide over the past two decades. It is more frightening that their concerns might not be enough to stop many of these cases from becoming more entrenched unless justices who share these views are prepared to do more than merely define the outer limits of the constitutional jurisprudence with which they disagree.

The nominations of John Roberts, Harriet Miers,[85] and Samuel Alito shed further light on these circumstances. Their respective confirmation proceedings reflected the Senate's functioning as a gatekeeper to weaken Supreme Court decisions with which it disagrees and strengthen those with which a critical mass of senators agree.[86] The respective journeys of these nominees through the confirmation process were different from those followed by the embattled judicial nominees of the 1980s and early 1990s. Though Republicans controlled the Senate in 2005–2006, the nominees and their supporters in the Senate deliberately avoided discussions of—or expressions of support for—particular judicial ideologies.

John Roberts avoided controversy by rejecting fidelity to any particular theory of constitutional interpretation. Instead, he espoused a philosophy of "judicial modesty." He likened judging to umpiring, and he referred to himself as a proponent of "bottom-up" judging, which included a healthy degree of respect for stare decisis.[87] Roberts' descriptions of himself were politically astute because he invented new concepts with which to discuss judicial philosophy that had the multiple advantages of not appearing to be inconsistent with substantial amounts of constitutional law, appealing to those evaluating him, and not backing him into a corner on the cases likely to come before him.

Yet, Roberts, Miers, and Alito each owed their respective nominations to a president who had vowed not to make the mistakes of his Republican predecessors—namely President Reagan and his father—in appointing justices who had failed to fulfill their agenda of overturning liberal decisions such as *Roe v. Wade*. President George W. Bush seemed determined to go further when he promised to nominate "strict constructionists" and implied that his nominees would be in the mold of Justice Antonin Scalia or Justice Clarence Thomas, both of whom had openly expressed their desire to overrule many precedents long criticized by conservative scholars and activists. But super precedent posed a problem for President Bush, and particularly his nominees. President Bush tellingly avoided nominees who had openly scorned not only arguably settled cases like *Roe* and *Griswold*, but also more deeply entrenched decisions supporting the constitutionality of the New Deal, the Great Society, and landmark environmental legislation. Someone who seems bent on producing havoc or chaos in constitutional law is a hard sell to the Senate and the American people.

Against this backdrop, Chief Justice Roberts set an important precedent for subsequent nominees to follow. He espoused respect for precedent throughout his hearings. He may have been a firebrand when he worked in the Office of the Attorney General, the White House, and the Office of the Solicitor General, but he was no firebrand when he appeared before the Senate Judiciary Committee. He no doubt understood that President Bush wanted him to move the Court further to the right than Chief Justice Rehnquist had. Yet, Roberts the nominee expressly accepted some judicial decisions inconsistent with that political agenda, including those recognizing a marital right of privacy,[88] the framework for analyzing separation of powers conflicts,[89] the constitutionality of the 1965 Voting Rights Act,[90] and heightened scrutiny for gender classifications.[91] Moreover, Roberts acknowledged *Roe* as "settled law," and cautioned against excessive overrulings.[92] He made abundantly clear that his philosophy of judicial modesty is grounded, at least in part, in respect for others' decisions, including those of his predecessors on the Court, members of Congress, and presidents.

Roberts acknowledged that predictability, stability, consistency, and reliance are values to be taken into account in constitutional adjudication, and it would seem to follow that these values ought to count in most cases.[93] It follows that there may be at least some instances in which the values promoted by fidelity to precedent are compelling. A Court that overrules too many precedents not only sets a bad example—a bad precedent—because it provides no incentive to respect the work of its predecessors, but also invites other branches and lower courts to view its decisions with the same lack of respect with which it views previous decisions. A healthy respect for precedent means learning to live with decisions with which one disagrees.

When Roberts went further to describe himself as a "bottom-up" kind of judge,[94] he was signaling a preference to decide cases incrementally and to infer principles from the records of the cases below. A bottom-up judge is willing to learn from experience, which means that much of our experience has to be left intact.

Harriet Miers, in her brief period as a Supreme Court nominee, took pains to avoid appearing as if she favored any radical thinking, or results, in constitutional law. The fact that she had little or no public record of radical opinions may have made her an attractive nominee to the president. She might have been a nominee who was committed to ruling as he would prefer, and she lacked a paper trail that could become a target in confirmation hearings. It was the president's supporters, not the Democrats, who questioned her credentials most vigorously, and their most vocal concern was whether she had the right kind of ideological commitments and whether she would become the "obsequious instrument of [the president's] pleasure," as Alexander Hamilton once described the kind of nominee the Senate ought to reject.[95] She tried to answer the concerns of her critics with assurances that she believed judges needed to be "humble," language that had undoubtedly been designed to echo Chief Justice Roberts. When Republican senators, among others, demanded to see some of her work as chief White House counsel to get a better idea of her ideological commitments and professional competence, the president refused on the basis of executive privilege. In the end, she withdrew her nomination to avoid jeopardizing the confidentiality of her work as chief White House counsel.[96]

Enter Samuel Alito. As a federal appellate judge for 15 years, he had made more than a few decisions with which Democratic senators could take issue.[97] He explained those decisions largely rested on the basis of Supreme Court precedent. He explained he had merely been helping his client—the Justice Department—when as a Reagan Justice Department official he wrote several memoranda that criticized Court decisions on executive power, abortion, and apportionment.[98] He stressed further that his personal views would play no role in his work as a Supreme Court justice.[99] He even expressed almost as much respect for stare decisis as had Chief Justice Roberts in his confirmation hearings.[100] While, prior to his hearings, Justice Alito had expressed his opinion that the Court had probably been mistaken in not allowing more religion into public life,[101] no one pressed him on that subject in his hearings. He hastened to reassure senators of his acceptance of the right to privacy recognized in *Griswold*,[102] and it was understandable he identified Justice John Marshall Harlan II as among the justices he most admired, since he was the first justice since Harlan to have attended Princeton. Alito's supporters repeatedly praised his temperament and characterized him as a humble person—a man with a "great heart"—likely to appreciate and embody the importance of humility and modesty in judging.[103] Republican senators defending Alito discounted any possibility that his appointment could destabilize the Court or constitutional doctrine.

In retrospect, the Roberts and Alito hearings may be most important for the nonjudicial precedents they established. First, Roberts and Alito followed the pattern of successful Supreme Court nominees with prior judicial experience. Had Miers made it to the Court, she would have been the first person without judicial experience to have been appointed to the Court since William Rehnquist in 1971.

Second, for many Republican senators, the successful confirmations of Roberts, and particularly Alito, buried the Bork precedent—their confirmations arguably demonstrated that two justices with conservative judicial philosophies (and histories of opposing liberal precedents) could be approved.

Third, the Roberts and Alito hearings may have extended the Judiciary Committee's practice of rigorously questioning Supreme Court nominees about their records and their philosophies. Try as the nominees did to avoid discussing their philosophies in any meaningful detail, most senators asked questions about their judicial philosophies (and prior statements about particular decisions) either in the hearings or in closed-door meetings with the nominees before the hearings. The Roberts and Alito hearings established two additional precedents supporting the long-standing practice of senators' taking judicial philosophy into account in assessing Supreme Court nominations. Such questioning dates back to at least the 1950s, while senators have been taking nominees' politics and likely judicial philosophies into account since Washington was president.

Fourth, neither the chief justice nor Justice Alito presented himself as a threat to settled doctrine. The chief justice construed his confirmation as an affirmation of the distinction between judging and politics, though almost all of the discussion about his judicial philosophy was obscured by platitudes and characterizations of judging in elusive, non-self-defining terms. While Justice Alito refrained from endorsing the notion of super precedents, the chief justice did not dispute (at least expressly) that some precedents may be so politically, socially, and legally important as to be effectively immune to reconsideration. Even Justice Alito was careful to acknowledge that he supported the reapportionment decisions he once derided, and both Chief Justice Roberts and Justice Alito finished their first two years on the Court without voting to overrule precedent.

Last, but not least, super precedents pose serious challenges to aspiring Supreme Court nominees, the justices, other leaders, and constitutional theorists. Super precedents are a fact of constitutional life. Successful Supreme Court nominees tend not to question these precedents or risk putting their nominations in jeopardy. Posing a threat to settled doctrine places nominees outside the mainstream of American jurisprudence and invites opposition and condemnation, not support, from national leaders and their colleagues. Successful nominees are pragmatic and moderate, in part because our political system rewards pragmatism and moderation. They sound like Chief Justice Roberts and Justice Alito, who eschewed grand theories. The Court, too, tends to reward pragmatism and moderation. The justices tend therefore to employ conventional modalities of argumentation. They are invested in, not hostile to, the constitutional status quo. The Court is not in the business of fashioning or endorsing particular theories of interpretation. The Court does not settle disputes about theory; it decides real cases or controversies. Extremists rarely command votes, or steer the Court, in part because extreme positions on precedent, particularly excessive hostility to precedent, are prone to undercut, not encourage, respect on and off the Court.

Constitutional theorists, too, cannot ignore how cases are actually adjudicated. They must adjust their descriptive theories of the Court to account for super precedents. They cannot ignore the impediments—on and off the Court—to implementing particular approaches to deciding cases that are incompatible with super precedents. Stability, uniformity, predictability, and consistency have enormous normative appeal on and off the Court. In practice, this means that any theory that requires justices to deviate from the Court's traditions (including requiring justices to prioritize sources in any particular manner or to espouse grand theories) will be difficult, if not impossible, to implement on the Court, not to mention the difficulties their decisions may confront off the Court. Justices consider their independence in these matters to be inviolable, and valuing judicial independence may be one of our most important nonjudicial precedents which our national political leaders consistently recognize (and pay homage to). Thus, as an integral part of the Court and of our constitutional culture, super precedents are bound to endure.

Conclusion

The Future of Precedent

In the first two terms of the Roberts Court, all the usual dynamics relating to precedent were apparent. First, the Roberts Court exhibited respect for precedent generally: Precedent was, by far, the most common basis for its decisions. Even when the Court deviated from or weakened some precedents, it did so on the basis of precedent. Moreover, the Roberts Court did not overrule a single constitutional case in either of its first two terms. Hence, it is the first Court in more than four decades not to overrule at least one constitutional precedent in a term. In addition, neither of the Court's two newest justices—Chief Justice Roberts and Justice Alito—voted to overrule, or joined any opinion urging the overruling of, a constitutional precedent. Chief Justice Roberts went further to expressly reaffirm the Court's embattled decision on federal campaign finance law, *Buckley v. Valeo*.

Second, the Roberts Court demonstrated the limited path dependency of precedent. Indeed, a common criticism of the Roberts Court is that, in three cases decided in 2007, it ruled exactly the opposite from what the Court had previously ruled in practically identical cases. In *Federal Election Commission v. Wisconsin Right to Life*,[1] the five-member majority of the Roberts Court held unconstitutional a provision of the Bipartisan Campaign Reform Act that limited expenditures by corporations, even though the Court had upheld the same provision four years earlier.[2] Similarly, in *Gonzales v. Carhart*,[3] the same five-member majority upheld the constitutionality of a federal partial-birth abortion law, even though the Court had struck down a nearly identical state partial-birth abortion law in 2000.[4] Moreover, in *Hein v. Freedom from Religion Foundation*,[5] the same five-member majority held that individual taxpayers had no standing to assert an Establishment Clause challenge to President George W. Bush's faith-based initiatives, even though the Court, in *Flast v. Cohen*,[6] had recognized nearly four decades earlier that taxpayers had standing to assert an Establishment Clause challenge to the constitutionality of congressional expenditures.

The Court's failure to strictly follow liberal precedents in these three cases reflects the consequences of weak or nonexistent network effects.

The meaning of a precedent depends more on what subsequent justices think (and say) it means than on what the justices were thinking (and saying) when they created it. Consequently, if a precedent has never been cited or followed by the Court, it has no network effects, and generates no meaningful power to constrain. Indeed, there were no network effects for *Gonzales v. Carhart* and *FEC v. Wisconsin Right to Life* to follow: They were the Court's first opportunities for a majority to determine the meaning and significance of *Stenberg* and *McConnell*, respectively. The absence of network effects made it easy for the Court to deviate from the latter precedents.

Even the constraining force of a seminal case depends on its network effects. The more often it is cited for the same proposition, the more fixed its meaning or significance in constitutional law becomes; but the less often it is cited for some proposition, the less clearly it stands for that proposition. Such was the case in *Parents Involved in Community Schools v. Seattle School District*.[7] There, the Court considered the constitutionality of Seattle's and Louisville's voluntary *Brown v. Board of Education* desegregation plans which employed race as a factor in school assignments. The Court struck down both plans, and found that neither was compelled by Brown and its progeny, including *Grutter v. Bollinger*[8] which barely upheld the constitutionality of the State's employing race as a factor in graduate and professional school admissions. While *Grutter* had virtually no meaningful network effects, *Brown* and its progeny have been cited, at least since the mid-1990s, to support subjecting any race-based classification to strict scrutiny. Thus, Chief Justice Roberts in *Parents Involved* claimed this string of citations when he subjected Seattle's and Louisville's voluntary desegregation plans to strict scrutiny. Applying strict scrutiny in *Parents Involved* was not unusual; indeed, *Grutter* followed precedent in employing strict scrutiny.[9]

Of course, things may change. They always do. But not everything is likely to change, particularly everything that relates to precedent. Consequently we can expect some patterns in the Court's handling of precedent to persist. First, precedent will continue to function as a popular mode of constitutional argument or justification. Precedent is endemic to our legal system and our culture. For more than two centuries, justices and nonjudicial authorities have made precedents, and have been trained (and are expected) to argue in terms of precedent. Precedent is a fundamental, enduring unit in the language of law.[10]

Second, Supreme Court justices—and other public authorities—will continue to adhere to a golden rule of precedent. On the Court, the justices recognize the need to give the same level of respect to the precedents of others as they expect their preferred precedents to deserve. The golden rule does more than just preserve collegiality on the Court (and in other institutional settings). Adherence to the golden rule of precedent is the bridge between the Court's general respect for precedent and the limited path dependency of particular precedents. But the adherence to the golden rule is further premised on justices' appreciation for the institutional values of stability, consistency, and predictability in constitutional adjudication. Justices who are disposed to value—or to balance—these institutional considerations over any personal preferences to do otherwise are likely to maintain—if not expand—their influence both on and off the Court.

The appeal of the golden rule is stronger than one might expect. It may be inferred, for instance, from the statistics in the first chapter showing that Justice Thomas had the highest average number of pleas for overruling per year on the Rehnquist Court and that his average was about two. As a practical matter, this means that Justice Thomas is accepting a large number of precedents with which he probably disagrees. The same is true for all the other justices on the Rehnquist Court.

Off the Court, the golden rule of precedent persists. It is evident in national political leaders' caution in disrupting tradition, respecting the rule of law, and relying heavily on precedent to justify their decisions. Moreover, the golden rule appeals to the American people, who are not likely to follow leaders who express wholesale disdain for the constitutional judgments of their predecessors.

However, the importance (and consequences) of the golden rule should not be overstated. Adhering to the golden rule does not oblige public officials, or justices, to accept any particular precedents—with the obvious exception of super precedents—with which they disagree. Indeed, it hardly obliges public authorities to do much. It does not dictate how public authorities, including the Court, should construe—or apply—specific precedents. Nor does it impose much constraint on their decisions for many reasons, including constitutional design, the indeterminacy of the constitutional text, how constitutional decisions are framed, and cycling.

Third, the Supreme Court selection process will continue to favor justices who express respect for precedent. For one thing, this respect is basic to the cultural ideal of the law and of judging. Moreover, it signals—if not ensures—nominees as falling within the mainstream of American constitutional jurisprudence. The process rewards moderation in tone and outlook, and it tends to discourage or even punish people who are prone to wreak havoc on established traditions and well-settled precedents. The process therefore tends to encourage the appointments of jurists committed to judicial modesty, which I understand as favoring bottom-up judging. Top-down judging brooks no compromise and allows no margin for error. Being a member of a collegial body, such as the Court, requires give and take; it requires compromise, adjustment, and valuing institutional considerations. It encourages deciding cases incrementally and allowing principles to percolate up from lower courts and other institutions. Most justices learn from their experiences and the experiences of others. Most justices learn, in other words, from precedent.[11]

Fourth, judicial and nonjudicial precedents will continue to perform multiple functions, of which constraint is but one. All precedents have the potential to perform multiple functions, including serving as heuristics for legal discourse, modalities of constitutional argumentation, and the means for implementing constitutional values, facilitating public dialogues about the Constitution, clarifying constitutional structure, chronicling constitutional history, forging national identity, and shaping (and being shaped by) culture.

Moreover, it is impossible to understand constitutional law without fully appreciating not only that nonjudicial authorities produce (and maintain) precedents, but also that super precedents are an enduring part of constitutional law. Nonjudicial precedents are much more extensive than judicial ones, but just as enduring. The case for judicial supremacy is undermined not only by their prominence, but particularly by their settlement of numerous constitutional conflicts in the absence of judicial review. Among the more familiar of these are the president's powers to unilaterally remove executive officials, to negotiate treaties, and to veto legislation on policy grounds; the respective understanding of the House and Senate of the scope of their respective authorities in the federal impeachment process; the respective understanding of the House and Senate of their respective authorities to determine rules for their respective proceedings; the persistence of "senatorial courtesy" in the federal appointments process; and the multiple ways in which Congress may authorize presidents to go to war or to extend military campaigns.[12]

Enduring judicial and nonjudicial precedents are, of course, super precedents. While it is always possible that the Court—or other public institutions—may revisit some earlier, very well settled precedents which are supported by extensive, deep-rooted network effects, it is unlikely they will overturn them. It is a basic fact of constitutional law that there are some precedents whose network effects are so well developed (both on and off the Court) and so long-standing that they are practically impossible to dismantle. Among these is the Court's doctrine on stare decisis, which puts a premium on institutional values including the golden rule— a super precedent that is much older than any of our public institutions, but which they will likely maintain as long as they endure.

Fully appreciating constitutional law further requires recognizing the value and utility of bridging legal and social science methodologies. Neither group of scholars has anything to fear from the other. To the contrary, each enriches our understanding of how the Court operates and particularly how precedent functions in constitutional law. The bridge between these disciplines, which I have proposed in this book, requires scholars and other students of constitutional law to study more than just judicial outcomes; it requires appreciating the content and consequences of judicial opinions—why justices write them as they do. Understanding precedent requires appreciating the constitutional significance of the precedents that nonjudicial authorities produce and especially the interdependence between different kinds of precedents.

Understanding precedent requires recognizing that we can break with some particular precedents, but we cannot break away from precedent. Understanding precedent requires scholars to be modest about their own limitations, about how they, like everyone else, are historically, socially, and culturally bound. All of us, including our public authorities, are a part of history and culture. None of us can stand apart from them, and understanding the difference is crucial to the study of precedent. While justices proclaim what they believe—or hope—are timeless expressions of the principles of constitutional law, these expressions can only become timeless if they are enduringly supported by subsequent generations of justices and other public authorities. Nor can these expressions be fully understood apart from the cultural, political, social, legal, and historical contexts in which they are made or subsequently evaluated. No matter how strongly justices may feel that their decisions are both correct and timeless, they have little sway over how subsequent justices and other public authorities will understand those decisions within the contexts in which they are functioning. In fact, they can do little, apart from relying on the power of their reasoning and the golden rule of precedent, to cultivate enduring public support and to immunize the precedents they create from manipulation, modification, or reconstruction by the justices who follow them.

It is for these reasons that the study of precedent—in all of its forms—needs to focus not just on the contexts in which precedent is made but also on the enduring institutions that construct precedents (and their patterns and practices of decision making).[13] For these institutions and their leaders cannot function without precedent. The power of precedents to rigidly constrain these institutions and their leaders may not always be strong, but their power to illuminate is constant and enduring.

Appendix

Appendix Table 1

Case	Date	Case Overruled	Vote	Operative Language	Change in Composition of Court	Clause	Subject Matter	Court
The Propeller Genesee Chief v. Fitzhugh, 53 U.S. 443 (1851)	1851	The Thomas Jefferson, 23 U.S. 428 (1825); The Orleans v. Phoebus, 36 U.S. 175 (1837)	8 to 1	"If we follow [Thomas Jefferson], we follow an erroneous decision," 53 U.S. at 456	All; All	Art III, § 2, cl. 1	martime jurisdiction	Taney
Knox v. Lee, 79 U.S. 457 (1871)	1871	Hepburn v. Griswold, 75 U.S. 603 (1869)	5 to 4	"overrule," 79 U.S. at 553	2 New	Art. I, § 2, cl. 1	impairment of contracts	Chase
Kilbourn v. Thompson, 103 U.S. 168 (1880)	1880	Anderson v. Dunn, 19 U.S. 204 (1821)	7 to 0	"notwithstanding what is said in the case Anderson v. Dunn," 103 U.S. at 199–200	All	Art. I, § 5	power of Congress to punish witness for contempt	Waite
In re Ayers, 123 U.S. 443 (1887)	1887	Osborn v. United States Bank, 22 U.S. 738 (1824)	8 to 0	"decision distinguished" at 123 U.S. at 488; Justice Harlan dissents, 123 U.S. 510	All	Amend. XI	soveign immunity	Waite

Philadelphia and S. Steamship Co. v. Pennsylvania, 122 U.S. 326 (1887)	1887	In re State Tax on Railway Gross Receipts, 82 U.S. 284 (1872)	8 to 0	"the first ground on which the decision in state Tax ... was placed is not tenable," 122 U.S. at 342	5 New	Art. I, § 8, cl. 3 (commerce clause)	commerce clause, state taxation in violation of	Waite
LeLoup v. Port of Mobile, 127 U.S. 640 (1888)	1888	Osborne v. Mobile, 83 U.S. 479 (1872)	9 to 0	"an ordinance [of the type in Osborne] would now be regarded as repugnant to the power conferred upon Congress," 127 U.S. at 647	6 New	Art. I, § 8, cl. 3 (commerce clause)	commerce clause, state taxation in violation of	Waite
Leisy v. Hardin, 135 U.S. 100 (1890)	1890	Peirce v. New Hampshire, 46 U.S. 504 (1847)	6 to 3	"Peirce v. New Hampshire ... must be regarded as having been distinctly overthrown by the numerous cases hereinafter referred to," 135 U.S. at 118	All	Art. I, § 8, cl. 3 (commerce clause)	commerce clause, Interpretation of Congressional silence concerning interstate commerce	Fuller
Garland v. Washington, 232 U.S. 642 (1914)	1914	Crain v. United States, 162 U.S. 625 (1896)	9 to 0	"overruled," 232 U.S. at 647	All	Amend. XIV	due process and criminal procedure	White

(Continued)

Appendix Table 1 (*Continued*)

Case	Date	Case Overruled	Vote	Operative Language	Change in Composition of Court	Clause	Subject Matter	Court
United States v. Nice, 241 U.S. 591 (1916)	1916	Matter of Heff, 197 U.S. 488 (1905)	9 to 0	"overruled," 241 U.S. at 601	6 New	Art. I, § 8, cl. 3 (commerce clause)	commerce clause, commerce with Indian tribes	White
Pennsylvania R.R. v. Towers, 245 U.S. 6 (1917)	1917	Lake Shore Ry. v. Smith, 173 U.S. 684 (1899)	9 to 0	"overruled," 245 U.S. at 17	8 New	Amend. XIV	due process and rate fixing	White
Terral v. Burke Constr. Co., 257 U.S. 529 (1922)	1922	Doyle v. Continental Ins. Co., 94 U.S. 535 (1876); Security Mut. Life Ins. Co. v. Prewitt, 202 U.S. 246 (1906)	9 to 0	"overruled," 257 U.S. at 533	6 New	Art. III	right to resort to federal courts	Taft
Alpha Cement Co. v. Massachusettes, 268 U.S. 203 (1925)	1925	Baltic Mining Co. v. Massachusettes, 231 U.S. 68 (1913)	8 to 1	"definitely disapproved," 268 U.S. at 218	6 New	Art. I, § 8, cl. 3 (commerce clause)	state taxation in violation of commerce clause	Taft
Farmer's Loan and Trust Co. V. Minnesota, 280 U.S 204 (1930)	1930	Blackstone v. Miller, 188 U.S. 189 (1903)	7 to 2	"definitely overruled," 280 U.S. at 209	8 New	Amend. XIV	due process and inheritance tax	Taft

	Year	Prior case	Vote	Quotation	New	Provision	Subject	Chief Justice
East Ohio Gas Co. v. Tax Comm'n, 283 U.S. 465 (1931)	1931	Pennsylvania Gas Co. v. Public Serv. Comm'n, 252 U.S. 23 (1920)	9 to 0	"disapproved to the extent it is in conflict with our decision here," 283 U.S. at 472	5 New	Art. I, § 8, cl. 3 (commerce clause)	commerce clause, state taxation under	Hughes
Chicago & E. Ill. R.R. v. Industrial Comm'n, 284 U.S. 296 (1932)	1932	Erie R.R. v. Collins, 253 U.S. 77 (1920); Erie R.R. v. Szary, 253 U.S. 86 (1920)	9 to 0	"definitely overruled," 284 U.S. at 299	6 New; 6 New	Art. I, § 8, cl. 3 (commerce clause)	commerce clause and FELA	Hughes
Fox Film Corp. v. Doyal, 286 U.S. 123 (1932)	1932	Long v. Rockwood, 277 U.S. 142 (1928)	9 to 0	"definitely overruled," 286 U.S. at 131	3 New	Art. VI, cl. 2	supremacy clause and immunity from state taxation of federal instrumentalities	Hughes
West Coast Hotel Co. v. Parrish, 300 U.S. 379 (1937)	1937	Adkins v. Children's Hosp., 261 U.S. 525 (1923)	5 to 4	"overruled," 300 U.S. at 400	4 New	Amend. XIV	due process and minimum wage law	Hughes
Erie R.R. v. Tompkins, 304 U.S. 64 (1938)	1938	Swift v. Tyson, 41 U.S. 1 (1842)	8 to 0	"In disapproving [the Swift] doctrine," 304 U.S. at 79 to 80.	All	Amend. X	rights reserved to the states	Hughes

(Continued)

Appendix Table 1 (*Continued*)

Case	Date	Case Overruled	Vote	Operative Language	Change in Composition of Court	Clause	Subject Matter	Court
Helvering v. Mountain Producers Corp., 303 U.S. 376 (1938)	1938	Burnet v. Colorado Oil & Gas Co., 285 U.S. 393 (1932); Gillispie v. Oklahoma, 257 U.S. 501 (1922)	5 to 2	"overruled," 303 U.S. at 387	3 New; 7 New	Amend. X	Immunity of state instrumentality from federal tax	Hughes
Graves v. New York ex rel. O'Keefe, 306 U.S. 466 (1939)	1939	Dobbins v. Erie County, 41 U.S. 435 (1842); Collector v. Day, 78 U.S. 113 (1870); New York ex rel. Rogers v. Graves, 299 U.S. 401 (1937); Brush v. Commissioner, 300 U.S. 352 (1937)	7 to 2	"overruled," 306 U.S. at 486	All; All; 3 New; 3 New	Amend. X	immunity of federal and state officers from income taxes	Hughes
O'Malley v. Woodrough, 307 U.S. 277 (1939)	1939	Evans v. Gore, 253 U.S. 245 (1920)	7 to 1	"to the extent that what the Court now says is inconsistent ... [Miles] cannot survive," 307 U.S. at 282–83	8 New; 7 New	Art. III, § 1	diminution of judges' salaries through taxation	Hughes

Case	Year	Overruled Case(s)	Vote	Quotation	Justices	Provision	Subject	Chief Justice
Helvering v. Halock, 309 U.S. 106 (1940)	1940	Becker v. St. Louis Union Trust Co., 296 U.S. 48 (1935), Helvering v. St. Louis Union Trust Co., 296 U.S. 39 (1935)	7 to 2	"We therefore reject as untenable the diversities taken in the St. Louis Trust Cases in applying the Klein doctrine…" 309 U.S. at 122	4 New; 4 New		value of remainder interest is part of decedent's gross estate under the Revenue Act of 1926	Hughes
Madden v. Kentucky, 309 U.S. 83 (1940)	1940	Colgate v. Harvey, 296 U.S. 404 (1935)	7 to 2	"overruled," 309 U.S. at 93	4 New	Amend. XIV	privileges and immunities clause and the right to engage in certain incidents of business	Hughes
Tigner v. Texas, 310 U.S. 141 (1940)	1940	Connolly v. Union Sewer Pipe Co., 184 U.S. 540 (1902)	8 to 1	"Connolly's case … is no longer controlling," 310 U.S. at 147	All	Amend. XIV	equal protection of various industries under criminal laws to deter monopolies	Hughes
Alabama v. King & Boozer, 314 U.S. 1 (1941)	1941	Panhandle Oil Co. v. Knox, 277 U.S. 218 (1928); Graves v. Texas Co, 298 U.S. 393 (1936)	9 to 0	"[S]o far as a different view has prevailed [in Panhandle and Graves], we think it no longer tenable," 314 U.S. at 9	All; 7 New	Art. VI, § 2	supremacy clause, immunity of federal government from state taxation under	Hughes

(Continued)

Appendix Table 1 (*Continued*)

Case	Date	Case Overruled	Vote	Operative Language	Change in Composition of Court	Clause	Subject Matter	Court
California v. Thompson, 313 U.S. 109 (1941)	1941	DiSanto v. Pennsylvania, 273 U.S. 34 (1927)	9 to 0	"overruled," 313 U.S. at 116	7 New	Art. I, § 8, cl. 3 (commerce clause)	commerce clause, Licensing criteria for free agents under	Hughes
Edwards v. California, 314 U.S. 160 (1941)	1941	City of New York v. Miln, 36 U.S. 102 (1837)	6 to 0	"we do not consider ourselves bound," 314 U.S. at 177	All	Art. I, § 8, cl. 3 (commerce clause)	commerce clause, Interstate transport of persons under	Hughes
Olsen v. Nebraska, 313 U.S. 236 (1941)	1941	Ribnik v. McBride, 277 U.S. 350 (1928)	9 to 0	"The drift away from [*Ribnik*] has been so great that it can no longer be deemed a controlling authority," 313 U.S. at 244	7 New	Amend. XIV	due process concerns of business affected with a public interest	Hughes
United States v. Chicago-Milwaukee, St. Paul & Pac. R.R., 312 U.S. 592 (1941)	1941	United States v. Heyward, 250 U.S. 633 (1919); United states v. Lynah, 188 U.S. 445 (1903)	9 to 0	"So far as [*Lynah* and *Heyward*] sanction such a principle, it is in irreconcilable conflict with our later decisions and cannot be considered as expressing the law," 312 U.S. at 598	All; All	Amend. V	authorized takings and just compensation	Hughes

1941	United States v. Darby, 312 U.S. 100 (1941)	9 to 0	"overruled," 312 U.S. at 116 to 117	Art. I, § 8, cl. 3 (commerce clause)	All	commerce clause, Fair Labor Standards within	Hughes
1942	Graves v. Schmidlapp, 315 U.S. 657 (1942)	8 to 1	"overruled," 315 U.S. at 665	Amend. XIV	All	due process	Stone
1942	First Nat'l Bank v. Maine, 316 U.S. 174 (1942)	7 to 2	"overruled," 316 U.S. at 181	Amend. XIV	8 New	due process and death tax	Stone
1942	Williams v. North Carolina, 317 U.S. 287 (1942)	7 to 2	"overruled," 317 U.S. at 304	Art. IV, § 1	All	full faith and credit clause concerning divorce decree	Stone
1943	Jones v. Opelika, 319 U.S. 103 (1943) (per curiam); Murdock v. Pennsylvania, 319 U.S. 105 (1943)	5 to 4	"The judgment in Jones v. Opelika has this day been vacated," 319 U.S. at 117	Amend. I	0 New	freedom of religion, license tax imposed on religious colporteurs	Stone
1943	Oklahoma Tax Comm'n v. U.S., 319 U.S. 598 (1943)	5 to 4	"Childers ... was in effect overruled by the Mountain Producers decision," 319 U.S. at 604	Art. VI, § 2	All	supremacy clause and state estate taxes imposed on federally restricted indian property	Stone

(Continued)

Appendix Table 1 (*Continued*)

Case	Date	Case Overruled	Vote	Operative Language	Change in Composition of Court	Clause	Subject Matter	Court
West Virginia Bd. of Educ. v. Barnette, 319 U.S. 624 (1943)	1943	Minersville Sch. Dist. v. Gobitis, 319 U.S. 642 (1940)	6 to 3	"overruled," 319 U.S. at 1187	2 New	Amend. I, XIV	freedom of expression	Stone
Smith v. Allwright, 321 U.S. 649 (1944)	1944	Grovery v. Townsend, 295 U.S. 45 (1935)	8 to 1	"overruled," 321 U.S. at 666	7 New	Amend. XV	right to vote	Stone
Girouard v. United States, 328 U.S. 61 (1946)	1946	United States v. Schwimmer, 279 U.S. 644 (1929); United States v. Macintosh, 283 U.S. 605 (1931); United States v. Bland, 283 U.S. 636 (1931)	5 to 3	"We conclude that the *Schwimmer*, *Macintosh*, and *Bland* cases do not state the correct rule of law," 328 U.S. at 69	8 New	Amend. I	freedom of religion, Construction of the Naturalization Act in light of freedom of religion guarantee	Stone
Angel v. Bullington, 330 U.S. 183 (1947)	1947	Lupton's Sons Co. v. Automobile Club, 225 U.S. 489 (1912)	6 to 3	"Cases like *Lupton's*... are obsolete insofar as they are based on a view of diversity jurisdiction which came to an end with *Erie*," 330 U.S. at 192	All	Art. III, § 2	diversity jurisdiction	Vinson

Case	Year	Vote	Quotation	Extent	Constitutional provision	Subject	Chief Justice
Lincoln Union v. Northwestern Iron & Metal Co., 335 U.S. 525 (1948); Adair v. United States, 208 U.S. 161 (1908); Coppage v. Kansas, 236 U.S. 1 (1915)	1948	9 to 0	"This Court has steadily rejected the due process philosophy enunciated in the *Adair Coppage* line of cases," 335 U.S. at 536	All; All	Amend. XIV	due process and state legislation prohibiting injurious business practices	Vinson
Sherrer v. Sherrer, 334 U.S. 343 (1948); Andrews v. Andrews, 188 U.S. 14 (1903)	1948	7 to 2	"superseded by subsequent decisions," 334 U.S. at 353	All	Art. IV, § 1	full faith and credit clause	Vinson
Oklahoma Tax Comm'n v. Texas Co., 336 U.S. 342 (1949); Choctaw, Okla. & Gulf R.R. v. Harrison, 235 U.S. 292 (1914); Indian Territory Illuminating Oil Co. v. Oklahoma, 240 U.S. 522 (1916); Howard v. Gipsy Oil Co., 247 U.S. 503 (1917); Large Oil Co. v. Howard, 248 U.S. 549 (1919); Oklahoma v. Barnsdall Refineries, 296 U.S. 521 (1936)	1949	9 to 0	"overruled," 336 U.S. at 365	All; All; All; All; All	Amend. X	non-Indian leases of restricted Indian lands are subject to state production and excise taxes	Vinson

(Continued)

Appendix Table 1 (*Continued*)

Case	Date	Case Overruled	Vote	Operative Language	Change in Composition of Court	Clause	Subject Matter	Court
United States v. Rabinowitz, 339 U.S. 56 (1950)	1950	Trupiano v. United States, 334 U.S. 699 (1948)	5 to 3	"overruled," 339 U.S. at 66	2 New	Amend. IV	search and seizure, reasonableness goes to the the search, not the procurement of a warrant	Vinson
Burstyn v. Wilson, 343 U.S. 495 (1952)	1952	Mutual Film Co. v. Industrial Comm'n, 236 U.S. 230 (1915)	9 to 0	"overruled," 343 U.S. at 502	All	Amend. I	freedoms of speech and press	Vinson
Brown v. Board of Ed., 347 U.S. 483 (1954)	1954	Plessy v. Ferguson, 163 U.S. 537 (1896)	9 to 0	"any language in Plessy v. Ferguson to the contrary to this finding is rejected," 347 U.S. at 494 to 495	All	Amend. XIV	equal protection in public education	Warren
Elkins v. United States, 364 U.S. 206 (1960)	1960	Weeks v. United States, 232 U.S. 383 (1914)	5 to 4	"reason and experience ... point to the rejection of [the Weeks] doctrine," 364 U.S. at 222	All	Amend. IV	search and seizure, admissibility of evidence obtained by state search in federal court	Warren

United States v. Raines, 362 U.S. 17 (1960)	1960	Barney v. City of New York, 193 U.S 430 (1904)	9 to 0	"*Barney* must be regarded as having 'been work away by the erosion of time,' and of contrary authority," 362 U.S. at 26	All	Amend. XV	racial discrimination in voting	Warren
Mapp v. Ohio, 367 U.S. 643 (1961)	1961	Wolf v. Colorado, 338 U.S. 25 (1949)	5 to 4	"[w]e can no longer permit that right [to be secure against invasions of privacy by state officers] to remain an empty promise," 367 U.S. at 660	6 New	Amend. IV	search and seizure, admissibility of evidence obtained in an illegal federal search in state court	Warren
Ferguson v. Skrupa, 372 U.S. 726 (1963)	1963	Adams v. Tanner, 244 U.S. 590 (1917)	8 to 1	"[R]eliance on [*Adams*] is mistaken as would be adherance to [*Adkins* ... overruled by *West Coast Hotel*]," 372 U.S. at 731	All	Amend. XIV	due process and state restrictions on operation of certain businesses.	Warren

(Continued)

Appendix Table 1 (*Continued*)

Case	Date	Case Overruled	Vote	Operative Language	Change in Composition of Court	Clause	Subject Matter	Court
Gideon v. Wainwright, 372 U.S. 335 (1963)	1963	Betts v. Brady, 316 U.S. 455 (1942)	9 to 0	Amici "argue that *Betts* 'was an anachronism when handed down' and that it should now be overruled. We agree," 372 U.S. at 345	7 New	Amend. VI, XIV	applicability of constitutional right to counsel in state court	Warren
Escobedo v. Illinois, 378 U.S. 478 (1964)	1964	Crooker v. California, 357 U.S. 433 (1958); Cicenia v. La Gay, 357 U.S. 504 (1958)	5 to 4	"[T]o the extent that *Cicenia* or *Crooker* may be inconsistent with the principles announced today, they are not to be regarded as controlling," 378 U.S. at 492	3 New; 3 New	Amend. VI, XIV	statements made prior to reading of rights when investigation is focused on one individual are inadmissible	Warren
Jackson v. Denno, 378 U.S. 368 (1964)	1964	Stein v. New York, 346 U.S. 156 (1953)	5 to 4	"overruled," 378 U.S. at 391	6 New	Amend. XIV	due process and determination of voluntariness of a confession	Warren

Case	Year	Vote		All/New	Amend.	Right	Court
Malloy v. Hogan, 378 U.S. 1 (1964)	1964	5 to 4	"Decisions of the Court since *Twinning* and *Adamson* have departed from the contrary view expressed in those cases," 378 U.S. at 6	All; 7 New	Amend. V, XIV	privilege against self-incrimination is applicable to state actions.	Warren
Murphy v. Waterfront Comm'n, 378 U.S. 52 (1964)	1964	7 to 2	Jack v. Kansas, 199 U.S. 372 (1905); United States v. Murdock, 284 U.S. 141 (1931), Feldman v. United States, 322 U.S. 487 (1944); Knapp v. Schweitzer, 357 U.S. 371 (1958); Mills v. Louisiana, 360 U.S. 230 (1959) "The Court today rejected [the rule of the aforementioned cases], and with it, all the earlier cases resting on that rule," 378 U.S. at 77	All; All; 7 New; 2 New	Amend. V, XIV	use of federally compelled evidence to incriminate at state level	Warren
Pointer v. Texas, 380 U.S. 400 (1965)	1965	7 to 2	West v. Louisiana, 194 U.S. 258 (1904) "In the light of *Gideon* … the statements made in West … can no longer be regarded as the law," 380 U.S. at 406	All	Amend. VI, XIV	right to confrontation applicable to state court	Warren

(Continued)

Case	Date	Case Overruled	Vote	Operative Language	Change in Composition of Court	Clause	Subject Matter	Court
Harper v. Virginia Bd. of Elections, 383 U.S. 663 (1966)	1966	*Breedlove v. Shuttles,* 302 U.S. 277 (1937); *Butler v. Thompson,* 341 U.S. 937 (1951)	6 to 3	*Breedlove* "overruled," 383 U.S. at 669. The *Butler* decision is only mentioned in dissent, but stands for the same overruled proposition.	All; 6 New	Amend. XIV	equal protection, state conditioning of right to vote is violation of	Warren
Afroyim v. Rusk, 387 U.S. 253 (1967)	1967	*Perez v. Brownell,* 356 U.S. 44 (1958)	5 to 4	"overruled," 387 U.S. at 268	3 New	Amend. XIV	citizenship clause, state's attempt to revoke citizenship violative of	Warren
Camara v. Municipal Court, 387 U.S. 523 (1967)	1967	*Frank v. Maryland,* 359 U.S. 360 (1959)	6 to 3	"overruled," 387 U.S. at 528	2 New	Amend. IV	search and seizure, warrantless searches by municipal health inspector	Warren

Katz v. United States, 389 U.S. 347 (1967)	1967	Olmstead v. United States, 277 U.S. 438 (1928); Goldman v. United States, 316 U.S. 129 (1942)	7 to 1	"We conclude that the underpinnings of Olmstead and Goldman have been so eroded by our subsequent decisions that the "trespass" doctrine there enunciated can no longer be regarded as controlling," 389 U.S. at 353	All; 7 New	Amend. IV	search and seizure, recordation of oral statements unaccompanied by actual trespass	Warren
Keyishian v. Board of Regents, 385 U.S. 589 (1967)	1967	Adler v. Board of Educ., 342 U.S. 485 (1952)	5 to 4	"[C]onstitutional doctrine which has emerged since that decision has rejected [Adler's] major premise," 385 U.S. at 605	6 New	Amend. I	public employment conditioned upon surrender of constitutional rights	Warren
Spevack v. Klein, 385 U.S. 511 (1967)	1967	Cohen v. Hurley, 366 U.S. 117 (1961)	5 to 4	"overruled," 385 U.S. at 514	3 New	Amend. V, XIV	equal protection of lawyers asserting right against self-incrimination	Warren
Bruton v. United States, 391 U.S. 123 (1968)	1968	Delli Paoli v. United States, 352 U.S. 232 (1957)	6 to 2	"overruled," 391 U.S. at 126	4 New	Amend. IV	codefendant confession at joint trial	Warren

(Continued)

Appendix Table 1 (*Continued*)

Case	Date	Case Overruled	Vote	Operative Language	Change in Composition of Court	Clause	Subject Matter	Court
Jones v. Alfred H. Mayer Co., 392 U.S. 409 (1968)	1968	Hodges v. United States, 203 U.S. 1 (1906)	7 to 2	"overruled," 392 U.S. at 441 n. 78	All	Amend. XIII	Congressional power to decide what are incidents of slavery and enact legislation	Warren
Benton v. Maryland, 395 U.S. 784 (1969)	1969	Palko v. Connecticut, 302 U.S. 319 (1937)	7 to 2	"overruled," 395 U.S. at 794	8 New	Amend. V, XIV	double jeopardy prohibition is applicable to the states	Warren
Brandenburg v. Ohio, 395 U.S. 444 (1969)	1969	Whitney v. California, 274 U.S. 357 (1927)	8 to 0	"overruled," 395 U.S. at 449	All	Amend. I	freedom of speech	Warren
Chimel v. California, 395 U.S. 752 (1969)	1969	Harris v. United States, 331 U.S. 145 (1947); United States v. Rabinowitz 339 U.S. 56 (1950)	6 to 2	"It is time … to hold that … insofar as the principles [that Harris and Rabinowitz] stand for are inconsistent with those that we have endorsed today, they are not longer to be followed," 395 U.S. at 768	7 New; 7 New	Amend. Iv.	search and seizure, searches at the time of arrest must be limited to the person and the area within his reach	Warren

Case	Year	Overruled case	Vote	Disposition		Amendment	Holding	Court
Moore v. Ogilvie, 394 U.S. 814 (1969)	1969	MacDougall v. Green, 335 U.S. 281 (1948)	7 to 2	"overruled," 394 U.S. at 819	7 New	Amend. XIV	due process and residency requirements for political parties	Warren
Ashe v. Swenson, 397 U.S. 436 (1970)	1970	Hoag v. New Jersey, 356 U.S. 464 (1958)	7 to 1	*Hoag* is implicitly overruled since the Court reaches the opposite result on nearly the same facts, 396 U.S. at 445	6 New	Amend. V	double jeopardy, guarantee against double jeopardy includes collateral estoppel as a constitutional requirement	Burger
Price v. Georgia, 398 U.S. 323 (1970)	1970	Brantley v. Georgia, 217 U.S. 284 (1910)	8 to 0	"overruled," 398 U.S. at 330 n. 9	All	Amend. V, XIV	new trial for defendant convicted of lesser offense limited to that lesser charge	Burger
Williams v. Florida, 399 U.S. 78 (1970)	1970	Thompson v. Utah, 170 U.S. 343 (1898); Rasmussen v. United states, 197 U.S. 516 (1905)	6 to 2	The overruled cases are cited as authority for a twelve-man jury, 399 U.S. at 91 to 92, and are implicitly overruled by the announcement of the new rule allowing six-man juries. Id.	All; All	Amend. VI, XIV	six-person jury is not violative of defendant's Sixth Amendment right	Burger

(Continued)

Appendix Table 1 (*Continued*)

Case	Date	Case Overruled	Vote	Operative Language	Change in Composition of Court	Clause	Subject Matter	Court
Perez v. Campbell, 402 U.S. 637 (1971)	1971	Reitz v. Mealy 314 U.S. 33 (1941); Kesler v. Department of Pub. Safety, 369 U.S. 153 (1962)	5 to 4	"We can no longer adhere to the aberrational doctrine of *Kesler*," 402 U.S. at 651	7 New; 4 New	Art. VI, § 2	supremacy clause, state legislation that frustrates full effectiveness of federal law is invalid under supremacy clause even if supported by legitimate state purpose	Burger
Dunn v. Blumstein, 405 U.S. 330 (1972)	1972	Pope v. Williams, 193 U.S. 621 (1904)	5 to 2	"To the extent that the dicta in [*Pope*] are inconsistent with the test we apply or result we reach today, those dicta are rejected," 405 U.S. at 337 n. 7	All	Amend. XIV	equal protection, one-year residency requirement to voting violative of	Burger

Case	Year	Overruled case	Vote	Holding		Provision	Description	Chief Justice
Lehnhausen v. Lake Shore Auto Parts Co., 410 U.S. 356 (1973)	1973	Quaker City Cab Co. v. Pennsylvania, 277 U.S. 389 (1928)	9 to 0	"overruled," 410 U.S. at 366	All	Amend. XIV	equal protection, state law requiring payment of ad valorum taxes on corporations but not individuals not violative of	Burger
Miller v. California, 413 U.S. 15 (1973)	1973	A Book Named "John Cleland's Memoirs of a Woman of Pleasure" v. Attorney Gen. of Mass., 383 U.S. 413 (1966)	5 to 4	"*Memoirs* test has been abandoned as unworkable by its author, and no Member of the Court today supports the *Memoirs* formulation," 413 U.S. at 23	5 New	Amend. I	freedom of speech, obscenity test	Burger
North Dakota Pharmacy Bd. v. Snyder's Drug Stores, 414 U.S. 156 (1973)	1973	Liggett Co.v. Baldridge, 278 U.S. 105 (1929)	9 to 0	"overruled," 414 U.S. at 167	All	Amend. XIV	equal protection, state law requiring pharmacists to be registered, or majority of stock to be owned by pharacists in good standing no violative of	Burger

(Continued)

Appendix Table 1 (*Continued*)

Case	Date	Case Overruled	Vote	Operative Language	Change in Composition of Court	Clause	Subject Matter	Court
Edelman v. Jordan, 415 U.S. 651 (1974)	1974	Shapiro v. Thompson, 394 U.S. 618 (1969); State Dep't of Health and Rehab. Serv. v. Zarate, 407 U.S. 918 (1972); Sterrett v. Mothers' and Childrens' rights Org., 409 U.S. 809 (1972)	5 to 4	"we disapprove the Eleventh Amendment holdings of those cases to the extent that they are inconsistent with our holding today," 415 U.S. at 671	3 New; 0 New; 0 New	Amend. XI	retroactive payment of benefits under AABD programs which were withhold wrongfully by state officials prohibited	Burger
Taylor v. Louisiana, 419 U.S. 522 (1975)	1975	Hoyt v. Florida, 368 U.S. 57 (1961)	8 to 1	"We cannot follow the contracy implications of the prior cases, including Hoyt v. Florida," 419 U.S. at 537	3 New	Amend. VI	automatic exemptions cannot be used to exclude women from jury to obtain male venire	Burger
City of New Orleans v. Dukes, 427 U.S. 297 (1976)	1976	Morey v. Doud, 354 U.S. 457 (1957)	8 to 0	"overruled," 427 U.S. at 306	8 New	Amend. XIV	due process, purely economic legislation given deferential treatment	Burger

Case	Year	Precedent	Vote	New	Quote	Provision	Subject	Chief
Craig v. Boren, 429 U.S. 190 (1976)	1976	Goesaert v. Cleary, 335 U.S. 464 (1948)	7 to 2	All	"Insofar as *Goesaert* ... may be inconsistent, that decision is disapproved," 429 U.S. at 210 n. 23	Amend. XIV	equal protection, gender discrimination	Burger
Hudgens v. NLRB, 424 U.S. 507 (1976)	1976	Almalgamated Food Employees Union Local 590 v. Logan Valley Plaza, 391 U.S. 308 (1968)	5 to 3	5 New	"[W]e make it clear now ... that the rationale of *Logan Valley* did not survive the Court's decision in the *Lloyd* case," 424 U.S. at 518	Amend. I, XIV	freedom of speech, picketing is not protected speech on private shopping center property.	Burger
Michelin Tire Corp. v. Wages, 423 U.S. 276 (1976)	1976	Low v. Austin, 80 U.S. 29 (1971)	7 to 1	5 New	"overruled," 423 U.S. at 301	Art. I, § 10, cl. 2	state may assess nondiscriminatory ad valorem tax on imported items.	Burger
National League of Cities v. Usery, 426 U.S. 833 (1976)	1976	Maryland v. Wirtz, 392 U.S. 183 (1968)	5 to 4	4 New	"overruled," 426 U.S. at 855	Art. I, § 8, cl. 3 (commerce clause)	commerce clause, Congress cannot force states to make certain choices in the guise of regulating interstate commerce.	Burger

(Continued)

Appendix Table 1 (*Continued*)

Case	Date	Case Overruled	Vote	Operative Language	Change in Composition of Court	Clause	Subject Matter	Court
Virginia Bd. of Pharmacy v. Virginia Citizens Consumer Council, 425 U.S. 748 (1976)	1976	Valentine v. Chrestensen, 316 U.S. 52 (1942)	7 to 1	Overruling is implicit in the discussion of *Valentine* and the following contrary holding, 425 U.S. at 760 to 62	All	Amend. I	freedom of speech, purely commercial speech is protected speech but is subject to regulation	Burger
Complete Auto Transit v. Brady, 430 U.S. 274 (1977)	1977	Spector Motor Serv. v. O'Connor, 340 U.S. 602 (1951)	9 to 0	"overruled," 430 U.S. at 289	All	Art. I, § 8, cl. 3 (commerce clause)	commerce clause, state tax levied for the privilege of doing business is not per se unconstitional	Burger
Oregon v. Corvallis Sand & Gravel Co., 429 U.S. 363 (1977)	1977	Bonelli Cattle Co. v. Arizona, 414 U.S. 313 (1973)	6 to 3	"*Bonelli*'s application of federal common law to cases such as this must be overruled," 429 U.S. at 382	1 New	disputed ownership of riverbed lands must be determined as a matter of state law	disputed ownership of riverbed lands must be determined as a matter of state law.	Burger

Shaffer v. Heitner, 433 U.S. 186 (1977)	1977	Pennoyer v. Neff, 95 U.S. 714 (1877)	8 to 0	The jurisdictional framework of Pennoyer is implicitly rejected in the Court's discussion, 433 U.S. at 197–206	All	Amend. XIV	due process and personal jurisdiction	Burger
Burks v. United States, 437 U.S. 1 (1978)	1978	Bryan v. United States, 338 U.S. 552 (1950); Sapir v. United States, 348 U.S. 373 (1955); Yates v. United States, 354 U.S. 298 (1957); Forman v. United States, 361 U.S. 416 (1960)	8 to 0	"overruled," 437 U.S. at 18	All; All; 8 New; 7 New	Amend. V	double jeopardy, appellate court's determination of insufficient evidence required it to acquit under the double jeopardy clause	Burger
Department of Revenue v. Association of Washington Stevedoring Cos., 435 U.S. 734 (1978)	1978	Puget Sound Stevedoring Co. v. State Tax Comm'n, 302 U.S. 90 (1937); Joseph v. Carter & Weekes Stevedoring Cos., 330 U.S. 422 (1947)	8 to 0	"overruled," 435 U.S. at 750	All; All	Art. I, § 8, cl. 3 (commerce clause)	commerce clause, business and occupation tax does not violate commerce clause when applied to the commercial activity of stevedoring	Burger

(Continued)

Appendix Table 1 *(Continued)*

Case	Date	Case Overruled	Vote	Operative Language	Change in Composition of Court	Clause	Subject Matter	Court
United States v. Scott, 437 U.S. 82 (1978)	1978	United States v. Jenkins, 420 U.S. 358 (1975)	5 to 4	"overruled," 437 U.S. at 87	1 New	Amend. V	double jeopardy clause is not violated when a state appeals from a decision in favor of defendant when defendant sought termination of proceeding on a basis other than guilt/innocence.	Burger
Hughes v. Oklahoma, 441 U.S. 322 (1979)	1979	Geer v. Connecticut, 161 U.S. 519 (1896)	7 to 2	"overruled," 441 U.S. at 335	All	Art. I, § 8, cl. 3 (commerce clause)	commerce clause, state regulation of wildlife is to be analyzed by same rules in respect to commerce clause as other natural resources	Burger

	Case	Vote	Quote		Provision	Holding	Chief Justice
1980	United States v. Salvucci, 448 U.S. 83 (1980) / Jones v. United States, 362 U.S. 257 (1960)	7 to 2	"We are convinced that the automatic standing rule of *Jones* has outlived its usefulness in this Court's Fourth Amendment jurisprudence," 448 U.S at 95	7 New	Amend. IV	search and seizure, defendant's charged with possession may only claim benefits of exclusionary rule if their own Fourth Amendment rights have not been violated.	Burger
1981	Commonwealth Edison Co. v. Montana, 453 U.S. 609 (1981) / Heisler v. Thomas Colliery Co., 260 U.S. 245 (1922)	6 to 3	"Any contrary statements in *Heisler* and its progeny are disapproved," 453 U.S. at 617	All	Art. I, § 8, cl. 3 (commerce clause)	commerce clause, state tax is not protected from the commerce clause scrutiny by a claim that the tax is imposed on goods before they enter the stream of commerce.	Burger
1982	Sporhase v. Nebraska ex rel. Douglas, 458 U.S. 941 (1982) / Hudson County Water Co. v. McCarter, 209 U.S. 349 (1908)	7 to 2	Court explains that *Hudson* was based on *Geer* which was expressly overruled previously, 458 U.S. at 950–51	All	Art. I, § 8, cl. 3 (commerce clause)	commerce clause, ground water is an article of commerce and is subject to commerce clause regulation.	Burger

(Continued)

Appendix Table 1 (*Continued*)

Case	Date	Case Overruled	Vote	Operative Language	Change in Composition of Court	Clause	Subject Matter	Court
United States v. Ross, 456 U.S. 798 (1982)	1982	Robbins v. California, 453 U.S. 420 (1981)	6 to 3	"[W]e reject the precise holding of *Robbins*," 456 U.S. at 824	1 New	Amend. IV	search and seizure, scope of search in automobile not limited to the container, but by the object of the search and probable cause giving rise to the search.	Burger
Illinois v. Gates, 462 U.S. 213 (1983)	1983	Aguilar v. Texas, 378 U.S. 108 (1964); Spinelli v. United States, 393 U.S. 410 (1969)	6 to 3	The Court discussed the tests contained in *Aguilar* and *Spinelli* and concludes that "it is wiser to abandon the 'two-pronged test,' established by our decision in *Aguilar* and *Spinelli*," 462 U.S. at 238	5 New	Amend. IV	"totality of the circumstances" determines probable cause questions.	Burger

Limbach v. Hooven & Allison Co., 466 U.S. 353 (1984)	1984	Hooven & Allison Co. v. Evatt, 324 U.S. 652 (1945)	9 to 0	"*Hooven I*, to the extent it espouses the [original package] doctrine, is not to be regarded as authority and is overruled," 466 U.S. at 361	All	Art. I, § 10, cl. 2	focus on validity of ad valorem tax on imports should be on whether the tax is an "impost" or a "duty"	Burger
Pennhurst State Sch. & Hosp. v. Halderman, 465 U.S. 89 (1984)	1984	Rolston v. Missouri Fund Comm'rs, 120 U.S. 390 (1887); Siler v. Louisville & Nashville R.R. Co., 213 U.S. 175 (1909); Atchinson T. & S.F. Ry. V. O'Connor, 223 U.S. 280 (1912); Green v. Lousiville & Interurban R.R., 244 U.S. 499 (1917); Johnson v. Lankford, 245 U.S. 541 (1918); 28 additional cases listed at 465 U.S.89, 109 nn. 17–21, 165–68 nn. 50 & 52, and accompanying text	5 to 4	"In sum, contrary to the view implicit in decisions such as *Green*, ..., neither pendent jurisdiction, nor any other basis of jurisdiction may override the Eleventh Amendment," 465 U.S. at 121	All; All; All; All; All; All	Amend. XI	rule that claim against state officials is a claim against the state and is barred by the 11th Amendment also applies to state claims in federal court under pendent jurisdiction.	Burger

(Continued)

Appendix Table 1 (*Continued*)

Case	Date	Case Overruled	Vote	Operative Language	Change in Composition of Court	Clause	Subject Matter	Court
United States v. One Assortment of 89 Firearms, 465 U.S. 354 (1984)	1984	Coffey v. United States, 116 U.S. 436 (1886)	9 to 0	"[W]e reject the contrary rationale of Coffey v. United States," 465 U.S. at 366	All	Amend. V	double jeopardy, remedial forfeiture proceeding following an acquittal on related criminal charges is not barred under the double jeopardy Clause	Burger
Garcia v. San Antonio Metro. Transit Auth., 469 U.S. 528 (1985)	1985	National League of Cities v. Usery, 426 U.S. 833 (1976)	5 to 4	"overruled," 469 U.S. at 557	1 New	Art. I, § 8, cl. 3 (commerce clause)	commerce clause, determination of state immunity does not turn on whether the government function is traditional or integral	Burger

Case	Year	Precedent	Vote	Quote		Amendment	Holding	Chief Justice
United States v. Miller, 471 U.S. 130 (1985)	1985	Ex parte Bain, 121 U.S. 1 (1887)	8 to 0	"[T]o the extent that *Bain* stands for the proposition...to avoid further confusion, we now explicitly reject that proposition," 471 U.S. at 144	All	Amend. V	to drop allegations unnecessary to an offense that is clearly contained within an indictment is not an unconstitutional amendment	Burger
Batson v. Kentucky, 476 U.S. 79 (1986)	1986	Swain v. Alabama, 380 U.S. 202 (1965)	7 to 2	"For the reasons that follow, we reject this evidentiary formulation as inconsistent with standards that have developed since *Swain*," 476 U.S. at 93	7 New	Amend. XIV	equal protection, defendant may present a prima facie case of discriminatory selection of venire based on prosecutorial conduct in his case, which gives rise to an inference of unconstitutional behavior	Burger

(Continued)

Appendix Table 1 (*Continued*)

Case	Date	Case Overruled	Vote	Operative Language	Change in Composition of Court	Clause	Subject Matter	Court
Daniels v. Williams, 474 U.S. 327 (1986)	1986	Parratt v. Taylor, 451 U.S. 527 (1981)	9 to 0	"overruled," 474 U.S. at 330	1 New	Amend. XIV	due process, lack of due care by state official which amounts to negligence does not "deprive" a person of life or liberty and therefore does not implicate due process Clause	Burger
Puerto Rico v. Branstad, 483 U.S. 219 (1987)	1987	Kentucky v. Dennison, 65 U.S. 66 (1861)	9 to 0	"Kentucky v. Dennison is the product of another time ... We conclude that it may stand no longer," 483 U.S. at 230	8 New	Art. IV, §2, cl. 2	federal courts have authority to compel performance by asylum state to deliver fugitive upon proper demand.	Rehnquist

Year	Case	Vote	Quote	Number	Provision	Holding	Author
1987	Solorio v. United States, 483 U.S. 435 (1987)	6 to 3	"overruled," 483 U.S. at 436	6 New	Art. I, §8, cl. 14	jurisdiction of court martial depends upon status as a member of the military and not on the relationship between the offense and service	Rehnquist
1987	Welch v. Texas Dep't of Highway's and Pub. Transp., 483 U.S. 468 (1987)	5 to 4	"overruled," 483 U.S. at 478	7 New	Amend. XI	if Congress intends to abrogate the Eleventh Amendment in exercising commerce clause power, it may do so expressly in the statute	Rehnquist
1988	South Carolina v. Baker, 485 U.S. 505 (1988) / Pollock v. Farmers' Loan & Trust Co., 157 U.S. 429 (1895)	6 to 2	"We thus confirm that subsequent case law had overruled the holding in *Pollock*," 485 U.S. at 524	All	Amend. XVI	state bond interest is not immune from nondiscriminatory federal tax	Rehnquist

(Continued)

Appendix Table 1 (*Continued*)

Case	Date	Case Overruled	Vote	Operative Language	Change in Composition of Court	Clause	Subject Matter	Court
Alabama v. Smith, 490 U.S. 794 (1989)	1989	Simpson v. Rice, 395 U.S. 711 (1969)	8 to 1	"Believing as we do that there is no basis for the presumption of vindictiveness where a second sentence imposed after a trial is heavier than a first sentence imposed after a guilty plea, we overrule Simpson v. Rice ... to that extent," 490 U.S. at 803	6 New	Amend. VI	sentencing	Rehnquist
Healy v. Beer Inst. Inc., 491 U.S. 324 (1989)	1989	Joseph E. Seagram & Sons, Inc. v. Hostetter, 384 U.S. 35 (1966)	6 to 3	"to the extent that Seagram holds that retrospective affirmation statutes do not facially violate the commerce clause, it is no longer good law," 491 U.S. at 343	7 New	Art. I, § 8, cl. 3 (commerce clause)	commerce clause	Rehnquist

Case	Year	Overruled Case(s)	Vote	Quotation	New	Provision	Subject	Author
Thornburgh v. Abbott, 490 U.S. 401 (1989)	1989	Procunier v. Martinez, 416 U.S. 396 (1974)	6 to 3	"overrule," 490 U.S. at 413	4 New	Amend. VIII	distinction between correspondence from prisoners or nonprisoners in prison regulations	Rehnquist
Collins v. Youngblood, 497 U.S. 37 (1990)	1990	Kring v. Missouri, 107 U.S. 221 (1883); Thompson v. Utah, 170 U.S. 343 (1898)	9 to 0	"overrule," 497 U.S. at 51–52	All; All	Art. I, §10, cl. 1	ex post facto clause	Rehnquist
California v. Acevedo, 500 U.S. 565 (1991)	1991	Arkansas v. Sanders, 442 U.S. 753 (1979)	6 to 3	"We conclude that it is better to adopt one clear-cut rule to govern automobile searches and eliminate the warrant requirement for closed containers set forth in *Sanders*," 500 U.S. at 579	4 New	Amend. IV	search and seizure	Rehnquist
Estelle v. McQuire, 502 U.S. 62 (1991)	1991	Cage v. Louisiana, 498 U.S. 39 (1990); Yates v. Evatt, 500 U.S. 391 (1991)	6 to 2	"We now disapprove the standard of review language in *Cage* and *Yates*," 502 U.S. at 71, n. 4	1 New; 0 New	Amend. XIV	due process standard of review for jury instruction	Rehnquist

(Continued)

Appendix Table 1 (*Continued*)

Case	Date	Case Overruled	Vote	Operative Language	Change in Composition of Court	Clause	Subject Matter	Court
Harmelin v. Michigan, 501 U.S. 957 (1991)	1991	Solem v. Helm, 463 U.S. 277 (1983)	5 to 4	"we conclude from this examination that *Solem* was simply wrong," 501 U.S. at 965	3 New	Amend. VIII	proportionality of crime and punishment under cruel and unusual punishment clause	Rehnquist
Payne v. Tennessee, 501 U.S. 808 (1991)	1991	South Carolina v. Gathers, 490 U.S. 805 (1989); Booth v. Maryland, 482 U.S. 496 (1987)	5 to 4	"Reconsidering these decisions now, we conclude for the reasons heretofore stated, that they were wrongly decided and should be, and now are, overruled," 501 U.S. at 830	1 New, 1 New	Amend. VI	admissibility of victim impact evidence	Rehnquist
Planned Parenthood v. Casey, 505 U.S. 833 (1992)	1992	City of Akron v. Akron Center for Reproductive Health, 462 U.S. 416 (1983); Thornburgh v. American College of Obstetricians and Gynecologists, 476 U.S. 747 (1986)	plurality	"overruled," 505 U.S. at 870	4 New; 4 New	Amend. XIV	due process and right of privacy	Rehnquist

Case	Year	Vote	Overruled citation	Amend.	Description	Court
Quill Corp. v. North Dakota, 504 U.S. 298 (1992)	1992	9 to 0	"overruled," 504 U.S. at 302	8 New	Amend. XIV	due process and minimum contacts analysis	Rehnquist
United states v. Dixon, 509 U.S. 688 (1993)	1993	5 to 4	"overruled," 509 U.S. at 704	2 New	Amend. V	double jeopardy, definition of same offense under	Rehnquist
Nichols v. United States, 511 U.S. 738 (1994)	1994	6 to 3	"overruled," 511 U.S. at 748	6 New	Amend. V, XIV	prior conviction enhancing subsequent conviction	Rehnquist
Adarand Constructors, Inc. v. Pena, 515 U.S. 200 (1995)	1995	5 to 4	"overruled," 515 U.S. at 227	4 New	Amend. V, XIV	equal protection and level of scrutiny for racial classifications	Rehnquist
United States v. Gaudin, 515 U.S. 506 (1995)	1995	9 to 0	"other reasoning in *Sinclair* not yet repudiated, we repudiate now," 515 U.S. at 520	All	Amend. VI	jury determination of pertinency and materiality	Rehnquist

National Bella Hess, Inc., v. Dept. of Revenue, 386 U.S. 753 (1967)

Grady v. Corbin, 495 U.S. 508 (1990)

Baldasar v. Illinois, 446 U.S. 222 (1980)

Metro Broadcasting, Inc. v. FCC, 497 U.S. 547 (1990)

Sinclair v. United states, 279 U.S. 263 (1929)

(Continued)

Appendix Table 1 *(Continued)*

Case	Date	Case Overruled	Vote	Operative Language	Change in Composition of Court	Clause	Subject Matter	Court
44 Liquormart, Inc. v. Rhode Island, 517 U.S. 484 (1996)	1996	California v. LaRue, 409 U.S. 109 (1972); New York State Liquor Auth. v. Bellanca, 452 U.S. 714 (1981); City of Newport v. Iacobucci, 479 U.S. 92 (1986)	9 to 0	"we now disavow its reasoning," 517 U.S. at 516	7 New, 7 New, 5 New	Amend. XXI	state regulation of the use or delivery of intoxicating beverages	Rehnquist
Seminole Tribe v. Florida, 517 U.S. 44 (1996)	1996	Pennsylvania v. Union Gas Co., 491 U.S. 1 (1989)	5 to 4	"overruled," 517 U.S. at 66	4 New	Amend. XI	state immunity in federal court.	Rehnquist
Agostini v. Felton, 521 U.S 203 (1997)	1997	School Dist. Grand Rapids v. Ball, 473 U.S. 373 (1985); Aquilar v. Felton, 473 U.S. 402 (1985)	5 to 4	"overruled," 521 U.S. at 236	6 New; 6 New	Amend. I	freedom of religion, funding of religious schools under the etablishment clause	Rehnquist
Hudson v. United States, 522 U.S. 93 (1997)	1997	Halper v. United States, 490 U.S. 435 (1989)	9 to 0	"ill considered," 522 U.S. at 101	4 New	Amend. V	double jeopardy, civil and criminal punishment for the same conduct under	Rehnquist

College Savings Bank v. Florida Prepaid PostSecondary Education Expense Board, 527 U.S. 666 (1999)	1999	Parden v. Terminal R. Co. of Ala. Docks Dept., 377 U.S. 184 (1964)	5 to 4	"expressly overruled," 527 U.S. at 680	All	Amend. XI	state immunity in federal court.	Rehnquist
Mitchell v. Helms, 530 U.S. 793 (2000)	2001	Meek v. Pettenger, 421 U.S. 349 (1975); Wolman v. Walter, 433 U.S. 229 (1977)	6 to 3	"overrule," 530 U.S. at 835	8 New; 7 New	Amend. I	freedom of religion, government aid to public and private schools under the etablishment clause	Rehnquist
United States v. Hatter, 532 U.S. 557 (2001)	2001	Evans v. Gore, 253 U.S. 245 (1920)	6 to 1	"overrule," 532 U.S. at 567	All	Art. III, §1	nondiscriminatory taxes on federal judges under the compensation clause	Rehnquist
Atkins v. Virginia, 536 U.S. 304 (2002)	2002	Penry v. Lynaugh, 492 U.S. 302 (1989)	6 to 3	"Much has changed since … our decision in Penry," 536 U.S. at 314	4 New	Amend. VIII	cruel and unusual punishment prohibits death penalty for mentally retarded.	Rehnquist

(Continued)

Appendix Table 1 (*Continued*)

Case	Date	Case Overruled	Vote	Operative Language	Change in Composition of Court	Clause	Subject Matter	Court
Lapides v. Bd. of Regents, 535 U.S. 613 (2002)	2002	Ford Motor Co. v. Dept. of Treasury of Ind., 323 U.S. 459 (1945)	9 to 0	"*Ford*, which is inconsistent with the basic rationale of those cases, is overruled insofar as it would otherwise apply," 535 U.S. at 623	All	Amend. XI	state immunity in federal courts.	Rehnquist
Ring v. Arizona, 536 U.S. 584 (2002)	2002	Walton v. Arizona, 497 U.S. 639 (1990)	7 to 2	"overrule," 536 U.S at 589	4 New	Amend. VI	sentencing	Rehnquist
United States v. Cotton, 535 U.S. 625 (2002)	2002	Ex parte Bain, 121 U.S. 1 (1887)	9 to 0	"overruled," 535 U.S. at 631	All	Amend. VI	right to jury trial	Rehnquist
Lawrence v. Texas, 539 U.S. 558 (2003)	2003	Bowers v. Hardwick, 478 U.S. 186, (1986)	6 to 3	"overruled," 539 U.S. 578	6 New	Amend. XIV	due process and the right to sexual autonomy	Rehnquist

Case	Year	Precedent overruled	Vote		Quote	Amendment	Issue	Court
Crawford v. Washington, 541 U.S. 36 (2004)	2004	Ohio v. Roberts, 448 U.S. 56 (1980)	7 to 2	7 New	"[*Roberts*] was a fundamental failure on our part to interpret the Constitution" 541 U.S. 67	Amend. VI	confrontation clause	Rehnquist
Roper v. Simmons, 543 U.S. 551 (2005)	2005	Stanford v. Kentucky, 492 U.S. 361 (1989)	6 to 3	4 New	"Stanford v. Kentucky should be deemed no longer controlling on this issue" 543 U.S. 574	Amend. VIII	cruel and unusual punishment prohibits death penalty for minors	Rehnquist

Appendix Table 2
Overrulings by Subject Matter

Subject Matter	Overrulings
Art. I (tax, ex post facto, etc.)	6
Art. I (commerce clause)	18
Art. III (jurisdiction / access to courts)	5
Art. IV (full faith and credit, etc.)	3
Art. VI, cl 2 (supremacy clause)	4
Amend. I—religion	3
Amend. I—speech	6
Amend. I—public employment	1
Amend. IV—search and seizure	11
Amend. V (double jeopardy, grand jury, self-incrimination, takings, due process)	15
Amend. VI (sentencing, trial by jury, confrontation)	11
Amend. VIII (proportionality, cruel and unusual)	3
Amend. X	4
Amend. XI	7
Amend. XIII	1
Amend. XIV—due process	19
Amend. XIV—equal protection	8
Amend. XIV—privileges and immunities	1
Amend. XIV—citizenship clause	1
Amend. XV	2
Amend. XVI	1
Amend. XXI	1
Other	2

Appendix Table 3

Number of Overrulings by Change in Court Composition

New justices	Overrulings
0	4
1	8
2	8
3	10
4	17
5	7
6	18
7	23
8	12
9	101

Appendix Table 4
Number of Overrulings by Court

Court	Overrulings
Marshall Court	0
Taney	2
Chase	1
Waite	4
Fuller	1
White	3
Taft	4
Hughes	25
Stone	10
Vinson	11
Warren	32
Burger	76
Rehnquist	39
Roberts	0

Appendix Table 5

Number of Overrulings by Justices Who Served on Rehnquist Court

Justice	Overrulings
White	55
Marshall	36
Blackmun	38
Powell	31
Rehnquist	59
Stevens	42
O'Connor	42
Scalia	35
Kennedy	32
Souter	21
Thomas	29
Ginsburg	12
Breyer	14

Appendix Table 6

Samples of Occasions Cases Urged Overruled and Eventual Results

Case Urged Overruled	Number of Times Overruling Urged	Issue	Eventually Overruled?
Bacchus v. Dias, 468 U.S. 263 (1984)	1	Art. I, § 8, cl. 3	No
Davis v. Bandemer, 478 U.S. 109 (1986)	1	Amend. XIV (equal protection)	No
New York v. Belton, 453 U.S. 454 (1981)	1	Amend. IV	No
Nevada Dept. of Human Resources v. Hibbs, 538 U.S. 721 (2003)	1	Amends. XI, XIV	No
Austin v. Michigan Chamber of Commerce, 494 U.S. 652 (1990)	1	Amend. I	No
Buckley v. Valeo, 424 U.S. 1 (1976)	3	Amend. I	No
Apprendi v. New Jersey, 530 U.S 466 (2000)	3	Amends. V, VI	No
McMillan v. Pennsylvania, 477 U.S. 79, 153 L.Ed.2d 524 (1986)	1	Amends. V, VI	No
Jones v. United States, 526 U.S. 227 (1999)	1	Amends. V, VI	No
Employment Div., Dept. of Human Resources of Oregon v. Smith, 494 U.S. 872, (1990)	1	Amend. I	No
BMW v. Gore, 517 U.S. 559 (1996)	1	Amends. VIII, XIV	No
Planned Parenthood v. Casey, 505 U.S. 833 (1992)	1	Amend. XIV (due process)	No

Case		Provision	
Powers v. Ohio, 499 U.S. 400 (1991)	1	Amend. XIV (equal protection)	No
Wilson v. Seiter, 501 U.S. 294 (1991)	1	Amend. VIII	No
Penry v. Lynaugh, 492 U.S. 302 (1989)	2	Amend. VIII	Yes
Roe v. Wade, 410 U.S. 113 (1973)	2	Amend. XIV (due process)	No
National Bellas Hess v. Department of Revenue of State of Ill., 386 U.S. 753 (1967)	1	Art. I, § 8, cl. 3	No
Branti v. Finkel, 445 U.S. 507 (1980)	1	Amend. I	No
Elrod v. Burns, 427 U.S. 347 (1976)	1	Amend. I	No
Booth v. Maryland, 482 U.S. 496 (1987)	1	Amend. VIII	Yes
Hans v. Louisiana, 134 U.S. 1 (1890)	2	Amend. XI	No
Joseph E. Seagram & Sons, Inc. v. Hostetter, 384 U.S. 35, 86 S.Ct. 1254, 16 L.Ed.2d 336 (1966)	1	Art. I, § 8, cl. 3 (commerce clause)	Yes
Gertz v. Robert Welch, Inc., 418 U.S. 323 (1974)	1	Amend. I	No
Estes v. State of Tex., 381 U.S. 532 (1965)	1	Amend. XIV	No
Mapp v. Ohio, 367 U.S. 643 (1961)	1	Amend. IV	No
Ker v. California, 374 U.S. 23 (1963)	1	Amend. IV	No
Trimble v. Gordon, 430 U.S. 762 (1977)	1	Amend. XIV (equal protection)	No

(Continued)

Appendix Table 6 *(Continued)*

Case Urged Overruled	Number of Times Overruling Urged	Issue	Eventually Overruled?
Texas v. Florida, 306 U.S. 398 (1939)	1	Art. III, § 2	No
Board of Education v. Allen, 392 U.S. 236 (1968)	1	Amend. I	No
Washington v. Louisiana, 428 U.S. 906 (1976)	1	Amend. VIII	No
Younger v. Gilmore, 404 U.S. 15 (1971)	1	Amends. I, XIV	No
Davis v. Beason, 133 U.S. 333 (1890)	1	Amend. XIV	No
Murphy v. Ramsey, 114 U.S. 15 (1885)	1	Amend. XIV	No
O'Callahan v. Parker, 395 U.S. 258	1	Art. I, § 8, cl. 14	Yes
Spinelli v. United States, 393 U.S. 410 (1969)	1	Amend. IV	Yes
Aguilar v. Texas, 378 U.S. 108 (1964)	1	Amend. IV	Yes
Yee Hem v. United States, 268 U.S. 178 (1925)	1	Amend. V	No
Roth v. United States, 354 U.S. 476	1	Amend. I	No
Beauharnais v. Illinois, 343 U.S. 250	1	Amend. I	No
Braunfeld v. Brown, 366 U.S. 599	1	Amends. I, XIV	No
On Lee v. United States, 343 U.S. 747 (1952)	1	Amend. IV	No
Adamson v. California, 332 U.S. 46 (1947)	1	Amends. V, XIV	Yes
Betts v. Brady, 316 U.S. 455 (1942)	1	Amends. VI, XIV	Yes

Appendix Table 7

Implicit Overrulings

Case	Date	Case Overruled	Vote	Subject Matter
Bunting v. Oregon, 243 U.S. 426	1917	Lochner v. New York, 198 U.S. 45 (1904)	5–3	Due Process
West Coast Hotel v. Parrish, 300 U.S. 379	1937	Morehead v. New York ex. rel. Tipaldo, 298 U.S. 587 (1936)	5–4	Due Process
O'Malley v. Woodrough, 307 U.S. 277	1939	Evans v. Gore, 253 U.S. 245 (1920)	7–1	Nondiscriminatory taxes on federal judges under the Compensation Clause
United States v. Chicago, Milwaukee, St. Paul & Pacific RR, 312 U.S. 592	1941	US v. Heyward, 250 U.S. 633 (1919)	9–0	Commerce Clause
Oklahoma Tax Commission v. Texas Co, 336 U.S. 342, 365–66	1949	Howard v. Gipsy Oil Co., 247 U.S. 503 (1918); Large Oil Co. v. Howard, 248 U.S. 549 (1919); State of Oklahoma v. Bamsdall Refineries, 296 U.S. 521 (1936); Helvering v. Mountain Producers Corp., 303 U.S. 376 (1938)	9–0	Taxation and intergovernmental immunity
Brown v. Board of Education, 347 U.S. 483	1954	Cumming v. Board of Education, 175 US 528 (1899); Gong Lum v. Rice, 275 U.S. 78 (1927)	9–0	Equal Protection
Gayle v. Browder, 352 U.S. 903	1956	Plessy v. Ferguson, 163 U.S. 537 (1896)	9–0	Equal Protection

(Continued)

Appendix Table 7 *(Continued)*

Case	Date	Case Overruled	Vote	Subject Matter
Elkins v. United States, 364 U.S. 206	1960	Weems v. United States, 232 U.S. 383 (1914); Center v. U.S., 267 U.S. 575 (1925); Byers v. U.S., 273 U.S. 28 (1927)	5–4	Search & Seizure
Baker v. Carr, 369 U.S. 186	1962	Colegrove v. Green, 328 U.S. 549 (1946)	7–2	Equal Protection
Gray v. Sanders, 372 U.S. 368	1963	Overruling 3 Cases	8–1	Equal Protection & Due Process
Schneider v. Rusk, 377 U.S. 163	1964	Mackenzie v. Hare, 239 U.S. 299 (1915)	5–3	Naturalization
Dunn v. Blumstein, 405 U.S. 330	1972	Pope v. Williams, 193 U.S. 621 (1904)	6–1	Equal Protection
Furman v. Georgia, 408 U.S. 238	1972	McGautha v. California, 402 U.S. 183 (1971)	5–4	Cruel and Unusual Punishment and Due Process
Dept. of Human Resources of Oregon v. Smith, 485 U.S. 660	1988	Sherbet v. Verner, 374 U.S. 398 (1963)	5–3	Free Exercise Clause
Arizona v. Fulminate, 499 U.S. 279	1991	Chapman v. California, 386 U.S. 18 (1967)	5–4	Self Incrimination & Due Process
U.S. v. Booker, 543 U.S. 220	2005	Apprendi v. New Jersey, 530 U.S. 466 (2000)	5–4	Right to Jury Trial

Introduction

1. The eight justices are President Reagan's four appointees (Sandra Day O'Connor, William Rehnquist as Chief Justice, Antonin Scalia, and Anthony Kennedy), President George H. W. Bush's two appointees (David Souter and Clarence Thomas), and President George W. Bush's two appointees (John Roberts as Chief Justice and Samuel Alito, Jr.). The other three justices are John Paul Stevens (appointed by President Ford with no apparent agenda in mind regarding *Roe*) and Ruth Bader Ginsburg and Stephen Breyer (both appointed by President Clinton to fortify *Roe*). There may be other, cynical explanations for *Roe*'s endurance, including mistakes made in the selection process or the likelihood that the relatively small pool from which Republican presidents selected their nominees is mostly filled with people who agree with *Roe*.

2. Legal scholars have begun recently to pay more attention to social science analyses of the Court. For two noteworthy efforts to harmonize what law and political science say about the Court and precedent, see Barry Friedman, *The Politics of Judicial Review*, 84 Tex. L. Rev. 257 (2005) (demonstrating the need for normative theories of judicial review "to come to grips with what positive scholarship teaches about the political environment in which constitutional judges act and about the constraints they necessarily face"); Stephen Feldman, *The Rule of Law or the Rule of Politics? Harmonizing the Internal and External Views of Supreme Court Decision Making*, 30 Law & Soc. Inquiry 89, 93 (2005) (proposing "to harmonize the internal and external views of Supreme Court decision making").

Chapter 1

1. U.S. 419 (1793).
2. U.S. 393 (1856).
3. U.S. 601 (1895).
4. U.S. 112 (1970).
5. Laurence Tribe notes the Nineteenth Amendment effectively reversed *Minor v. Happersett*, 88 U.S. (21 Wall.) 162 (1874), which denied women the right to vote. See Tribe, 1 *American Constitutional Law* § 3–6, 309 n.19 (3d ed. West 2000).
6. See, e.g., *Ex Parte Klein*, 80 U.S. 128 (1871); *United States v. Eichman*, 496 U.S. 310 (1990); *City of Boerne v. Flores*, 521 U.S. 507 (1997); *Dickerson v. United States*, 530 U.S. 428 (2000).
7. John Marshall served as Chief Justice for 34 years and several months.

8. The cases enumerated include instances in which the Court overruled more than one precedent in one decision.

9. Although Justice Story believed *United States v. Hudson and Goodwin*, 11 U.S. 32 (1812), was wrongly decided, the Court reaffirmed the decision in *United States v. Coolidge*, 14 U.S. 415, 416 (1816).

10. See, e.g., Jeffrey A. Segal & Harold J. Spaeth, *The Supreme Court and the Attitudinal Model Revisited* 288–310 (Cambridge Univ. Press 2002).

11. *Walton v. Arizona*, 497 U.S. 639, 674–75 (1990) (Brennan, J., joined by Marshall, J., dissenting); *McCray v. Florida*, 454 U.S. 1041, 1041 (1981) (Brennan, J., & Marshall, J., separately dissenting); *Gregg v. Georgia*, 428 U.S. 153, 230–31, 241 (1976) (Brennan, J., & Marshall, J., separately dissenting).

12. See, e.g., Akhil Amar, *The Supreme Court, 1999 Term, Foreword: The Document and the Doctrine*, 114 Harv. L. Rev. 26, 40–44 (2000); Cass R. Sunstein, *Supreme Court Term, Foreword: Leaving Things Undecided*, 110 Harv. L. Rev. 6 (1996).

13. U.S. (6 Cranch) 281 (1810).

14. U.S. (4 Cranch) 241 (1808).

15. Hudson, 10 U.S. at 285 ("He was still of opinion that the construction then given was correct.... However, the principle of that case (Rose v. Himely) is now overruled").

16. U.S. 443 (1851).

17. U.S. 428 (1825).

18. *Id*. at 456. A few years earlier Chief Justice Taney recognized the need for the Court to have the power to reconsider its decisions because of the near impossibility of correcting the Court's mistakes through other means. See *Passenger Cases*, 48 U.S. (7 How.) 283 (1849).

19. *Propeller Genesee Chief*, 53 U.S. at 458–59.

20. U.S. (8 Wall.) 603 (1870).

21. *Knox v. Lee*, 79 U.S. 457, 572 (1870) (Chase, J., dissenting).

22. *Id*. at 553–54.

23. *Id*. at 569–70 (Bradley, J., concurring).

24. *Id*. at 570.

25. Geoffrey R. Stone, *Precedent, the Amendment Process, and Evolution in Constitutional Doctrine*, 11 Harv. J.L. & Pub. Pol'y 67, 70 (1988).

26. See Benjamin Cardozo, *The Nature of the Judicial Process* 150 (Yale Univ. Press 1925) ("I think that when a rule, after it has been duly tested by experience, has been found to be inconsistent with the sense of justice or with the social welfare, there should be less hesitation in frank avowal and full abandonment"); *Vasquez v. Hillery*, 474 U.S. 254, 266 (1986) ("every successful proponent of overruling precedent has borne the heavy burden of persuading the Court that changes in society or in the law dictate that the values served by *stare decisis* yield in favor of a greater objective").

27. See generally James H. Fowler & Sangick Jeon, *The Authority of Supreme Court Precedent: A Network Analysis*, June 29, 2005, at 1 (copy on file with

author) (finding "the Court is careful to ground overruling decisions in past precedent").

28. See, e.g., *Vieth v. Jubelirer*, 541 U.S. 267, 306 (U.S. 2004) ("Eighteen years of essentially pointless litigation have persuaded us that *Bandemer* is incapable of principled application. We would therefore overrule that case"). It may be significant that Chief Justice Roberts noted in his confirmation hearings in September 2005 that "to avoid an arbitrary discretion in the judges, they need to be bound down by rules and precedents," yet indicated a willingness to overturn precedent if the "doctrinal bases of a decision had been eroded by subsequent developments" rendering the precedent "unworkable."

29. *Burnet v. Coronado Oil & Gas Co.*, 285 U.S. 393, 406–8 (1932) (Brandeis, J., dissenting).

30. *Smith v. Allwright*, 321 U.S. 649, 669 (1944) (Roberts, J., dissenting), overruling *Grovey v. Townsend*, 295 U.S. 45 (1935).

31. U.S. 643 (1961).

32. U.S. 25 (1949).

33. *Id.* at 33.

34. See *Mapp*, 367 U.S. at 673 & nn. 4–5 (Harlan, J., dissenting).

35. *Id.* at 660.

36. *Id.* at 666 (Black, J., concurring).

37. *Id.* at 670 (Douglas, J., concurring).

38. *Id.* at 672 (Harlan, J., dissenting).

39. *Id.* at 674.

40. See *id.* at 676.

41. See *id.* at 677.

42. *Id.*

43. U.S. 808 (1991).

44. U.S. 805 (1989).

45. U.S. 496 (1987).

46. See 501 U.S. at 828–29 ("[*Booth* and *Gathers*] were decided by the narrowest of margins, over spirited dissents challenging the basic underpinnings of those decisions").

47. See *id.* at 828 ("Considerations in favor of *stare decisis* are at their acme in cases involving property and contract rights, where reliance interests are involved … the opposite is true in cases such as the present one involving procedural and evidentiary rules").

48. See *id.* at 827 ("when governing decisions are unworkable or badly reasoned, 'this Court has never felt constrained to follow precedent'") (quoting *Smith v. Allwright*, 321 U.S. 649, 665 (1949)).

49. *Id.* at 832 (O'Connor, J., concurring).

50. *Id.* at 835 (Scalia, J., concurring).

51. See *United States v. Virginia*, 518 U.S. 515, 568 (1996) (Scalia, J., dissenting) (noting the Court, when adopting tests, should craft them "so as to reflect

those constant and unbroken national traditions that embody the people's understanding of ambiguous constitutional texts. [When text is supported by] a long tradition of open, widespread, and unchallenged use that dates back to the beginning of the Republic, we have no proper basis for striking it down").

52. See *Planned Parenthood v. Casey*, 505 U.S. 833, 983 (1992) (Scalia, J., concurring in the judgment and dissenting in part) ("*Roe* was plainly wrong—even on the Court's methodology of 'reasoned judgment,' and even more so (of course) if the proper criteria of text and tradition are applied").

53. See *Payne*, 501 U.S. at 839–40 (Souter, J., concurring) ("*Booth* sets an unworkable standard of constitutional relevance that threatens, on its own terms, to produce such arbitrary consequences and uncertainty of application as virtually to guarantee a result far diminished from the case's promise of appropriately individualized sentencing for capital defendants").

54. *Id.* at 844 (Marshall, J., dissenting).

55. See *id.*

56. *Id.* at 845.

57. *Id.* at 848.

58. *Id.* at 854.

59. *Id.* at 867 (Stevens, J., dissenting) (citation omitted).

60. U.S. 113 (1973).

61. U.S. 833 (1992).

62. *Id.* at 854–55 (citations omitted).

63. *Id.* at 855.

64. *Id.* at 855–56.

65. *Id.* at 856.

66. See *id.* at 859–861.

67. U.S. 45 (1905).

68. U.S. 537 (1896).

69. *Planned Parenthood*, 505 U.S. at 862.

70. U.S. 483 (1954).

71. *Planned Parenthood*, 505 U.S. at 867.

72. *Id.* at 869.

73. U.S. (19 How.) 393 (1857).

74. See *Planned Parenthood*, 505 U.S. at 998, 1001 (Scalia, J., concurring in the judgment and dissenting in part).

75. *Id.* at 954 (Rehnquist, C.J., concurring in the judgment and dissenting in part).

76. See *id.* at 955–966.

77. *Id.* at 964.

78. *Id.* at 966.

79. U.S. 200 (1995).

80. U.S. 547 (1990).

81. *Adarand*, 515 U.S. at 231 (quoting *Helvering v. Hallock*, 309 U.S. 106, 119 (1940)).

82. *Id.* at 231.
83. *Id.* at 231–32.
84. *Id.* at 232.
85. *Id.*
86. *Id.* at 233.
87. *Id.* at 234.
88. *Id.* at 234.
89. U.S. 448 (1980).
90. U.S. 469 (1989).
91. *Adarand*, 515 U.S. at 256–57.
92. U.S. 1 (1890).
93. U.S. 1 (1989).
94. Article I, section 8, clause 3 of the Constitution provides in pertinent part that "Congress shall have the power … [t]o regulate Commerce with foreign nations, and among the several states, and with the Indian tribes."
95. U.S. 44 (1996).
96. U.S. at 66.
97. *Id.* at 63.
98. *Id.* at 64 (citations omitted).
99. *Id.* at 66.
100. U.S. at 36–42.
101. *Seminole Tribe*, 517 U.S. at 66.
102. *Id.* at 94 (citation omitted).
103. *Id.* (citation omitted).
104. *Id.* at 102 (Souter, J., dissenting).
105. *Id.* at 116–117 (citations omitted).
106. *Id.* at 102.
107. *Id.* at 166.
108. *Id.* at 166–167.
109. *Id.* at 159.
110. *Id.* at 183.
111. U.S. 666 (1999).
112. U.S. 184 (1964).
113. *Welch v. Texas Department of Highways and Public Transportation*, 483 U.S. 468, 478 (1987), quoted in *College Savings Bank*, 527 U.S. at 678.
114. *College Savings Bank*, 527 U.S. at 680.
115. *Id.* at 696 (Breyer, J., dissenting).
116. *Id.*
117. *Id.* In his majority opinion, Justice Scalia contested the dissent's likening of *Seminole Tribe* to *Lochner* as unfounded and irrational. He suggested *Seminole Tribe*

> resembles *Lochner* … in the respect that it rejects a novel assertion
> of governmental power which the legislature believed to be justified.
> But if that alone were enough to qualify as a mini-*Lochner*,

the list of mini-*Lochners* would be endless. Most of our judgments invalidating state and federal laws fit that description. We had always thought that the distinctive feature of *Lochner* … was that it sought to impose a particular economic philosophy upon the Constitution. And we think that feature aptly characterizes, not our opinion, but Justice Breyer's dissent, which believes that States should not enjoy the normal constitutional protections of sovereign immunity when they step out of their proper economic role to engage in "ordinary commercial ventures". … Whatever happened to the need for "legislative flexibility"?

Id. at 690–91 (citation omitted).

118. *Id.* at 704–5 (citations omitted).
119. U.S. 793 (2000).
120. U.S. 349 (1975).
121. U.S. 229 (1977).
122. *Mitchell v. Helms*, 530 U.S. at 850 (O'Connor, J., concurring in the judgment).
123. *Id.* at 835.
124. *Id.*
125. *Id.* at 849 (O'Connor, J., concurring in the judgment).
126. *Id.* at 857.
127. *Id.* at 858 (Souter, J., dissenting).
128. U.S. 558 (2003).
129. U.S. 186 (1986).
130. U.S. at 576.
131. *Evans v. Roemer*, 517 U.S. 620, 634 (2000).
132. See 539 U.S. at 586–605 (Scalia, J., dissenting).
133. *Id.* at 594 (citation omitted).
134. *Id.* at 602.
135. *Id.* at 604.
136. S. Ct. 1183 (U.S. 2005).
137. U.S. 361 (1989).
138. S. Ct. at 1193.
139. *Id.* (citations omitted).
140. *Id.* at 1206 (O'Connor, J., dissenting).
141. *Id.* at 1218 (Scalia, J., dissenting).
142. In each of the six past years, more than 7000 cases were filed with the Court, from which the Court chose 81 to 86 to be argued and disposed of 71 to 77 cases through signed opinions. The Court decided 5 to 11 constitutional cases in each of the past six years, which works out to be 5 to 15 percent of the Court's signed opinions (depending on the term). Explicit overrulings were a tiny fraction of signed opinions—1.4 to 2.8 percent, depending on the term.
143. See *Marsh v. Alabama*, 326 U.S. 501 (1946) (reversing the conviction of a Jehovah's Witness for distributing religious literature on the premises of a

company-owned town); *Amalgamated Food Employees Union Local* 590 *v. Logan Valley Plaza*, 391 U.S. 308 (1968) (holding that the prohibition of peaceful labor picketing of a store within a shopping center violated the First Amendment); *Lloyd Corp. v. Tanner*, 407 U.S. 1 (1972) (upholding a privately owned shopping center's prohibition of union picketing of a store on the premises); *Hudgens v. NLRB*, 424 U.S. 507 (1976) (clarifying *Lloyd* effectively had overruled *Logan Valley*).

144. U.S. 45 (1905).

145. U.S. 426 (1917) (sustaining a regulation of work hours for men in manufacturing establishments).

146. U.S. 537 (1896).

147. U.S. 484 (1954).

148. *Id.* at 487 (footnote omitted).

149. U.S. 903 (1956).

150. See 142 F. Supp. 707, 717 (1956) ("we think that *Plessy v. Ferguson* has been impliedly, though not explicitly, overruled, and that, under later decisions, there is now no rational basis upon which the separate but equal doctrine can be validly applied [to public busing]").

151. Compare *Sweatt v. Painter*, 339 U.S. 629 (1950) (ordering the admission of a black student to a white law school because there was no substantially equal black law school in the same state); *McLaurin v. Oklahoma State Regents for Higher Education*, 339 U.S. 637 (1950) (holding unconstitutional a state's admitting a black student into an all white school but separating him physically from other students); and *Sipuel v. Board of Regents*, 332 U.S. 631 (1948) (holding that a state was constitutionally obliged to provide a black student with an equal legal education) with *Henderson v. United States*, 339 U.S. 816 (1950) (holding that the rules and practices of a railway to separate black and white diners violated the Interstate Commerce Act which prohibited railroads from subjecting any person to prejudicial treatment) and *Buchanan v. Warley*, 245 U.S. 60 (1917) (holding that a statute barring blacks from occupying a residence in a block in which whites owned a majority of the houses, and vice versa, violated the Fourteenth Amendment). After *Brown*, the Court issued a series of terse per curiam opinions in which it held unconstitutional segregation in a wide variety of other public facilities. See *Gayle v. Browder*, 352 U.S. 903 (1956) (busing); *Holmes v. City of Atlanta*, 350 U.S. 879 (1955) (municipal golf courses); *Mayor of Baltimore v. Dawson*, 350 U.S. 877 (1955) (public beaches and bathhouses).

152. *Brown*, 347 U.S. 483, 493 (1954) (acknowledging that "education is perhaps the most important function of state and local governments").

153. U.S. 279 (1991).

154. U.S. 176 (2004).

155. U.S. 36 (1983).

156. U.S. at 182–83.
157. *Id.* at 189 (Thomas, J. concurring).
158. *Id.* at 192 (Souter, J., dissenting).
159. U.S. 833 (1976).
160. U.S. 528 (1985).
161. See *EEOC v. Wyoming*, 460 U.S. 226, 243 (1983); *Fed. Energy Regulatory Comm'n v. Mississippi*, 456 U.S. 742, 753 (1982); *United Transp. Union v. Long Island R.R. Co.*, 455 U.S. 678, 686 (1982); *Hodel v. Indiana*, 452 U.S. 314, 330 (1981).
162. See *id.* at 589 (Rehnquist, J., dissenting).
163. U.S. 144 (1992).
164. See, e.g., *Printz v. United States*, 521 U.S. 898 (1997).
165. U.S. 263 (1980).
166. See *Weems v. United States*, 217 U.S. 349, 372, 377, 380 (1910) (striking down a penalty for falsifying a public record that included a 12 year prison term with "accessories" or "accompaniments" such as hard labor while chained).
167. U.S. 277 (1983). In an intervening case, *Hutto v. Davis*, 454 U.S. 370 (1982), the Court upheld a criminal sentence of 40 years' imprisonment and a $20,000 fine for possession of marijuana with intent to sell.
168. *Solem*, 463 U.S. at 304 (Burger, C.J., dissenting) (complaining that "[a]lthough today's holding cannot rationally be reconciled with *Rummel*, the Court does not purport to overrule *Rummel*").
169. U.S. 957 (1991).
170. See *id.* at 965 ("*Solem* was scarcely the expression of clear and well accepted constitutional law. ... [*Solem* is] in apparent tension with other decisions. [After paying particular attention to the background of the Eighth Amendment] we conclude from this examination that *Solem* was simply wrong").
171. *Id.* at 1001 (Kennedy, J. concurring in part).
172. *Lockyer v. Andrade*, 535 U.S. 969 (2002).
173. *Lockyer v. Andrade*, 583 U.S. 63 (2003).
174. *Id.* at 71–72.
175. *Id.* at 71.
176. U.S. 557 (1969).
177. U.S. 103 (1990).
178. U.S. 377 (1992).
179. See *Wisconsin v. Mitchell*, 508 U.S. 476 (1993).
180. U.S. 343 (2003).
181. See *Texas v. Johnson*, 491 U.S. 397, 414 (1989); *United States v. Eichman*, 496 U.S. 110 (1990).
182. U.S. 444 (1969) (per curiam).
183. U.S. 494 (1951).
184. *Brandenburg*, 395 U.S. at 447 & n.2.
185. U.S. at 510 (citation omitted).
186. See *Nebraska Press Association v. Stuart*, 427 U.S. 539, 563 (1976).

187. 274 U.S. 357 (1927).

188. *Texas v. Johnson*, 491 U.S. 397, 419 (1989).

189. See, e.g., Alexander M. Bickel, *The Supreme Court and the Idea of Progress* 87 (Yale Univ. Press 1978) ("The Court is the place for principled judgment, disciplined by the method of reason familiar to the discourse of moral philosophy, and in constitutional adjudication, the place only for that").

190. See, e.g., *Payne*, 501 U.S. at 844 (Marshall, J., dissenting) ("Power, not reason, is the new currency of this Court's decisionmaking ... Neither the law nor the facts supporting *Booth* and *Gathers* underwent any change in the last four years. Only the personnel of this Court did"); *Id.* at 859 (Stevens, J., dissenting) ("Today's majority has obviously been moved by an argument that has strong political appeal but no proper place in a reasoned judicial opinion"). See also *Webster v. Reproductive Health Services*, 492 U.S. 490, 565 (1989) (Stevens, J., concurring in part and dissenting in part) (noting a correlation between changes in the Court's composition and its increasing disposition to overrule *Roe*).

191. See *Nichols v. United States*, 511 U.S. 738 (1994); *United States v. Dixon*, 509 U.S. 688 (1993); *Harmelin v. Michigan*, 501 U.S. 957 (1991).

192. See *New York v. United States*, 505 U.S. 144 (1992).

193. See *Mitchell v. Helms*, 530 U.S. 793 (2000); *Agostini v. Felton*, 521 U.S. 203 (1997).

194. See *Adarand Constructors, Inc. v. Pena*, 515 U.S. 200 (1995).

195. U.S. 146 (1990).

196. U.S. 477 (1981) (holding that once an accused individual requests counsel, officials may not reinitiate questioning until counsel has been made available to the individual).

197. U.S. 436 (1966) (holding that police must terminate interrogation of an accused in custody if the accused requests the assistance of counsel).

198. *Minnick*, 498 U.S. at 153.

199. U.S. 428 (2000).

200. *Id.* at 443 (citation omitted).

201. U.S. 203, 235 (1997).

202. *Dickerson*, 530 U.S. at 443 (citation omitted).

203. *Id.* at 443–44 (citations omitted).

204. *Id.* at 444.

205. *Id.*

206. *Id.* (footnote omitted).

207. *Id.* at 448 (Scalia, J., dissenting).

208. *Id.* at 451, 454.

209. *Id.* at 462 (citations omitted).

210. *Id.* at 464–65 (citations omitted).

211. *Id.* at 465.

212. U.S. 1 (1976) (per curiam).

213. 540 U.S. 93 (2003).

214. 548 U.S. 1165 (2006).

215. Richard H. Fallon, Jr., *The Conservative Path of the Rehnquist Court's Federalism Decisions*, 69 U. Chi. L. Rev. 429, 432 (2002).

216. *Id.* at 475.

217. U.S. 549 (1995).

218. U.S. 598 (2000).

219. See, e.g., *Lopez*, 514 U.S. at 558–59 ("we have identified three broad categories that Congress may regulate under its commerce power … the channels of interstate commerce … the instrumentalities of interstate commerce … [and] those activities that substantially affect interstate commerce"); *Morrison*, 529 U.S. at 610 ("a fair reading of *Lopez* shows that the non-economic, criminal nature of the conduct at issue was central to our decision").

220. Act of June 27, 1988, Pub. L. No. 100–352, 102 Stat. 662 (eliminating the Supreme Court's mandatory appeal jurisdiction).

221. See, e.g., *Turner v. California*, 498 U.S. 1053 (1991) (Marshall, J., dissenting from the Court's denial of certiorari) (dissenting to the Court's refusal to reconsider his argument, rejected in previous cases, that the Court should recognize that "comparative, proportionality review" is constitutionally required in capital cases); *Snead v. Stringer*, 454 U.S. 988, 989 (1981) (Rehnquist, J., dissenting from the Court's denial of certiorari) (protesting the Court's adherence to a line of precedents that culminated in the Court's failure to reverse a lower court's erroneous construction of the Sixth Amendment as mandating a new criminal trial for a defendant who, by telephone, but without consulting counsel, volunteered a statement to a prosecutor); See also H. W. Perry, *Deciding to Decide: Agenda Setting in the United States Supreme Court* (Harvard Univ. Press 1991) (discussing how the justices make initial decisions in the certiorari process about the precedents they wish to leave alone and those they would like to revise).

222. See, e.g., *Benton v. Maryland*, 395 U.S. 784 (1969) (incorporating the Fifth Amendment's prohibition on double jeopardy); *Duncan v. Louisiana*, 391 U.S. 145 (1968) (recounting the Court's decisions from 1897 through 1967 incorporating most of the guarantees of the Bill of Rights through the Fourteenth Amendment's due process clause and holding the Sixth Amendment's right to a jury trial applicable to the states through the same clause); *Pointer v. Texas*, 380 U.S. 400 (1965) (incorporating the Sixth Amendment's right to confrontation of opposing witnesses).

223. See, e.g., *Reynolds v. Sims*, 377 U.S. 533 (1964) (striking down an Alabama apportionment scheme); *Wesberry v. Sanders*, 376 U.S. 1 (1964) (striking down a Georgia apportionment scheme); *Baker v. Carr*, 369 U.S. 186 (1962) (holding that malapportionment does not constitute a nonjusticiable political question).

224. U.S. 444 (1969).

225. See, e.g., *South Dakota v. Dole*, 483 U.S. 203 (1987) (upholding a federal statute passed pursuant to Congress' spending power that directed the secretary of transportation to withhold a portion of federal highway funds from states that do not agree to prohibit the purchase of alcohol by people under the age of 21); *United States v. Kahriger*, 345 U.S. 22 (1953) (upholding an occupational tax on gamblers as long as the congressional measure was revenue producing on its face); *Woods v. Cloyd W. Miller Co.*, 333 U.S. 138 (1948) (upholding the use of Congress' war powers to remedy the effects of war after the end of conflict).

226. Fallon, 69 U. Chi. L. Rev. at 477.

227. *Id*. at 480 (citation omitted).

Chapter 2

1. See Thomas R. Lee, *Stare Decisis in Historical Perspective: From the Founding Era to the Rehnquist Court*, 52 Vand. L. Rev. 647 (1999); see also Thomas R. Lee & Lance S. Lehnhof, *The Anastasoff Case and the Judicial Power to 'Unpublish' Opinions*, 77 Notre Dame L. Rev. 135 (2001).

2. Lee, *supra* note 1, at 718.

3. Lee & Lehnof, *supra* note 1, at 155 (citation omitted).

4. Lee, *supra* note 1, at 661.

5. Lee, *supra* note 1, at 718–19 ("the notion of a diminished standard of deference to constitutional precedent was generally rejected by founding-era commentators, and drew only isolated support in opinions in the Taney era. Under the prevailing view in the founding era and through the Marshall and Taney years, exceptions to the rule of stare decisis might condone the rejection of constitutional precedent, but any exceptions were applied across the board, irrespective of the constitutional nature of the decision. The first majority opinion to suggest otherwise appears to be Justice Strong's opinion for the Court in the Legal Tender Cases").

6. See James H. Fowler & Sangick Jeon, *The Authority of Supreme Court Precedent: A Network Analysis*, June 29, 2005. These authors note that "hardly any 18th century cases cited at least one precedent, but starting in about 1800 there is a slow and steady increase in the practice. This increase levels off by 1900, when about 90% of the cases are citing precedent. Thus, justices were clearly in the habit of connecting their decisions to previous rulings by the turn of the century." *Id*. at 8–9. See also Richard H. Fallon, Jr., *Stare Decisis and the Constitution: An Essay on Constitutional Methodology*, 76 N.Y.U. L. Rev. 570, 580 (2001).

7. Lee & Lehnof, *supra* note 1, at 171. See also *Federalist No. 78* (Alexander Hamilton) ("[t]o avoid an arbitrary discretion in the courts, it is indispensable that they should be bound down by strict rules and precedents, which serve to define and point out their duty in every particular case that comes before them").

8. See generally *United States v. Arredondo*, 31 U.S. (6 Pet.) 691, 710, 8 L. Ed. 547 (1832) (different circumstances from *Foster & Elam v. Neilson*, 27 U.S. (2 Pet.) 253, 7 L. Ed. 415 (1829)); *Sullivan v. Burnett*, 105 U.S. (15 Otto) 334, 341, 26 L. Ed. 1124 (1881) (not governed by *McCreery's Lessee v. Somerville*, 22 U.S. 354 (9 Wheat.) 354, 6 L. Ed. 109 (1824)); *Meath v. Phillips County*, 108 U.S. 553, 555, 2 S. Ct. 869, 870, 27 L. Ed. 819 (1883) (distinguishing *County of Cass v. Johnston*, 95 U.S. (5 Otto) 360, 24 L. Ed. 416 (1877) and *Davenport v. Dodge Co.*, 105 U.S. (15 Otto) 237, 26 L. Ed. 1018 (1881)); *Board of Com'rs of Chaffee County v. Potter*, 142 U.S. 355, 366, 12 S. Ct. 216, 220, 35 L. Ed. 1040 (1892) (distinguishing *Dixon Co. v. Field*, 111 U.S. 83, 4 Sup. Ct. Rep. 315 (1884) and *Lake Co. v. Graham*, 130 U.S. 674, 9 Sup. Ct. Rep. 654 (1889)); *Warner v. Baltimore & O.R. Co.*, 168 U.S. 339, 346, 18 S. Ct. 68, 71, 42 L. Ed. 491 (1897) (distinguishing *Elliot v. Railway Co.*, 150 U.S. 245, 14 Sup. Ct. 85 (1893).

9. Lee, *supra* note 1, at 727.

10. *Legal Tender Cases*, 79 U.S. (12 Wall.) 457, 553–54, 20 L. Ed. 287 (1871); *Washington University v. Rouse*, 75 U.S. (8 Wall.) 439, 444, 19 L. Ed. 498 (1869); *License Cases*, 46 U.S. (5 How.) 504, 612, 12 L. Ed. 256 (1847) (Daniel, J., concurring).

11. Thomas M. Cooley, *A Treatise on the Constitutional Limitations Which Rest Upon the Legislative Power of the States of the American Union* 62 (5th ed., Little, Brown 1883) ("Precedents, therefore, become important, and counsel are allowed and expected to call the attention of the court to them, not as concluding controversies, but as guides to the judicial mind"); *id.* at 65 ("It will of course sometimes happen that a court will find a former decision so unfounded in law, so unreasonable in its deductions, or so mischievous in its consequences, as to feel compelled to disregard it").

12. D. H. Chamberlain, *The Doctrine of Stare Decisis As Applied to Decision of Constitutional Questions*, 3 Harv. L. Rev. 125, 131 (1889).

13. Larry D. Kramer, *The Supreme Court 2000 Term Foreword: We the Court*, 115 Harv. L. Rev. 4, 74 (2001). Kramer expanded this article into a book, *The People Themselves: Popular Constitutionalism and Judicial Review* (Oxford Univ. Press 2004).

14. *Hayburn's Case*, 2 U.S. (2 Dall.) 409, 410 n.*, 1 L. Ed. 436 (1792) (declaring, "if we can be convinced this opinion is a wrong one, we shall not hesitate to act accordingly, being so far from the weakness of supposing that there is any reproach in having committed an error, to which the greatest and best men are sometimes liable, as we should be, from so low a sense of duty, as we think it would not be the highest and most deserved reproach that could be bestowed on any men (much more on judges) that they were capable, from any motive, of persevering against conviction, in apparently maintaining an opinion, which they really thought to be erroneous").

15. U.S. (2 Dall.) 419, 1 L. Ed. 440 (1793).

16. Charles Garner Geyh & Emily Field Van Tassel, *The Independence of the Judicial Branch in the New Republic*, 74 Chi.-Kent L. Rev. 31 (1999) (conclud-

ing the Framers had not considered judicial independence at any length, but that during the battles over the judiciary of 1801 and 1802, it was argued that the judiciary was not independent.)

17. *License Cases*, 48 U.S. (7 How.) 283, 12 L. Ed. 702 (1849); *Genesee Chief*, 53 U.S. (12 How.) 443, 458–59, 13 L. Ed. 1058 (1851); *Legal Tender Cases*, 79 U.S. (12 Wall.) 457, 554, 20 L. Ed. 287 (1870).

18. *Legal Tender Cases*, 79 U.S. (12 Wall.) 457, 554, 20 L. Ed. 287 (1871).

19. *Briscoe v. Commonwealth's Bank*, 33 U.S. (8 Pet.) 118, 122, 33 U.S. 120, 8 L. Ed. 887 (1834) ("The practice of this court is, not (except in cases of absolute necessity) to deliver any judgment in cases where constitutional questions are involved, unless four judges concur in opinion, thus making the decision that of a majority of the whole court").

20. *Legal Tender Cases*, 79 U.S. (12 Wall.) 457, 569, 20 L. Ed. 287 (1871).

21. *Id.* at 634 (Though Chief Justice Chase refers to the Court's overturning of its prior decision as "unprecedented," the context in which he made this statement suggests he was referring to an overruling of a precedent due to change in the composition of the Court.).

22. Edward A. Purcell, Jr., *Reconsidering the Frankfurterian Paradigm: Reflections on Histories of Lower Federal Courts*, 24 Law & Soc. Inquiry 679, 725 (1999).

23. William O. Douglas, *Stare Decisis*, 49 Colum. L. Rev. 735, 736 (1949).

24. *Id.* at 737.

25. *Id.* at 750.

26. *Id.* at 754.

27. *Glidden Company v. Zdanok*, 370 U.S. 530, 592, 82 S. Ct. 1459, 1495 (1962) (Douglas, J., dissenting).

28. *United Gas Improvement Co. v. Continental Oil Co.*, 381 U.S. 392, 406, 85 S. Ct. 1517, 1525 (1965) (Douglas, J., dissenting).

29. See *Columbia Broadcasting System, Inc. v. Democratic Nat'l Committee*, 412 U.S. 94, 154, 93 S. Ct. 2080, 2112, 36 L. Ed. 2d 772, 813 (1972) (Douglas, J., concurring); *Furman v. Georgia*, 408 U.S. 238, 248 n.1, 92 S. Ct. 2726, 2731 n.1, 33 L. Ed. 2d 346, 355 n.1 (1972) (Douglas, J., concurring); *McNeal v. Culver*, 356 U.S. 109, 119, 81 S. Ct. 413, 419, 5 L. Ed. 2d 445, 452 (1961) (Douglas, J., concurring); *Flood v. Kuhn*, 407 U.S. 258, 286, 92 S. Ct. 2099, 2114, 32 L. Ed. 2d 728, 746 (1972) (Douglas, J., dissenting).

30. Hugo L. Black, *A Constitutional Faith* 14 (Knopf 1968).

31. *Connecticut General Life Insurance Co. v. Johnson*, 303 U.S. 77, 85, 58 S. Ct. 436, 440, 82 L. Ed. 673 (1938) (Black, J., dissenting).

32. See Maurice Kelman, *The Forked Path of Dissent*, 1985 Sup. Ct. Rev. 227, 251.

33. Phillip B. Kurland, *Politics, the Constitution, and the Warren Court*, 91 (Univ. of Chicago Press 1970).

34. *Id.* at xx.

35. See, e.g., *Lamb's Chapel v. Center Moriches Union Free Sch. Dist.*, 1135 S. Ct. 2141, 2150 (1993) (Scalia, J., concurring) (establishment clause); *Lee v.*

Weisman, 112 S. Ct. 2649, 2685 (1992) (Scalia, J., dissenting) (establishment clause); *Mistretta v. United States*, 488 U.S. 361, 417 (1989) (Scalia, J., dissenting) (separation of powers); *Morrison v. Olson*, 487 U.S. 654, 710–12 (1988) (Scalia, J., dissenting) (separation of powers); *American Trucking Ass'ns v. Scheiner*, 483 U.S. 266, 303–6 (1987) (Scalia, J., dissenting) (dormant commerce clause); *Barnes v. Glen Theatre, Inc.*, 111 S. Ct. 2456, 2463 (1991) (Scalia, J., concurring) (nude dancing); *Pope v. Illinois*, 481 U.S. 497, 505 (1987) (Scalia, J., concurring) (obscenity); *California v. Acevedo*, 111 S. Ct. 1982, 1992 (1991) (Scalia, J., concurring) (criminal procedure); *Powers v. Ohio*, 499 U.S. 400, 417 (1991) (Scalia, J., dissenting) (criminal procedure).

36. *South Carolina v. Gathers*, 490 U.S. 805, 825, 109 S. Ct. 2207, 104 L. Ed. 2d 876 (1989) (Scalia, J., dissenting) ("I agree with Justice Douglas: 'A judge looking at a constitutional decision may have compulsions to revere past history and accept what was once written. But he remembers above all else that it is the Constitution which he swore to support and defend, not the gloss which his predecessors may have put on it.' Douglas, *Stare Decisis*, 49 Colum. L. Rev. 735, 736 (1949)").

37. U.S. 677 (2005).

38. *Id.* at 690.

39. *Id.*

40. Richard A. Posner, The Problems of Jurisprudence 94 (Harvard Univ. Press 1990); Cass R. Sunstein, *Foreword: Leaving Things Undecided*, 110 Harv. L. Rev. 4, 25–26 (1995).

41. See, e.g., *Hearings Before the Committee on the Judiciary United States Senate on the Nomination of Robert H. Bork to be Associate Justice of the Supreme Court of the United States*, Part I, 523–24, quoted in *Battle for Justice: How the Bork Nomination Shook America*, Ethan Bonner 260 (W. W. Norton 1989) ("I don't think that in the field of constitutional law precedent is all that important … If you become convinced that a prior court has misread the Constitution, I think it's your duty to go back and correct it.… I don't think precedent is all that important. I think the importance is what the framers were driving at, and to go back to that").

42. See, e.g., Michael Perry, *The Constitution, the Courts, and Human Rights* 64–67 (Yale Univ. Press 1982); Henry Monaghan, *Stare Decisis and Constitutional Adjudication*, 88 Colum. L. Rev. 723, 723–24 (1988).

43. Robert Bork, *The Tempting of America: The Political Seduction of the Law* 156–69 (Free Press 1989).

44. Raoul Berger, *Original Intent and Boris Bittker*, 66 Ind. L.J. 723, 747 (1991) (citation omitted).

45. *Id.* at 754.

46. *Id.* at 725.

47. See, e.g., Michael Stokes Paulsen, *Abrogating Stare Decisis by Statute: May Congress Remove the Precedential Effect of Roe and Casey?* 109 Yale L.J. 1535, 1543–44 (2000); John Harrison, *The Power of Congress Over the Rules of*

Precedent, 50 Duke L.J. 503 (2000); Gary Lawson, *The Constitutional Case against Precedent*, 17 Harv. J.L. & Pub. Pol'y 23 (1994). See also Steven Calabresi, *The Tradition of the Written Constitution: Text, Precedent, and Burke*, 57 Alabama L. Rev. 635 (2006).

48. Kelman, *Forked Path*, at 251.

49. 356 U.S. 165, 78 S. Ct. 632, 2 L. Ed. 2d 672 (1958).

50. *Id.* at 195.

51. Douglas, too, sometimes recognized precedent as having some weight, albeit tiny, in constitutional adjudication. Douglas, at 736 ("Stare decisis provides some moorings so that men may trade and arrange their affairs with confidence. Stare decisis serves to take the capricious element out of law and to give stability to a society").

52. Felix Frankfurter, *The Present Approach to Constitutional Decision on the Bill of Rights*, 28 Harv. L. Rev. 790, 791 (1915).

53. Felix Frankfurter & Thomas Corcoran, *Petty Federal Offenses and Trial by Jury*, 39 Harv. L. Rev. 917, 922 (1926).

54. Letter from Frankfurter to Stone (Dec. 28, 1943), quoted in Alpheus T. Mason, Harlan Fiske Stone 610 (1956).

55. *United States v. Rabinowitz*, 339 U.S. 56, 86, 70 S. Ct. 430, 94 L. Ed. 653 (1950) (Frankfurter, J., concurring).

56. *Graves v. New York*, 306 U.S. 466, 487, 59 S. Ct. 595, 83 L. Ed. 927 (1939) (Frankfurter, J., concurring).

57. *Green v. United States*, 356 U.S. 165, n.2, 78 S. Ct. 632, 2 L. Ed. 2d 672 (1958) (Frankfurter, J., concurring).

58. *Id.* at 193.

59. *Casey*, at 944 (Rehnquist, C.J, dissenting).

60. See *Johnson v. Transportation Agency, Santa Clara County, Cal.*, 480 U.S. 616, 673, 107 S. Ct. 1442, 1473, 94 L. Ed. 2d 615 (1987) (Scalia, J., dissenting); *South Carolina v. Gathers*, 490 U.S. 805, 823, 109 S. Ct. 2207, 2217, 104 L. Ed. 2d 876 (1989) (Scalia, J., dissenting); *Welch v. Texas Dept. of Highways and Public Transp.*, 483 U.S. 468, 496, 107 S. Ct. 2941, 2958, 97 L. Ed. 2d 389 (1987) (Scalia, J., concurring in part and in the judgment); *Healy v. Beer Institute, Inc.*, 491 U.S. 324, 344, 109 S. Ct. 2491, 2504, 105 L. Ed. 2d 275 (1989) (Scalia, J., concurring in part and in the judgment); *Webster v. Reproductive Health Services*, 492 U.S. 490, 532, 109 S. Ct. 3040, 3064, 106 L. Ed. 2d 410 (1989) (Scalia, J., concurring in part and in the judgment).

61. *U.S. v. International Business Machines Corp.*, 517 U.S. 843, 856, 116 S. Ct. 1793, 1801, 135 L. Ed. 2d 124, (1996) (opinion written by Thomas).

62. Antonin Scalia, *A Matter of Interpretation: Federal Courts and the Law* 138–39 (Princeton Univ. Press 1997).

63. *Id.* at 139.

64. See, e.g., *U.S. v. Dixon*, 509 U.S. 688, 704, 113 S. Ct. 2849, 2860, 125 L. Ed. 2d 556 (1993) (Scalia, J., majority) (arguing that *Grady v. Corbin*, 495 U.S. 508, 110 S. Ct. 2084, 109 L. Ed. 2d 548 (1990), should be overruled because it is

"wholly inconsistent with earlier Supreme Court precedent and with the clear common-law understanding of double jeopardy"); *Board of Educ. of Kiryas Joel Village School Dist. v. Grumet*, 512 U.S. 687, 751, 114 S. Ct. 2481, 2515, 129 L. Ed. 2d 546 (1994) (Scalia, J., dissenting) (arguing that the *Lemon* test, in *Lemon v. Kurtzman*, 403 U.S. 602, 91 S. Ct. 2105, 29 L. Ed. 2d 745 (1971), should be abandoned because it has become "utterly meaningless"); *Allied-Bruce Terminix Companies, Inc. v. Dobson*, 513 U.S. 265, 285, 115 S. Ct. 834, 845, 130 L. Ed. 2d 753 (1995) (Scalia, J., dissenting) (arguing *Southland Corp. v. Keating,* 465 U.S. 1, 104 S. Ct. 852, 79 L. Ed. 2d 1 (1984), should be overruled because, in addition to being wrongly decided, overruling would not impair any reliance interests); *Hubbard v. U.S.*, 514 U.S. 695, 716, 115 S. Ct. 1754, 1765, 131 L. Ed. 2d 779 (1995) (Scalia, J., concurring in part and concurring in the judgment) (arguing that *United States v. Bramblett,* 348 U.S. 503, 75 S. Ct. 504, 99 L. Ed. 594 (1955), should be overruled because it has "unacceptable consequences"); *U.S. v. Gaudin*, 515 U.S. 506, 520, 115 S. Ct. 2310, 2318, 132 L. Ed. 2d 444, (1995) (Scalia, J., majority) (arguing that the reasoning supporting *Sinclair v. United States,* 279 U.S. 263, 49 S. Ct. 268, 73 L. Ed. 692 (1929), had been repudiated by subsequent cases); *College Sav. Bank v. Florida Prepaid Postsecondary Educ. Expense Bd.*, 527 U.S. 666, 683, 119 S. Ct. 2219, 2229, 144 L. Ed. 2d 605, (1999) (arguing that *Parden v. Terminal R. of Ala. Docks Dept.,* 377 U.S. 184, 84 S. Ct. 1207, 12 L. Ed. 2d 233 (1964), was inconsistent with other privilege doctrine and had been effectively overruled by previous cases); *Dickerson v. U.S.*, 530 U.S. 428, 448, 120 S. Ct. 2326, 2339, 147 L. Ed. 2d 405 (2000) (Scalia, J., dissenting) (arguing that *Miranda v. Arizona,* 384 U.S. 436, 86 S. Ct. 1602, 16 L. Ed. 2d 694 (1966), should be overruled because it is "objectionable for innumerable reasons, not least the fact that cases spanning more than 70 years had rejected its core premise"); *Stenberg v. Carhart*, 530 U.S. 914, 955, 120 S. Ct. 2597, 2622, 147 L. Ed. 2d 743 (2000) (Scalia, J., dissenting) (arguing *Planned Parenthood of Southeastern Pa. v. Casey,* 505 U.S. 833, 112 S. Ct. 2791, 120 L. Ed. 2d 674 (1992), should be overruled because it was "hopelessly unworkable in practice").

65. Richard A. Posner, *In Memoriam: William J. Brennan, Jr.*, 111 Harv. L. Rev. 9, 11 (1997).

66. William J. Brennan, *In Defense of Dissents*, 37 Hastings L.J. 427, 435–37 (1986).

67. *Id.* at 432.

68. U.S. Const. art. III, § 2, cl. 1.

69. Fallon, at 592.

70. *Marbury v. Madison*, 5 U.S. (1 Cranch) 137, 177, 2 L. Ed. 60 (1803).

71. James B. Thayer, *The Origin and Scope of the American Doctrine of Constitutional Law*, 7 Harv. L. Rev. 129, 144 (1893) (He didn't say clearly erroneous, but he did say "It can only disregard the Act when those who have the right to make laws have not merely made a mistake, but have made a very clear one—so clear that it is not open to rational question").

72. The constitutionality of the third statute turns on the extent to which one regards it as indistinguishable from a regulation of the Court's jurisdiction.

If one were to accept the statute as the latter, then its constitutionality turns on the scope of congressional authority to regulate federal jurisdiction. If the Congress had unfettered discretion to regulate federal jurisdiction, it would follow that Congress may decide to foreclose an entire realm of the Constitution from further judicial review once the Court reached what Congress considered to be a correct interpretation of the Constitution. A statute that effectively regulated the Court's jurisdiction in this manner would be similarly constitutional.

73. U.S. Const. art. II, § 4 ("The President, Vice President and all civil officers of the United States, shall be removed from office on impeachment for, and conviction of, treason, bribery, or other high crimes and misdemeanors").

74. There is no persuasive or good evidence to suggest that the Framers had ever believed that a mistake in constitutional interpretation could plausibly constitute a legitimate basis for impeaching and removing a judge from office. See Michael J. Gerhardt, *Chancellor Kent and the Search for Elements of Impeachable Offenses*, 74 Chi.-Kent L. Rev. 91, 123 (1998).

75. See Evan H. Caminker, *Sincere and Strategic Voting Norms on Multimember Courts*, 97 Mich. L. Rev. 2297, 2329 (1999).

76. See generally, *U.S. v. Lopez*, 514 U.S. 549, 574, 115 S. Ct. 1624, 1637, 131 L. Ed. 2d 626, (1995) (Kennedy, J., concurring) ("The second, related to the first but of even greater consequence, is that the Court as an institution and the legal system as a whole have an immense stake in the stability of our Commerce Clause jurisprudence as it has evolved to this point. Stare decisis operates with great force in counseling us not to call in question the essential principles now in place respecting the congressional power to regulate transactions of a commercial nature"); *Quill Corp. v. North Dakota*, 504 U.S. 298, 317, 112 S. Ct. 1904, 1916, 119 L. Ed. 2d 91, (1992) ("The 'interest in stability and orderly development of the law' that undergirds the doctrine of stare decisis, see *Runyon v. McCrary*, 427 U.S. 160, 190–191, 96 S. Ct. 2586, 2604–2605, 49 L. Ed. 2d 415 (1976) (Stevens, J., concurring), therefore counsels adherence to settled precedent"); *Williams v. North Carolina*, 317 U.S. 287, 323, 63 S. Ct. 207, 225, 87 L. Ed. 279 (1942) (Jackson, J., dissenting) ("This Court may follow precedents, irrespective of their merits, as a matter of obedience to the rule of stare decisis. Consistency and stability may be so served. They are ends desirable in themselves, for only thereby can the law be predictable to those who must shape their conduct by it and to lower courts which must apply it. But we can break with established law, overrule precedents, and start a new cluster of leading cases to define what we mean, only as a matter of deliberate policy"); *Pollock v. Farmers' Loan & Trust Co.*, 158 U.S. 601, 663, 15 S. Ct. 912, 930, 39 L. Ed. 1108, (1895) (Harlan, J., dissenting) ("While, in a large sense, constitutional questions may not be considered as finally settled, unless settled rightly, it is certain that a departure by this court from a settled course of decisions on grave constitutional questions, under which vast transactions have occurred, and under which

the government has been administered during great crises, will shake public confidence in the stability of the law").

77. U.S. (1 Wheat.) 304, 4 L. Ed. 97 (1816).

78. U.S. (4 Wheat.) 316, 4 L. Ed. 579 (1819).

79. See Christopher J. Peters, *Foolish Consistency: On Equality, Integrity, and Justice in Stare Decisis*, 105 Yale L.J. 2031, 2050 (1996); Michael C. Dorf, *The Supreme Court, 1997 Term—Foreword: The Limits of Socratic Deliberation*, 112 Harv. L. Rev. 4, 8 (1998).

80. See, e.g., Richard A. Posner, *The Problematics of Moral and Legal Theory* (Harvard Univ. Press 1999).

81. U.S. Const. art. I, § 2, cl. 1.

82. See *Knox v. Lee*, 79 U.S. 457 (1870).

83. See *Santa Clara County v. Southern P.R. Co.*, 118 U.S. 394 (1886).

84. For comments on the tension between legal tender and original meaning, see, e.g., Henry P. Monaghan, *Stare Decisis and Constitutional Adjudication*, 88 Colum. L. Rev. 723, 744 (1988); Kenneth W. Dam, *The Legal Tender Cases*, 1981 Sup. Ct. Rev. 367, 389 (1981); Peter B. McMutchen, *Mistakes, Precedent, and the Rise of the Administrative State: Toward a Constitutional Theory of Second Best*, 80 Cornell L. Rev. 1, 17 (1994). While some scholars claim legal tender is consistent with original meaning, their claim turns, among other things, on ignoring the fact that it inexplicably eluded the dissenters in *Knox v. Lee*, including Chief Justice Chase, who as treasury secretary had been a leader in the administration's production of legal tender. For comments on the original understanding of the Fourteenth Amendment as not including corporations within the term "person", see, e.g., Raoul Berger, *Colloquy: Original Intent and Boris Bittker*, 66 Ind. L.J. 723, 749 (1991); Howard Jay Graham, *The Conspiracy Theory of the Fourteenth Amendment*, 47 Yale L.J. 371, 381 (1938).

85. U.S. 419 (1793).

86. U.S. Const. amend. XI ("The judicial power of the United States shall not be construed to extend to any suit in law or equity, commenced or prosecuted against one of the United States by citizens of another state, or by citizens or subjects of any foreign state").

87. For commentaries that Eleventh Amendment doctrine is driven principally by precedent, see, e.g., John T. Noonan, Jr., *Narrowing the Nation's Power: The Supreme Court Sides with the States* 153 (Univ. of California Press 2002); Vicki C. Jackson, *The Supreme Court, the Eleventh Amendment, and State Sovereign Immunity*, 98 Yale L.J. 1, 3 (1988). See also David J. Cloherty, *Exclusive Jurisdiction and the Eleventh Amendment: Recognizing the Assumption of State Court Availability in the Clear Statement Compromise*, 82 Cal. L. Rev. 1287, 1312 (1994); William A. Fletcher, *A Historical Interpretation of the Eleventh Amendment: A Narrower Construction of an Affirmative Grant of Jurisdiction Rather than a Prohibition Against Jurisdiction*, 35 Stan. L. Rev. 1033, 1060 (1983).

88. *Seminole Tribe v. Fla.*, 517 U.S. 44, 95 (1996) (Stevens, J., dissenting) ("Except insofar as it has been incorporated into the text of the Eleventh Amendment, the doctrine [of sovereign immunity] is entirely the product of judge-made law").

89. U.S. 1 (1890).

90. *Welch v. Texas Department of Highways and Public Transportation*, 483 U.S. 468, 496 (Scalia, J., concurring in part and concurring in the judgment) ("Regardless of what one may think of *Hans*, it has been assumed to be nearly the law for nearly a century. During that time, Congress has enacted many statutes ... on the assumption that States were immune from suits by individuals. Even if we were to find that assumption to have been wrong, we could not, in reason, interpret the statutes as though the assumption never existed").

91. See, e.g., *Alden v. Maine*, 527 U.S. 706 (1999); *College Savings Bank v. Florida Board*, 527 U.S. 666 (1999); *Seminole Tribe*, 517 U.S. at 44.

92. The Seventh Amendment provides in pertinent part that "the right of trial by jury shall be preserved, and no fact tried by jury, shall be otherwise re-examined in any Court of the United States, than according to the rules of the common law." U.S. Const. amend. VII.

93. See, e.g., Margaret L. Moses, *What the Jury Must Hear: The Supreme Court's Evolving Seventh Amendment Jurisprudence*, 68 Geo. Wash. L. Rev. 183 (2000) (noting that the Supreme Court's "evolving Seventh Amendment jurisprudence" in the 20th century emerged in four distinct strands).

94. See *Markman v. Westview Instruments, Inc.*, 517 U.S. 370, 384 (1996) ("Since evidence of common-law practice at the time of the framing does not entail application of the Seventh Amendment's jury guarantee to the construction of the claim document, we must look elsewhere to characterize this determination of meaning in order to allocate it as between court or jury. We accordingly consult existing precedent and consider both the relative interpretive skills of judges and juries and the statutory policies that ought to be furthered by the allocation").

95. See Jeffrey A. Segal & Harold J. Spaeth, *The Supreme Court and the Attitudinal Model Revisited* 298 (Cambridge Univ. Press 2002) ("The justices are rarely influenced by stare decisis").

96. Burkeans tend to accept the evolution of constitutional decisions in a common-law-like manner (issues dealt with on a case-by-case or incremental basis) and our entire history since the Founding. See, e.g., Ernest A. Young, *Rediscovering Conservatism: Burkean Political Theory and Constitutional Interpretation*, 72 N.C. L. Rev. 619 (1994).

97. For empirical analysis supporting this conclusion, see James H. Fowler & Sangick Jeon, *The Authority of Supreme Court Precedent: A Network Analysis* (June 29, 2005), available at http://jhfowler.ucdavis.edu/authority_of_supreme_court_precedent.pdf.

98. Akhil Reed Amar, *Foreword: The Document and the Doctrine*, 114 Harv. L. Rev. 26 (2000). Amar divides constitutional theorists into two camps—those who put the document first and those who put precedent first. While the latter differ in their reasons for putting precedent first, their common ground is a strong view of precedent.

99. Bruce Ackerman, *We the People, Volume II, Transformations*, at 5 (Belknap Press 1988) [hereinafter *Volume II*].

100. *Id.* at 418.

101. *Id.* at 419.

102. See generally Ronald Dworkin, *Taking Rights Seriously* 22–39 (Harvard Univ. Press 1997). For Dworkin's most recent articulation and defense of his legal philosophy and critique of rival theories, see *Justice in Robes* (Harvard Univ. Press 2006).

103. Ronald Dworkin, *Law's Empire* 228–38 (Belknap Press 1986).

104. Dworkin argues that empirically judges regard themselves as bound by the law and decide cases as if they are bound to find what the law is. This approach is consistent with their constitutional obligations. Judges are not entitled to exercise broad discretion because they have no democratic mandate to do so.

105. David A. Strauss, *Common Law Constitutional Interpretation*, 63 U. Chi. L. Rev. 877, 833, 879 (1996) (suggesting, inter alia, constitutional decisions evolve like the common law). See also Henry P. Monaghan, *The Supreme Court, 1974 Term—Foreword: Constitutional Common Law*, 89 Harv. L. Rev. 1 (1975) (suggesting Supreme Court precedents have the status of constitutional common law, which is superior to legislation or statutes but may be displaced by the Court or constitutional amendment); Kermit Roosevelt, *Constitutional Calcification*, 91 Va. L. Rev. 1649, 1693 (2005) (discussing how "when a stable jurisprudential regime has persisted for a period of time, decision rules can be mistaken for constitutional operative principles"); Mitchell Berman, *Constitutional Decision Rules*, 90 Va. L. Rev. 1, 9, 13, 80 n.145 (2004) (dividing constitutional doctrine into (1) "constitutional operative propositions," which "represent the judiciary's understanding of the proper meaning of a constitutional power, right, duty, or other sort of provision," and (2) "constitutional decision rules," which are "doctrines that direct courts how to decide whether a constitutional operative proposition is satisfied").

106. Kathleen M. Sullivan, *Foreword: The Justices of Rules and Standards*, 106 Harv. L. Rev. 22 (1992).

107. Kathleen M. Sullivan, *The Jurisprudence of the Rehnquist Court*, 22 Nova L. Rev. 743 (1998).

108. Lawrence Solum proposes the Court should "abandon its adherence to its doctrine that it is free to overrule its own decisions." Lawrence B. Solum, *The Supreme Court in Bondage: Constitutional Stare Decisis, Legal Formalism, and the Future of Unenumerated Rights*, 9 U. Pa. J. Const. Law 155 (2006).

He defends a "revival of formalist revival that would create theoretical space for the idea that the Supreme Court should regard itself as bound by precedent." He expects this revival to have the virtue of making justices more hesitant to take liberties, or to experiment, with broader, more aggressive constructions of the text. Another benefit might be encouraging justices to draft narrower opinions to allow themselves more discretion in future cases. See also Thomas W. Merrill, *Orginalism, Stare Decisis, and the Promotion of Judicial Restraint*, 22 Const. Comm. 271 (2005) (arguing that "a strong theory of precedent is more likely to produce judicial restraint").

109. See, e.g., Michael J. Gerhardt, *The Role of Precedent in Constitutional Decisionmaking and Theory*, Geo. Wash. L. Rev. 68, 116 (1991).

110. For a similar view, see Ward Farnsworth, *Signatures of Ideology: The Case of the Supreme Court's Criminal Docket*, 104 Mich. L. Rev. 71 (2005).

111. Farnsworth suggests "in cases where it's close—where maybe the rationale is present or maybe it isn't, or where the formal statement of the rule from the first case leaves a little room to question its fit in the second one—where should a judge look for guidance? There is really nothing to consider but his own immediate perception of which makes more sense, and this will trade heavily on intuitions about the underlying policies at stake." *Id.* at 81. On my view, the "underlying policies at stake" whenever justices are considering what to count as precedent, depends on many other factors, including their constructions of other precedents.

112. Jeffrey A. Segal & Harold J. Spaeth, *The Supreme Court and the Attitudinal Model* (Cambridge Univ. Press 1993).

113. See Harold J. Spaeth & Jeffrey A. Segal, *Majority Rule or Minority Will: Adherence to Precedent on the U.S. Supreme Court* (Cambridge Univ. Press 1999).

114. See Segal & Spaeth, *supra* note 95, at 48 (citations omitted.)

115. *Id.* (quoting *Law's Empire, supra* note 103, at 255).

116. See *Taking Rights Seriously, supra* note 102, at 401.

117. *Id.* at 47.

118. *Id.* at 292.

119. See *id.* at 401.

120. See Segal & Spaeth, *supra* note 95, at 292 (quoting Ronald Kahn, *Interpretive Norms and Supreme Court Decision-Making: The Rehnquist Court on Privacy and Religion*, in *Supreme Court Decision-Making: New Institutionalist Approaches* 75 (C. W. Clayton & H. Gillman eds., Univ. of Chicago Press 1999)).

121. See Segal & Spaeth, *supra* note 95, at 298 (quoting C. Herman Pritchett, *The Development of Judicial Research*, in *Frontiers of Judicial Research* 42 (J. B. Grossman & J. Tanenhaus eds., John Wiley & Sons 1969)).

122. See Segal & Spaeth, *supra* note 95, at 296.

123. *Id.* at 298.

124. *Id.* at 300.

125. *Id.* at 306.

126. *Id.* at 309–10.

127. See Edward L. Rubin, *The New Legal Process, the Synthesis of Discourse, and the Microanalysis of Institutions* 109 Harv. L. Rev. 1393, 1406 (1996) ("Positive political theory is similar to public choice theory in its view of public officials as rational self-interest maximizers. Instead of restricting self-interest to the individual, however, positive political theory analyzes institutional interests as well and views members of the institution as maximizing the power or discretion of the institution as a whole"). For a discussion of motivations, including formulating policy, political goals, the desire to reach "principled" decisions, and upholding institutional legitimacy, see Lee Epstein & Jack Knight, *The Choices Justices Make* 22–51 (CQ Press 1998).

128. Attitudinalists question rational choice theorists' assumption that the institutional framework provides constraints sufficient to cause justices to manipulate the law or vote outside of their personal policy preferences. See Segal & Spaeth, *supra* note 15, at 111. See also Jeffrey A. Segal, *Separation-of-Powers Games in the Positive Theory of Congress and Courts*, 91 Amer. Pol. Sci. Rev. 28, 42–43 (1997) (citing evidence that "suggests that justices can act in a sophisticated fashion *when they need to do so.* But the institutional protections granted the Court mean that with respect to Congress and the presidency, they almost never need to do so") (emphasis in original)).

129. See Segal & Spaeth, *supra* note 95, at 99–100 (citation omitted, ellipsis in original).

130. *Id.*

131. *Id.*

132. *Id.* at 102.

133. *Id.* at 111.

134. Jack Knight & Lee Epstein, *The Norm of Stare Decisis*, 40 Am. J. Pol. Sci. 1018–39 (1996).

135. Jeffrey A. Segal & Harold J. Spaeth, *Norms, Dragons, and Stare Decisis: A Response*, 40 Am. J. Pol. Sci. 1064–82 (1996).

136. See Andrew D. Martin & Kevin M. Quinn, *Dynamic Ideal Point Estimation via Markov Chain Monte Carlo for the Supreme Court, 1953–1999*, 10 Pol. Analysis 134 (2002).

137. Jack Goldsmith & Adrien Vermeule, *Empirical Methodology and Legal Scholarship*, 69 U. Chi. L. Rev. 153, 154–55 (2002).

138. *Id.* at 155.

139. See Segal & Spaeth, *supra* note 95, at 298 ("The levels of precedential behavior that we find in the U.S. Supreme Court are simply not consistent with the sorts of arguments we find, for example, in Dworkin, Kahn, or any of the other legalists that we have discussed").

140. Gerald N. Rosenberg, *The Supreme Court and the Attitudinal Model*, 4 Law & Cts. 6, 7 (1994).

141. Vincent Blasi, *Praise for the Court's Unpredictability*, N.Y. Times, July 16, 1986, at 23.

142. See Goldsmith & Vermeule, *supra* note 137, at 155 ("The substance of much legal scholarship is doctrinal, interpretive, and normative. Subgenres in this category include articles and books that attempt to reconcile or distinguish lines of precedent displaying internal tensions; that provide conceptual analysis of the internal logic of statutes, cases, and other materials; and that provide novel readings of canonical legal sources. The best legal scholarship combines these features, fitting confused canonical materials together in a coherent way and presenting the materials in a normatively attractive light. Work in this vein contains no empirical claims in any important or contestable sense—at least not if 'contestable' is defined by reference to the internal consensus of legal academics").

143. Only recently have some social scientists begun to test the extent to which sources other than precedent constrain courts. See, e.g., Robert M. Howard & Jeffrey A. Segal, *An Original Look at Originalism*, 36 Law & Soc'y Rev. 113, 133 (2002) (questioning whether justices base their decisions on the meaning of the text and the intent of the Framers).

144. See generally *Should Ideology Matter? Judicial Nominations* 2001: *Hearing before the Subcommittee on Administrative Oversight and the Courts of the Senate Committee on the Judiciary*, 107th Cong. App. (2001).

145. See Segal & Spaeth, *supra* note 95, at 295.

146. See, e.g., *Eldred v. Ashcroft*, 537 U.S. 186 (2003) (upholding 7–2 Congress' repeated extensions of the rights of copyright ownership in spite of constitutional language allowing Congress to do so for "limited terms"); *Reno v. Condon*, 528 U.S. 141 (2000) (unanimously upholding Congress' power to bar states from disclosing or selling personal information required for drivers' licenses); *Saenz v. Roe*, 526 U.S. 489 (1999) (reinvigorating, 7–2, the privileges or immunities clause); *Clinton v. Jones*, 520 U.S. 681 (1997) (unanimously holding that sitting presidents are not entitled to any immunity from civil lawsuits based on their unofficial misconduct); *United States v. Virginia*, 518 U.S. 515 (1996) (ruling 7–1 Virginia Military Academy's policy of excluding women as students violated equal protection); *Nixon v. United States*, 506 U.S. 224 (1993) (unanimously agreeing that the Court lacked the power to review the constitutionality of the procedures employed by the Senate in judicial impeachment trials); *Morrison v. Olson*, 487 U.S. 654 (1988) (upholding 8–1 the constitutionality of the Independent Counsel Act); *United States v. Nixon*, 418 U.S. 683 (1974) (unanimously holding presidents are not entitled to absolute executive privilege that would allow them unilateral discretion over whether to comply with otherwise lawful subpoenas).

147. *Virginia v. Black*, 538 U.S. 343 (2003).

148. See U.S. Const., art. III., § 1.

149. See Posner, *supra* note 80, at 118–19.

150. For one of the rare efforts by political scientists to explain legal change, see Thomas G. Hansford & James F. Spriggs II, *The Politics of Precedent on the U.S. Supreme Court* (Princeton Univ. Press 2006). Hanford and Spriggs attribute legal change to both the ideological distance of the Court to a precedent and the vitality—or extent of authority—of that precedent. I discuss their methodology and its implications in each of the next two chapters.

151. See *id.* at 117 ("Unquestionably, John Marshall dominated his Court as no other justice has").

152. Republican appointees filled 10 of the 11 vacancies arising on the Court during Marshall's tenure.

153. William Winslow Crosskey, *Mr. Chief Justice Marshall*, in *Mr. Justice: Biographical Studies of Twelve Supreme Court Justices* 5 (Allison Dunham & Philip B. Kurland eds., Univ. of Chicago Press 1964).

154. *Id.* at 12.

155. *Id.* at 18.

156. The Court rejected this view in *Wheaton v. Peters*, 8 Pet. 591 (1834).

157. See Segal & Spaeth, *supra* note 95, at 323.

158. See Michael J. Gerhardt, *The Rhetoric of Judicial Critique: From Judicial Restraint to the Virtual Bill of Rights*, 10 Wm. & Mary Bill of Rights J. 585, 637–38 (2002).

159. Leonard Baker, *Brandeis and Frankfurter: A Dual Biography* 456 (New York Univ. Press 1984).

160. *Graves v. New York ex rel. O'Keefe*, 306 U.S. 466, 491 (1939) (Frankfurter, J., concurring).

161. See Segal & Spaeth, *supra* note 15, at 118–19, 130, 132–33, 135, 138, 153, 156, 159.

162. I review these decisions in chapters 2 and 6.

163. U.S. 436 (1966).

164. U.S. 428 (2000).

165. See *The Supreme Court in American Politics: New Institutionalist Interpretations* (H. Gillman & C. W. Clayton eds., Univ. Press of Kansas 1999); Keith Whittington, *Once More Unto the Breach: PostBehavioralists Approaches to Judicial Politics*, 25 Law & Soc. Inquiry, 601, 607 (2000) (reviewing *Supreme Court Decision-Making: New Institutionalist Approaches* (Clayton & Gillman eds., 1999)).

166. *Id.* at 617.

Chapter 3

1. For a basic introduction to historical institutionalism, see *Supreme Court Decision-Making: New Institutionalist Approaches* (C. W. Clayton & H. Gillman eds., Univ. of Chicago Press 1999).

2. The notion of path dependency which I employ derives from social science, especially economic theory. It describes a specific phenomenon of

past events within economic and social systems as foreclosing certain choices. See generally Douglas North, *Institutions, Institutional Change, and Economic Performance* 99 (Cambridge Univ. Press 1990) (describing the notion of path dependency); Paul A. David, *Historical Economics in the Long Run: Some Implications of Path Dependence*, in *Historical Analysis in Economics* 29 (Graeme D. Stokes ed., Routledge 1993) (describing path dependency as the inability "to shake off the effects of past events") (footnotes omitted).

3. See Theodore W. Ruger et al., *The Supreme Court Forecasting Project: Legal and Political Science Approaches to Predicting Supreme Court Decisionmaking*, 104 Colum. L. Rev. 1150 (2004).

4. See Jeffrey A. Segal & Harold J. Spaeth, *The Supreme Court and the Attitudinal Model Revisited* 432 (Cambridge Univ. Press 2002) (citation omitted).

5. See Howard Gillman, *What's Law Got to Do with It? Judicial Behavioralists Test the "Legal Model" of Judicial Decision Making* 26 Law & Soc. Inquiry 465, 490–91 (2001) (citations and footnotes omitted).

6. *Id.* at 490–91 (citations omitted).

7. *Id.* at 490 (citing Elizabeth Bussiere, *(Dis)Entitling the Poor: The Warren Court, Welfare Rights, and the American Political Tradition* (Pennsylvania State Univ. Press 1997); Ronald Dworkin, *Freedom's Law: The Moral Reading of the American Constitution* (Harvard Univ. Press 1996)).

8. *Id.* at 490 (citing Mark Graber, *Transforming Free Speech: The Ambiguous Legacy of Civil Libertarianism* (Univ. of California Press 1991)).

9. *Id.* at 490 (citing Lee Epstein & Joseph F. Kobylka, *The Supreme Court and Legal Chance: Abortion and the Death Penalty* (Univ. of North Carolina Press 1992)).

10. *Id.* at 480 (citing Jack Knight & Lee Epstein *The Norms of Stare Decisis*, 40 Am. J. Pol. Sci. 1018 (1996).

11. *Id.* at 481 (citations omitted).

12. *Id.* at 481 (citing Frank B. Cross, *Political Science and the New Legal Realism: A Case of Unfortunate Interdisciplinary Ignorance*, 92 Nw. U. L. Rev. 251, 305–9 (1997)).

13. *Id.* at 481 (citations omitted).

14. *Id.* at 491.

15. Herbert M. Kritzer & Mark J. Richards, *Jurisprudential Regimes in Supreme Court Decisionmaking*, 96 Am. Pol. Sci. Rev. 205 (2002). See also Kritzer & Richards, *Jurisprudential Regimes: The Lemon Regime and Establishment Clause Cases*, 37 Law & Soc'y. Rev. 827 (2003) (finding that the *Lemon* test of *Lemon v. Kurtzman* influences outcomes).

16. Kritzer & Richards, *Jurisprudential Regimes in Supreme Court Decisionmaking*, 96 Am. Pol. Sci. Rev., at 205. Emerson Tiller and Frank Cross note that Kritzer and Richards "did not address the questions of why the Justices crafted specific language or exactly how different language mattered, but [they] established the very important point that doctrine

does matter in future decisions." Emerson Tiller & Frank Cross, *What Is Legal Doctrine?* in *Symposium: The First Century: Celebrating* 100 *Years of Legal Scholarship* 100 Nw. U. L. Rev. 517, 525 (2006). See also Stefanie A. Lindquist & David E. Klein, *The Influence of Jurisprudential Considerations on Supreme Court Decisionmaking: A Study of Conflict Cases,* 40 Law & Soc'y Rev. 135, 135 (2006) (finding "that jurisprudential considerations, as well as attitudinal concerns, affect the justices' decisionmaking processes in a substantial minority of cases").

17. Lawrence Baum, *Judges and Their Audiences: A Perspective on Judicial Behavior* 174 (Princeton Univ. Press 2006).

18. *Id.* at 22.

19. *Id.* at 175.

20. See Cass R. Sunstein, David Schadke, Lisa M. Ellman, & Andres Sawicki, *Are Judges Political? An Empirical Analysis of the Federal Judiciary* (Brookings Institution Press 2006).

21. Stephanie A. Lindquist & Frank B. Cross, *Empirically Testing Dworkin's Chain Novel Theory: Studying the Path of Precedent,* 80 N.Y.U. L. Rev. 1156 (2005).

22. *Id.* at 1204.

23. *Id.* at 1168.

24. *Id.* at 1155.

25. *Id.* at 1172–73.

26. *Id.* at 1177–78.

27. *Id.* at 1178.

28. Thomas G. Hansford & James F. Spriggs II, *The Politics of Precedent on the U.S. Supreme Court* (Princeton Univ. Press 2006).

29. *Id.* at 13.

30. *Id.* at 24.

31. See Brannon P. Denning, *Means to Amend: Theories of Constitutional Change,* 65 Tenn. L. Rev. 155, 229 (1997) (arguing that "[w]ith recent cases tending to reaffirm the Court's holding in *Lopez,* and with more cases to follow, notions that the Supreme Court has 'settled' the issue of congressional Commerce Clause power are no longer valid").

32. See Richard H. Fallon, Jr., *The "Conservative" Paths of the Rehnquist Court's Federalism Decisions,* 69 U. Chi. L. Rev. 429, 432 (2002).

33. See Table I (listing all expressly overruled Supreme Court cases).

34. See, e.g., *United States v. Morrison,* 529 U.S. 598 (2000) (holding that a gender-motivated violent crime is not an economic activity); *United States v. Lopez,* 514 U.S. 549 (1995) (holding that the possession of guns in school zones is not an economic activity).

35. 410 U.S. 113 (1973).

36. 381 U.S. 479 (1965) (finding that a state statute prohibiting the use of contraceptives violates married couples' right to marital privacy and is thereby unconstitutional).

37. 262 U.S. 390 (1923) (striking a state law that prohibited teaching non-English to any child in the eighth grade or below).

38. 268 U.S. 510 (1925) (holding that an Oregon law compelling school children to attend school within their district of residence was an unconstitutional interference with parents' liberty to direct their children's education).

39. 316 U.S. 535 (1942) (finding that the Oklahoma Habitual Criminal Sterilization Act violated the equal protection clause of the Fourteenth Amendment).

40. 381 U.S. at 485–87 (noting that the opinion is confined to the right to privacy within marriage).

41. *Roe v. Wade*, 410 U.S. 113, 159 (1973) (stating that "[t]he situation ... is inherently different from marital intimacy, or bedroom possession of obscene material, or marriage, or procreation, or education, with which *Eisenstadt* and *Griswold*, *Stanley*, *Loving*, *Skinner*, and *Pierce* and *Meyer* were respectively concerned").

42. See *id.* at 152 (citing a litany of cases dealing with the right to personal privacy drawn from many different amendments).

43. 539 U.S. 558 (2003).

44. 478 U.S. 186 (1986).

45. *Lawrence*, 539 U.S. at 585–605 (2003) (Scalia, J., dissenting).

46. See *Vacco v. Quill*, 521 U.S. 793, 807–8 (1997) (unanimously rejecting the argument that New York's ban on physician-assisted suicide violates the equal protection clause because the state allowed competent persons to refuse lifesaving medical treatment); *Washington v. Glucksberg*, 521 U.S. 702, 728 (1997) ("[T]he asserted 'right' to assistance in committing suicide is not a fundamental liberty interest protected by the Due Process Clause"); *Cruzan v. Dir., Mo. Dep't of Health*, 497 U.S. 261, 280 (1990) (holding that a state may constitutionally impose higher evidentiary requirements in the matter of terminating treatment for incompetent patients); *Bowers*, 478 U.S. at 190–91 ("[W]e think it evident that none of the rights announced in [*Roe*] bears any resemblance to the claimed constitutional right of homosexuals to engage in acts of sodomy").

47. 517 U.S. 620, 623–25 (1996) (holding unconstitutional an amendment to the Colorado Constitution that prohibited state government action designed to protect homosexuals from discrimination).

48. 539 U.S. at 580 ("We have been most likely to apply rational basis review to hold a law unconstitutional under the Equal Protection Clause, where as here, the challenged legislation inhibits personal relationships").

49. *Bowers*, 478 U.S. at 186.

50. 514 U.S. 549 (1995).

51. See *id.* at 560 (reconciling with the test such decisions as *NLRB v. Jones & Laughlin Steel Corp.*, 301 U.S. 1 (1937); *Darby v. United States*, 312 U.S. 100 (1941); *Heart of Atlanta Motel, Inc., v. United States*, 379 U.S. 241 (1964); and *Wickard v. Filburn*, 317 U.S. 111 (1942)).

52. 540 U.S. 712 (2004).

53. *Id.* at 718.

54. 536 U.S. 639 (2002).

55. See *Locke*, 540 U.S. at 726 (Scalia, J., dissenting) (finding *Lukumi* to be "irreconcilable with *Locke*, which sustains a public benefits program that facially discriminates against religion").

56. 503 U.S. 520, 546 (1993) (quoted in *Locke*, 540 U.S. at 726 (Scalia, J., dissenting)).

57. *Id.* at 533 (quoted in *Locke*, 540 U.S. at 726 (Scalia, J., dissenting)).

58. 494 U.S. 872, 882–85 (1990) (discussing the reasons for rejecting heightened scrutiny).

59. See, e.g., *Wisconsin v. Yoder*, 406 U.S. 205, 221 (1972) ("Where fundamental claims of religious freedom are at stake … we must searchingly examine the interests the state seeks to promote"); *Sherbert v. Verner*, 374 U.S. 398, 406 (1963) ("We must … consider whether some compelling state interest justifies the substantial infringement of appellant's First Amendment right").

60. 395 U.S. 444 (1969).

61. *Id.* at 447.

62. *Yates v. United States*, 354 U.S. 298 (1957); *Dennis v. United States*, 341 U.S. 494, 505 (1951); *Abrams v. United States*, 250 U.S. 616, 627 (1919).

63. 515 U.S. 200 (1995).

64. 497 U.S. 547 (1990).

65. See *Adarand*, 515 U.S. at 225–27 (holding that *Metro Broadcasting* rejected long-standing jurisprudence requiring congruence of standards for evaluating federal and state racial classification).

66. *City of Richmond v. J.A. Croson Co.*, 488 U.S. 469, 511 (1989).

67. See, e.g., *Fullilove v. Klutznick*, 448 U.S. 448, 491–92 (1980) (upholding federal legislation requiring 10 percent of federal funding for local public works projects be set aside for minority applicants); *Regents of University of California v. Bakke*, 438 U.S. 265, 320 (1978) (reversing an injunction that would prevent the university from ever considering race in admissions procedures).

68. See *Adarand*, 515 U.S. at 256–57 (Stevens, J., dissenting) (finding that *Adarand* was "an unjustified departure from settled law").

69. 369 U.S. 186 (1962).

70. 531 U.S. 98 (2000).

71. See, e.g., Markenzy Lapointe, *Bush v. Gore: Equal Protection Turned on its Head, Perhaps for a Good Though Unintended Reason*, 2 Wyo. L. Rev. 435, 479 (2002) (arguing, inter alia, that "the result cannot be justified by any of the Court's prior equal protection decisions").

72. See, e.g., Rachel E. Barkow, *More Supreme than Court? The Fall of the Political Question Doctrine and the Rise of Judicial Supremacy*, 102 Colum. L. Rev. 237, 336 (2002).

73. 328 U.S. 549 (1946).

74. 541 U.S. 267 (2004).

75. 478 U.S. 109 (1986).

76. *Vieth*, 541 U.S. at 281.

77. *Id.* at 68. Justice Scalia stressed *Davis* required overruling, because "[e]ighteen years of essentially pointless litigation have persuaded [a plurality] that *[Davis v.] Bandemer* is incapable of principled application." *Id.* at 70. In a separate concurrence in *Vieth*, Justice Anthony Kennedy resisted overruling *Davis* because he would not "foreclose all possibility of judicial review if some limited and precise rationale were found to correct an established violation of the Constitution in some redistricting cases." *Id.* at 71 (Kennedy, J., concurring in the judgment).

78. At issue in *Bush v. Gore* were the meanings and significance of several voting rights decisions, including *Harper v. Virginia State Board of Elections*, 383 U.S. 663 (1966) (declaring the state poll tax unconstitutional); and *Wesberry v. Sanders*, 376 U.S. 1 (1964) (holding unconstitutional uneven apportionment of congressional districts in Georgia); *Baker v. Carr*, 369 U.S. 186 (1962) (finding justiciable a cause of action involving state reapportionment decisions).

79. 426 U.S. 88 (1976).

80. William N. Eskeridge, Jr., Philip P. Frickey & Elizabeth Garrett, *Cases and Materials on Legislation: Statutes and the Creation of Public Policy* 394 (3d ed., West 2001). The authors suggest the possibility that *Mow Sun Wong* may be the result of four justices abandoning their initial belief that the case should be decided on equal protection grounds in order "to avoid friction over [what was then Stevens'] first opinion." *Id.* These factors might explain *Mow Sun Wong*, but not the subsequent failure to sharply redefine or narrow the case.

81. 505 U.S. 833 (1992).

82. 506 U.S. 224 (1993).

83. The only impeachment proceeding to run its full course through the House and the Senate after Walter Nixon's was the impeachment and trial of President William Jefferson Clinton. President Clinton considered the suggestion, but ultimately declined to initiate any judicial challenge to his impeachment by the House.

84. The Eleventh Amendment provides that "[t]he Judicial power of the United States shall not be construed to extend to any suit in law or equity, commenced or prosecuted against one of the United States by Citizens of another State, or by Citizens or Subjects of any Foreign State." U.S. Const. amend. XI.

85. 134 U.S. 1 (1890).

86. See Christina Bohannan, *Beyond Abrogation of Sovereign Immunity: State Waivers, Private Contracts, and Federal Incentives*, 77 N.Y.U. L. Rev. 273, 281 (2002) (noting that the Court's holding in *Hans* is "contrary to the plain language of the Eleventh Amendment").

87. See *Dellmuth v. Muth*, 491 U.S. 223, 229 n.2 (1989) (declining "this most recent invitation to overrule [its] opinion in *Hans*").

88. See Ruger et al., *supra* note 3, at 1151–52 (noting that a machine did "significantly better at predicting [case] outcomes than did the [academic legal] experts").

89. Jeffrey A. Segal & Harold J. Spaeth, *The Supreme Court and the Attitudinal Model Revisited* 319 (Cambridge Univ. Press 2002) ("The model predicts 77 percent of the Court's cases correctly"). I hasten to add that a 77% success rate in predicting outcomes is not necessarily that good. Under most grading systems, 77% is a B or a C. In contrast, the 92% success rate of attorneys in the forecasting study is a high B or a low A.

90. *Griswold v. Connecticut*, 381 U.S. 479, 479–86 (1965).

91. Cf. *Stenberg v. Carhart*, 530 U.S. 914 (2000) (striking a state statute criminalizing performance of partial-birth abortions because the law lacked a health exception and thereby placed an undue burden on a woman's right to choose to have an abortion).

92. 347 U.S. 483 (1954).

93. See David A. Strauss, *Discriminatory Intent and the Taming of Brown*, 56 U. Chi. L. Rev. 935, 940–44 (1989) (identifying those principles as "lack of impartiality," "subordination," "stigma," "second-class citizenship," and "encouragement of prejudice").

94. *United States v. Lopez*, 514 U.S. 549 (1995).

95. See *id.* at 567 (declining to continue the history of automatic deference to Congress in rational basis analysis).

96. 469 U.S. 528, 551 (1985).

97. See *id.* at 557 ("*National League of Cities v. Usery* is overruled") (citation omitted).

98. 426 U.S. 833, 855 (1976) ("We are ... persuaded that *Wirtz* must be overruled").

99. See *Maryland v. Wirtz*, 392 U.S. 183 (1968) (stating that under the commerce clause the Fair Labor Standards Act could be applied to state-operated hospitals and schools).

100. *Garcia*, 469 U.S. at 580 (Rehnquist, J., dissenting) (holding that it is not "incumbent on those of us in dissent to spell out further the fine points of a principle that will, I am confident, in time again command the support of a majority of this Court").

101. See *New York v. United States*, 505 U.S. 144 (1992).

102. 517 U.S. 44, 53 (1996) ("[T]he Eleventh Amendment prevent[s] Congress from authorizing suits by Indian tribes against states for prospective injunctive relief to enforce legislation enacted pursuant to the Indian Commerce Clause").

103. 531 U.S. 98 (2000).

104. Compare *Bush*, 531 U.S. at 103 ("Our consideration is limited to the present circumstances") with Steven J. Mulroy, *Lemonade from Lemons: Can*

Advocates Convert Bush v. Gore into a Vehicle for Reform? 9 Geo. J. on Poverty L. & Pol'y 357, 357 (2002) ("[A] number of voting rights advocates have tried to use the *Bush* decision to push for long overdue electoral reform"). Moreover, the obvious difficulties with predicting *Bush*'s impact on voting rights law were apparent in the days leading up to the 2004 presidential election: Experts were predicting all sorts of dire legal scenarios, none of which came to pass.

105. See *Bush*, 531 U.S. at 109 ("Our consideration is limited to the present circumstances, for the problem of equal protection in election processes generally presents many complexities").

106. *McCulloch v. Maryland*, 17 U.S. (4 Wheat.) 316, 407 (1819) (stating that a constitution's "nature ... requires that only its great outlines should be marked").

107. For a discussion of how the indeterminacy of the law facilitates its unpredictability, see Jules L. Coleman & Brian Leiter, *Determinacy, Objectivity, and Authority*, 142 U. Pa. L. Rev. 549, 579–84 (1993).

108. Michael C. Dorf, *Legal Indeterminacy and Constitutional Design*, 78 N.Y.U. L. Rev. 875, 884 (2003).

109. Oona A. Hathaway, *Path Dependence in the Law: The Course and Pattern of Legal Change in a Common Law System*, 86 Iowa L. Rev. 601, 604 (2001).

110. See Frank H. Easterbrook, *Abstraction and Authority*, 59 U. Chi. L. Rev. 349, 366 (1992) (criticizing the argument that—because of the phenomenon of path dependency—"the meaning of the Constitution varies with the order in which cases reach the Court"); Richard H. Fallon, Jr., *The "Conservative" Paths of the Rehnquist Court's Federalism Decisions*, 69 U. Chi. L. Rev. 429, 434–35 (2002) (describing how the Rehnquist Court's federalism decisions reflect the conventional conception of path dependency); Richard A. Posner, *The Supreme Court, 2004 Term—Foreword: A Political Court*, 119 Harv. L. Rev. 31, 45 (2005) ("Honoring precedent injects path dependence in constitutional law: where you end depends to a significant degree on where you began"); Richard A. Posner, *Past-Dependency, Pragmatism, and Critique of History in Adjudication and Legal Scholarship*, 67 U. Chi. L. Rev. 573, 585–86 (2000) (acknowledging that because of path dependency the "structure of common law doctrine (broadly understood as doctrine forged in the process of deciding cases, whether or not they technically are common law cases) seems on the whole pretty efficient"); see also Barry Friedman & Scott B. Smith, *The Sedimentary Constitution*, 147 U. Pa. L. Rev. 1, 9–33 (1998) (employing the conventional conception of path dependency to describe the process of constitutional adjudication). But see Fallon, *supra*, at 436 (urging "capacious conception of path dependence [a]s the idea that as the Court proceeds along a doctrinal path, both it and the attentive public assess what the justices may properly do next in light of past experience"); Posner, *Past-Dependency*, at 586 (recommending conceiving of the law as "a servant of social need, a conception which severs the law from any inherent dependence on its past").

111. See, e.g., Charles Fried, *Saying What the Law Is: The Constitution in the Supreme Court* 4 (Harvard Univ. Press 2004); Henry P. Monaghan, *Foreword to Constitutional Common Law*, 89 Harv. L. Rev. 1, 3 (1975) (analyzing the Supreme Court's 1974 term to illustrate the use of common-law reasoning in constitutional cases); David Strauss, *Common Law Constitutional Interpretation*, 63 U. Chi. L. Rev. 877 (1996) (arguing in favor of constitutional interpretation based on common law).

112. On differences between rules and standards, see generally Kathleen M. Sullivan, *The Justices of Rules and Standards*, 106 Harv. L. Rev. 22 (1992).

113. See Kathleen M. Sullivan, *The Jurisprudence of the Rehnquist Court*, 22 Nova L. Rev. 741, 753–58 (1998) (demonstrating the application of constitutional standards).

114. See *Terry v. Ohio*, 392 U.S. 1, 21 (1968) (holding that reasonableness of search or seizure can be determined by "balancing the need to search (or seize) against the invasions which the search (or seizure) entails").

115. 488 U.S. at 473 (1989) ("Even if the level of equal protection scrutiny could be said to vary according to the ability of different groups to defend their interests in the representative process, heightened scrutiny would still be appropriate in the circumstances of this case").

116. 515 U.S. at 227 (1995) ("[A]ll racial classifications … must be analyzed by a reviewing court under strict scrutiny. In other words, such classifications are constitutional only if they are narrowly tailored measures that further compelling governmental interests").

117. 539 U.S. at 343 (2003) (upholding a narrowly tailored affirmative action program in a law school admissions program).

118. 541 U.S. 36 (2004).

119. See *id.* at 1373 ("By replacing constitutional guarantees with open-ended balancing tests, we do violence to their design. Vague standards are manipulable").

120. *Id.* at 1370 ("[T]he [Confrontation] Clause's ultimate goal is to ensure reliability of evidence, but it is a procedural rather then a substantive guarantee … The Clause thus reflects a judgment, not only about the desirability of reliable evidence, but about how reliability can be best determined").

121. *Crawford*, 541 U.S. at 1374 ("Where testimonial statements are at issue, the only indicum of reliability sufficient to satisfy constitutional demands is the one the Constitution actually prescribes: confrontation"); U.S. Const. amend. VI ("In all criminal prosecutions … the accused shall enjoy the right … to be confronted with the witnesses against him").

122. See, e.g., Mitchell Berman, *Constitutional Decision Rules*, 90 Va. L. Rev. 1 (2004); Kermit Roosevelt, *Aspiration and Underenforcement*, 119 Harv. L. Rev. 193 (2006); Jack Balkin, *Abortion and Original Meaning* (August 28, 2006), Yale Law School Public Working Paper No. 128, available at SSRN: http//ssrn.com/abstract=925558.

123. Barry Friedman and Scott Smith have referred to this phenomenon as our "sedimentary constitution," in which different doctrines have been built up over time one atop the other, just like different layers of sediment. See Barry Friedman & Scott Smith, *The Sedimentary Constitution*, 147 U. Pa. L. Rev. 1 (1998).

124. One study shows that changes in the Court's composition affect justices short- and long-term strategies in handling precedent. See Scott R. Meinke & Kevin M. Scott, *Explaining Vote Changes on the U.S. Supreme Court: The Effect of Membership Change on Continuing Justices*, November 16, 2005.

125. See John W. Dean, *The Rehnquist Choice: The Untold Story of the Nixon Appointment That Redefined the Supreme Court* 16 (Free Press 2001) (discussing Nixon's search for a strict constructionist justice).

126. *Id*. at 15.

127. See Michael J. Gerhardt, *The Pressure of Precedent: A Critique of the Conservative Approaches to Stare Decisis in Abortion Cases*, 10 Const. Comment. 67, n.2 (1993) (citing Reagan's and Bush's positions on abortion).

128. See Christopher E. Smith & Thomas R. Hensley, *Unfulfilled Aspirations: The Court Packing Efforts of Presidents Reagan and Bush*, 57 Alb. L. Rev. 1111, 1122 (1994) ("The Supreme Court approved governmental regulations affecting women's choices about abortion that would never have been approved by the Justices comprising the majority in *Roe v. Wade*").

129. See *The Republicans: The Convention in New York, The Platform on Gay Marriage*, N.Y. Times, Aug. 30, 2004, at A8 (reprinting text of the Republican platform).

130. See Vikram D. Amar & Evan H. Caminker, *Equal Protection, Unequal Political Burdens and the CCRI*, 23 Hastings Const. L.Q. 1019, 1028 (1996) (arguing that "[l]ower courts are generally obligated to interpret and apply existing Supreme Court precedents faithfully, having little discretion to determine that old precedent has lost its binding force").

131. See Evan H. Caminker, *Why Must Inferior Courts Obey Supreme Superior Court Precedents?* 46 Stan. L. Rev. 817, 818 (1994) ("[L]ongstanding doctrine dictates that a court is *always* bound to follow a precedent established by a court 'superior' to it").

132. See *Don E. Williams Co. v. Comm'r of Internal Revenue.*, 429 U.S. 569, 573 (1977) (observing that because the Seventh Circuit Court of Appeals had not yet ruled on an issue, the Tax Court was free to decline to follow decisions of the Third, Ninth, and Tenth Circuits).

133. Caminker, *supra* note 131, at 853 ("[I]nternal consistency strengthens external credibility").

134. Adrien Vermeule, *The Judiciary is a 'They,' Not an 'It': Two Fallacies of Interpretive Theory* 1–2 (Univ. Chi. Pub. Law & Legal Theory Working Paper No. 49, 2003) (pointing to the underlying assumptions about the judiciary's collective character that render generally accepted views on statutory interpretation tenuous).

135. See Maxwell L. Stearns, *Constitutional Process: A Social Choice Analysis of Supreme Court Decision Making* 46 (Univ. of Michigan Press 2000) ("Cycling arises when, for any given outcome, another has majority support in a direct binary comparison. ... [W]hen a [voting paradox] rule is employed, no outcome is stable. For this reason, we can conceive of [voting paradox] rules as possessing the characteristic feature of unlimited majority veto").

136. See *Legal Tender Cases*, 79 U.S. (12 Wall.) 457, 553–54 (1870), overruling *Hepburn v. Griswold*, 75 U.S. (8 Wall.) 603 (1869).

137. See generally *Should Ideology Matter? Judicial Nominations 2001: Hearing before the Subcommittee on Administrative Admin. Oversight and the Courts of the Senate Committee on the Judiciary*, 107th Cong. App. 1–2 (2001) (explaining the relevance of ideology to federal judicial selection).

138. On the unpredictability of Supreme Court appointments, see generally Henry J. Abraham, *Justices and Presidents: A Political History of Appointments to the Supreme Court* (rev. ed., Oxford Univ. Press 1993).

139. *Lawrence v. Texas*, 539 U.S. 558 (2003), is an excellent example. Both appointees by President George H. W. Bush fractured, with Souter joining the majority and Thomas in dissent. President Reagan's appointees also divided, with Justice Kennedy writing for the majority, Justice O'Connor concurring on separate grounds, and Justice Scalia writing a fiery dissent. *Id.*

140. Ward Farnsworth recognizes that the absence of formal rules for construing or constructing precedents leaves justices with considerable room for manipulating precedents on the bases of their respective personal preferences or ideological commitments. See Ward Farnsworth, *Signatures of Ideology: The Case of the Supreme Court's Criminal Docket*, 104 Mich. L. Rev. 71, 88–89 (2005).

141. Adrian Vermeule, *Veil of Ignorance Rules in Constitutional Law*, 111 Yale L.J. 399, 399 (2001) (explaining the use of the veil rule to suppress self-interested behavior).

142. *Id.*

143. See U.S. Const. art. V (requiring two-thirds of each house of Congress to propose amendments and three-fourths of the state legislatures to ratify them).

144. See Cass R. Sunstein, *President Versus Precedent: Bush's Reckless Bid for an Amendment Defies an Oval Office Tradition*, L.A. Times, Feb. 26, 2004, at B13 (explaining how President Bush's deviation from previously successful efforts to amend the Constitution likely dooms his proposed amendment to ban gay marriage).

145. See *Goodridge v. Dep't of Pub. Health*, 798 N. E. 2d 941, 969 (Mass. 2003) ("[B]arring an individual from the protections, benefits, and obligations of civil marriage solely because that person would marry a person of the same sex violates the Massachusetts Constitution").

146. See, e.g., H. W. Perry Jr., *Deciding to Decide: Agenda Setting in the United States Supreme Court* 127 (Harvard Univ. Press 1991) (arguing that certain

highly respected interest groups have better success in the certiorari process); Lee Epstein, *Interest Group Litigation During the Rehnquist Court Era*, 9 J.L. & Pol'y 639 (1993) (examining the frequency, goals, kinds, issues, and efficacy of interest group litigation).

147. Joseph D. Kearney & Thomas W. Merrill, *The Influence of Amicus Curiae Briefs on the Supreme Court*, 148 U. Pa. L. Rev. 743 (2000) (studying cases from 1946 to 1995 that triggered 20 or more amicus briefs).

148. *Grutter v. Bollinger*, 539 U.S. 306, 371 (2003) (Thomas, J., concurring in part and dissenting in part) (contesting the majority's use of the amicus briefs in their opinions).

149. 530 U.S. 428 (2000).

150. *Miranda v. Arizona*, 384 U.S. 436 (1966).

151. See, e.g., Gerald N. Rosenberg, *Bringing Politics Back In*, 95 Nw. U. L. Rev. 309 (2000) (reviewing Lucas A. Powe, Jr., *The Warren Court and American Politics* (Belknap Press 2000)) (criticizing Powe for placing too much emphasis on *Brown*'s influence over the Civil Rights Movement); Michael J. Klarman, *Rethinking the Civil Rights and Civil Liberties Revolutions*, 82 Va. L. Rev. 1, 7 (1996) ("*Brown* is better understood as the product of a civil rights movement spawned by World War II than as the principal cause of the 1960s civil rights movement").

152. 531 U.S. 98 (2000).

153. Judge Richard Posner favors this approach. See Richard A. Posner, *Breaking the Deadlock: The 2000 Election, the Constitution, and the Courts* (Princeton Univ. Press 2001) (viewing the decision in terms of "judicial pragmatism").

154. 323 U.S. 214 (1944).

155. See *Adarand*, 515 U.S. at 214 (citing *Korematsu*); *Croson Co.*, 488 U.S. at 494 ("We thus reaffirm the view expressed by the plurality in *Wygant* that the standard of review [of compelling state interest] … is not dependent on the race of those burdened or benefited by a particular classification").

156. James H. Fowler & Sangick Jeon, *The Authority of Supreme Court Precedent: A Network Analysis* (June 29, 2005).

157. *Id.* at 31.

158. *Id.* at 31.

159. Stephen Choi and Mitu Gulati found circuit court judges do not engage in citation bias—citing more precedents from judges from their own party than from opinions by the other party's judges—in mundane areas, but are more likely to engage in citation bias in opinions dealing with salient subjects or with another judge in opposition. See Choi & Gulati, *Bias in Judicial Citations: A Window into the Behavior of Judges?* (Nov. 26, 2006).

Chapter 4

1. For how lawyers generally define precedent, see *Black's Law Dictionary* 1214 (Deluxe 8th ed., West 2004) (defining precedent alternatively as either

"the making of law by a court in recognizing and applying new rules while administering justice" or "a decided case that furnishes a basis for determining later cases involving similar facts or issues"). For social scientists' understandings of precedent, see, e.g., Thomas G. Hansford & James F. Spriggs II, *The Politics of Precedent on the U.S. Supreme Court* 5 (Princeton Univ. Press 2006) (defining precedent as "the legal doctrines, principles, or rules established by prior court opinions").

2. For a notable exception among casebooks, see, e.g., Paul Brest, Sanford Levinson, J. M. Balkin, & Akhil Reed Amar eds., *Processes of Constitutional Decisionmaking: Cases and Materials* (4th ed., Aspen 2000).

3. See, e.g., *Atkins v. Virginia*, 536 U.S. 304, 348 (2002) (Scalia, J., dissenting) (deriding the "arrogance" of the majority's ruling that the Eighth Amendment bars executions of people with cognitive disabilities found guilty of certain crimes); Laurence H. Tribe, *Erog v. Hsub and Its Disguises: Freeing Bush v. Gore from its Hall of Mirrors*, 115 Harv. L. Rev. 170, 288 (2001) (claiming "[t]he Court's self-confidence in matters constitutional is matched only by its disdain for the meaningful participation of other actors in constitutional debate"); Samuel Issacharoff, *Political Judgments*, in *The Vote: Bush, Gore, and the Supreme Court* 55, 57 (Cass R. Sunstein & Richard A. Epstein eds., Univ. of Chicago Press 2001) (describing *Bush v. Gore* as a "swaggeringly confident").

4. On how nonjudicial actors' constitutional decision making helps to construct constitutional law, see generally Keith Whittington, *Constitutional Construction: Divided Powers and Constitutional Meaning* (Harvard Univ. Press 1999).

5. See Ruth C. Silva, *Presidential Succession* 39–41 (Univ. of Michigan Press 1951); Carl Brent Swisher, *Roger B. Taney* 269–72 (Archon Books 1961).

6. Edward P. Crapol, *John Tyler: The Accidental President* 10 (Univ. of North Carolina Press 2006).

7. *Id.* (citation omitted in original).

8. *Id.* at 11.

9. John Tyler, Inaugural Address, April 9, 1861.

10. Crapol, *supra* note 6, at 12–13.

11. Norma Lois Peterson, *The Presidencies of William Henry Harrison and John Tyler* 49–50 (Univ. Press of Kansas 1989).

12. *Id.* at 49–50.

13. Crapol, *supra* note 6, at 10.

14. The seven other vice presidents who succeeded to the presidency are Millard Fillmore (1850), Andrew Johnson (1865), Chester Arthur (1881), Theodore Roosevelt (1901), Calvin Coolidge (1923), Harry Truman (1945), and Lyndon Johnson (1963).

15. See *infra* note 22 and accompanying text.

16. Article I, § 7, cl. 2 (provides that a president "shall sign" a bill of which he approves, while in vetoing a measure he is required to return the measure "with his Objections to that House in which it shall have originated").

17. T. J. Halstead, CRS Report for Congress, *Presidential Signing Statements: Constitutional and Institutional Implications*, September 20, 2006, at 2.

18. See *id.* at 3–4.

19. See *id.* at 5.

20. See *id.* at 5–8.

21. See *id.* at 8–11.

22. See, e.g., Charlie Savage, *Takeover: The Return of the Imperial Presidency and the Subversion of American Democracy* 230 (Little, Brown and Company 2007) ("By the seventh year of [his] presidency, Bush had attached signing statements to about 150 bills …, challenging the constitutionality of well over 1,100 separate sections in the legislation"). See also Philip J. Cooper, *George W. Bush, Edgar Allan Poe and the Use and Abuse of Presidential Signing Statements*, Presidential Studies Q. 35, no. 3, at 517, 522 (September 2005) (characterizing the constitutional objections raised by President Bush as falling across 17 categories, ranging from generalized assertions of presidential authority to supervise the "unitary executive branch" to federalism limits imposed on Congress by the Supreme Court).

23. For comprehensive discussions of the first impeachment, see Buckner Meltner, Jr., *The First Impeachment: The Constitution's Framers and the Case of Senator William Blount* (Mercer Univ. Press 1998); David P. Currie, *The Constitution in Congress: The Federalist Period, 1789–1801* 275–81 (Univ. of Chicago Press 1997).

24. See *Responses of the Presidents to Charges of Misconduct* 8 (C. Vann Woodward ed., Dell 1974) (special report to the Judiciary Committee on the history of impeachment).

25. *Id.*

26. U.S. Const., art. II, § 4.

27. On the possible significance of the Senate votes on Blount's defenses, see Michael J. Gerhardt, *The Federal Impeachment Process: A Constitutional and Historical Analysis* 47–50 (rev. ed., Univ. of Chicago Press 2000).

28. *Id.* at 49–50.

29. See, e.g., D. Currie, *supra* note 23, at 281 (referring to "Blount's case … [a]s commonly cited to have established" the "proposition" that "members of Congress are not 'officers of the United States'") (citations omitted).

30. Blount's lawyers argued that expulsion was the exclusive remedy for sanctioning the misconduct of members of Congress and that it was absurd to construe the Constitution as allowing two modes for removing senators, particularly since expulsion is easier to accomplish than removal, as the former depends only on the Senate's judgment. In response, the House managers stressed that the two procedures were not in tension with each other, because the impeachment process allows for one sanction—disqualification—that expulsion does not. See *id.* at 279–80. While this latter argument is perfectly sensible, neither representatives nor senators

have shown any interest in rethinking the impeachability of members of Congress.

31. See Sean Wilentz, *The Rise of American Democracy: Jefferson to Lincoln* 399–401, 436–47, 443 (W. W. Norton 2005).

32. *Id.* at 398.

33. Andrew Jackson, Message of Protest to Senate, April 15, 1834; Message to the Senate Clarifying the Protest, April 21, 1834.

34. Wilentz, *supra* note 31, at 454.

35. See Michael J. Gerhardt, *The Constitutionality of Censure*, 33 U. Rich. L. Rev. 33 (1999) (discussing the constitutionality of proposed censure of President Clinton and other arguably similar resolutions previously passed by the House and Senate).

36. See Jack H. Maskell, CRS Report 98–843, *Censure of the President*, December 8, 1998 (reviewing House and Senate resolutions critical of presidents); *Alternatives to Impeachment: What May Congress Do?* Association of the Bar of the City of New York, Committee on Federal Legislation, December 11, 1998 (identifying as constitutionally significant resolutions passed by the House criticizing Presidents Tyler, Polk, Lincoln, Buchanan, and T. Roosevelt).

37. See Mildred L. Amer, Congressional Research Service, *The Congressional Record: Content, History, and Issues*, January 1993, at 3.

38. See *id.*

39. Charles Schamel et Al., U.S. National Archives and Records Administration, *Guide to the Records of the United States House of Representatives at the National Archives, 1789–1989: Bicentennial Edition* (Doct. No. 100–245, 1989).

40. *Id.*

41. *Id.*

42. *Id.*

43. Before 1934, presidential and executive branch records had serious deficiencies. In the early 1900s, the State Department implemented, for the first time, a numbering system to record executive orders, beginning with President Lincoln's Emancipation Proclamation. From 1934 onward, the *Federal Register* has published presidential proclamations and executive orders. In 1934 Congress enacted the Federal Register Act, which requires, inter alia, the preservation of administrative rules and regulations. In 1957 the Office of the Federal Register began publishing materials that presidents and other executive officials donated as historical materials to the National Archives, but it was not until the Presidential Records Act of 1978 that Congress made presidents' papers the official property of the United States.

44. S. Doc No. 106–1, R. XXII, § 2, at 21.

45. For a description of the controversy generated by Democrats' filibusters against President Bush's judicial nominees and Republican responses, see

Thomas E. Mann & Norman J. Ornstein, *The Broken Branch: How Congress Is Failing and How to Get It Back on Track* 162–69 (Oxford Univ. Press 2006).

46. See, e.g., Catherine Fisk & Erwin Chemerinsky, *The Filibuster*, Stan. L. Rev. 181 (1997); John O. McGinnis & Michael B. Rappaport, *The Constitutionality of Legislative Super Majority Voting Requirements: A Defense*, 105 Yale L.J. 483, 496–500 (1995).

47. See Mann & Ornstein, *supra* note 45, at 162–69 (describing how the nuclear option works); Martin B. Gold & Dimple Gupta, *The Constitutional Option to Change Senate Rules and Procedures: A Majoritarian Means to Overcome the Filibuster*, 28 Harv. J.L. & Pub. Pol'y 205 (2004) (describing the "constitutional option" for a majority's successfully prohibiting judicial filibusters).

48. See Mann & Ornstein, *supra* note 45, at 168.

49. See *id.* at 209. See also *id.* at 210 (acknowledging that "each time the Senate rules have been amended, the body has followed the rules change procedures set forth in the rules themselves").

50. See Hearing on Rule XXII and Proposals to Amend the Rule, Committee on Rules and Administration, U.S. Senate, June 5, 2003.

51. See Betsy Palmer, Congressional Research Service Report, *Changing Senate Rules: The "Constitutional" or "Nuclear" Option*, April 15, 2005. For one incident that is an arguable precedent on point, see *infra* notes 58–64 and accompanying text.

52. See Joseph R. Biden, Jr., *Floor Statement: Jumping Off the Precipice: The "Nuclear Option" and the United States Senate*, April 27, 2005 (discussing the significance of the senators' rejection of Dawes' suggestion), available at http://biden.senate.gov/newsroom/details.cfm?id=237030&&.

53. Senate Committee on Rules and Administration, 99th Congress, Senate Cloture Rule, Limitation of Debate in the Congress of the United States and Legislative History of Rule XXII of the Standing Rules of the United States Senate (Cloture Rule) at 29 (Comm. Print 1985) (citation omitted).

54. *Id.*

55. *Id.*

56. *Id.*

57. See, e.g., Gold & Gupta, *supra* note 47, at 98.

58. Senate Cloture Rule, *supra* note 53, at 28–29.

59. *Id.* at 30 (citation omitted in the original).

60. *Id.* at 30.

61. *Id.*

62. *Id.*

63. *Id.* at 31 (citation omitted in original).

64. *Id.* at 31.

65. See generally Richard S. Beth, Congressional Research Service Memorandum, *Supermajority Vote Requirements Currently in Effect in Congress*, 3–4 (January 20, 1995).

66. Bill Frist, *It's Time for an Up-or-Down Vote*, USA Today, May, 16, 2005, at 12A.

67. T. Mann & N. Ornstein, *supra* note 45, at 167 (making reference to holds, the blue-slip process, the discretion of committee chairs not to schedule committee votes, and negative committee votes as the various means through which differently sized minorities nullify judicial nominations and other legislative business in the Senate).

68. See *id.* at 251 n.14 ("Proponents of the nuclear option argued that Fortas had not been filibustered, even though virtually every news account at the time and the comments of Fortas opponents viewed the actions against him as a filibuster. Moreover, the official Senate Web site, in its section on history, has as its headline 'October 1, 1968: Filibuster Derails Supreme Court Appointee'") (citation omitted in original).

69. Gold & Gupta, *supra* note 47, at 262–69 (describing the "Byrd" precedents).

70. *Id.*

71. See *supra* notes 44–70 and accompanying text.

72. For an account of the rejections of the Versailles Treaty and the League of Nations Covenant, see Samuel Eliot Morison, *The Oxford History of the American People* 880–882 (Oxford Univ. Press 1965).

73. Article 5, North Atlantic Treaty Organization, August 24, 1949, 63 Stat. 2241, TIAS No. 1964, 34 UNTS 243. But the United Nations Security Council has the power under the United Nations Charter (to which the United States is a party via a statute) to move UN members into a state of hostilities with malefactor nations. Although President George H. W. Bush cited the UN Security Council's authorization as the basis for his mobilization of American troops in response to Iraq's invasion of Kuwait, he agreed in the eleventh hour to seek—and got—congressional approval for the use of force in what ensued as Desert Storm.

74. U.S. Const., art. I, § 7, cl. 1.

75. For one eminent scholar's approval of treaty authorizations of president's use of force, see Philip C. Bobbitt, *War Powers: An Essay on John Hart Ely's War and Responsibility: Constitutional Lessons of Vietnam and its Aftermath*, 92 Mich. L. Rev. 1364, 1394 (1994). For a similarly expansive view of a president's options to go to war, see H. Jefferson Powell, *The President's Authority Over Foreign Affairs: An Essay in Constitutional Interpretation* (Carolina Academic Press, 2002).

76. See, e.g., Nicholas Quinn Rosenkranz, *Executing the Treaty Power*, 118 Harv. L. Rev. 1867, 1869 (2005) (arguing against the declaration that "there are no subject-matter limitations on the treaty power" in the Restatement (Third) of the Foreign Relations Law of the United States, in part because it allows treaties to expand congressional and presidential powers beyond those explicitly recognized in the Constitution).

77. U.S. Const., art. VI, cl. 2.

78. See, e.g., Bobbitt, *supra* note 75, at 1394.

79. See, e.g., *Goldwater v. Carter*, 444 U.S. 996 (1979) (four justices maintained that presidential rescission of treaties is a nonjusticiable, political question, while Justice Powell argued that the claim was not yet ripe for judicial review because Congress had taken no action to assert its constitutional authority).

80. See *Youngstown Sheet & Tube v. Sawyer*, 343 U.S. 634–55 (1952) (Jackson, J., concurring).

81. *Id.*, art. II, § 2, cl. 2 (the president "shall have Power, by and with Advice and Consent of the Senate, to make Treaties, provided two-thirds of the Senators present concur").

82. Bobbitt, *supra* note 75, at 1383–84.

83. See Catherine Drinker Bowen, *Miracle at Philadelphia: The Story of the Constitutional Convention May to September 1787*, 22–23 (Back Bay Books 1986).

84. See Michael A. Gillespie & Michael Lienesch, *Introduction* to *Ratifying the Constitution* 1 (Michael A. Gillespie & Michael Lienesch eds., Univ. Press of Kansas 1989).

85. See generally Steven G. Calabresi, *The ABA in Law and Social Policy: What Role?* (Federalist Society for Law & Public Policy Studies 1994) (surveying the participation of the ABA in making policy decisions and recommendations on judicial nominees).

86. See, e.g., *Lawyers Committee for Civil Rights Under Law Urges Rejection of John D. Ashcroft as Attorney General of the United States*, U.S. Newswire, Jan. 22, 2001, available in 2001 WL 4139263; Robert Belton, *A Comparative Review of Public and Private Enforcement of Title VII of the Civil Rights Act of 1964*, 31 Vand. L. Rev. 905, 923–33 (1978) (noting that the Lawyers' Committee for Civil Rights Under Law contributed to early enforcement of Title VII through litigation); Susan M. Olson, *How Much Access to Justice from State "Equal Access to Justice Acts"?* 71 Chi.-Kent. L. Rev. 547, 555 (noting the committee's opposition to the Equal Access to Justice Act).

87. U.S. Const., amend. XXVII.

88. See *With Little Fanfare, Amendment Is Signed*, N.Y. Times, May 19, 1992, at A14.

89. See S. Rep. No. 75–711, at 13–14 (1937) (summarizing senators' explanations for their rejection of the Court-packing plan).

90. See, e.g., Betsy Palmer, *Changing Senate Rules: The "Constitutional" or "Nuclear" Option*, CRS Report for Congress, April 5, 2005, at 1 (describing the presiding officer's and institution's formal judgments on rules and their operation as governing "precedents" within the Senate).

91. See Arthur T. Denzau & Robert J. Mackay, *Gatekeeping and Monopoly Power of Committees: An Analysis of Sincere and Sophisticated Behavior*, 27 Am. J. Pol. Sci. 740, 741–44 (1983).

92. See generally Congressional Quarterly, *CQ Guide to Congress* 425 (3d ed., 1982).

93. See, e.g., *id.* at 195–96 (discussing the "norm" of senatorial courtesy and other long-standing practices of the Senate).

94. See Elizabeth Garrett, *Term Limitations and the Myth of the Citizen Legislator*, 81 Cornell L. Rev. 623, 662–63 (1996) (charting the peaks and valleys of the seniority system over the course of the 20th century).

95. U.S. Const., art. I, § 5.

96. H. W. Brands, *Woodrow Wilson* 30–31 (Times Books 2003) (describing this innovation as "one of [Wilson's] lasting contributions to American governance").

97. See, e.g. Cal. Health & Safety Code § 7180(a) (2005) (defining "death" as "irreversible cessation of circulatory and respiratory functions" and /or "irreversible cessation of all functions of the entire brain").

98. See Anna Badkhen, *In Massachusetts, Gay Weddings are Now Routine; Growing Acceptance of Same-Sex Nuptials on First Anniversary*, S.F. Chronicle, May 17, 2005, at A4.

99. See Lynne M. Ross ed., *State Attorneys General: Powers and Responsibilities* 61–75 (National Association of Attorneys General 1990); see also Robert Toepfer, *Some Legal Aspects of the Duty of the Attorney General to Advise*, 19 U. Cin. L. Rev. 201, 203 (1950).

100. For instance, former Virginia governor Doug Wilder appointed special legal counsel to represent the Virginia Retirement System because he perceived that Mary Sue Terry, the attorney general, would have a conflict of interest. Though Terry filed suit, the state assembly resolved the impasse under Va. Code Ann. § 2.1-122(a) (1994) (current version at 2.2-510.1 (2006)) (specifying that the governor may appoint special counsel when the Attorney General's office is "unable" to render the service at issue).

101. See, e.g., Cal. Const. art. VII, § 8 (disqualification from office; bribery; improper election practices); Mo. Const. art. VII, §§ 1, 4 (impeachment and removal of officers not subject to impeachment); N.C. Const. art. VI, § 8 (disqualifications for office).

102. Charlie LeDuff, *The California Recall: The Governor-Elect*, N.Y. Times, Oct. 8, 2003, at A26.

103. William Yardley, *Under Pressure, Rowland Resigns Governor's Post*, N.Y. Times, June 22, 2004, at Al.

104. Laura Mansnerus, *McGreevey Steps Down After Disclosing a Gay Affair*, N.Y. Times, Aug. 13, 2004, at A1.

105. U.S. Const. art. I, § 10 ("No State shall ... pass any ... Law impairing the Obligation of Contracts").

106. See, e.g., *Indiana ex rel. Anderson v. Brand*, 303 U.S. 96 (1938); *Ogden v. Saunders*, 25 U.S. 213, 256–59, 326 (1827).

107. U.S. Const. amend. XIV ("nor shall any State deprive any person of life, liberty, or property, without due process of law").

108. U.S. Const. amend. V ("nor shall private property be taken for public use, without just compensation").

109. See, e.g., *Memphis Light, Gas & Water Div. v. Craft*, 436 U.S. 1 (1978); *Board of Regents v. Roth*, 408 U.S. 564 (1972); *Fox River Paper v. Railroad Commission*, 274 U.S. 651 (1927); *Sauer v. New York*, 206 U.S. 536 (1907).

110. U.S. Const. amend. VIII ("Excessive bail shall not be required, nor excessive fines imposed, nor cruel and unusual punishments inflicted").

111. See, e.g., *Lockyer v. Andrade*, 538 U.S. 63 (2003); *Ewing v. California*, 538 U.S. 11 (2003).

112. 539 U.S. 558 (2003).

113. *Id*. at 571–72.

114. *Id*. at 568.

115. U.S. 186 (1986).

116. See generally Larry Kramer, *The People Themselves: Popular Constitutionalism and Judicial Review* (Oxford Univ. Press 2004).

117. See generally Michael J. Klarman, *From Jim Crow to Civil Rights: The Supreme Court and the Struggle for Racial Equality* (Oxford Univ. Press 2004).

118. See Civil Rights Act of 1957, Pub. L. No. 71–634 (1957) and Civil Rights Act of 1964, Pub. L. No. 88–352 (1964).

119. See Mark V. Tushnet, *The NAACP's Legal Strategy Against Segregated Education, 1925–1950* 144 (Univ. of North Carolina Press 1987) (describing a common perception of the litigation strategy used by the NAACP, Inc. Fund to dismantle segregation as a model for public interest law generally); see also Richard Thompson Ford, *Courting Trouble: A Story of Love, Marriage, and Litigation Strategy* from Slate.com (June 1, 2004), available at http://www.slate.com/id/2101537 (arguing that gay marriage activism in California failed because parties in that state failed to follow litigation strategy established by the civil rights movement).

120. See Robert L. Tienken, *Precedents of the House of Representatives Relating to Exclusion, Expulsion and Censure* (Library of Congress, Congressional Research Service, 1973); but see *Powell v. McCormack*, 395 U.S. 486 (1969) (overturning exclusion of Adam Clayton Powell on grounds that he wrongfully diverted House funds for personal use and made false reports regarding expenditures of foreign currency).

121. Jack Maskell, *Expulsion, Censure, Reprimand, and Fine: Legislative Discipline in the House of Representatives*, CRS Report RL 31382, 24–25 (Library of Congress, Congressional Research Service, 2002). At the time this book went to press, House leaders were threatening to expel Bob Ney, who resigned after pleading guilty to several felonies.

122. *Id*. at 22–23.

123. *Id*. at 23–24.

124. Anne M. Butler & Wendy Wolff, *U.S. Senate Election, Expulsion, and Censure Cases, 1793–1990*, S. Doc. No. 103–33 xviii (1995).

125. *Id*. at xxviii.

126. *Id*. at xxix.

127. Andrew Jackson, Veto Message, July 10, 1832, 2 *Messages and Papers of the Presidents* 578–79 (Richardson ed., 1897); available at http://onlinebooks. library.upenn.edu/webbin/metabook?id=mppresidents. Jackson argued that the "authority of the Supreme Court must not ... be permitted to control the Congress or the Executive when acting in their legislative capacities, but to have only such influence as the force of their reasoning may deserve." *Id.*

128. See Sandy Levinson, *Against the Veto*, The New Republic (2006).

129. See, e.g., *Guide to the Presidency* 816 (Michael Nelson ed., CQ Press 2002) (describing President Franklin D. Roosevelt's efforts to modernize the organization of the White House).

130. See Michael A. Fletcher, *Quiet but Ambitious White House Counsel Makes Life of Law*, Wash. Post, June 21, 2005, at A19 (mentioning White House Counsel Harriet Miers' staff of 13 lawyers); see also Dan Froomkin, *2004 White House Office Staff List*, Wash. Post, available at http://www.washingtonpost.com/wp-srv/politics/administration/whbriefing/2004stafflistc.html.

131. See *Guide to the Presidency* 1220–1221 (Michael Nelson ed., CQ Press 2002) (describing the changing priorities of the attorney general and the Department of Justice through the Nixon, Ford, Carter, and Reagan administrations).

132. See generally Douglas W. Kmiec, *OLC's Opinion Writing Function: The Legal Adhesive for a Unitary Executive*, 15 Cardozo L. Rev. 337 (1993).

133. U.S. Const. amend. XII.

134. See Bruce A. Ackerman, *The Failure of the Founding Fathers: Jefferson, Marshall, and the Rise of Presidential Democracy* (Harvard Univ. Press 2006).

135. U.S. Const. art. I, § 2, cl. 5.

136. *Id.*, art. I, § 3, cl. 5.

137. U.S. 996 (1979). The Supreme Court vacated the claim. Four Justices based their decision on the political question doctrine, while Justice Powell concurred on the ground that the claim was not yet ripe for judicial review because Congress had taken no action to assert its constitutional authority.

138. See also Peter M. Shane & Harold H. Bruff eds., *Separation of Powers Law* 807 (2d ed., Carolina Academic Press 2005) ("[T]he Executive has adhered to a constitutional view ... that the President has unreviewable authority (a) to determine when the interests of the United States demand U.S. military action and (b) to commit our troops to the protection of U.S. interests, even without clear legislative authority").

139. See Archibald Cox, *The Role of the Supreme Court in American Government* 18 (Oxford Univ. Press 1976) (noting the limitation that the courts may only decide constitutional issues as questions of law "in the course of ordinary litigation").

140. See generally Richard H. Fallon et al., *Hart and Wechsler's The Federal Courts and the Federal System* 320–323 (5th ed., Foundation Press 2003). See also Daniel Meltzer, *The History and Structure of Article III*, 138 U. Pa. L. Rev. 1569 (1990).

141. For the 12-month period ending in March 2004, 1,654,847 cases were filed in the bankruptcy courts; 278,212 cases were filed in the U.S. District Courts; and 60,505 cases were filed in the U.S Court of Appeals. See Statistics Division of the Administrative Office of the United States Courts, *Federal Judicial Caseload Statistics* (March 31, 2005), available at http://www.uscourts.gov/caseload2005/contents.html. During the 2004 term, the Supreme Court considered 1727 petitions from the appellate docket, granting certiorari to 69, and 5815 petitions from the miscellaneous docket, granting certiorari to only 11. See *The Supreme Court—The 2004 Term: The Statistics*, 119 Harv. L. Rev. 415, 426 (2005).

142. See, e.g., Jonathan D. Glater, *As a Private Lawyer, Miers Left Little for the Public Record*, N.Y. Times, October 10, 2005, at A17 (citing statistics that, of 80 cases before the Supreme Court in the previous term, only 33 raised questions of constitutional law, and that such numbers are typical).

143. For instance, during the 2004 term of the Supreme Court, three cases dealt with constitutional judgments of the federal government outside the criminal context. Of these cases, at least two were decided for the government. Likewise, 13 cases dealt with the constitutional judgments of state or local actors. Of these, the Court decided nine in favor of the government. (Note, however, that this percentage shifts in the criminal context—of the three federal criminal cases involving constitutional issues, all were decided against the government, while six of eight state criminal cases involving constitutional issues were decided against the government.)

144. *Hart and Wechsler, supra* note 140, at 320–21.

145. See *Black's Law Dictionary* 1290 (Deluxe 8th ed., West 2004) ("Rational basis is the most deferential of the standards of review that courts use").

146. For some notable exceptions, see *Lawrence v. Texas*, 539 U.S. 558 (2003); *Romer v. Evans*, 517 U.S. 620 (1996); *City of Cleburne v. Cleburne Living Center*, 437 U.S. 432 (1985).

147. See Erwin Chemerinsky, *Federal Jurisdiction* 58 (4th ed., Aspen 2003) ("The notion is that by restricting who may sue in federal court, standing limits what matters the judiciary will address and minimizes judicial review of the actions of the other branches of government"); see also Antonin Scalia, *The Doctrine of Standing as an Essential Element of the Separation of Powers*, 17 Suffolk U. L. Rev. 881 (1983) (arguing that standing "is a crucial and inseparable element of [the separation of powers] principle, whose disregard will inevitably produce … an overjudicialization of the processes of self-governance").

148. *Elk Grove Unified Sch. Dist. v. Newdow*, 124 S. Ct. 2301 (2004).

149. U.S. Const. amend. I ("Congress shall make no law respecting an establishment of religion, or prohibiting the free exercise thereof").

150. See Act of June 14, 1954, Pub. L. No. 396, Ch. 297, 68 Stat. 249 (1954).

151. See 148 Cong. Rec. S6100, 6101–4 (2002) (quoting various senators referring to the decision as "twisted" (Sen. Lieberman), "nuts" (Sen. Daschle), and "stupid" (Sen. Reid)).

152. See, e.g., *Nixon v. United States*, 506 U.S. 224 (1993); *Coleman v. Miller*, 307 U.S. 433 (1939); *Foster v. Neilson*, 27 U.S. 253 (1829).

153. See *Coleman*, 307 U.S. at 450.

154. See *Nixon*, 506 U.S. at 229–30 (determining that constitutional text, historical practices, and original understanding supported treating judicial challenges to Senate trial committees as nonjusticiable).

155. See *Luther v. Borden*, 48 U.S. 1 (1849).

156. *Id.* at 10–12.

157. For one thoughtful examination of custom's significance in constitutional analysis, see Michael J. Glennon, *The Use of Custom in Resolving Separation of Powers Disputes*, 64 B.U. L. Rev. 109 (1984).

158. See, e.g., *Eldred v. Ashcroft*, 537 U.S. 186, 204 (2003); *Marsh v. Chambers*, 463 U.S. 783 (1983).

159. See *infra* notes 165 and 166 and accompanying text.

160. See, e.g., *Vacco v. Quill*, 521 U.S. 793, 807 (1997) (referring to traditional rights to bodily integrity and freedom from unwanted touching); *Washington v. Glucksberg*, 521 U.S. 702, 725 (1997) (referring to the "long legal tradition protecting the decision to refuse unwanted medical treatment").

161. See, e.g., *Am. Ins. Ass'n v. Garamendi*, 539 U.S. 396, 416 (2003) (referring to the "historical practice" of the executive making postwar reparations settlements). In *Hudson v. Michigan*, 547 U.S. 1096 (2006), the Court construed "changed circumstances" in police practices as an additional basis for deferring to nonjudicial activities—in that case, violations of the ancient "knock-and-announce" rule.

162. U.S. 299 (1803).

163. *Id.* at 308–9.

164. See, e.g., Statute of the International Court of Justice, art. 38, 59 Stat. 1055, 1060 (1945) (listing "international custom" as a traditional source of international law).

165. See generally William N. Eskeridge, Jr., et al., *Cases and Materials on Legislation Statutes and the Creation of Public Policy* 1062–70 (3d ed., West 2000) (describing the commonality of agencies' constructions of ambiguous federal statutes and the Court's consistent deference to them).

166. See, e.g., Thomas Merrill, *Judicial Deference to Executive Precedent*, 101 Yale L.J. 969 (1992) (finding the Court before 1984 deferred to agencies in 75 percent of surveyed cases but after *Chevron, U.S.A., Inc., v. Natural Resources Defense Council*, 467 U.S. 837 (1984), it deferred to agencies in 59 percent of the cases in which it applied *Chevron's* framework). See also

Gregg J. Polsky, *Can Treasury Overrule the Supreme Court?* 84 B.U. L. Rev. 85 (2004); Comment, *The NMF's National Standard Guidelines: Why Judicial Deference*, 91 Cal. L. Rev. 1375 (2003).

167. For three notable exceptions, see *United States v. Virginia*, 518 U.S. 515 (1996); *Lee v. Weisman*, 505 U.S. at 583; *Loving v. Virginia*, 388 U.S. 1 (1967).

168. See, e.g., *Edelman v. Jordan*, 415 U.S. 651, 663–69 (1974); *Hans v. Louisiana*, 134 U.S. 1 (1890); *Louisiana v. Jumel*, 107 U.S. 711 (1883).

169. U.S. Const. amend. XI.

170. See *Alden v. Maine*, 527 U.S. 705, 724 (1999).

171. See, e.g., *College Sav. Bank v. Fla. Prepaid Postsecondary Ed. Expense Bd.*, 527 U.S. 666, 675 (1999) (holding that court will only find a waiver of immunity if the state voluntarily invokes the Supreme Court's jurisdiction, or if it makes a "clear declaration" that it intends to submit itself to Supreme Court jurisdiction); *Clark v. Barnard*, 108 U.S. 436, 447 (1883) (holding that a state's sovereign immunity "is a personal privilege which it may waive at pleasure"); *Beers v. Arkansas*, 61 U.S. 527, 529 (1858) (holding that the decision for a state to waive its immunity "is altogether voluntary on the part of the sovereignty").

172. S. Ct. 2195 (2005).

173. *Id.* at 2221 (O'Connor, J., dissenting).

174. S. Ct. 2655 (2005).

175. Audrey G. McFarlane, *The New Inner City: Class Transformation, Concentrated Affluence and the Obligations of the Police Power*, 8 U. Pa. J. Const. L. 1, 49 (2006) ("the holding in *Kelo* affirms the guarantee … of local government autonomy, not just in matters of development, but also as in matters of property ownership in general").

176. S. Ct. 769 (2003).

177. *Id.* at 778.

178. U.S. Const. art. I, § 8, cl. 7.

179. See generally Michael J. Gerhardt, *The Federal Impeachment Process: A Constitutional and History Analysis* passim (2d ed., Univ. of Chicago Press 2000) (discussing these and other constitutional issues arising in impeachment proceedings).

180. See *Judicial Nominations, Filibusters, and the Constitution: When a Majority is Denied Its Right to Consent: Hearing before the S. Comm. on the Judiciary*, 108th Cong. (2003) (statement of Douglas Kmiec) ("The original understanding gives unfettered nomination authority to the President"); Michael J. Gerhardt, *The Federal Appointments Process as Constitutional Interpretation*, in *Congress and the Constitution* 110 (Neal Devins & Keith Whittington eds., Duke Univ. Press 2005) (discussing the ways in which the Senate effects unreviewable constitutional interpretation through its authority over federal appointments).

181. See generally Jack M. Beerman & William P. Marshall, *The Constitutional Law of Presidential Transitions*, 84 N.C. L. Rev. 1253 (2006).

182. See generally Keith E. Whittington, *Hearing about the Constitution in Congressional Committees*, in *Congress and the Constitution*, *supra* note 132, at 87 (suggesting that committees engage constitutional issues as evidenced through their hearings).

183. Courts routinely have deferred to Congress' internal procedural rules. In *United States v. Ballin*, 144 U.S. 1 (1892), the Court upheld the rule under the rational basis test, while lower courts dismissed judicial challenges to procedural rules on standing and political question grounds. See *Skaggs v. Carlyle*, 110 F.3d 831 (D.C. Cir. 1997); *Hoffman v. Jeffords*, 175 F. Supp. 2d 49 (D.D.C. 2001); *Page v. Shelby*, 995 F. Supp. 23 (D.D.C. 1998).

184. Homeland Security Act of 2002, Pub. L. No. 107–296, 116 Stat. 2135 (codified as amended in scattered sections of 6 U.S.C.).

185. See, e.g., *Schick v. Reed*, 419 U.S. 256, 266 (1974) ("Presidents throughout our history as a Nation have exercised the power to pardon or commute sentences upon conditions that are not specifically authorized by statute [and] such conditions have generally gone unchallenged").

186. See *Adarand Constructors v. Pena*, 515 U.S. 200, 237 (1995) (declaring that "we wish to dispel the notion that strict scrutiny is 'strict in theory, but fatal in fact'") (citation omitted).

187. *Grutter v. Bollinger*, 539 U.S. 306 (2003).

188. U.S. 265 (1978).

189. See *McConnell v. Fed. Election Comm'n*, 540 U.S. 93 (2003) (upholding the constitutionality of the Bipartisan Campaign Finance Reform Bill).

190. See *Nevada Dep't of Human Resources v. Hibbs*, 538 U.S. 721 (2003) (upholding the constitutionality of the Family Leave Act).

191. Through the 2002 term, the Supreme Court had struck down only 169 federal laws as unconstitutional. Of those, 13 were struck down during the 1930s, while the Rehnquist Court struck down 41. See Linda Greenhouse, *Because We Are Final: Judicial Review Two Hundred Years After Marbury*, 56 SMU L. Rev. 781, 786 (2003). For a table providing the number of federal and state laws struck down by decade, see Harold W. Stanley & Richard G. Niemi, *Vital Statistics on American Politics 2003–2004* 292 (CQ Press 2003); see also Lee Epstein, Jeffrey A. Segal, Harold J. Spaeth, & Thomas Walker, *The Supreme Court Compendium* 163–66 (3d ed., CQ Press 2003).

192. See Neal Devins, *Conservative and Progressive Legal Orders: The Majoritarian Rehnquist Court?* 67 Law & Contemp. Prob. 63 (2004).

193. From 1986 through April 30, 2006, the Senate passed 11,642 total measures, while the House passed 13,257, for a grand total of 24,899. In 2004 the Senate passed 663 of 1318 measures introduced, while the House passed 747 of 2338 measures introduced. In 1997 the Senate passed 385 of 1840 measures introduced, while the House passed 544 of 3728 measures introduced.

194. From 1980 to 1989, the Supreme Court struck down 169 state or local laws, but this number dropped to 61 from 1990 to 1999. From 2000 to 2002, the Court struck down nine state or local laws, fewer than the number of federal

laws struck down in the same period (11). See Stanley & Niemi, *supra* note 191, 163–66. In the 2004 term, the Court struck down 9 of the 13 state or local acts it reviewed. See *Supreme Court Compendium, supra* note 191, at 193.

195. See, e.g., *Clinton v. Jones,* 520 U.S. 681 (1997); *United States v. Nixon,* 418 U.S. 683 (1974).

196. See *Hamdi v. Rumsfeld,* 124 S. Ct. 2633 (2004); *Rumsfield v. Padilla,* 124 S. Ct. 2711 (2004); *Rasul v. Bush,* 124 S. Ct. 2686 (2004).

197. See Jerry Markon, *U.S. to Free Hamdi, Send Him Home,* Wash. Post, Sept. 23, 2004, at A01.

198. See, e.g., *Clinton v. City of New York,* 524 U.S. 417 (1998); *Youngstown Sheet & Tube Co. v. Sawyer,* 343 U.S. 579 (1952).

199. See Michael Les Benedict, *The Impeachment and Trial of Andrew Johnson* 46–47 (W. W. Norton 1973).

200. See generally *id.* passim.

201. See *Myers v. United States,* 272 U.S. 52 (1926).

202. The Oregon Death With Dignity Act, Or. Rev. Stat §§ 127.800–897 (2003).

203. *Gonzales v. Oregon,* 126 S. Ct. 904 (2005).

204. U.S. Const. art. II, § 2, cl. 1.

205. Proclamation No. 4311, 39 Fed. Reg. 32601 (Sept. 8, 1974).

206. *United States v. Klein,* 80 U.S. 128 (1871) (overturning a congressional enactment aimed at limiting the effects of presidential pardons); *Ex Parte Garland,* 71 U.S. 333 (1867) (holding, among other things, that the president's pardon power is "not subject to legislation" that "Congress can neither limit the effect of his pardon, nor exclude from its exercise any class of offenders…. It was competent for the President to annex to his offer of pardon any conditions or qualifications he should see fit").

207. *Pardon of Richard M. Nixon and Related Matters: Hearing Before the House Subcomm. On Criminal Justice,* 94th Cong. (1975).

208. *Id.* Nor, for that matter, did the courts have the power to adjudicate its merits. The only person with standing to challenge Nixon's pardon would probably have been Nixon, but he of course had no reason to challenge the pardon. It is quite likely the Court would have dismissed any challenge to the pardon power as nonjusticiable.

209. See Kmiec, *supra* note 132, at 337.

210. See generally Lou Fisher, *The Politics of Executive Privilege* (Carolina Academic Press 2004). Legislators' privileges to maintain the confidentiality of information produced in the course of the exercise of their official functions are shaped, much like executive privilege, by decision making outside the courts. For an interesting, comparative analysis of legislative privilege, see Josh Chafetz, *Democracy's Privilege and Democratic Norms in the British and American Constitutions* (Yale University Press, 2007).

211. See Julie Hirschfield Davis, *Bush to Nominate Rehnquist's Successor on Court 'Promptly'; President Must Choose Nominee, Chief Justice; Transition in the Supreme Court,* Baltimore Sun, Sept. 5, 2005, at 1A.

212. See Charles Fried, *Saying What the Law Is: The Constitution in the Supreme Court* 1–12 (Harvard Univ. Press 2004); see also Jack Knight & Lee Epstein, *The Norm of Stare Decisis*, 40 Am. J. Pol. Sci. 1018, 1021 (1996) (stating that "precedent can serve as a constraint on Justices acting on their personal policy preferences").

213. See *supra* notes 90–96 and accompanying text.

214. *See* Barry R. Weingast, *A Rational Choice Perspective on Congressional Norms*, 23 Am. J. Pol. Sci. 245 (1979).

215. Gerhardt, *supra* note 27, at 175 (describing the views expressed in the written statements of senators released in the aftermath of Clinton's acquittal).

216. *Id.* at 50–51.

217. *Id.* at 50 (citation omitted).

218. *Id.* (citation omitted).

219. *Id.* at 51 (citation omitted).

220. *Id.*

221. *Id.*

222. See, e.g., William H. Rehnquist, Grand Inquests: The Historic Impeachments of Justice Samuel Chase and President Andrew Johnson 127–28 (Harper 1992).

223. There is no consensus on how to determine, or even to approach, tradition as a relevant source in constitutional interpretation. Consequently, non-judicial authorities routinely disagree on a wide range of issues relating to tradition, including how to find it.

224. A number of Clinton nominees did not get hearings because they lacked requisite paperwork or were nominated too late in the congressional session to allow meaningful committee consideration. See also Carl Tobias, *Federal Judicial Selection in a Time of Divided Government*, 47 Emory L.J. 527 (1998) (referring to the Judiciary Committee's "inability or reluctance" to hold hearings for and vote on nominees); Helen Dewar, *Estrada Abandons Court Bid*, Wash. Post, Sept. 5, 2003, at A01 (explaining that Senate Republicans "bottled up" nearly 60 of President Clinton's judicial nominees).

225. Senator Durbin seemed to regard the Republican blockage of several of President Clinton's nominees as a precedent in his decision to reject President Bush's nomination of Charles Pickering. See 148 Cong. Rec. S 1915, 1918 (2002).

226. S. Doc. No. 106-1, R. XXXI § 6, at 55 (2003).

227. See *Confirmation Hearing on Federal Appointments*, S. Hrg. 108–35, Pt. 1, 11–12 (Jan. 29, 2003) (statement by Sen. Leahy).

228. See *Confirmation Hearing on the Nomination of Janice R. Brown, of California, to be Circuit Judge for the District of Columbia Circuit*, S. Hrg. 108–463, 4 (Oct. 22, 2003) (statement by Sen. Durbin).

229. See *Confirmation Hearing on Federal Appointments*, S. Hrg. 108–35, Pt. 1, 7 (Jan. 29, 2003) (statement by Sen. Leahy).

230. See, e.g., 151 Cong. Rec. S 10631, Sep. 29, 2005 (containing statements from various senators explaining at length the reasons for their votes on the Roberts nomination).

231. See Neil A. Lewis, *Democrats Reject Bush Pick in Battle Over Court Balance*, N.Y. Times, Sept. 6, 2002, at A1.

232. Audrey Hudson, *Texas Judge Rejected for the Federal Bench; Came under Fire for Being a Court 'Activist,'* Wash. Times, Sept. 6, 2002, at A4.

233. See Bob Dart, *Democrats Block Vote on Judgeship*, Atlanta J. Const., Nov. 7, 2003, at 15A.

234. See Neil A. Lewis, *Judicial Nominee Advances Amid Dispute over Religion*, N.Y. Times, July 24, 2003, at A17.

235. See Michael J. Gerhardt, *The Federal Appointments Process: A Constitutional and Historical Analysis* 51–52 (Duke University Press rev. edition 2003).

236. See Henry Flanders, *The Lives and Times of the Chief Justices of the Supreme Court* 640 (William S. Hein 1971) (1875).

237. See Norman Vieira & Leonard Gross, *Supreme Court Appointments: Judge Bork and the Politicization of Senate Confirmations* 247 (Southern Illinois Univ. Press 1998); Senator Orrin Hatch, *The Dangers of Political Law*, 75 Cornell L. Rev. 1338, 1351 (1990) (reviewing Robert H. Bork, *The Tempting of America: The Political Seduction of the Law* (Touchstone 1989)); Stephen L. Carter, *The Confirmation Mess: Cleaning Up the Federal Appointments Process* 133 (Basic Books 1994).

238. See Gerhardt, *supra* note 235, at 163.

239. Ethan Bronner, *Battle for Justice: How the Bork Nomination Shook America* 241–246 (Anchor 1989).

240. See Gerhardt, *supra* note 235, at 83. See also Michael Gerhardt, *Interpreting Bork*, 75 Cornell L. Rev. 1358, 1386–91 (1990) (reviewing Robert H. Bork, *The Tempting of America: The Political Seduction of the Law* (Touchstone 1989)).

241. See Louis Fisher, *Constitutional Interpretation by Members of Congress*, 63 N.C. L. Rev. 707 (1985).

242. Gerhardt, *supra* note 235, at 314.

243. Gerhardt, *supra* note 27, at 112–16.

244. Senate Majority Leader Bill Frist, who has vigorously protested the use of the filibuster on judicial nominees, had previously participated in filibusters against President Clinton's judicial nominees. See Democratic Policy Committee, *The Republican Flip-Flop on Filibusters* (2003), available at http://democrats.senate.gov/dpc/dpc-new.cfm?doc_name=sr-108-1-199.

245. Eric Shickler, *Disjointed Pluralism: Institutional Innovation and the Development of the U.S. Congress* (Princeton Univ. Press 2001).

246. See U.S. Const., art. II, § 2, cl. 2.

247. See U.S. Const., Preamble ("We the People of the United States …"). See also Ernest A. Young, *State Sovereign Immunity and the Future of Federalism*, 1999 Sup. Ct. Rev. 1 (1999) (recognizing "We the People" as the ultimate

sovereign under our Constitution); Akhil Reed Amar, *A Neo-Federalist View of Article III*, 65 B.U. L. Rev. 511 (1985) (same).

248. 545 U.S. 469 (2005).

249. See *Ballot Questions Reveal Public Moods*, Las Vegas Review-Journal, Nov. 10, 2006, at 10B (noting that Nevada's passage of a measure restricting taking private property for the benefit of private entities "rais[ed] to 35 the number of states that have now sought to limit eminent domain abuses").

250. *Kelo*, 545 U.S. at 492.

251. See Monica Davey, *Voter Initiatives: Liberals Find Rays of Hope in Ballot Measures*, N.Y. Times, Nov. 9, 2006, at P1.

252. For a recent, thorough discussion of this controversy and its constitutional ramifications, see Bruce A. Ackerman, *The Failure of the Founding Fathers: Jefferson, Marshall, and the Rise of Presidential Democracy* (Harvard Univ. Press 2006).

253. U.S. Const., amend. XII.

254. For a small sampling of books recounting the pivotal efforts of nonjudicial actors in response to secession and the Civil War, see Nicolas Leman, *Redemption: The Last Battle of the Civil War* (Farrar, Straus and Giroux 2006); Eric Foner, *Reconstruction: America's Unfinished Revolution, 1863–1877* (Harper 2002); James M. McPherson, *Ordeal By Fire: The Civil War and Reconstruction* (McGraw-Hill 2000).

255. See generally William H. Rehnquist, *Centennial Crisis: The Disputed Election of 1876* (Knopf 2004).

Chapter 5

1. H. Jefferson Powell, *A Community Built on Words: The Constitution in History and Politics* 6 (Univ. of Chicago Press 2002).

2. See Philip C. Bobbitt, *Is Law Politics?* 41 Stan. L. Rev. 1233, 1303 (1989) (explaining that modalities "are not true in themselves, but provide criteria by which we can determine whether statements about the American Constitution are true"); see also Philip C. Bobbitt, *Constitutional Fate: Theory of the Constitution* (Oxford Univ. Press 1982) (describing the six modalities under which a constitutional argument may be made).

3. 531 U.S. 98 (2000).

4. Hansford and Spriggs recognize that precedent performs functions besides attempting to constrain the justices' policy preferences. Precedent allows the justices "to legitimize their policies." Thomas G. Hansford & James F. Spriggs II, *The Politics of Precedent on the U.S. Supreme Court* 21 (Princeton Univ. Press 2006). Their data suggest that "while the justices make decisions based on their policy preferences, they are also constrained by the need to legitimize policy choices by relying on vital precedents." *Id.* at 67. Moreover, "Court opinions set precedents that affect the behavior of a wide range of actors." *Id.* at 124.

5. Compare *U.S. Term Limits, Inc. v. Thornton*, 514 U.S. 779, 806–15 (1995) (looking to the Framers' intent in holding that a provision of the Arkansas Constitution that imposes term limits for members of Congress violates the federal Constitution) with *Brown v. Board of Education* 347 U.S. 483, 492 (1954) (stating that "[the Court] cannot turn the clock back to 1868 when the Amendment was adopted," in holding that racial segregation in public schools violates the equal protection guarantee of the Fourteenth Amendment).

6. See Akhil Reed Amar, *Intratextualism*, 112 Harv. L. Rev. 747, 749–76 (1999) (discussing use of intratextualism by the Court in *McCulloch v. Maryland, Martin v. Hunter's Lessee, Marbury v. Madison, Brown v. Board of Education, Bolling v. Sharpe*, and *Roe v. Wade*).

7. See generally Ronald Dworkin, *Law's Empire* 225–238 (Belknap 1986) (incorporating a conception of precedent into his notion of law as integrity); Ronald Dworkin, *Taking Rights Seriously* 110–15 (Harvard Univ. Press 1977) (describing precedent as a "gravitational force" that constrains judgments).

8. 60 U.S. 393 (1856).

9. 198 U.S. 45 (1905).

10. 17 U.S. (4 Wheat.) 316 (1819).

11. 304 U.S. 144, 152–53 n.4 (1938).

12. See generally Bruce A. Ackerman, *Beyond Carolene Products*, 98 Harv. L. Rev. 713, 715 (1985) (arguing *Carolene Products* established an enduring "premise" for judicial interpretation).

13. See generally Martin B. Gold & Dimple Gupta, *The Constitutional Option to Change Senate Rules and Procedures: A Majoritarian Means to Overcome the Filibuster*, 28 Harv. J.L. & Pub. Pol'y 205 (2004).

14. See, e.g., 145 Cong. Rec. S 1337, 1355 (1999) (statement by Rep. McCollum) ("Can you imagine how damaging that would be to our constitutional form of government, to set the precedent that no President will be removed from office for high crimes and misdemeanors unless polls show that the public wants that to happen?"); 144 Cong. Rec. H 11774, 11800 (statement by Sen. Lofgren) ("By [voting for conviction] … you will set the dangerous precedent that the certainty of presidential terms, which has so benefited our wonderful America, will be replaced by the partisan use of impeachment").

15. Cong. Rec. S 1791, 1792–3 (1999).

16. Cong. Rec. S 869, 873 (1999).

17. See 145 Cong. Rec. S 1775, 1778 (1999) (statement by Sen. Sessions) (citing argument that Nixon's alleged tax evasion was not an impeachable offense because it was not directly related to one of the president's duties); see also Sen. Patrick Leahy, *Procedural and Factual Insufficiencies in the Impeachment of William Jefferson Clinton*, reprinted in 145 Cong. Rec. S 1564, 1588 (1999) (citing Professor Tribe's argument that Clinton's

behavior, like Nixon's tax evasion, presents no threat of becoming a model of emulation).

18. See *Senator Joseph Biden's Comprehensive Statement on Impeachment*, reprinted in 145 Cong. Rec. S 1462, 1481 (1999) (arguing that Clinton's impeachment proceedings, like Johnson's, were motivated by "policy disagreements and personal animosity").

19. 124 S. Ct. 2686 (2004).

20. 124 S. Ct. 2633 (2004).

21. In a related case, the Court considered the legality of designating an American citizen as an "enemy combatant" and denying him the opportunity to challenge the conditions of his detention in court. See *Rumsfeld v. Padilla*, 124 S. Ct. 2711 (2004).

22. 418 U.S. 683 (1974).

23. 520 U.S. 621 (1997).

24. See generally Cass R. Sunstein, *One Case at a Time: Judicial Minimalism on the Supreme Court* (Harvard Univ. Press 1999). For a thoughtful critique of Sunstein's theory of judicial minimalism, see Neil S. Siegel, *A Theory in Search of a Court*, 103 Mich. L. Rev. 1951 (2005).

25. See Cass R. Sunstein, *Burkean Minimalism*, 105 Mich. L. Rev. 336 (2006).

26. *Id*. at 348.

27. See generally Henry Campbell Black, *Handbook on the Law of Judicial Precedents* § 81 (West 1912) ("[T]he rule of res judicata prevents the parties ... from maintaining a new and different suit upon the same cause of action ... or from raising the same issues which were settled for them by a former judgment.").

28. See *id*. §§ 1, 15 (discussing the relationship between degrees of factual similarity in cases and their precedential value).

29. Cf. Keith E. Whittington, *Extrajudicial Constitutional Interpretation: Three Objections and Responses*, 80 N.C. L. Rev. 773, 784 (2002) ("Judicial supremacy requires deference by other government officials to the constitutional dictates of the Court, even when other government officials think that the Court is substantively wrong about the meaning of the Constitution."). For an excellent article on legitimacy and the Constitution, see Richard H. Fallon, Jr., *Legitimacy and the Constitution*, 118 Harv. L. Rev. 1787 (2005).

30. This deliberation is framed by litigants' choices of which cases to try to bring before the Court. While there may be many issues on which justices would like to rule, they are bound by the Court's rule requiring the approval of at least four justices to grant petitions for certiorari.

31. See U.S. Const. amend. II (providing that "[a] well-regulated Militia, being necessary to the security of a free State, the right of the people to keep and bear Arms, shall not be infringed.").

32. See *United States v. Miller*, 307 U.S. 174, 178 (1939) (determining that the Second Amendment did not guarantee a citizen's right to possess a "shotgun

having a barrel of less than eighteen inches in length" because that weapon had not been shown to be "ordinary military equipment" that "could contribute to the common defense").

33. On November 20, 2007, the Supreme Court agreed to review a decision by the U.S. Court of Appeals for the District of Columbia striking down the District's 31-year-old law banning ownership of handguns and requiring other guns that may be legally kept in the home to be disassembled or kept under a trigger lock. The issue before the Court is whether the law violates "the Second Amendment rights of individuals who are not affiliated with any state-regulated militia, but who wish to keep hanguns and other firearms for private use in their homes." Previously, the Ninth and Tenth Circuit Courts of Appeals had each upheld state laws restricting the displaying or carrying of certain firearms, while the Fifth Circuit Court of Appeals had upheld a federal law restricting a person under a court order for prevention of domestic violence from transporting a firearm.

34. See Thomas W. Merrill, *The Making of the Second Rehnquist Court: A Preliminary Analysis*, 47 St. Louis U. L.J. 569, 570 (2003) (describing the dominant theme of the "second" Rehnquist Court, which began in October 1994, as "constitutional federalism").

35. See *id.* at 569–70 (contrasting the "first" Rehnquist Court's tendency to hear controversial social issues with the "second" Rehnquist Court's federalism theme).

36. See generally Neal Devins & Louis Fisher, *The Democratic Constitution* (Oxford Univ. Press 2004); Louis Fisher, *Constitutional Dialogue: Interpretation as Political Process* (Princeton Univ. Press 1988) (observing several examples of forces external to the courts that influence constitutional interpretation); Barry Friedman, *Dialogue and Judicial Review*, 91 Mich. L. Rev. 577, 668–70 (1993) (explaining how the courts synthesize society's views and turn them back to society for further discourse).

37. Alexander M. Bickel, *The Supreme Court and the Idea of Progress* 91 (Yale Univ. Press 1978/1970).

38. 347 U.S. 483 (1954).

39. Robert A. Burt, *The Constitution in Conflict* 295 (Belknap 1992).

40. *Id.*

41. Robert C. Post, *The Supreme Court, 2002 Term, Foreword: Fashioning the Legal Constitution: Culture, Courts, and Law*, 117 Harv. L. Rev. 4, 104–5 (2003) (footnote omitted).

42. *Id.* at 8.

43. *Id.*

44. *Id.* Post agrees with Jeff Powell that constitutional culture consists of "an historically extended tradition of argument" whose "integrity and coherence … are to be found in, not apart from, controversy." H. Jefferson Powell, *A Community Built on Words: The Constitution in History and Politics* 6 (Univ. of Chicago Press 2002). More generally, philosopher Alistair

MacIntyre saw that "[a] living tradition ... is an historically extended, socially embodied argument, and argument precisely in part about the goods which constitute that tradition." Alistair MacIntyre, *After Virtue: A Study in Moral Theory* 207 (Univ. of Notre Dame Press 1981).

45. Post, *supra* note 41, at 8.

46. *Id.*

47. *Id.*

48. Dr. Rice agreed to testify before the special commission on September 11, 2001, after her initial refusal to testify provoked significant public backlash. See generally Philip Shenon, *Rice Questioners May Avoid Partisanship*, N.Y. Times, April 8, 2004, at A25; Vincent Morris, *Condi Won't Say Sorry*, N.Y. Post, April 8, 2004, at A10; Greg Miller, *Rice's Comments to Face Scrutiny at Hearings*, L.A. Times, April 8, 2004, at A14; Charlie Savage, *Rice Set to Detail Bush's Side Testimony before 9/11 Panel as Seen as Response to Clarke*, The Boston Globe, April 8, 2004, at A3.

49. See Letter from Judge Alberto Gonzalez (March 30, 2004) (stating, inter alia, "we have now received assurances from the Speaker of the House and the Majority Leader of the Senate that, in their view, Dr. Rice's public testimony in connection with the extraordinary events of September 11, 2001, does not set, and should not be cited as, a precedent for future requests for a National Security Adviser or any other White House official to testify before a legislative body"), available at http://www.whitehouse.gov/news/releases/2004/03/20040330-3.html.

50. Charles Fried suggests "precedent is only a presumption. If constitutional doctrine is not to become rigid, driven by the path-dependence of common law adjudication, there must be room for distinguishing, narrowing, and abandoning precedent altogether. The dissent contains the germ of such changes of direction." Charles Fried, *Saying What the Law Is: The Constitution in the Supreme Court* 11–12 (Harvard Univ. Press 2004). I differ with Fried in that I believe that the "germ of ... changes of direction" is not present only within dissents, but rather is a function of the limited path dependency of precedent. Fried seems to agree, for he concedes on the same page that "doctrine and precedent constrain more or less loosely." *Id.* at 12. Where I might part further from Fried is the various factors I identify beyond dissents as explanations for the limited path dependency of precedent.

51. Hansford & Spriggs, *supra* note 4, at 8.

52. See, e.g., Ronald C. Kahn, *Presidential Power and the Appointments Process: Structuralism, Legal Scholarship, and the New Historical Institutionalism*, 47 Case W. Res. L. Rev. 1419, 1446–49 (1997) (examining how historical institutionalists view the Supreme Court with respect to other political actors).

53. See, e.g., Matthew D. Adler & Michael C. Dorf, *Constitutional Existence Conditions and Judicial Review*, 89 Va. L. Rev. 1101 (2003) (proposing a theory of judicial review based on the Court's determining the "existence conditions" for certain governmental action).

54. See, e.g., *Planned Parenthood v. Casey*, 505 U.S. 833 (1992) (considering the abortion issue); *Griswold v. Connecticut*, 381 U.S. 479 (1965) (examining the issue of marital privacy for the use contraception); *Youngstown Sheet & Tube Co. v. Sawyer*, 343 U.S. 579 (1952) (dealing with the reach of executive authority).

55. 491 U.S. 110 (1990) (plurality opinion) (finding no substantive due process right of a natural father to establish his paternity).

56. 521 U.S. 702 (1997) (holding that Washington's ban on physician-assisted suicide did not violate substantive due process, with only five justices supporting the majority opinion).

57. 60 U.S. (19 How.) 393 (1856) (denying freedom to a slave, even though he had traveled to a free state).

58. See Michael J. Gerhardt, *Crisis and Constitutionalism*, 63 Mont. L. Rev. 277, 296 n.65 (2002).

59. 531 U.S. 98 (2000).

60. See *Texas v. Johnson*, 491 U.S. 397 (1989) (overturning a Texas flag desecration statute).

61. See *United States v. Eichman*, 496 U.S. 310 (1990) (striking down the federal Flag Protection Act of 1989 in part because of the fact that the federal law could not be distinguished from the Texas statute struck the previous year).

62. 550 U.S. __ (2007).

63. 530 U.S. 914 (2000).

64. James C. Scott, *Seeing Like a State: How Certain Schemes to Improve the Human Condition Have Failed* 9 (Yale Univ. Press 1998). Scott explains how governments have systematically designed projects intended "to arrange the population in ways that simplified the classic state functions of taxation, conscription, and prevention of rebellion," and that the legibility of such projects has been "a central problem in statecraft." *Id.* at 2.

65. See Ken I. Kersch, *The Reconstruction of Constitutional Privacy Rights and the New American State*, 16 Stud. Am. Pol. Dev. 61, 67 (2002) (describing the project of legibility for constitutional rights to privacy).

66. 529 U.S. 598 (2000).

67. *Id.* at 619–21.

68. 109 U.S. 3 (1883).

69. See 529 U.S. at 613.

70. See generally Henry Paul Monaghan, *Stare Decisis and Constitutional Adjudication*, 88 Colum. L. Rev. 723, 730–34, 749–52 (1988) (demonstrating how precedents have shaped governmental structure).

71. See, e.g., *Chevron v. Natural Res. Def. Council*, 467 U.S. 837 (1984) (holding that absent a finding of clear congressional intent, courts should defer to agency interpretation of organic statutes); *Citizens to Pres. Overton Park, Inc. v. Volpe*, 401 U.S. 402 (1971) (holding that even in an informal adjudication, an agency must give an adequate explanation and supply a sufficient

factual record to permit a reviewing court to determine if the agency has engaged in reasoned decision making); *Humphrey's Exec'r v. United States*, 295 U.S. 602 (1935) (upholding a statute restricting the power of the president to remove heads of nonexecutive agencies).

72. See *Tahoe-Sierra Pres. Council, Inc. v. Tahoe Reg'l Planning Agency*, 535 U.S. 302 (2002) (holding that agency ordered moratoria on development are not per se Fifth Amendment takings); *Lucas v. S.C. Coastal Council*, 505 U.S. 1003 (1992) (defining categorical regulatory takings and creating an exception for regulations rooted in background principles of law); *Tenn. Valley Auth. v. Hill*, 437 U.S. 153 (1978) (interpreting the Endangered Species Act as prohibiting further construction of a multimillion dollar dam in order to preserve an endangered species); see generally Michael J. Gerhardt, *On Revolution and Wetland Regulations*, 90 Geo. L.J. 2143, 2156–66 (2002) (detailing the Court's reliance on existing rather than revolutionary constitutional doctrine to shape the course of environmental regulations).

73. U.S. Const. art. II, § 2.

74. See John N. Moore, *The National Law of Treaty Implementation* 378–405 (Carolina Academic Press 2001).

75. B. Ackerman & D. Golove, *Is NAFTA Constitutional?* 108 Harv. L. Rev. 801, 820 (1995).

76. U.S.C. § 112b (2004).

77. Restatement (3rd) Foreign Relations Law of the United States § 303 cmt. f (1987).

78. *Id.*, § 303 cmt. e.

79. *Id.*, § 303 cmt. g.

80. See *United States v. Belmont*, 301 U.S. 324 (1937).

81. See generally W. Taylor Reveley III, *War Powers of the President and Congress: Who Holds the Arrows and Olive Branch?* (Univ. Press of Virginia 1981).

82. Bobbitt, *supra* note 2, at 1393.

83. *Id.*

84. *Id.* at 1365.

85. *Id.* at 1394.

86. 60 U.S. (19 How.) 393 (1856).

87. 531 U.S. 98 (2000).

88. See, e.g., Jack M. Balkin, *Bush v. Gore and the Boundary Between Law and Politics*, 110 Yale L.J. 1407 (2001) (discussing the politicization of the *Bush v. Gore* decision).

89. Reva B. Siegel, *Constitutional Culture, Social Movement Conflict, and Constitutional Change: The Case of the de facto ERA*, 94 Cal. L. Rev. 1323, 1324 (2006). Siegel argues that because cultural meaning is a key part of the intellectual and working environment within which the Court functions, cultural understandings affect legal outcomes in ways of which the justices are not consciously aware.

90. See David Currie, *The Constitution in Congress: The Jeffersonians, 1801–1829*, 232–49 (Univ. of Chicago Press 2001).

91. *Id.* at 112–13.

92. *Id.* at 124.

93. See Robert Caro, *Master of the Senate: The Years of Lyndon Johnson*, 683–1012 (Knopf 2002).

94. See, e.g., Anthony T. Kronman, *Precedent and Tradition*, 99 Yale L.J. 1029, 1043–47 (1990) (arguing that our judicial precedents and traditions have shaped our current attitudes and practices).

95. See, e.g., *United States v. Butler*, 297 U.S. 1, 65–66 (1936) (agreeing with Hamilton's rather than Madison's understanding of the scope of Congress' spending power); *McCulloch v. Maryland*, 17 U.S. (4 Wheat.) 316, 332 (1819) (agreeing with Hamilton's rather than Madison's understanding of the necessary and proper clause); see also Harold Hongju Koh, *The National Security Constitution: Sharing Power After the Iran-Contra Affair*, 134–49 (Yale Univ. Press 1990) (detailing the regularity with which the Court has cited historical support for its siding with the president on separation of powers issues).

96. 506 U.S. 224, 229–30 (1993).

97. 392 U.S. 409, 428–32 (1968).

98. 376 U.S. 254, 270–71 (1964).

99. 501 U.S. 957, 978 n.9 (1991).

100. 463 U.S. 783, 786–89 (1983).

101. 539 U.S. 558 (2003).

102. 478 U.S. 186 (1986).

103. *Id.* at 192.

104. *Lawrence*, 539 U.S. at 571–73.

105. On President Bush's call for a constitutional amendment to protect states' efforts to preserve traditional marriage and outlaw same-sex marriage, see Peter S. Canellos, *Bush Seeks Marriage Amendment; From Both Sides, Danger of Alienating Moderates*, Boston Globe, Feb. 25, 2004, at A1.

106. See, e.g., *Deputization of Members of Congress as Special Deputy U.S. Marshals*, 18 Op. Off. Legal Counsel 125 (1994) (arguing that deputizing members of Congress as special deputy U.S. marshals conflicts with historical practices); *Recess Appointments During an Intrasession Recess*, 16 Op. Off. Legal Counsel 15, 16 (1992) (arguing that past practice indicates presidents may exercise recess appointment power during intrasession recesses of 18 days); *Reimbursement for Detail of Judge Advocate General Corps Personnel to a United States Attorney's Office*, 13 Op. Off. Legal Counsel 188, 189 n.2 (1989) (arguing that historical practices suggest the executive branch is not bound by legal opinions of the comptroller general when they conflict with legal opinions of the attorney general or Office of Legal Counsel).

107. C. Vann Woodward, *Responses of the Presidents to Charges of Misconduct* (Dell 1974).

108. See 6–11 Clarence Cannon, *Cannon's Precedents of the House of Representatives of the Untied States Including References to Provisions of the Constitution, the Laws, and Decisions of the United States Senate* 10–16; Lewis Deschler & William Holmes Brown, *Deschler-Brown Precedents of the United States House of Representatives*; Lewis Deschler, *Procedure in the U.S. House of Representatives, 97th Congress: A Summary of the Modern Precedents and Practices of the House 86th Congress-97th Congress* (1982); 1–6 Asher C. Hinds, *Hinds' Precedents of the House of Representatives of the United States, Including References to Provisions of the Constitution, the Laws, and Decisions of the United States Senate.*

109. Memorandum from the Office of the Legal Advisor, U.S. Dep't of State, *The Legality of United States Participation in the Defense of Viet-Nam* (1966), reprinted in 1 *The Vietnam War and International Law* 583, 597 (Richard A. Falk ed., Princeton Univ. Press 1968).

110. 408 U.S. 238, 313 (1972) (White, Jr., concurring) (observing the death penalty "has for all practical purposes run its course").

111. Michael J. Klarman, *Brown and Lawrence (and Goodridge)*, 104 Mich. L. Rev. 431, 482 (2005) (citing and quoting John Hart Ely, *Democracy and Distrust: A Theory of Judicial Review* 67–70 (Harvard Univ. Press 1981) (suggesting that "there is no reason to suppose judges are well qualified to foresee the future of popular opinion" and that "by predicting the future the justices will unavoidably help to shape it").

112. See, e.g., Eugene Rostow, *The Democratic Character of Judicial Review*, 66 Harv. L. Rev. 193, 208 (1952) (providing a well-known defense of the Court as educator on constitutional questions); see generally Christopher L. Eisgruber, *Is the Supreme Court an Educative Institution?* 67 N.Y.U. L. Rev. 961 (1992) (commenting on the literature on the Court as educator).

113. See Alexander M. Bickel, *The Least Dangerous Branch: The Supreme Court at the Bar of Politics* (2d ed., Yale Univ. Press 1986); see also Cass R. Sunstein, *One Case at a Time: Judicial Minimalism on the Supreme Court* 3–6 (Harvard Univ. Press 1999); Cass R. Sunstein, *Foreword*, in *Leaving Things Undecided*, *The Supreme Court 1995 Term*, 110 Harv. L. Rev. 4, 48 (1996) (observing that the narrowness of Justice Powell's *Bakke* opinion "left the democratic process ample room to maneuver" and was "an effort to promote both democracy and deliberation").

114. Obviously, each of the other branches issue public commentaries on the Constitution. They do so through a much wider variety of means than do the justices, and they are much freer than justices with respect to the people whom they may consult in formulating constitutional judgments.

115. 347 U.S. 483, 490 (1954).

116. 358 U.S. 1 (1958).

117. 505 U.S. 833, 867 (1992).

118. 125 S. Ct. 1183, 1194–95 (2005).

119. 539 U.S. 558, 572 (2003).

120. See *Roper*, 125 S. Ct. at 1203 (Scalia, J., dissenting) (suggesting foreign law on which both the majority and Justice O'Connor rely in her dissent has no place in the construction of uniquely American constitutional provisions or traditions); *Lawrence*, 539 U.S. at 590, 595 (Scalia, J., dissenting)("The Court's discussion of [foreign] views (ignoring, of course, the many countries that have retained criminal prohibitions on sodomy) is ... meaningless dicta. Dangerous dicta, however, since "this Court ... should not impose foreign moods, fads, or fashions on Americans") (citation omitted).

121. See Laurence H. Tribe, *Lawrence v. Texas: The "Fundamental Right" that Dare not Speak Its Name*, 117 Harv. L. Rev. 1893, 1901 n.28 (2004).

122. See Joseph R. Biden, *The Constitution, The Senate, and the Court*, 24 Wake Forest L. Rev. 951 (1989) (arguing that the Senate should be able to reject judicial nominees on the basis of their judicial philosophies).

123. See 151 Cong. Rec. S 10461, 10467–68 (daily ed. Sept. 27, 2005) (statement of Senator Graham) (approvingly reciting Justice Ginsburg's refusals to answer questions in her own confirmation hearings); but see 151 Cong. Rec. S 9908, 9909 (daily ed. Sept. 12, 2005) (statement of Senator Boxer) (suggesting that Justice Ginsburg was far more forthcoming than Republican senators at the Roberts hearing were suggesting).

124. Cong. Rec. S 9211, 9212–13 (July 28, 2005) (citing Senator Hatch urging the application of the Ginsburg rule ("no hints, no forecasts, no previews") at the Roberts hearing).

125. See Stephen Carter, *The Confirmation Mess: Cleaning Up the Federal Appointments Process* xi (Basic Books 1994).

126. John G. Roberts, President's Remarks at Swearing-In Ceremony of Chief Justice Roberts (Sept. 29, 2005) (available at http://www.whitehouse.gov/news/releases/2005/09/20050929-3.html) ("I view the vote this morning as confirmation of what is for me a bedrock principle, that judging is different from politics").

127. Klarman, *supra* note 111, at 453.

128. 798 N.E. 2d 941 (Mass. 2003).

129. U.S. (1 Cranch) 137, 176 (1803).

130. U.S. (4 Wheat.) 316, 415 (1819).

131. U.S. (4 Wheat.) 316, 415 (1819).

132. *Missouri v. Holland*, 252 U.S. 416, 433 (1920).

133. *Elk Grove Unified School District v. Newdow*, 542 U.S. 1, 26–29 (2004) (Rehnquist, C.J., concurring in judgment).

134. See generally Anders Stephanson, *Manifest Destiny: American Expansionism and the Empire of Right* (Hill and Wang 1995); Albert K. Weinberg, *Manifest Destiny: A Study of Nationalist Expansionism in American History* (Johns Hopkins Press 1935).

135. See, e.g., Editorial, *The War President: Spying without Oversight, No Mere Matter of Trust*, Detroit Free Press, Dec. 20, 2005, at 10 (arguing that the

president's use of secret military tribunals violates "the liberty fundamental to the American system of government"; Editorial, *Spying on Americans*, Wash. Post, Dec. 18, 2005, at B06 (arguing that many of the president's policies in fighting terrorists "are not consistent with a democratic society").

136. See, e.g., *Blanchard v. Bergeron*, 489 U.S. 939, 962 (Scalia, J., concurring in part and concurring in the judgment) ("As anyone familiar with modern-day drafting of congressional committee reports is well aware, the references [in the committee report on which the majority relies] were inserted, at least by a committee staff member on his or her own initiative, or at worst by a committee staff member at the suggestion of a lawyer-lobbyist; and the purpose of those references was not primarily to inform the Members of Congress what the bill meant but rather to influence judicial construction.").

137. See, e.g., *U.S. Term Limits, Inc. v. Thornton*, 514 U.S. 779, 865 (Thomas, J., dissenting) ("As far as the Federal Constitution is concerned, ... the States can exercise all powers that the Constitution does not withhold from them. The Federal Government and the States thus face different default rules: where the Constitution is silent about the exercise of a particular power—that is, where the Constitution does not speak either expressly or by necessary implication—the Federal Government lacks that power and the States enjoy it. These basic principles are enshrined in the Tenth Amendment.").

138. See, e.g., *id.* at 793 (""The Tenth Amendment ... provides no basis for concluding that the States possess reserved power to add qualifications to those that are fixed in the Constitution. In the absence of any constitutional delegation to the States of power to add qualifications to those enumerated in the Constitution, such a power does not exist.").

139. Daryl J. Levinson, *Rights Essentialism and Remedial Equilibrium*, 99 Colum. L. Rev. 857, 890 (1999).

140. Richard H. Fallon, Jr., *Judicially Manageable Standards and Constitutional Meaning*, 119 Harv. L. Rev. 1274, 1314 (2006).

141. *Id.* at 1324–25.

142. Kermit Roosevelt III, *Aspiration and Underenforcement*, 119 Harv. L. Rev. 193 (2006).

143. Kermit Roosevelt III, *Constitutional Calcification: How the Law Becomes What the Court Does*, 91 Va. L. Rev. 1649 (2005); Mitchell N. Berman, *Constitutional Decision Rules*, 90 Va. L. Rev. 1 (2004).

144. Fallon, *supra* note 140, at 1316.

145. 462 U.S. 919 (1983).

146. Neal Devins & Lou Fisher, *The Democratic Constitution* (Oxford Univ. Press 2004).

147. See, e.g., Seth B. Tillman, *A Textualist Defense of Article I, Section 7, Clause 3*, 83 Tex. L. Rev. 1 (2005); Peter L. Strauss, *Legislative Theory and the Rule of Law: Some Comments on Rubin*, 89 Colum. L. Rev. 427 (1989); Laurence

H. Tribe, *The Legislative Veto Decision: A Law By Any Other Name?* 21 Harv. J. Legis. 1 (1984); E. Donald Elliott, *INS v. Chadha: The Administrative Constitution, the Constitution, and the Legislative Veto*, 1983 Sup. Ct. Rev. 125.

148. See generally Louis Fisher, Congressional Research Service Report, *Legislative Vetoes after Chadha.*, May 2, 2005 (counting more than 400 legislative vetoes enacted after *Chadha*).

149. See generally William N. Eskeridge, Jr., Philip P. Frickey, & Elizabeth Garrett, *Cases and Materials on Legislation: Statutes and the Creation of Public Policy* 787–800, 1036–39 (3d ed., West 2001) (discussing the implications of social science research on equilibrium for understanding the strategic interaction of public institutions over questions of public law).

150. U.S. Const., art. IV, § 2.

151. See, e.g., Leo Sandon, *Religious Tests for Public Office: Enough Already*, Tallahassee Democrat, Nov. 5, 2005, at D1; Editorial, *Faith and the Court*, N.Y. Times, Oct. 18, 2005, at A26.

Chapter 6

1. *Spicer v. Spicer*, 79 Eng. Rep. 451 (1620).

2. U.S. 299, 308–9 (1803).

3. Abraham Lincoln, *Response to Douglas in Representatives' Hall in the Illinois State House* (June 26, 1857), in *The Living Lincoln: The Man, His Mind, His Times, and the War He Fought, Reconstructed from His Own Writings* 201 (Paul M. Angle & Earl Schenck Miers eds., Rutgers Univ. Press 1955).

4. See Jeffrey Rosen, *So, Do You Believe in 'Superprecedent'?* N.Y. Times, Oct. 30, 2005, § 4 at 1 ("The term superprecedent first surfaced at the Supreme Court confirmation hearings of Judge John Roberts, when Senator Arlen Specter of Pennsylvania, the chairman of the Judiciary Committee, asked him whether he agreed that certain cases like *Roe* had become superprecedents or 'super-duper' precedents—that is, that they were so deeply embedded in the fabric of law they should be especially hard to overturn").

5. U.S. 113 (1973).

6. *Richmond Med. Ctr. for Women v. Gilmore*, 219 F.3d 376, 376–77 (4th Cir. 2000); see also Rosen, *supra* note 4 ("An origin of the idea [of super precedent] was a 2000 opinion written by J. Michael Luttig, a judge on the U.S. Court of Appeals for the Fourth Circuit, who regularly appears on short lists for the Supreme Court"). In an unrelated development, Judge Luttig resigned from the Fourth Circuit in the spring of 2006.

7. See, e.g., Robert H. Bork, *Slouching Toward Gomorrah: Modern Liberalism and American Decline* 117 (Regan Books 1996) (arguing for the abolition of judicial review); Mark V. Tushnet, *Taking the Constitution Away from the Courts* 6–53 (Princeton Univ. Press 1999) (challenging judicial review);

Girardeau A. Spann, *Neutralizing Grutter*, 7 U. Pa. J. Const. L. 633, 656–67 (2005) (arguing for the abandonment of judicial review in the context of affirmative action).

8. 5 U.S. (1 Cranch) 137 (1803).

9. *City of Boerne v. Flores*, 521 U.S. 507, 516 (1997) (citing *Marbury*, 5 U.S. (1 Cranch) at 176, in an attempt to limit judicial authority); *United States v. Nixon*, 418 U.S. 683, 703 (1974) (citing *Marbury*, 5 U.S. (1 Cranch) at 177, for the exercise of judicial review in an executive official case).

10. U.S. (1 Wheat.) 304 (1816).

11. *Id.* at 379–80. *Cohens v. Virginia*, 19 U.S. (6 Wheat.) 264 (1821), is equally important for its recognition of the constitutional necessity for Supreme Court review over state criminal cases, 19 U.S. (6 Wheat.) at 264, 375–431.

12. Oliver Wendell Holmes, *Law and the Court*, in *Collected Legal Papers* 291, 295–96 (Harcourt Brace 1920).

13. 463 U.S. 1032 (1983).

14. *Id.* at 1044 (holding that when state court decisions rest on federal law, the Court will infer that the state court believed that federal law required it to do so).

15. The most prominent example of this resistance can be seen in the Southern Manifesto. For a general discussion of the resistance to *Martin* during this period, see Walter F. Murphy, James E. Fleming, Sotirios A. Barber, & Stephen Macedo, *American Constitutional Interpretation* 271–384 (3d ed., Foundation Press 2003).

16. See *Elk Grove Unified Sch. Dist. v. Newdow*, 542 U.S. 1, 49 (2004) (Thomas, J., concurring) ("I accept that the Free Exercise Clause, which clearly protects an individual right, applies against the States through the Fourteenth Amendment. … But the Establishment Clause is another matter").

17. Robert R. Baugh, *Applying the Bill of Rights to the States: A Response to William P. Gray, Jr.*, 49 Ala. L. Rev. 551, 571–72 (1998) ("Initially, the Supreme Court used the fundamental fairness approach to protect certain individual rights against state action. Later, the Court adopted the selective incorporation approach and applied the precise language of portions of the Bill of Rights against the states. Finally, although the total incorporation doctrine has never been accepted by a majority of the sitting members of the Court, the historical arguments made in favor of total incorporation provide an intellectual foundation for the application of the majority of the Bill of Rights against the states").

18. 367 U.S. 643 (1961).

19. *Id.* at 655 (incorporating the Fourteenth Amendment). *Mapp* is significant because of its recognition of the exclusionary rule that all evidence obtained in violation of the Fourth Amendment is inadmissible in state court. Persistent criticisms of the exclusionary rule reduce the likelihood that this particular holding of *Mapp* qualifies as a super precedent.

20. 391 U.S. 145, 147 (1968).

21. 48 U.S. (7 How.) 1 (1849).

22. *Id.* at 47.

23. *Id.* ("[A]ccording to the institutions of this country, the sovereignty in every State resides in the people of the State, and that they may alter and change their form of government at their own pleasure. But whether they have changed it or not by abolishing an old government, and establishing a new one in its place, is a question to be settled by the political power. And when that power has decided, the courts are bound to take notice of its decision, and to follow it").

24. 369 U.S. 186 (1962).

25. *Id.* at 210–11 ("We have said that 'In determining whether a question falls within [the political question] category, the appropriateness under our system of government of attributing finality to the action of the political departments and also the lack of satisfactory criteria for a judicial determination are dominant considerations.' The nonjusticiability of a political question is primarily a function of the separation of powers. Much confusion results from the capacity of the 'political question' label to obscure the need for case-by-case inquiry. Deciding whether a matter has in any measure been committed by the Constitution to another branch of government, or whether the action of that branch exceeds whatever authority has been committed, is itself a delicate exercise in constitutional interpretation, and is a responsibility of this Court as ultimate interpreter of the Constitution. To demonstrate this requires no less than to analyze representative cases and to infer from them the analytical threads that make up the political question doctrine" (quoting *Coleman v. Miller*, 307 U.S. 433, 454–55 (1939))).

26. Daniel A. Farber, William N. Eskridge, Jr., & Philip P. Frickey, *Cases and Materials on Constitutional Law* 1201 (3d ed., West 2006).

27. 531 U.S. 98 (2000).

28. 79 U.S. (12 Wall.) 457 (1871).

29. *Id.* at 80.

30. William N. Eskridge, Jr., & John Ferejohn, *Super Statutes*, 50 Duke L. J. 1215 (2001).

31. Pub. L. No. 88–352, 78 Stat. 241 (codified as amended in scattered sections of 5, 28, and 42 U.S.C. (2000)).

32. 15 U.S.C. §§ 1–2 (2000).

33. See Eskridge & Ferejohn, *supra* note 30, at 1231–46.

34. See *id.* at 1216–17.

35. *Id.* at 1217.

36. See *id.* at 1215–17.

37. 347 U.S. 483 (1954).

38. See Brad Snyder, *How the Conservatives Canonized Brown v. Board of Education*, 52 Rutgers L. Rev. 383, 396–98 (2000).

39. Michael Klarman, *An Interpretative History of Modern Equal Protection*, 90 Mich. L. Rev. 213, 241–43 (1991).

40. Snyder, *supra* note 38, at 468 ("Responding to a softball question from Senator Thurmond about this apparent conflict, Bork admitted that 'as a matter of original intent, I am not at all sure that segregation was not intended to be eliminated'" (quoting *Nomination of Robert H. Bork to be Associate Justice of the Supreme Court of the United States: Hearings Before the S. Comm. on the Judiciary*, 100th Cong. 132 (1987))).

41. *Nomination of Judge Clarence Thomas to be Associate Justice of the Supreme Court of the United States: Hearings Before the S. Comm. on the Judiciary*, 102d Cong. 489 (1991) ("I have no agenda to change existing case law. That is not my predisposition, and it is not the way that I approach my job" (statement of Judge Clarence Thomas)).

42. *Confirmation Hearing on the Nomination of John G. Roberts, Jr. to be Chief Justice of the United States: Hearing Before the S. Comm. on the Judiciary*, 109th Cong. 144, 167–68, 262–63 (2005) (statement of Judge John Roberts) [hereinafter *Roberts Confirmation Hearing*]; *U.S. Senate Judiciary Committee Holds a Hearing on Judge Samuel Alito's Nomination to the Supreme Court*, available at http://jurist.law.pitt.edu/alitoday2.php (Jan. 10, 2006) (transcript at 58) (statement of Judge Samuel Alito) [hereinafter *Alito Confirmation Hearing*].

43. 109 U.S. 3 (1883).

44. *Id.* at 6.

45. 529 U.S. 598, 599–600 (2000).

46. 426 U.S. 229 (1976).

47. *Id.* at 239 (holding that a law or official act, without regard to whether it reflects a racially discriminatory purpose, is not unconstitutional solely because it has a racially discriminatory impact).

48. 343 U.S. 579 (1952).

49. *Roberts Confirmation Hearing, supra* note 42, at 370 ("I agree with the basic proposition that the President's authority is at its greatest when he has the support of Congress" (statement of Judge John Roberts)).

50. *Alito Confirmation Hearing, supra* note 42, at 8 (statement of Judge Samuel Alito, responding affirmatively to Sen. Arlen Specter's question: "I want to … ask you first if you agree with the quotation from Justice Jackson's concurrence in the *Youngstown Steel [S]eizure* case about the evaluation of presidential power").

51. See, e.g., *id.* (statement of Sen. Arlen Specter).

52. 198 U.S. 45 (1905).

53. 60 U.S. (19 How.) 393 (1856).

54. 384 U.S. 436 (1966).

55. 530 U.S. 428, 432 (2000).

56. See, e.g., *Missouri v. Seibert*, 542 U.S. 600 (2004) (undermining *Miranda* in part); *New York v. Quarles*, 467 U.S. 649, 655–56 (1984) (creating a public safety exception to the *Miranda* warnings); *Rhode Island v. Innis*, 446 U.S. 291, 300–301 (1980) (holding that *Miranda* safeguards come into play

only when a person in custody is subject to either express questioning or its functional equivalent); *Harris v. New York*, 401 U.S. 222, 224–26 (1971) (allowing statements made before *Miranda* warnings for the purpose of impeaching defendant's credibility).

57. Undoubtedly, the fact that the constitutional scholar who mapped out a strategy for undoing *Miranda* lost his cause, but is now a federal district judge obliged to follow *Miranda*, further entrenches it in constitutional law. See Paul G. Cassell, *The Paths Not Taken: The Supreme Court's Failures in Dickerson*, 99 Mich. L. Rev. 898 (2001). Cassell was sworn in as a U.S. District Court judge for the District of Utah on July 2, 2002.

58. 317 U.S. 111 (1942).

59. *Id.* at 128–29.

60. 514 U.S. 549, 554–57 (1995).

61. *Id.* at 559–60.

62. 125 S. Ct. 2195, 2206–208 (2005).

63. *Id.* at 2235–37 (Thomas, J., dissenting).

64. *Roberts Confirmation Hearing, supra* note 42, at 261–63 ("But I would say that because [*Wickard*] has come up again so recently in the *Raich* case that it's an area where I think it's inappropriate for me to comment on my personal view about whether it's correct or not. ... Nobody in recent years has been arguing whether *Marbury v. Madison* is good law. Nobody has been arguing whether *Brown v. Board of Education* was good law. They have been arguing whether *Wickard v. Filburn* is good law" (statement of Judge John Roberts)).

65. 381 U.S. 479 (1965).

66. See *id.*; *Alito Confirmation Hearing, supra* note 42, at 129 ("[Y]ou've expressed admiration for ... Harlan") (statement of Sen. Charles Schumer).

67. See Linda Campbell, *Thomas Supports a Right to Privacy: Reply Surprises Democrats; Judge Won't Discuss Abortion*, Chi. Trib., Sept. 11, 1991, at A1.

68. *Nomination of Judge Antonin Scalia: Hearings Before the S. Comm. on the Judiciary*, 99th Cong. (1996).

69. See *Roberts Confirmation Hearing, supra* note 42, at 207 ("I agree with the *Griswold* court's conclusion that marital privacy extends to contraception and availability of that" (statement of Judge John Roberts)).

70. 410 U.S. 113 (1973).

71. See, e.g., Randy E. Barnett, *It's a Bird, It's a Plane, No, It's Super Precedent: A Response to Farber and Gerhardt*, 90 Minn. L. Rev. 1209, 1215–23 (2006).

72. *Id.* My response to Professor Barnett's and others' criticisms should not be construed, however, as a rejection of a "'formalist' commitment to stare decisis." *Id.* at 1218–19 n.38. I do not reject such a commitment, nor do I believe that the normative appeal of super precedent has any bearing, one way or another, on formalism in constitutional theory.

73. 163 U.S. 537 (1896).

74. 347 U.S. 483.

75. 198 U.S. 45 (1905), implicitly overruled by *West Coast Hotel Co. v. Parrish*, 300 U.S. 379, 397–98 (1937).

76. See *West Coast Hotel Co.*, 300 U.S. at 397–98.

77. See, e.g., *Ferguson v. Skrupa*, 372 U.S. 726 (1963); *Day-Brite Lighting, Inc. v. Missouri*, 342 U.S. 921 (1952); *Nebbia v. New York*, 291 U.S. 502 (1934); *Adkins v. Children's Hosp.*, 261 U.S. 525 (1923), overruled in part by *West Coast Hotel Co.*, 300 U.S. at 388–400.

78. See Daniel A. Farber & Suzanna Sherry, *Desperately Seeking Certainty: The Misguided Quest for Constitutional Foundations* 25 (Univ. of Chicago Press 2002).

79. Henry Paul Monaghan, *Stare Decisis and Constitutional Adjudication*, 88 Colum. L. Rev. 723, 724–27 (1988).

80. This tracks Barry Friedman's and Scott Smith's notion of the sedimentary Constitution. See generally Barry Friedman & Scott B. Smith, *The Sedimentary Constitution*, 147 U. Pa. L. Rev. 1 (1998).

81. 403 U.S. 602, 612–13 (1971) (establishing a three-pronged test for determining whether a government-sponsored message violates the establishment clause).

82. 469 U.S. 528, 546–47 (1985) (holding that the determination of state immunity from federal regulation does not turn on whether a particular governmental function is "integral" or "traditional").

83. 539 U.S. 558, 578–79 (2003) (striking down the ban on sodomy).

84. 543 U.S. 551, 568 (2005) (finding the execution of minors unconstitutional).

85. Michael Fletcher, *White House Counsel Miers Chosen for Court*, Wash. Post, Oct. 5, 2005, at A1.

86. The dynamic works in both directions—the Senate helps to shape the Court and the Court influences how the Senate functions in confirmation proceedings (and other settings in which it renders constitutional judgments). On the important relationship between the Supreme Court's constitutional decision making and the constitutional activities of nonjudicial actors (including the president and the Congress), see Robert C. Post, *The Supreme Court, 2002 Term—Foreword: Fashioning the Legal Constitution: Culture, Court, and Law*, 117 Harv. L. Rev. 4 (2003).

87. See Jeffrey Rosen, *Answer Key*, New Republic, Nov. 21, 2005, at 16, 20.

88. *Roberts Confirmation Hearing*, *supra* note 42, at 186 (statement of Judge John Roberts).

89. *Id.* at 382 (statement of Judge John Roberts).

90. *Id.* at 169 (statement of Judge John Roberts).

91. *Id.* at 190–91 (statement of Judge John Roberts).

92. Gwyneth K. Shaw, *Roberts: Roe 'Settled as Precedent'*, Balt. Sun, Sept. 14, 2005, at 1A.

93. See Rosen, *supra* note 87, at 20.

94. See *id.*

95. *Federalist No.* 76, at 426 (Alexander Hamilton) (Clinton Rossiter ed., Signet 1999).
96. Edward Epstein, *Miers Withdraws as Court Nominee*, S.F. Chron., Oct. 28, 2005, at A1.
97. See Rosen, *supra* note 87, at 18–20.
98. Peter Baker, *Alito Nomination Sets Stage for Ideological Battle*, Wash. Post, Nov. 1, 2005, at A1.
99. See *Alito Confirmation Hearing, supra* note 42, at 29–32 (statement of Judge Samuel Alito, responding to questions and comments from Sen. Ted Kennedy); *id.* at 41–42 (statement of Judge Samuel Alito, responding to questions from Sen. Charles Grassley); *id.* at 93–101 (statement of Judge Samuel Alito, responding to questions from Sen. Jeff Sessions).
100. *Alito Confirmation Hearing, supra* note 42, at 3, 4, 6, 7, 28, 124, 128, 131, 133 (statements of Judge Samuel Alito).
101. Charles Babington, *Senators Praise Nominee's Candor: Alito Shows Willingness to Discuss Controversial Issues Facing Supreme Court*, Wash. Post, Nov. 5, 2005, at A7 ("Many liberal groups fear further erosion of the separation of church and state if the court shifts to the right … Sen. John Cornyn (R-Tex.) told reporters that Alito 'did commiserate with me a little bit about the problems that the Supreme Court has had in coming up with a coherent body of law that is clear and can be easily applied, and can be predictable in a way that doesn't discourage people from expressing their religious views.'").
102. *Alito Confirmation Hearing, supra* note 42, at 2, 134 (statements of Judge Samuel Alito).
103. *Roberts Confirmation Hearing, supra* note 42, at 546 (statement of Sen. Tom Coburn).

Conclusion

1. 127 S. Ct. 2652 (2007).
2. See McConnell v. Federal Election Commission, 540 U.S. 93 (2003).
3. 127 S. Ct. 1610 (2007).
4. See Stenberg v. Carhart, 530 U.S. 914 (2000).
5. 127 S. Ct. 2553 (2007).
6. 392 U.S. 83 (1968).
7. 127 S. Ct. 2738 (2007).
8. 539 U.S. 306 (2003).
9. 127 S. Ct. 2738 (2007).
10. On the persistence of traditional legal reasoning in constitutional adjudication and commentary, see, e.g., J. M. Balkin & Sanford Levinson, *Getting Serious about "Taking Legal Reasoning Seriously,"* 74 Chi.-Kent L. Rev. 543 (1999); J. M. Balkin & Sanford Levinson, *Constitutional Grammar,* 72 Tex. L. Rev. 1771 (1994).

11. Cass Sunstein takes issue with the notion of judicial modesty (and bottom-up judging) that I have advanced here. See Cass Sunstein, *Burkean Minimalism*, 105 Mich. L. Rev. 353 (2006). Sunstein suggests that Burkeans value tradition (because it likely reflects society's best thinking on the practice in question) and favor several kinds of minimalism. It is, however, not clear why Burkeans need to explain their affinity for tradition any more than the Court does. Nor do I agree that Burkean minimalists are, or should all be, skeptical of the Warren Court's activism. Surely there are minimalists, perhaps including Sunstein, who are supportive of at least some, if not many, Warren Court decisions. Some may prefer minimalism as a way to avoid the wholesale disassembling of Warren Court decisions. Indeed, minimalism generally is undertaken at the expense of some clarity, candor, and comprehensiveness. Minimalism also would generally seem to eschew attacking or eviscerating precedents except perhaps as a last resort. But, judicial minimalists are not likely to disclose more than they have to. The critical question has to do with justices' fundamental assumptions about precedent in any given case—how much of the Court's precedent do they have to accept generally? I suggest that the answer is that justices today have to accept—or at least are challenged to accept—a lot more precedents than 19th-century justices had to accept as a faithful application of the golden rule of precedent.

12. Keith Whittington discusses these and other extrajudicial constitutional interpretations as largely if not wholly settled in the absence of judicial review. See Keith E. Whittington, *Extrajudicial Constitutional Interpretation: Three Objections and Responses*, 80 N.C. L. Rev. 786 (2002). While Whittington does not describe these extrajudicial interpretations as precedents, the ones he discusses have the distinctive features of nonjudicial precedents which I have discussed, including discoverability.

13. In addition to the approaches surveyed in chapter 2, game theory has become a popular perspective from which to analyze the patterns and practices of the decision making processes of public institutions. For an excellent collection of essays on how game theory may be used to illuminate the Court's decision making process, see *Institutional Games and the U.S. Supreme Court* (James R. Rogers et al. eds., Univ. Press of Virginia, 2006).

Index

abortion, 20, 199, 324*n*3. See also *Gonzales v. Carhart*; *Planned Parenthood v. Casey*; *Roe v. Wade*; *Stenberg v. Carhart*

Ackerman, Bruce, 66, 274*n*99, 298*n*134, 307*n*12, 312*n*75

activism, 148
  appointees and presidents against, 101–2
  Bush, George W., and, 101–02
  economic liberties and, 11, 35
  minority rights and, 12
  nominations and, 141–42
  Reagan and, 101, 126
  symbolism and, 170
  of Warren Court, 101, 110, 325*n*6

Adams, John, 117

Adams, John Quincy, 115, 140

Adarand Constructors, Inc. v. Pena, 24–26, 29, 90, 99, 109, 282*n*65, 286*n*116

administrative law, 160, 311*n*71

administrative practices, 111, 132–33

adversarial system, 165

affirmative action, 20, 25, 90, 99, 107, 109, 282*n*67, 296*nn*115–17

agendas, 6, 126, 153–55, 308*n*30, 309*n*33

Agostini v. Felton, 41

Alito, Samuel, Jr.
  as Bush, George W., appointee, 176, 199–200, 255*n*1
  confirmation hearings of, 38, 169, 176, 184, 193–97, 320*n*50, 321*n*66, 323*n*99, 323*n*101
  golden rule and, 7
  Harlan and, 186, 321*n*66
  overrulings and, 44, 199
  Roberts, J., and, 193–97, 199–200, 323*n*3, 324*n*4

Amar, Akhil Reed, 274*n*98, 306*n*247, 307*n*6

amendments, constitutional
  First, 10, 20, 32, 39–40, 43–44, 58, 132, 159, 164, 180, 282*n*59, 300*n*149, 311*nn*60–61
  Second, 88, 154, 308*n*31, 309*nn*32–33
  Fourth, 10, 39, 181, 318*n*19
  Fifth, 10, 42, 91
  Sixth, 10, 264*n*222
  Seventh, 65, 273*n*94
  Eighth, 38–39, 128–29, 164, 262*n*170, 290*n*3
  Tenth, 10, 37, 98, 316*nn*137–38
  Eleventh, 9, 10, 26–30, 64–65, 92, 133, 272*nn*86–87, 273*n*88, 283*n*84, 283*n*86, 284*n*87, 284*n*102
  Twelfth, 146
  Thirteenth, 164
  Fourteenth, 9, 27, 45, 64, 85, 98, 133, 160, 180–81, 184, 264*n*222, 272*n*84, 307*n*5,

318*n*19, 318*nn*16–17
Sixteenth, 9
Nineteenth, 255*n*5
Twenty-Fifth, 115–16
Twenty-sixth, 9
Twenty-Seventh, 126
Article V and, 60–61, 66, 107, 288*n*143
ERA, 163
history and, 163
overrulings and, 9, 10, 49, 62, 63, 255*n*5
ratification of, 64, 65, 132
Reconstruction, 163
on same-sex/gay marriage, 146, 165, 288*n*144, 313*n*105

American Bar Association, 116, 126, 295*n*85

amicus briefs, 107, 289*nn*147–48

Am. Ins. Ass'n v. Garamendi, 300*n*161

Annals of Congress, 119

appeals, to Supreme Court, 131, 299*n*141

appointees/nominees. *See* justices; Supreme Court nominees/appointees

argumentation, modalities of, 6, 147–49, 201, 306*n*2, 307*n*12
  foundational institutional practice and, 178–79
  impeachment and, 149, 307*n*14, 307*n*17, 308*n*18

Arizona v. Fulminante, 36

armistice agreements, 162

Arthur, Chester, 290*n*14

attitudinal model, 67, 68–77
  golden rule and, 110
  limits of rational choice theory and, 71–77
  postpositivists and, 80–81
  rational choice theory, mixed models and, 68–71

attorneys general
  opinions and, 136–37
  states, governors and, 128–29, 296*n*100

Baker v. Carr, 90–91, 181–82, 283*n*78

Bakke v. California Regents, 134, 282*n*67, 314*n*113

Baldwin, Mr. Justice, 53

Balkin, Jack, 286*n*122, 290*n*2, 312*n*88

Barr, Bob, 112

Baum, Lawrence, 81–82, 280*n*17

BedRoc Ltd., LLC v. United States, 36

Benton, Thomas Hart, 118

Berger, Raoul, 55

Berman, Mitchell, 173, 274*n*105, 286*n*122, 316*n*143

Bickel, Alexander, 155–56, 167